Communications
in Computer and Information Science    76

Samir Kumar Bandyopadhyay   Wael Adi
Tai-hoon Kim   Yang Xiao (Eds.)

# Information Security and Assurance

4th International Conference, ISA 2010
Miyazaki, Japan, June 23-25, 2010
Proceedings

 Springer

Volume Editors

Samir Kumar Bandyopadhyay
University of Calcutta
Calcutta, India
E-mail: skb1@vsnl.com

Wael Adi
Braunschweig University of Technology
Braunschweig, Germany
E-mail: w.adi@tu-braunschweig.de

Tai-hoon Kim
Hannam University
Daejeon, South Korea
E-mail: taihoonn@hnu.kr

Yang Xiao
The University of Alabama
Tuscaloosa, AL, USA
E-mail: yangxiao@ieee.org

Library of Congress Control Number: 2010928128


CR Subject Classification (1998): C.2, K.6.5, D.4.6, E.3, H.4, I.2

ISSN        1865-0929
ISBN-10     3-642-13364-9 Springer Berlin Heidelberg New York
ISBN-13     978-3-642-13364-0 Springer Berlin Heidelberg New York

springer.com

© Springer-Verlag Berlin Heidelberg 2010
Printed in Germany

Typesetting: Camera-ready by author, data conversion by Scientific Publishing Services, Chennai, India
Printed on acid-free paper      06/3180      5 4 3 2 1 0

# Foreword

Advanced Science and Technology, Advanced Communication and Networking, Information Security and Assurance, Ubiquitous Computing and Multimedia Applications are conferences that attract many academic and industry professionals. The goal of these co-located conferences is to bring together researchers from academia and industry as well as practitioners to share ideas, problems and solutions relating to the multifaceted aspects of advanced science and technology, advanced communication and networking, information security and assurance, ubiquitous computing and multimedia applications.

This co-located event included the following conferences: AST 2010 (The second International Conference on Advanced Science and Technology), ACN 2010 (The second International Conference on Advanced Communication and Networking), ISA 2010 (The 4th International Conference on Information Security and Assurance) and UCMA 2010 (The 2010 International Conference on Ubiquitous Computing and Multimedia Applications).

We would like to express our gratitude to all of the authors of submitted papers and to all attendees, for their contributions and participation. We believe in the need for continuing this undertaking in the future.

We acknowledge the great effort of all the Chairs and the members of advisory boards and Program Committees of the above-listed events, who selected 15% of over 1,000 submissions, following a rigorous peer-review process. Special thanks go to SERSC (Science & Engineering Research Support soCiety) for supporting these co-located conferences.

We are grateful in particular to the following speakers who kindly accepted our invitation and, in this way, helped to meet the objectives of the conference: Hojjat Adeli (The Ohio State University), Ruay-Shiung Chang (National Dong Hwa University), Adrian Stoica (NASA Jet Propulsion Laboratory), Tatsuya Akutsu (Kyoto University) and Tadashi Dohi (Hiroshima University).

We would also like to thank Rosslin John Robles and Maricel O. Balitanas, graduate students of Hannam University, who helped in editing the material with great passion.

April 2010                                                                 Tai-hoon Kim

# Preface

We would like to welcome you to the proceedings of the 4th International Conference on Information Security and Assurance (ISA 2010), which was held on June 23–25, 2010, at Sheraton Grande Ocean Resort, in Miyazaki, Japan.

ISA 2010 focused on various aspects of advances in information security and assurance with computational sciences, mathematics and information technology. It provided a chance for academic and industry professionals to discuss recent progress in the related areas. We expect that the conference and its publications will be a trigger for further related research and technology improvements in this important subject. We would like to acknowledge the great effort of all the Chairs and members of the Program Committee. Out of around 280 submissions to ISA 2010, we accepted 42 papers to be included in the proceedings and presented during the conference. This gives an acceptance ratio firmly below 15%. Twelve of the papers accepted for ISA 2010 were published in a special volume, LNCS 6059, by Springer. The remaining 30 accepted papers can be found in this CCIS volume.

We would like to express our gratitude to all of the authors of submitted papers and to all the attendees, for their contributions and participation. We believe in the need for continuing this undertaking in the future.

Once more, we would like to thank all the organizations and individuals who supported this event as a whole and, in particular, helped in the success of ISA 2010.

April 2010

Samir Kumar Bandyopadhyay
Wael Adi
Tai-hoon Kim
Yang Xiao

# Organization

## Organizing Committee

| | |
|---|---|
| Honorary Chair | Hojjat Adeli (The Ohio State University, USA) |
| General Co-chairs | Samir Kumar Bandyopadhyay (University of Calcutta, India)<br>Wael Adi (Technische Universitaet Braunschweig, Germany) |
| Program Co-chairs | Tai-hoon Kim (Hannam University, Korea)<br>Yang Xiao (The University of Alabama, USA) |
| Workshop Co-chairs | Muhammad Khurram Khan (King Saud University, Kingdom of Saudi Arabia)<br>Seok-soo Kim (Hannam University, Korea) |
| International Advisory Board | Haeng-kon Kim (Catholic University of Daegu, Korea)<br>Kouich Sakurai (Kyushu University, Japan)<br>Justin Zhan (CMU, USA)<br>Hai Jin (Huazhong University of Science and Technology, China)<br>Edwin Sha (University of Texas at Dallas, USA)<br>Dominik Slezak (Infobright, Poland and Canada) |
| Publicity Co-chairs | Debnath Bhattacharyya (Heritage Institute of Technology, India)<br>Ching-Hsien Hsu (Chung Hua University, Taiwan)<br>Duncan S. Wong (City University of Hong Kong, Hong Kong)<br>Deepak Laxmi Narasimha (University of Malaya, Malaysia)<br>Prabhat K. Mahanti (University of New Brunswick, Canada) |
| Publication Chair | Bongen Gu (Chungju National University, Korea) |
| Local Arrangements Co-chairs | G.S. Tomar (VITM, India)<br>Debnath Bhattacharyya (Heritage Institute of Technology, India) |

## Program Committee

Abdelwahab Hamou-Lhadj
Ahmet Koltuksuz
Albert Levi
Andreas Jacobsson
Bonnefoi Pierre-Francois
Chantana Chantrapornchai
Chun-Ying Huang
Daniel Port
Debasis Giri
Dharma P. Agrawal
Eduardo Fernandez
Fangguo Zhang
Filip Orsag
Han-Chieh Chao
Hiroaki Kikuchi
Hironori Washizaki
Hongji Yang
Hyun Sung Kim

J.H. Abawajy
Jan deMeer
Jari Veijalainen
Javier Garcia-Villalba
Jeng-Shyang Pan
Jonathan Lee
Josef Bigun
Kenichi Takahashi
Mario Freire
Martin Drahansky
N. Jaisankar
Paolo D'Arco
Paolo Falcarin
Petr Hanacek
Pierre-François Bonnefoi
Qi Shi
Reinhard Schwarz
Rodrigo Mello

Rolf Oppliger
Rui Zhang
S. K. Barai
Serge Chaumette
Slobodan Petrovic
Stan Kurkovsky
Stefanos Gritzalis
Swee-Huay Heng
Tony Shan
Victor Winter
Wei Yan
Yannis Stamatiou
Yi Mu
Yong Man Ro
Yoshiaki Hori
Yeong Deok Kim

# Table of Contents

# Maximized Posteriori Attributes Selection from Facial Salient Landmarks for Face Recognition

Phalguni Gupta[1], Dakshina Ranjan Kisku[2], Jamuna Kanta Sing[3],
and Massimo Tistarelli[4]

[1] Department of Computer Science and Engineering,
Indian Institute of Technology Kanpur,
Kanpur - 208016, India
[2] Department of Computer Science and Engineering,
Dr. B. C. Roy Engineering College / Jadavpur University,
Durgapur – 713206, India
[3] Department of Computer Science and Engineering,
Jadavpur University, Kolkata – 700032, India
[4] Computer Vision Laboratory, DAP
University of Sassari, Alghero (SS), 07041, Italy
{drkisku,jksing}@ieee.org, pg@cse.iitk.ac.in, tista@uniss.it

**Abstract.** This paper presents a robust and dynamic face recognition technique based on the extraction and matching of devised probabilistic graphs drawn on SIFT features related to independent face areas. The face matching strategy is based on matching individual salient facial graph characterized by SIFT features as connected to facial landmarks such as the eyes and the mouth. In order to reduce the face matching errors, the Dempster-Shafer decision theory is applied to fuse the individual matching scores obtained from each pair of salient facial features. The proposed algorithm is evaluated with the ORL and the IITK face databases. The experimental results demonstrate the effectiveness and potential of the proposed face recognition technique also in case of partially occluded faces.

**Keywords:** Face biometrics, Graph matching, SIFT features, Dempster-Shafer decision theory, Intra-modal fusion.

## 1 Introduction

Face recognition can be considered as one of most dynamic and complex research areas in machine vision and pattern recognition [1-2] because of the variable appearance of face images. The appearance changes in face occur either due to intrinsic and extrinsic factors and due to these changes, face recognition problems become ill posed and difficult to authenticate faces with outmost ease. Auxiliary complexities like the facial attributes compatibility complexity, data dimensionality problem, the motion of face parts, facial expression changes, pose changes, partly occlusion and illumination changes cause major changes in appearance. In order to make the problem well-posed, vision researchers have adapted and applied an abundance of algorithms for pattern classification, recognition and learning.

S. K. Bandyopadhyay et al. (Eds.): ISA 2010, CCIS 76, pp. 1 – 8, 2010.

There exist the appearance-based techniques which include Principal Component Analysis (PCA) [1], Linear Discriminant Analysis (LDA) [1], Fisher Discriminant Analysis (FDA) [1] and Independent Component Analysis (ICA) [1]. Some local feature based methods are also investigated [4-5]. A local feature-based technique for face recognition, called Elastic Bunch Graph Matching (EBGM) has been proposed in [3]. EBGM is used to represent faces as graphs and the vertices localized at fiducial points (e.g., eyes, nose) and the geometric distances or edges labeled with the distances between the vertices. Each vertex contains a set known as Gabor Jet, of 40 complex Gabor wavelet coefficients at different scales and orientations. In case of identification, these constructed graphs are searched and get one face that maximizes the graph similarity function. There exists another graph-based technique in [6] which performs face recognition and identification by graph matching topology drawn on SIFT features [7-8]. Since the SIFT features are invariant to rotation, scaling and translation, the face projections are represented by graphs and faces can be matched onto new face by maximizing a similarity function taking into account spatial distortions and the similarities of the local features.

This paper addresses the problem of capturing the face variations in terms of face characteristics by incorporating probabilistic graphs drawn on SIFT features extracted from dynamic (mouth) and static (eyes, nose) salient facial parts. Differences in facial expression, head pose changes, illumination changes, and partly occlusion, result variations in facial characteristics and attributes. Therefore, to combat with these problems, invariant feature descriptor SIFT is used for the proposed graph matching algorithm for face recognition which is devised pair-wise manner to salient facial parts (e.g., eyes, mouth, nose).

The goal of the proposed algorithm is to perform an efficient and cost effective face recognition by matching probabilistic graph drawn on SIFT features whereas the SIFT features [7] are extracted from local salient parts of face images and directly related to the face geometry. In this regard, a face-matching technique, based on locally derived graph on facial landmarks (e.g., eye, nose, mouth) is presented with the fusion of graphs in terms of the fusion of salient features. In the local matching strategy, SIFT keypoint features are extracted from face images in the areas corresponding to facial landmarks such as eyes, nose and mouth. Facial landmarks are automatically located by means of a standard facial landmark detection algorithm [8-9]. Then matching a pair of graphs drawn on SIFT features is performed by searching a most probable pair of probabilistic graphs from a pair of salient landmarks. This paper also proposes a local fusion approach where the matching scores obtained from each pair of salient features are fused together using the Dempster-Shafer decision theory. The proposed technique is evaluated with two face databases, viz. the IIT Kanpur and the ORL (formerly known as AT&T) databases [11] and the results demonstrate the effectiveness of the proposed system.

The paper is organized as follows. The next section discusses SIFT features extraction and probabilistic graph matching for face recognition. Experimental results are presented in Section 3 and conclusion is given in the last section.

## 2   SIFT Feature Extraction and Probabilistic Matching

### 2.1   SIFT Keypoint Descriptor for Representation

The basic idea of the SIFT descriptor [6-7] is detecting feature points efficiently through a staged filtering approach that identifies stable points in the scale-space. Local feature points are extracted by searching peaks in the scale-space from a difference of Gaussian (DoG) function. The feature points are localized using the measurement of their stability and orientations are assigned based on local image properties. Finally, the feature descriptors which represent local shape distortions and illumination changes, are determined.

Each feature point is composed of four types of information – spatial location $(x, y)$, scale $(S)$, orientation $(\theta)$ and Keypoint descriptor $(K)$. For the sake of the experimental evaluation, only the keypoint descriptor [6-7] has been taken into account. This descriptor consists of a vector of 128 elements representing the orientations within a local neighborhood. In Figure 1, the SIFT features extracted from a pair of face images are shown.

### 2.2   Local Salient Landmarks Representation with Keypoint Features

Deformable objects are generally difficult to characterize with a rigid representation in feature spaces for recognition. With a large view of physiological characteristics in biometrics including iris, fingerprint, hand geometry, etc, faces are considered as highly deformable objects. Different facial regions, not only convey different relevant and redundant information on the subject's identity, but also suffer from different time variability either due to motion or illumination changes. A typical example is the case of a talking face where the mouth part can be considered as dynamic facial landmark part. Again the eyes and nose can be considered as the static facial landmark parts which are almost still and invariant over time. Moreover, the mouth moves changing its appearance over time. As a consequence, the features extracted from the mouth area cannot be directly matched with the corresponding features from

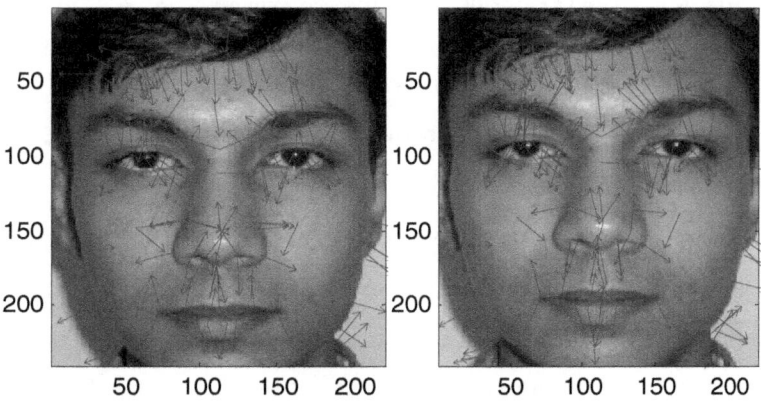

**Fig. 1.** Invariant SIFT Feature Extraction on a pair of Face Images

a static template. Moreover, single facial features may be occluded making the corresponding image area not usable for identification. For these reasons to improve the identification and recognition process, a method is performed which searches the matching features from a pair of facial landmarks correspond to a pair of faces by maximizing the posteriori probability among the keypoints features. The aim of the proposed matching technique is to correlate the extracted SIFT features with independent facial landmarks. The SIFT descriptors are extracted and grouped together by searching the sub-graph attributes and drawing the graphs at locations corresponding to static (eyes, nose) and dynamic (mouth) facial positions.

The eyes and mouth positions are automatically located by applying the technique proposed in [8]. The position of nostrils is automatically located by applying the technique proposed in [9]. A circular region of interest (ROI), centered at each extracted facial landmark location, is defined to determine the SIFT features to be considered as belonging to each face area.

SIFT feature points are then extracted from these four regions and gathered together into four groups. Then another four groups are formed by searching the corresponding keypoints using iterative relaxation algorithm by establishing relational probabilistic graphs [12] on the four salient landmarks of probe face.

### 2.3   Probabilistic Interpretation of Facial Landmarks

In order to interpret the facial landmarks with invariant SIFT points and probabilistic graphs, each extracted feature can be thought as a node and the relationship between invariant points can be considered as geometric distance between the nodes. At the level of feature extraction, invariant SIFT feature points are extracted from the face images and the facial landmarks are localized using the landmark detection algorithms discussed in [8], [9]. These facial landmarks are used to define probabilistic graph which is further used to make correspondence and matching between two faces.

To measure the similarity of vertices and edges (geometric distances) for a pair of graphs [12] drawn on two different facial landmarks of a pair of faces, we need to measure the similarity for node and edge attributes correspond to keypoint descriptors and geometric relationship attributes among the keypoints features. Let, two graphs be $G' = \{N', E', K', \varsigma'\}$ and $G'' = \{N'', E'', K'', \varsigma''\}$ where $N'$, $E'$, $K'$, $\zeta'$ denote nodes, edges, association between nodes and association between edges respectively. Therefore, we can denote the similarity measure for nodes $n'_i \in N'$ and $n''_j \in N''$ by $s^n_{ij} = s(k'_i, k''_j)$ and the similarity between edges $e'_{ip} \in E'$ and $e''_{jq} \in E''$ can be denoted by $s^e_{ipjq} = s(e'_{ip}, e''_{jq})$.

Further, suppose, $n'_i$ and $n''_j$ are vertices in gallery graph and probe graph, respectively. Now, $n''_j$ would be best probable match for $n'_i$ when $n''_j$ maximizes the posteriori probability [12] of labeling. Thus for the vertex $n'_i \in N'$, we are searching the most probable label or vertex $\overline{n}'_i = n''_j \in N''$ in the probe graph. Hence, it can be stated as

$$\overline{n}'_i = \arg \max_{j,n''_j \in N''} P(\psi_i^{n''_j} \mid K', \varsigma', K'', \varsigma'') \tag{1}$$

To simplify the solution of matching problem, we adopt a relaxation technique that efficiently searching the matching probabilities $\overline{P}^n_{ij}$ for vertices $n'_i \in N'$ and $n''_j \in N''$. By reformulating Equation (1) can be written as

$$\overline{n}'_i = \arg \max_{j,n''_j \in N''} \overline{P}^n_{ij} \tag{2}$$

This relaxation procedure considers as an iterative algorithm for searching the best labels for $\overline{n}'_i$. This can be achieved by assigning prior probabilities $P^n_{ij}$ proportional to $s^n_{ij} = s^n(k'_i, k''_j)$. Then the iterative relaxation rule would be

$$\hat{P}^n_{ij} = \frac{P^n_{ij} \cdot Q_{ij}}{\displaystyle\sum_{q,n''_q \in N''} P^n_{iq} \cdot Q_{iq}} \tag{3}$$

$$Q_{ij} = p^n_{ij} \prod_{p,n'_p \in N'_i} \sum_{q,n''_q \in N''_j} s^e_{ipjq} \cdot P^n_{pq} \tag{4}$$

Relaxation cycles are repeated until the difference between prior probabilities $P^n_{ij}$ and posteriori probabilities $\hat{P}^n_{ij}$ becomes smaller than certain threshold $\Phi$ and when this is reached then it is assumed that the relaxation process is stable. Therefore,

$$\max_{i,n'_i \in N', j,n''_j \in N''} \left| P^n_{ij} - \hat{P}^n_{ij} \right| < \Phi \tag{5}$$

Hence, the matching between a pair of graphs is established by using the posteriori probabilities in Equation (2) about assigning the labels from the gallery graph $G'$ to the points on the probe graph $G''$.

From these groups pair-wise salient feature matching is performed in terms of graph matching. Finally, the matching scores obtained from these group pairs are fused together by the Dempster-Shafer fusion rule [10] and the fused score is compared against a threshold for final decision.

## 3 Experimental Evaluation

To investigate the effectiveness and robustness of the proposed graph-based face matching strategy, experiments are carried out on the IITK face database and the ORL face database [11]. The IITK face database consists of 1200 face images with four images per person (300X4), which have captured in control environment with ±20 degree changes of head pose and with almost uniform lighting and illumination conditions, and the facial expressions keeping consistent with some ignorable changes. For the face matching, all probe images are matched against all target images. On the other hand, the ORL face database consists of 400 images taken from 40 subjects. Out of these 400 images, we use 200 face images for experiment, in which ±20 to ±30 degrees orientation changes have been considered. The face images show variations of pose and facial expression (smile/not smile, open/closed eyes). When the faces have been taken, the original resolution is 92 x 112 pixels for each one. However, for our experiment we set the resolution as 140×100 pixels in line with IITK database.

The ROC curves of the error rates obtained from the face matching applied to the face databases are shown in Figure 2. The computed recognition accuracy for the IITK database is 93.63% and for the ORL database is 97.33%. The relative accuracy of the proposed matching strategy for ORL database increases of about 3% over the IITK database. In order to verify the effectiveness of the proposed face matching algorithm for recognition and identification, we compare our algorithm with the algorithms that are discussed in [6], [13], [14], and [15]. There are several face matching algorithms discussed in the literatures which tested on different face databases or with different processes. It is duly unavailable of such uniform experimental environment, where the experiments can be performed with multiple attributes and characteristics. By extensive comparison, we have found that, the proposed algorithm is solely different from the algorithms in [6], [13], [14], [15] in terms of performance and design issues. In [13], the PCA approach discussed for different view of face images without transformation and the algorithm achieved 90% recognition accuracy for some specific views of faces. On the other hand, [14] and [15] use Gabor jets for face processing and recognition where the first one has used

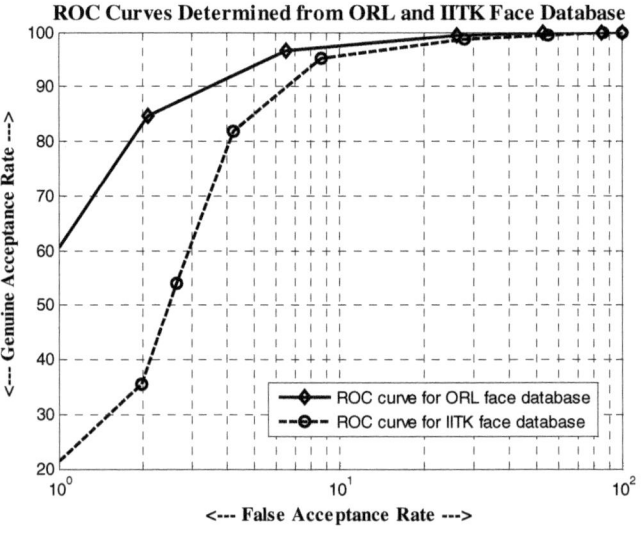

**Fig. 2.** ROC curves for the proposed matching algorithm for ORL and IITK databases

the Gabor jets without transformation and later one has used the Gabor jets with geometrical transformation. Both the techniques are tested on Bochum and FERET databases which are characteristically different from the IITK and the ORL face databases and the recognition rates are 94% and 96%, respectively at maximum, while all the possible testing are done with different recognition rates. Also, another two graph based face recognition techniques drawn on SIFT features have been discussed in [6] where the graph matching algorithms are developed by considering the whole face instead of the local landmark areas. The proposed face recognition algorithm not only devised keypoints from the local landmarks, but it also combines the local features for robust performance.

## 4 Conclusion

This paper has proposed an efficient and robust face recognition techniques by considering facial landmarks and using the probabilistic graphs drawn on SIFT feature points. During the face recognition process, the human faces are characterized on the basis of local salient landmark features (e.g., eyes, mouth, nose). It has been determined that when the face matching accomplishes with the whole face region, the global features (whole face) are easy to capture and they are generally less discriminative than localized features. On contrary, local features on the face can be highly discriminative, but may suffer for local changes in the facial appearance or partial face occlusion. In the proposed face recognition method, local facial landmarks are considered for further processing rather than global features. The optimal face representation using probabilistic graphs drawn on local landmarks allow matching the localized facial features efficiently by searching and making correspondence of keypoints using iterative relaxation by keeping similarity measurement intact for face recognition.

## References

1. Shakhnarovich, G., Moghaddam, B.: Face Recognition in Subspaces. In: Li, S., Jain, A. (eds.) Handbook of Face Recognition, pp. 141–168. Springer, Heidelberg (2004)
2. Shakhnarovich, G., Fisher, J.W., Darrell, T.: Face Recognition from Long-term Observations. In: IEEE European Conference on Computer Vision, pp. 851–865 (2002)
3. Wiskott, L., Fellous, J., Kruger, N., Malsburg, C.: Face recognition by Elastic Bunch Graph Matching. IEEE Transactions on Pattern Analysis and Machine Intelligence 19, 775–779 (1997)
4. Zhang, G., Huang, X., Wang, S., Li, Y., Wu, X.: Boosting Local Binary Pattern (lbp)-based Face Recognition. In: Li, S.Z., Lai, J.-H., Tan, T., Feng, G.-C., Wang, Y. (eds.) SINOBIOMETRICS 2004. LNCS, vol. 3338, pp. 179–186. Springer, Heidelberg (2004)
5. Heusch, G., Rodriguez, Y., Marcel, S.: Local Binary Patterns as an Image Preprocessing for Face Authentication. In: IDIAP-RR 76, IDIAP (2005)
6. Kisku, D.R., Rattani, A., Grosso, E., Tistarelli, M.: Face Identification by SIFT-based Complete Graph Topology. In: IEEE workshop on Automatic Identification Advanced Technologies, pp. 63–68 (2007)

7. Lowe, D.: Distinctive Image Features from Scale-invariant Keypoints. International Journal of Computer Vision 60(2), 91–110 (2004)
8. Smeraldi, F., Capdevielle, N., Bigün, J.: Facial Features Detection by Saccadic Exploration of the Gabor Decomposition and Support Vector Machines. In: 11th Scandinavian Conference on Image Analysis, vol. 1, pp. 39–44 (1999)
9. Gourier, N., James, D.H., Crowley, L.: Estimating Face Orientation from Robust Detection of Salient Facial Structures. In: FG Net Workshop on Visual Observation of Deictic Gestures, pp. 1–9 (2004)
10. Bauer, M.: Approximation Algorithms and Decision-Making in the Dempster-Shafer Theory of Evidence—An Empirical Study. International Journal of Approximate Reasoning 17, 217–237 (1996)
11. Samaria, F., Harter, A.: Parameterization of a Stochastic Model for Human Face Identification. In: IEEE Workshop on Applications of Computer Vision (1994)
12. Yaghi, H., Krim, H.: Probabilistic Graph Matching by Canonical Decomposition. In: IEEE International Conference on Image Processing, pp. 2368–2371 (2008)
13. Moghaddam, B., Pentland, A.: Face recognition using View-based and Modular Eigenspaces. In: SPIE Conf. on Automatic Systems for the Identification and Inspection of Humans. SPIE, vol. 2277, pp. 12–21 (1994)
14. Wiskott, L., Fellous, J.-M., Kruger, N., von der Malsburg, C.: Face recognition by Elastic Bunch Graph Matching. IEEE Transactions on Pattern Analysis and Machine Intelligence 19(7), 775–779 (1997)
15. Maurer, T., von der Malsburg, C.: Linear Feature Transformations to Recognize Faces Rotated in Depth. In: International Conference on Artificial Neural Networks, pp. 353–358 (1995)

# Security Improvement on a Remote User Authentication Scheme Using Smart Cards

Tien-Ho Chen[1], Han-Cheng Hsiang[2], and Wei-Kuan Shih[1]

[1] Department of Computer Science, National Tsing Hua University, No. 101,
Kuang Fu Rd, Sec. 2, 300 HsingChu, Taiwan, ROC
{riverchen,wshih}@rtlab.cs.nthu.edu.tw
[2] Department of Information Management, Vanung University, Taiwan, R.O.C
shc@rtlab.cs.nthu.edu.tw

**Abstract.** Authentication is a very important ingredient service for the network system to verify whether a remote user is legal through any insecure channel. Recently, Hsiang and Shih proposed a remote user authentication scheme as an improved scheme over Yoon-Ryu-Yoo's, and asserted that their scheme could escape from masquerade attack, parallel session attack, etc. In this paper, we show that Hsiang and Shih's scheme still suffers from parallel session attack. To mend the problem, we offer a procedure to improve Hsiang and Shih's scheme. Consequently, our scheme is suitable for applications with higher secure requirement.

**Keywords:** Authentication; Security; Cryptography; Password; Smart card.

## 1 Introduction

With current developed network technologies, people can launch various business activities in the Internet world, and therefore, how to assure the security of activities in an insecure communication channel has become the most important issue. In 1981, Lamport [12] proposed a password based remote user authentication scheme for a server to verify users' identifications, which is a good beginning for establishing efficient applications of Internet-based systems. Later, many studies provided similar approaches [2, 4, 8, 9, 13, 14, 15, 16, 17, 18, 19] to enhance Lamport's method which can verify remote users by hash function or verifier table. For instance, Hwang et al.'s [7] scheme can certify passwords without accessing passwords tables, which avoids the attack of stealing verifier table from servers. Later, Hwang-Li's [6] scheme provided an authentication method by using smart cards. In 2000, Lee and Chang [13] provided a method to verify remote users by their identifications and passwords in multi-server environment. Chien [1] proposed a password based remote user authentication scheme which provided mutual authentication without verification table in 2002. Later, an improved method was presented in Ku-Chen [10] to enhance Chine's flaws of reflection attack [3], inside attack [11], etc. After that, Yoon et al. [20] proposed an improvement of Ku-Chen's scheme which, however, was still vulnerable to parallel session attack and smart cards losing attack.

Recently, Hsiang-Shih [5] presented that Yoon et al's scheme could not prevent masquerading attack, off-line password guessing attack and parallel session attack by

S. K. Bandyopadhyay et al. (Eds.): ISA 2010, CCIS 76, pp. 9–16, 2010.

proposing an improved method. Unfortunately, we find that Hsiang and Shih's scheme is still vulnerable to parallel session attack.

To resolve the flaw, this paper proposes a robust remote user authentication mechanism using smart cards to improve preceding approaches, while the remainder of this paper is organized as follows. Section 2 reviews Hsiang and Shih's scheme, while Section 3 shows the cryptanalysis of Hsiang and Shih's scheme. Section 4 presents our enhanced security user authentication scheme using smart cards, and the security analysis is offered in Section 5. Finally, Section 6 concludes this paper.

## 2   Review of Hsiang and Shih's Scheme

The notations used throughout this paper are summarized as follows.

- U: the user.
- ID: the identity of U.
- PW: the password of U.
- S: the remote server.
- x: the permanent secret key of S.
- h ( ): a secure one-way hash function.
- $h_p$ ( ): a cryptographic hash function with secure s.
- => : a secure channel.
- →: a common channel.
- ||: string concatenation operation

In the following of this section, we briefly review Hsiang and Shih's scheme [5], while the four phases in their scheme, i.e., registration, login, verification and password change, are described as follows.

**Registration phase:** This phase is a registration procedure for the user $U_i$ to get a license from S. Before the user can access the services, s/he has to submit the identity ID and password PW to S. Then, S issues the license to $U_i$. The detailed steps are defined as follows.

First, $U_i$ selects a password PW, an arbitrary number b, computes $h(b \oplus PW)$ and then sends{ $ID, h(PW), h(b \oplus PW)$} to the server S by the secure channel. After S has received the message from $U_i$ and decided to accept the user's request, S calculates the results and sends { $V, R, h()$} to $U_i$ by the secure channel where $EID= h(ID||n)$, $P=h(EID \oplus x)$, $R=P \oplus h(b \oplus PW)$, $V=h(P \oplus h(b \oplus PW))$. And then, the smart card saves the data containing (V, R, h( )).

**Login phase:** When $U_i$ enters ID and password PW in order to login the service provider S, the smart card performs the following steps: The smart card computes $C_1= R \oplus h(b \oplus PW)$, $C_2= h(C_1 \oplus T_u)$, where $T_u$ denotes $U_i$'s current timestamp. And then, $U_i$ sends the message { $ID, C_2, T_u$ } to S.

**Verification phase:** After receiving the login request message {$ID, C_2, T_u$}, S executes the following to authenticate the user $U_i$.

First, S checks $T_s-T_u<\Delta T$ at the time $T_s$ (where $T_s$ denotes the current timestamp and $\Delta T$ the legal time interval for transmission delay), and then calculates

$C_2'=h(h(EID \oplus x) \oplus T_u)$ to check whether $C_2'$ is equal to $C_2$. If yes, the validity of $U_i$ can be assured, and S calculates $C_3 = h(h(EID \oplus x) \oplus h(T_s))$, then sends the message $\{C_3, T_s\}$ to $U_i$ by a common channel.

After that, $U_i$ checks whether $T_s = T_u$. If yes, $U_i$ terminates the session. Otherwise, $U_i$ calculates $C_3' = h(C_1 \oplus h(T_s))$ to check whether $C_3'$ is equal to $C_3$. If yes, the validity of S can be assured.

**Password change phase:** The user $U_i$ can change his original password to $PW_{new}$ freely without the help from S. The steps are as follows: $U_i$ inserts his smart card into the smart card reader. And then, $U_i$ enters $ID$ and $PW$, and requests to change the password. After that, the smart card computes the steps below:

$P^* = R \oplus h(b \oplus PW)$ and $V^* = h(P^* \oplus h(b \oplus PW))$

The smart card checks whether $V^* = V$. If yes, it selects the new password $PW_{new}$, calculates $R_{new} = P^* \oplus h(b \oplus PW_{new})$ which yields $h(EID \oplus x) \oplus h(b \oplus PW_{new})$ and $V_{new} = h(P^* \oplus h(b \oplus PW_{new}))$ , and then replaces $V$ and $R$ with $V_{new}$ and $R_{new}$, respectively.

## 3 Cryptanalysis of Hsiang and Shih's Scheme

In this section, we will show that Hsiang and Shih's scheme still can not escape from parallel session attack.

Assume that an intruder has intercepted one of the legal users $U_i$'s previous login message $\{ID_i, C_2, T_u\}$ and the message $\{C_3, T_s\}$ from S to $U_i$. If the intruder attempts to impersonate $U_i$ to login S at time $T^*$ for a new session (where $T^* = \Delta t + T_u = h(T_s) \oplus T_u$ is a valid special timestamp made by the adversary on purpose where the timestamp $T_s$ would be received by the server which checks the message at $T_s^*$), an impersonation attack can be performed as given below:

A1. The intruder computes $T^* = h(T_s) \oplus T_u$ and $C_2^* = C_3$
A2. Intruder $\rightarrow$ S: $\{ID, C_2^*, T^*\}$.
A3. Since $T^*$ is valid and S receives the message at the timestamp $T_s^*$, S will proceed to compute $C_2' = h(h(EID \oplus x) \oplus T^*)$ which will yield $C_2' = h(h(EID \oplus x) \oplus h(T_s) \oplus T_u) = h(C_3 \oplus T_u) = h(C_2^* \oplus T_u)$ and S will accept the intruder's login request due to the transmission delay or the adversary on purpose, that is, even if $T_s^*$ is not equal to $T^*$, S will still continue to process the authentication steps.

## 4 An Enhanced Scheme

This section presents our enhanced remote user authentication scheme for multi-server environment using smart cards. This scheme has four phases in our enhanced scheme as well, i.e., phrases of registration, login, verification and password change, while the details of our proposed scheme are descried as following.

**Registration phase:** This phase is a registration procedure for the user $U_i$ to get a license from S. Before the user grants the access permit from the service provider, s/he has to submit the identity $ID$ and password $PW$ to S. Then, S issues the license to $U_i$, while the steps are stated as below.

R1. $U_i =>S: \{ID, h(PW), h(b \oplus PW)\}$

U_i selects $PW_i$ and an arbitrary number $b$, computes $h(b \oplus PW)$, and then sends { $ID$, $h(PW)$, $h(b \oplus PW)$ } to the server S by the secure channel.

R2. $S => U_i: \{V, R, h( )\}$

After S received the message from $U_i$ and decided to accept the user's request, S calculates the results and sends $\{V, R, h()\}$ to $U_i$ by the secure channel where $EID = h(ID || n), P = h(EID \oplus x), R = P \oplus h(b \oplus PW)$ and $V = h(P \oplus h(b \oplus PW))$

R3. The smart card saves the data containing $(V, R, h( ))$

**Login phase:** When $U_i$ enters his identity $ID$ and password $PW$ in order to login the service provider S, the smart card performs the following steps.

L1. $U_i$ firstly must pass the verification of $V = h(h(EID \oplus x) \oplus h(b \oplus PW))$, and then generate a nonce $R_i$ and compute $C_1 = R \oplus h(b \oplus PW)$ and $C_2 = h(C_1 || R_i || T_u)$, where $T_u$ denotes $U_i$'s current timestamp .

L2. $U_i \rightarrow S: \{ID, C_2, T_u, R_i\}$
$U_i$ sends the message { $ID, C_2, T_u, R_i$ } to S

**Verification phase:** After receiving the login request message $\{ID, C_2, T_u, R_i\}$, S executes the following operations to verify the user $U_i$:

V1. $S \rightarrow U_i: \{ C_3, T_s \}$

S checks $T_s - T_u < \Delta T$ at the time $T_s$ (where $T_s$ denotes the current timestamp and $\Delta T$ the legal time interval for transmission delay), and then calculates $C_2' = h(h(EID \oplus x) || R_i || T_u)$ to check whether $C_2'$ is equal to $C_2$ or not. If yes, the validity of $U_i$ can be assured, and calculates $C_3 = h(h(EID \oplus x) || h(T_s))$, then S sends the message $\{C_3, T_s\}$ to $U_i$ by a common channel.

V2. $U_i$ checks $C_3' = C_3$?

$U_i$ checks whether $T_s = T_u$. If yes, $U_i$ terminates the session. Otherwise, $U_i$ calculates $C_3' = h(C_1 || h(T_s))$ to check whether $C_3'$ is equal to $C_3$. If yes, the validity of S can be assured and $h(C_1 || R_i || T_u || h(T_s))$ can be used between $U$ and $S$ as the session key for the subsequent private communication.

**Password change phase:** The user $U_i$ can change his original password to $PW_{new}$ freely without the help from S. The steps are as following:

P1. $U_i$ inserts his smart card into the smart card reader

$U_i$ enters $ID_i$ and $PW_i$, and requests to change the password..

P2. Smart card computes below:

$P* = R \oplus h(b \oplus PW)$ and $V* = h(P* \oplus h((b \oplus PW))$

The smart card checks whether $V* = V$. If yes, it selects the new password $PW_{new}$, calculates $R_{new} = P* \oplus h(b \oplus PW_{new})$ which yields $h(EID \oplus x) \oplus h(b \oplus PW_{new})$ and $V_{new} = h(P* \oplus h(b \oplus PW_{new}))$, and then replaces $V$ and $R$ with $V_{new}$ and $R_{new}$, respectively.

# 5  Security and Performance Analysis

In this section, we will discuss the enhanced security of our improved scheme, while it can be found that the security of our proposed scheme is higher than Hsiang and Shih's scheme.

## 5.1  Security analysis

**Resistance to replay attack:** The proposed remote user authentication mechanism resists replay attack .The details are as follows.

1. An intruder can not succeed in replay attack which needs the replay of the request message in Step L2: $U_i \rightarrow S$: $\{ID, C_2, T_u, R_i\}$ or V1: $S \rightarrow U_i$:$\{ C_3, T_s \}$ for the server S will check whether $T_s$-$T_u$< $\Delta T$ at the time $T_s$ and the intruder can not send the request message of $\{ID, C_2, T_u, R_i\}$ between the time interval $T_u$ and $T_s$.

2. An intruder can not succeed in Step V1: $S \rightarrow U_i$:$\{ C_3, T_s \}$ for the intruder does not have the cipher code $C_3$ where $C_3$= $h(h(EID \oplus x)|| h(T_s))$ and can not generate $C_3$ at the time $T_s$. It is infeasible to do that. That is, the proposed scheme can resist the reply attack.

**Resistance to parallel session attack:** Assume that an intruder has intercepted one of the legal users $U_i$'s previous login message $\{ID_i, C_2, T_u, R_i\}$ and the message$\{C_3, T_s\}$ from S to $U_i$ in the middle. If the intruder attempts to impersonate $U_i$ to login $S$ at the time $T^*$, an attack can be performed as given below: First, the intruder computes $T^* = h(T_s) \oplus T_u$ and $C_2^*$= $C_3$ $(C_3$= $h(h(EID \oplus x)|| h(T_s)))$. And then, the intruder sends the message $\{ ID_i, C_2^*, T^*, R_i\}$ to S. Since $T^*$ is valid, $S$ will proceed to compute $C_2$'=$h(h(EID \oplus x) ||R_i||T^*)$ which will yield $C_2$'= $h(h(EID \oplus x)||R_i||h(T_s) \oplus T_u)$ but $C_2$' is not equal to $h(C_2^*||R_i||T_u)$. Then S will not accept the intruder login request. The key solution is to change the original $C_2$ from $h(C_1 \oplus T_u)$ to $h(C_1||R_i||T_u)$ and the original $C_3$ from $h(h(EID \oplus x) \oplus h(T_s))$ to $h(h(EID \oplus x)||h(T_s))$.

**Resistance to stolen-verifier attack:** In the proposed scheme, there is no verifier table in the service providers firstly. Secondly, the user Ui's authentication data stored in smart card are $R=P \oplus h(b \oplus PW)$ and $V=h(P \oplus h(b \oplus PW))$. Suppose that an intruder has stolen the $V$ and $R$ , s/he can pass the authentication only if s/he has the information of $b$ and $PW$ , which implies he knows Ui's all information to pass the check point $V=h(h(EID \oplus x) \oplus h(b \oplus PW))$. It is infeasible to do that. That is, the proposed scheme can resist the stolen-verifier attack.

**Resistance to card-loss attack:** Assume that an intruder obtains a smart card and deciphers the $V$ and $R$ from it. It will be infeasible to cheat the service provider by off-line attack for the intruder must get the legal users $U_i$'s password and arbitrary number b to calculate $C_1$= $R \oplus h(b \oplus PW)$ and $C_2$= $h(C_1||R_i||T_u)$ to go next verification step. There is no password and b information at the smart card. That is, the proposed scheme can resist the card-loss attack.

**Resistance to guessing attack:** Assume that an intruder attempts to find out the password to access the server. It will fail for the intruder must send the request message "$C_2$" in Step L2:$U_i{\to}S$:$\{ID, C_2, T_u, R_i\}$ where $C_2 = h(C_1||R_i||T_u)$ ($T_u$ is the current timestamp) and the intruder can not find out the same random nonce $R_i$ which is generated by $U_i$' at the time $T_u$. It is infeasible to do that. That is, the proposed scheme can resist the guessing attack.

## 5.2 Comparison with the Eleven Properties of a Password Authentication Scheme

Liao et al. [15] proposed ten requirements for evaluating a password authentication scheme, described as follows:

R1. There is no password or verification tables are saved inside the server.
R2. The user can change password Freely.
R3. The server's administrator can not discern the password.
R4. The password must be transmitted in encryption type in an insecure network.
R5. The scheme can avoid impersonate attack.
R6. The scheme can avoid the replay attack, guessing attack, modification attack and stolen-verifier attack.
R7. The length of the password is suitable for memorization.
R8. The scheme must be efficient and practical.
R9. The scheme must be a mutual authentication scheme.
R10. The scheme can avoid the smart card losing attack.

In this section, we add a requirement,"R11. The scheme can avoid parallel session attack", and the comparison among the related schemes is shown in Table 1. Crucially, Ku-Chen's scheme can not serve to avoid guessing attack, forgery attack and parallel session attack [5,20] ; Yoon-Ryu-Yoo's scheme is vulnerable to masquerading attack, guessing attack and parallel session attack ; finally Hsiang-Shih's scheme suffers from parallel session attack. It is significant that our scheme satisfies the requirement of the eleven properties from R1 to R11.

**Table 1.** The comparison among the related schemes

|              | R1 | R2 | R3 | R4 | R5 | R6 | R7 | R8 | R9 | R10 | R11 |
|--------------|----|----|----|----|----|----|----|----|----|-----|-----|
| Ku-Chen      | Y  | N  | Y  | Y  | N  | N  | Y  | Y  | Y  | N   | N   |
| Yoon-Ryu-Yoo | Y  | Y  | Y  | Y  | N  | N  | Y  | Y  | Y  | Y   | N   |
| Hsiang-Shih  | Y  | Y  | Y  | Y  | Y  | Y  | Y  | Y  | Y  | Y   | N   |
| Ours         | Y  | Y  | Y  | Y  | Y  | Y  | Y  | Y  | Y  | Y   | Y   |

Ri:the Proposed requirement     N: not supported     Y: supported

## 5.3 Performance Analysis

In registration phase Ku-Chen and Yoon-Ryu-Yoo's schemes need $2T_h$ only (the computation cost of hash function). Hsiang-Shih's and ours need $5T_h$ .In verification phase Ku-Chen's and Yoon-Ryu-Yoo's schemes need $4T_h$ only (the computation cost of hash function). Hsiang-Shih's and ours need $6T_h$.

The computational cost of our proposed scheme is the same as that of Hsiang-Shih's scheme but our scheme has more security than Hsiang-Shih's. Further, the computational cost of our proposed scheme is higher than that of the others but the security is higher than the others, too. The comparison among the related schemes is shown in Table 2.

**Table 2.** The comparison of computation cost among the related schemes

|  | Registration phase | Login phase | Verification phase |
|---|---|---|---|
| Ku-Chen | $2T_h$ | $2T_h$ | $4T_h$ |
| Yoon-Ryu-Yoo | $2T_h$ | $2T_h$ | $4T_h$ |
| Hsiang-Shih | $5T_h$ | $2T_h$ | $6T_h$ |
| Ours | $5T_h$ | $2T_h$ | $6T_h$ |

$T_h$: the computation cost of hash function

## 6 Conclusion

After analyzed Hsiang-Shih's user authentication scheme and some other secure smart-card-based schemes, we found that Hsiang-Shih's scheme is better than the related user authentication schemes. However, in this paper, we point out that Hsiang-Shih's scheme is vulnerable to parallel session attack. The problems may render the scheme unsecured, because the attacker can successfully impersonate the legal user to login and use the server resources. Hence, we propose an improved approach. The proposed approach still does not need to maintain any verification table on the remote server. Furthermore , it not only inherits the merits of Hsiang-Shih's scheme but also enhances the security. As the result, the parallel session attack is completely solved under our proposed scheme.

## References

[1] Chien, H., Jan, J., Tseng, Y.: An efficient and practical solution to remote authentication smart card. Computers & Security 21(4), 372–375 (2002)
[2] Diffie, W., Hellman, M.: New directions in cryptography. IEEE Trans. Inf. Theory IT-21(6), 644–654 (1976)
[3] Duan, X., Liu, J., Zhang, Q.: Security improvement on Chien Et Al.'s remote user authentication scheme using smart cards. In: The 2006, IEEE International Conference on Computational Intelligence and Security (CIS 2006), vol. 2, pp. 1133–1135 (2006)
[4] Halevi, S., Krawczyk, H.: Public-key cryptography and password protocols. ACM Trans. Inf. Syst. Secur. 2(3), 230–268 (1999)
[5] Hsiang, H., Shih, W.: Weaknesses and improvements of the YoonRyuYoo remote user authentication scheme using smart cards. Computer Communications 32(4), 649–652
[6] Hwang, M., Li, L.: A new remote user authentication scheme using smart card. IEEE Transactions on Consumer Electronics 46(1), 28–30 (2000)
[7] Hwang, T., Chen, Y., Laih, C.: Non-interactive password authentication without password tables. In: IEEE region 10 conference on computer and communication system, September 1990, vol. 1, pp. 429–431 (1990)

[8]  Hwang, T., Ku, W.: Reparable key distribution protocols for Internet environments. IEEE Trans. Consum. Electron. 43(5), 1947–1949 (1995)

[9]  Joux, A.: A One Round Protocol for Tripartite Diffie–Hellman. J. Cryptology 17, 263–276 (2004), doi:10.1007/s00145-004-0312-y

[10] Ku, W., Chen, S.: Weaknesses and improvements of an efficient password based remote user authentication scheme using smart cards. IEEE Transactions on Consumer Electronics 50(1), 204–207 (2004)

[11] Ku, W., Chen, C., Lee, H.: Cryptanalysis of a variant of Peyravian–Zunic's password authentication scheme. IEICE Transactions on Communication E86-B(5), 1682–1684 (2003)

[12] Lamport, L.: Password authentication with insecure communication. Communications of the ACM 24(11), 770–772 (1981)

[13] Lee, W., Chang, C.: User identification and key distribution maintaining anonymity for distributed computer network. Comput. Syst. Sci. 15(4), 211–214 (2000)

[14] Lennon, R., Matyas, S., Mayer, C.: Cryptographic authentication of time invariant quantities. IEEE Transactions on Communications 29(6), 773–777 (1981)

[15] Liao, I., Lee, C., Hwang, M.: A password authentication scheme over insecure networks. J. Comput. System Sci. 72(4), 727–740 (2006)

[16] Mitchell, C.: Limitations of challenge-response entity authentication. Electronic Letters 25(17), 1195–1196 (1989)

[17] Sun, H.: An efficient remote use authentication scheme using smart cards. IEEE Transactions on Consumer Electronics 46(4), 958–961 (2000)

[18] Yang, G., Wong, D., Wang, H., Deng, X.: Two-factor mutual authentication based on smart cards and passwords. Journal of Computer and System Sciences (May 15, 2008) (in press) (corrected Proof)

[19] Yen, S., Liao, K.: Shared authentication token secure against replay and weak key attack. Information Processing Letters, 78–80 (1997)

[20] Yoon, E., Ryu, E., Yoo, K.: Further improvement of an efficient password based remote user authentication scheme using smart cards. IEEE Transactions on Consumer Electronics 50(2), 612–614 (2004)

# Dual-Byte-Marker Algorithm for Detecting JFIF Header

Kamaruddin Malik Mohamad[1], Tutut Herawan[1,2], and Mustafa Mat Deris[1]

[1] Faculty of Information Technology and Multimedia
Universiti Tun Hussein Onn Malaysia
Parit Raja, Batu Pahat 86400, Johor, Malaysia
[2] Department of Mathematics Education
Universitas Ahmad Dahlan
Yogyakarta 55166, Indonesia
malik@uthm.edu.my, tutut81@uad.ac.id, mmustafa@uthm.edu.my

**Abstract.** The use of efficient algorithm to detect JPEG file is vital to reduce time taken for analyzing ever increasing data in hard drive or physical memory. In the previous paper, single-byte-marker algorithm is proposed for header detection. In this paper, another novel header detection algorithm called dual-byte-marker is proposed. Based on the experiments done on images from hard disk, physical memory and data set from DFRWS 2006 Challenge, results showed that dual-byte-marker algorithm gives better performance with better execution time for header detection as compared to single-byte-marker.

**Keywords:** Forensics; JPEG JFIF; Data recovery.

## 1 Introduction

File carving for JPEG can be done much easier by using the file metadata (header, footer and marker) in a non-fragmented environment. Recently, there are some file carving researches that look into the file content rather than using metadata to solve corrupted and fragmented file. Thus, file carving is useful for both, data recovery and computer forensics [1].

The most common form of file carving is that they analyze headers and footers of a file and try to merge all the blocks in between [2]. One of the most popular JPEG file carving tool is Scalpel [3]. It is an enhancement done based on Foremost. However, most of these file carving tools still fail to merge files that are fragmented. File carving involving fragmented files are discussed in [1,2,4,5,6].

JPEG is a compression standard but does not specify a file format. JPEG File Interchange Format (JFIF) is a minimal JPEG file format to enable file exchanges between a wide variety of platforms and applications [7]. It is widely used in the internet. JFIF defines a number of details that are left unspecified by the JPEG standard [8,9]. Another JPEG format is called JPEG Extended File Information (Exif), created by Japan Electronic Industry Development Association for digital cameras [10].

S.K. Bandyopadhyay et al. (Eds.): ISA 2010, CCIS 76, pp. 17–26, 2010.
© Springer-Verlag Berlin Heidelberg 2010

Most forensics researchers do not discuss about the JPEG header detection algorithm in detail. Motivation of comparing algorithms for detecting headers is due to ever increasing hard disk size and the backlogs of law enforcement. By developing an automatic JPEG header detector, it would cut the time taken for analysis and can roughly predict the number of JPEG files that exists in a forensically investigated computer. For a forensics investigator who is currently working in the escalating child pornography cases in the internet, the existence of headers in the suspect's computer would mean that there is a possibility of evidence.

In this paper, a novel algorithm called dual-byte-marker for JPEG header detection is proposed. JFIF is used in the experimentations as it is the de-facto format for sharing in many applications and the internet [11]. Nevertheless, the proposed algorithm could also be applied for other JPEG file format by changing the data structure of the header in the algorithm.

The rest of the paper is organized as follows. Section 2 describes single-byte-marker algorithm. Section 3 describes the proposed dual-byte-marker algorithm. Section 4 describes the experimentations done. Section 5 describes the result and discussion. Finally section 6 concludes this paper.

## 2  Single-Byte-Marker Algorithm

Single-byte-marker has been found to be more efficient than 20-point-reference algorithm [12]. Therefore, comparison will only be made between the single-byte-marker and the newly proposed dual-byte-marker algorithm. Please refer to [12] for detail explaination of this algorithm. The algorithm is illustrated in Figure 1.

```
Do
  Read 1 byte                 // FIRST byte is read
  If (byte = 0xFF marker) then
     Read next 1 byte         // SECOND byte is read
     If (byte =  SOI marker) // SOI is 0xD8
        Read 18-byte structure
        If (Match JFIF string)
           Valid JFIF Header is FOUND
        Else
           Return the structure (18 BYTES) to input stream
           Position the pointer to the STARTING byte of the
                                    returned structure
        End-if
     Else if (byte = 0xFF) marker
        Return the second-byte
        Position the pointer to the returned byte
     End-if
While not end-of-image/file
```

**Fig. 1.** Algorithm for JFIF header detection using single-byte-marker algorithm [12]

# 3  The Proposed Algorithm

This section discusses on the development of the proposed algorithm called dual-byte-marker. The algorithm is designed to detect JFIF headers and then record the total processing time for JFIF headers' detection.

## 3.1  Dual-Byte-Marker Algorithm

Basically, the dual-byte-marker algorithm is made of these following steps:

STEP 1:  Identify start-of-image (SOI or 0xFFD8) marker (refer to Figure 2).
  • If two-byte structure read is a SOI marker, then read an eighteen-byte structure.
STEP 2:  Once SOI is found, locate JFIF identifier or "JFIF\0" (refer to Figure 2) ("JFIF" string terminated by NULL or "\0").
  • If 'JFIF\0' is found at the correct location in the 18-byte structure, then JFIF header is found.
STEP 3:  Repeat step 1 and 2 until end of data.

| SOI | A PP0 | Length | Identifier | | | | |
|------|--------|---------|------|----|----|----|------|
| 0xFF D8 | 0xFF E0 | 0x00 10 | 0x4A | 46 | 49 | 46 | 00 |
| | | | J | F | I | F | NULL |
| 2 bytes | 2 bytes | 2 bytes | 5 bytes | | | | |

**Fig. 2.** First 11 bytes of a JFIF header with valid hex codes sample

The name dual-byte-marker is used because two bytes are read from the data until SOI is found. For a successful JFIF header search, the first two bytes read must match 0xFFD8. After the first match, an eighteen-byte structure is obtained from the second read. The successful match scenario is shown in Figure 3.

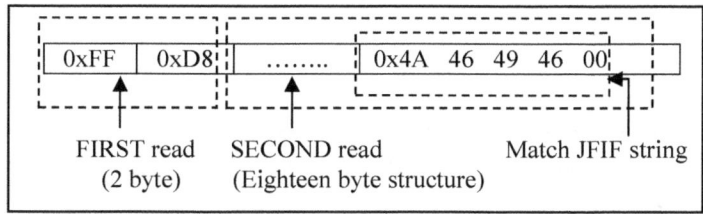

FIRST read    SECOND read    Match JFIF string
(2 byte)    (Eighteen byte structure)

**Fig. 3.** A match for JFIF header using "dual-byte-marker" algorithm

Now, let's consider few non-match situations when developing the dual-byte-marker. First non-match happens when the first two bytes read does not match 0xFFD8. In this case, the next read would obtained another two bytes that comes right after the previous read. This is illustrated Figure 4.

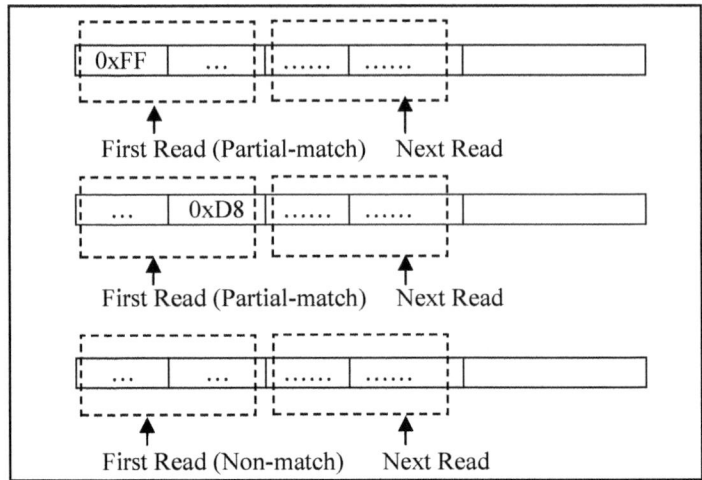

**Fig. 4.** First dual-byte-marker non-match case

Second non-match happens when the first two bytes read is a contiguous 0xFFFF instead of 0xFFD8. When this happens, these two bytes need to be returned to the input stream. So, the next read (second read) would start at the second byte of returned bytes. This is illustrated in Figure 5. These bytes (0xFFFF) are returned because there is a probability that the next two bytes (third read) is 0xFFD8.

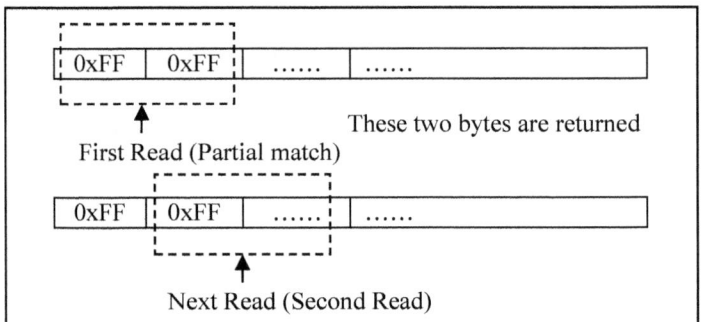

**Fig. 5.** Second dual-byte-marker non-match case

Next, the third non-match happens when the first two bytes read match 0xFFD8. Since the first read found its match, the second read would obtain an 18-byte structure. Nevertheless, the second read does not match 'JFIF\0' string. In this case, the 18-byte structure needs to be returned to the input stream. Therefore, the third read would take the first two bytes of the returned eighteen-byte structure. This is illustrated in Figure 6.

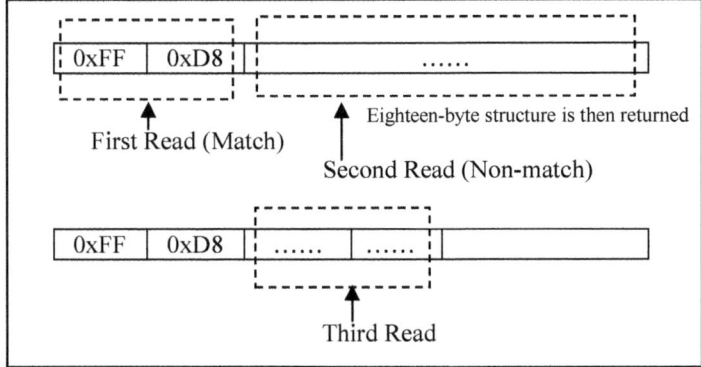

**Fig. 6.** Third dual-byte-marker non-match case

The algorithm can be generalized as:

Let $P(n)$ be 0xFFD8 (SOI).

Let $Q(n)$ be "JFIF\0" string.

$\exists n \in Z^+, P(n) \wedge Q(n) \Leftrightarrow$ *JFIF Header is found*

After considering all the cases, the algorithm for dual-byte-marker is illustrated as in Figure 7. The best and worst case scenarios are discussed below.

**Best case scenario:**

This happens when the first read (two bytes) is $P(n)$ and the second read (18 bytes) is $Q(n)$. Thus, for every two reads, there is one successful detection of JPEG header. Thus, the big O value for best case scenario is $O(n) = \dfrac{n}{20} \times 2$.

**Worst case scenario:**

This happens when no JFIF header is found because the data are filled with '0xFF's. Therefore, every time two bytes are read, the obtained values (0xFFFF) are returned to the input stream. The next two bytes read would start from the second byte of the previously returned bytes and the values obtained are still 0xFFFF. These steps will be repeated (read two bytes and then returned) until the end of the image. Thus, the big O value for worst case scenario is $O(n) = 2n - 1$.

The big O for best case scenario for single-byte-marker [12] is $O(n) = \dfrac{n}{20} \times 3$ while the big O for dual-byte-marker is $O(n) = \dfrac{n}{20} \times 2$. The big O for worst case

```
Do
   // FIRST read
   Read two-byte structure
   If two-byte structure = '0xFFD8'  marker then
      // SECOND read
      Read 18-byte structure
      If (the seventh-byte of the structure match JFIF
         string)
        Valid JFIF Header is FOUND
      Else
        Return the 18-byte structure to input stream
        Position the pointer to the FIRST byte of the
                        18-byte returned structure
      End-if
   // if contiguous 0xFFFF is found
   Else if second byte of the two-byte
                  structure = 0xFF
      Return the two-byte structure to the input stream
      Position the pointer to the second BYTE of the
                        returned structure
   End-if
While not end-of-image
```

**Fig. 7.** Algorithm for JFIF header detection using dual-byte-marker algorithm

scenario for both single-byte-marker and dual-byte-marker are the same; $O(n) = 2n - 1$. Thus, this shows that for best case scenario, dual-byte-marker is more efficient for detecting JPEG header.

## 4 Experimentation

This section discusses on the comparisons done for JFIF header detection between single-byte-marker and dual-byte-marker algorithms. These tests are done according to the FORIMAGE-JPEG model [12]. This model is illustrated in Figure 8. The inputs to be used with the model are an image taken from a hard disk, an image taken from the physical memory and finally a data set downloaded from Digital Forensics Research Workshop (DFRWS) 2006 Challenge [13]. The model is adapted from FORSIGS and FORWEB [14]. The FORIMAGE-JPEG model and the preparation of input for this model will not be discussed in this paper. Detail of it can be obtained from [12]. Both algorithms are implemented using C language in Windows Vista with Intel Core 2 Duo Processor and 2GB of physical memory. Single-byte-marker and dual-byte-marker algorithms will be referred to as 'single' and 'dual' respectively in the result tables shown in this section.

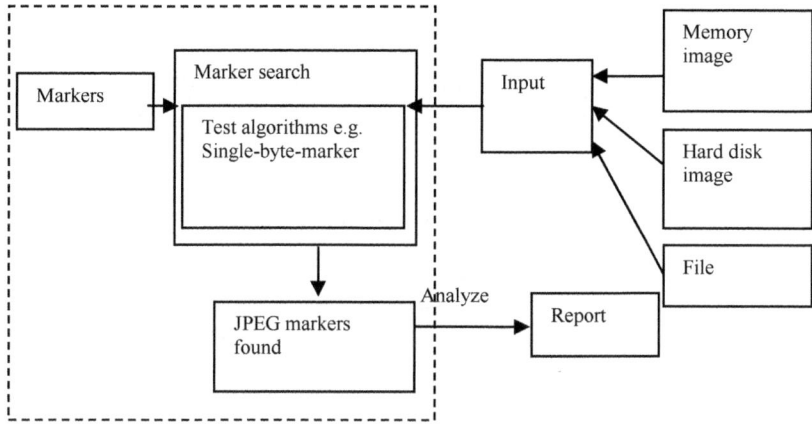

**Fig. 8.** Overview of FORIMAGE-JPEG model [12]

These algorithms are compared according to their processing time on the image data in seconds. The algorithm with the least overall processing time for all types of data being tested is considered as the most efficient one to be used for JFIF header detection. According to Gafinkel [1], only 16% of JFIF files are fragmented. Thus, it is much easier and faster to detect the existence of the majority of non-fragmented JFIF file through its header and footer.

### 4.1   Experiment Using Memory Image

A 1GB memory image mem.dd is used. This image is the same image used in [12], taken from a computer with 1GB physical memory using Helix Live CD [15,16,17]. Both, single-byte-marker and dual-byte-marker algorithms are tested few times using this image and each time they stop according to the predetermined varied incremented sizes (30MB, 60MB, 90MB, 120MB, 180MB, 600MB) as listed in Table 1. The results (processing time taken in seconds) are summarized in Table 1. Dual-byte-marker algorithm shows a faster processing time as the size of the image is increased.

**Table 1.** Results of tests done on memory image (mem.dd) of size 1GB

| Algorithm | Data read from mem.dd of size | | | | | |
| --- | --- | --- | --- | --- | --- | --- |
| | 30MB | 60MB | 90MB | 120MB | 180MB | 600MB |
| | Processing Time (seconds) | | | | | |
| single | 94.075 | 267.918 | 408.020 | 490.697 | 671.181 | 1959.070 |
| dual | 64.741 | 219.532 | 329.818 | 378.654 | 494.321 | 1365.277 |

### 4.2   Experiment Using Hard Disk Image

The second experiment is done using the hard disk image hdd.dd. This image is also the same image used in [12], taken from an 8MB hard disk partition. The results are summarized in Table 2. Again, dual-byte-marker algorithm shows a better performance in this experiment.

**Table 2.** Results of tests done on hard disk image (hdd.dd) of size 8MB

| Algorithm | Processing Time (seconds) |
|-----------|---------------------------|
| single | 21.860 |
| dual | 11.530 |

### 4.3   Experiment Using DFRWS 2006 Challenge Raw Data

Finally, these algorithms are tested using data set from DFRWS 2006 Challenge [13]. The dfrws-2006-challenge.zip (40.6 MB) file is downloaded from the internet and then extracted to obtain dfrws-2006-challenge.raw (47.6 MB). The results of these experiments are summarized in Table 3. As shown previously, dual-byte-marker algorithm again proved to give a better performance in this experiment. The screenshot of dual-byte-marker is shown in Figure 9.

**Table 3.** Results of tests done on dfrws-2006-challenge.raw (47.6MB)

| Algorithm | Processing time (seconds) |
|-----------|---------------------------|
| single | 131.330s<br>(2 minutes and 11.33 seconds) |
| dual | 69.7<br>(1 minute and 9.7 seconds) |

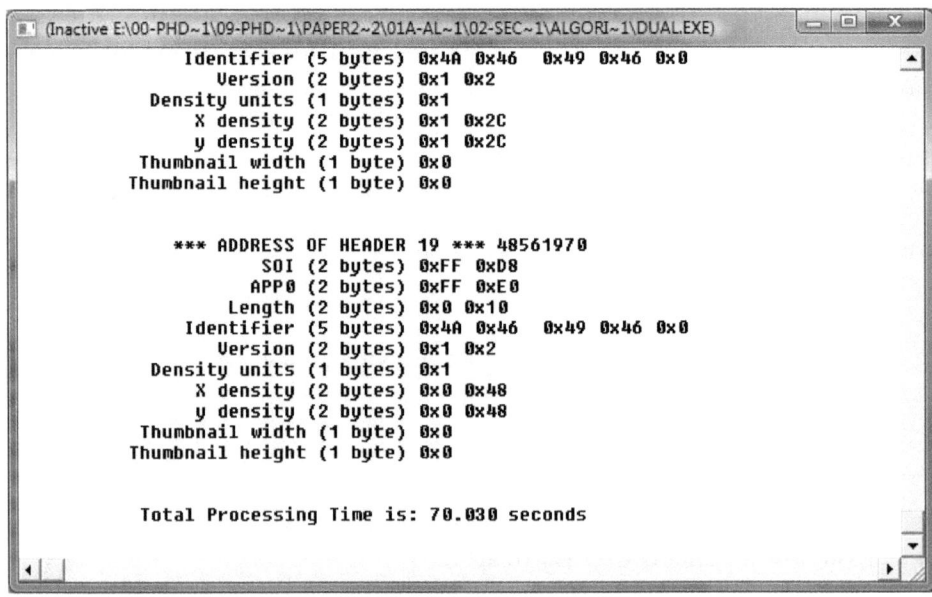

**Fig. 9.** The screenshot of dual-byte-marker

# 5 Result and Discussion

In the previous section, comparisons of two algorithms (single-byte-marker and dual-byte-marker algorithms) using FORIMAGE-JPEG model for detecting JFIF headers by their processing time are demonstrated. From these results, it is clearly shown that dual-byte-marker gives better performance in all three experiments done in detecting JFIF header. The performance can be further improved by minimizing the input output (i.e. writing information to the screen) in these algorithms [3].

# 6 Conclusion

In this paper, we have proposed a novel dual-byte-maker algorithm–for JFIF header detection. Comparison tests have been carried out between single-byte-marker and the proposed algorithm. The results clearly showed that dual-byte-marker algorithm gives better performance based on its processing time as compare to single-byte-marker.

## Acknowledgement

This work was supported by Universiti Tun Hussein Onn Malaysia.

## References

1. Garfinkel, S.L.: Carving Continuous and Fragmented Files with Fast Object Validation. Journal of Digital Investigation 4, 2–12 (2007)
2. Anadabrata, P., Husrev, T., Sencar, N.M.: Detecting File Fragmentation Point Using Sequential Hypothesis Testing. Journal of Digital Investigation 5, 2–13 (2008)
3. Golden, R., Roussev, G., Scalpel, V.: A Frugal, High Performance File Carver. In: The Proceedings of the 2005 digital forensics research workshop (2005)
4. Karresand, M., Shahmeri, N.: Reassembly of Fragmented JPEG Images Containing Restart Markers. IEEE press, Los Alamitos (2008)
5. Pal, A., Shanmugasundaram, K., Memon, N.: Automated Reassembly of Fragmented Images, AFOSR Grant F49620-01-1-0243 (2003)
6. Memon, N., Pal, A.: Automated Reassembly of File Fragmented Images Using Greedy Algorithms. IEEE press, Los Alamitos (2006)
7. Hamilton, E.: JPEG File Interchange File Format – Version 1.02, http://www.w3.org/Graphics/JPEG/jfif3.pdf
8. JPEG File Interchange Format, http://en.wikipedia.org/wiki/JFIF
9. Wallace, G.K.: The JPEG Still Picture Compression Standard. IEEE Transactions on Consumer Electronics (1991)
10. Alvarez, P.: Using Extended File Information (EXIF) File Headers in Digital Evidence Analysis. International Journal of Digital Evidence 2(3) (2004)
11. Swee, L.H.: JPEG for Digital Panel, Texas Instrument, http://focus.tij.co.jp/jp/lit/an/spra664/spra664.pdf
12. Mohamad, K.M., Mat Deris, M.: Single-byte-marker for detecting JPEG JFIF header using FORIMAGE-JPEG. In: Proceeding of NCM 2009, pp. 1693–1698 (2009)

13. Digital Forensics Research Workshop (DFRWS),
    http://www.dfrws.org/2006/challenge/dfrws-2006-challenge.zip
14. Haggerty, J., Liewellyn-Jones, D., Taylor, M.: FORWEB: File Fingerprinting for
    Automated Network Forensics Investigations (2007)
15. Austin, R.D.: Digital Forensics on the Cheap: Teaching Forensics Using Open Source
    Tools. ACM Press, New York (2007)
16. Helix Live CD, http://www.e-fense.com/helix
17. Helix Live CD, http://forensics.wikia.com/wiki/Helix_LiveCD

# Hiding Data in JPEG Using in-DQT Technique

Kamaruddin Malik Mohamad[1], Tutut Herawan[1,2], and Mustafa Mat Deris[1]

[1] Faculty of Information Technology and Multimedia
University of Tun Hussein Onn Malaysia
Parit Raja, Batu Pahat 86400, Johor, Malaysia
[2] Department of Mathematics Education
Universitas Ahmad Dahlan
Yogyakarta 55166, Indonesia
malik@uthm.edu.my, tutut81@uad.ac.id, mmustafa@uthm.edu.my

**Abstract.** Steganography techniques are useful to convey hidden information using various types of typically-transmitted multimedia data as cover file to conceal communication. When using JPEG as a cover file, normally message is hidden in the AC values of quantized DCT coefficients. However, concealment of message in quantization table is yet to be done. In this paper, a novel in-DQT technique for message hiding in JPEG's quantization table using bytewise insertion is proposed. By using in-DQT technique on standard JPEG test images for cover files with up to 24 bytes of message, results show that steganography image with minimal acceptable image distortion. Thus, in-DQT technique provides alternative for embedding message in quantization table.

**Keywords:** Steganography, Information Hiding, Data Hiding.

## 1 Introduction

Steganographic techniques are useful to convey hidden information by using various types of typically-transmitted multimedia data as cover for concealed communication [1]. Hiding message requires two files. The first is the innocent-looking image that will hold the hidden information, called the cover image. The second file is the message, the information to be hidden [2]. It is interesting to know that, many file formats e.g. JPEG, MP3 do not care if additional junk is appended to the end of a valid file [3]. The cover file format has a critical impact on the steganographic system. Using uncompressed format for a cover file, such as BMP, provide relatively more capacity but are more likely to be detected due to high redundant content. JPEG provides a good alternative for a cover file as it is the most popular compressed image file format used in communications and in the internet. Manipulation of JPEG images with the aim of reversible data hiding has been a challenge in recent years. Steganography in JPEG images using any space, rather than DCT coefficients, would create new challenges. One of the challenges is that, the hidden data should be correctly extractable and robust against JPEG lossy compression [4]. Steganalysis [5, 6, 7, 8, 9] is the art of detecting

S.K. Bandyopadhyay et al. (Eds.): ISA 2010, CCIS 76, pp. 27–36, 2010.

any hidden message on the communication channel. A basic of embedding introduces three different aspects in information hiding systems contend with each other: capacity, security and robustness. Capacity refers to the amount of information that can be hidden in the cover medium, security to an eavesdropper's inability to detect hidden information, and robustness to the amount of modification the steganography image can withstand before an adversary [10]. There are a number of ways exist to hide messages in cover images. Common approaches include least significant bit (LSB) insertion, masking and filtering, and finally algorithms and transformations. The message can be embedded into the image or selectively into noisy area (area with a great deal of color variations) [2]. Some of existing steganography tools using LSB insertion including Jsteg, Outguess, JPHide and Steghide. However, there are few drawbacks with these tools. Firstly, they are using LSB insertion method. The drawback of LSB insertion method is that it provides less capacity for hiding message. Only 1 bit of message can be hidden on the LSB of a chosen byte. Thus, a 24-byte messages needs up to $24 \times 8$ bytes (192 bytes) of cover size. Secondly, there is a limited number of data because normally the AC quantized values are mostly 0's, end-of-block or EOB. Thirdly, hiding message sequentially, e.g. Jsteg, is open for easy detection.

In this paper, a novel in-DQT technique for hiding message is proposed. It is using bytewise instead of LSB insertion. Thus, bigger message size can be hidden in smaller cover size. It is randomly hidden using scatter-code in quantization table. Many existing steganography techniques conceal message in AC quantized values, however, concealing in the quantization table is yet to be done. Quantization table normally does not have values of 0's. Thus, it provides bigger capacity for hiding message.

The rest of the paper is organized as follows. Section 2 describes quantization Table. Section 3 describes the proposed technique. Section 4 describes the experiment, result and discussion. Finally, the conclusions and future work are described in section 5.

## 2   Quantization Table (DQT Table)

Now, before concentrating on the hiding technique, we are going to discuss on the DQT table which is the location used for hiding the message. DQT table can be detected by 0xFFDB marker representing Define Quantization Table (DQT) segment. Each image can have up to 4 DQT tables. Every DQT table consists of a set of 64 DQT values used to quantize DCT coefficients. The specification for DQT table parameter sizes and values is shown in Table 1. The last DQT table normally ends prior to 0xFFC0 or SOF (Start-of-frame) marker for baseline DCT or baseline JPEG.

The DQT marker is followed by a two-byte of quantization table definition length (Lq), four-bit (MSB) DQT table element precision (Pq) with a valid value of 0 for baseline JPEG. DQT table element precision of value 0 specifies the precision of the Qk values using 8 bits. Then it is followed by another four-bit (LSB) DQT table destination identifier (Tq) with a valid value between 0 and 3 (0x00, 0x01, 0x10, 0x11) for baseline JPEG.

**Table 1.** DQT table, specification parameter sizes and values [11]

| Parameter | Size (bits) | Values | | | |
|-----------|-------------|--------|---|---|---|
| | | Sequential DCT | | Progressive DCT | Lossless |
| | | Baseline | Extended | | |
| Lq | 16 | $2 + \sum_{t=1}^{n} (65 + 64 \times \mathrm{Pq}(t))$ | | | Undefined |
| Pq | 4 | 0 | 0,1 | 0,1 | Undefined |
| Tq | 4 | 0–3 | | | Undefined |
| Qk | 8, 16 | 1–225, 1–65 535 | | | Undefined |

For example, the image used for message hiding in Figure 2 contains 2 tables with Pq+Tq (1 byte) of 0x00 and 0x01. The value for Lq is calculated as the formula given from [11], i.e., $2 + \sum_{t=1}^{n} (65 + 64 \times \mathrm{Pq}(t))$, where size of 2 bytes is the value for Lq. 65 bytes is the size for each DQT table which is comprise of Pq+Tq (1 byte) and 64 bytes of quantization elements. Pq in the formula is 0 for 8 bit sample precision P. The value n is the number of quantization tables specified in the DQT marker segment. In this experiment, 2 DQT tables are used or n is 2. Since, baseline JPEG is used, thus the size for each quantization element is 8 bits or 1 byte. Thus, the Lq value for 2 DQT tables in this experiment is $2 + 2(65 + (64 \times 0))$ which equals to 132 bytes. $Q_k$ is the quantization table element. It specifies the $k$th element out of 64 elements, where $k$ is the index in the zigzag ordering of the DCT coefficients. The quantization elements shall be specified in zig-zag scan order. There is no default DQT table recommended by [10]. Once a DQT table has been defined for a particular destination, it replaces the previous tables stored in that destination and shall be used, when referenced, in the remaining scans of the current image and in subsequent images represented in the abbreviated format for compressed image data. If a table has never been defined for a particular destination, then when this destination is specified in a frame header, the results are unpredictable. The last quantization table is used to conceal the message. The same experiments are then carried out using other cover files using standard test images. From these tests, the image quality degrades as the message capacity is increased. It shows an acceptable minimal image distortion for massage capacity up to 24 bytes.

## 3   The Proposed Technique

This section discusses on the in-DQT technique to embed message into DQT table (the last DQT table prior to SOF) using baseline JPEG [11] file. Baseline JPEG is used because it is the most widely used JPEG in the internet. A proof of concept program called myHide has been developed to hide the data (message) using a novel in-DQT technique and also to retrieve the message. Many image files including standard JPEG test images such as "lena" and "baboon" are used as cover media. The message embedding algorithm is illustrated in Figure 1.

```
Input: Message, over Image (JPEG)
Output: Steganography Image

1. Get the size of message m_size //max_embed_message_size is 24
2. if m_size < max_embed_message_size
3.    select the last DQT table (prior to SOF / 0xFFC0)
4.    go to last byte of DQT table
5.    replace DQT value with m_size // store size of message
6.    go one byte backwards in DQT table
7.    for (i=0; i<m_size; i++)
8.    // generate random number either 0 or 1 to simulate random
      walk
9.     r=random(0,1)
10.      scatter[i]=r  // 0 or 1
11.    end-for
12.    Fill remaining High Significant Bit (HSB) of  scatter[i]
       with 0's
     // 10110 (5 bits) now becomes 0001 0110 (1 byte)
13.    store scatter pattern  replacing DQT values // an array
       of m_size BITS (not bytes)
14.    go one byte backwards in DQT table
15.    for (i=m_size; i>0; i--)    // embed message
16.    if scatter[i] = 0  // if 0
17.      store 1 byte message
18.      go one byte backwards in DQT table
19.    else
20.      go one byte backwards in DQT table
21.      store 1 byte message
22.      go one byte backwards in DQT table
23.    endif
24.   end-for
25.endif
```

**Fig. 1.** in-DQT algorithm

The in-DQT technique is illustrated in Figure 1. Initially, (line 1) get the size of the message. The message hiding processes proceed if *m_size* (message size) is not more than the *max_embed_message_size* (maximum message size) of 24 bytes (line 2). Select the last DQT table prior to SOF (line 3). JPEG file can have up to four DQT tables. In this experiment, most of the tested files and the standard images used (baboon", "lena") has only two DQT tables. So, in this experiment, the second table is used. All the storing of additional information and embedding process is done in reverse order, from the last DQT value in the last DQT table backwards. Go to the last byte of the DQT table (line 4). Replace the current DQT value in the table with a byte of *m_size* (line 5). Go backwards by one byte (line 6). Generate m_size series of 0's and 1's (scatter-code) to implement random walk algorithm to scatter the message randomly in the DQT table (line 7–10). In a graph, random walk is implemented as Brownian motion where the value in the graph is either increased by 1 (upward) or decreased by 1 (downward). In this algorithm, a value 0 means no skip and a value of 1 means skip 1 byte. Once the variable size scatter-code is generated, store the code into the table by replacing DQT values i.e. if the message size is 5 byte, and the randomly generated code is 1, 0, 1, 1, 0, thus the scatter-code is 10110 which implemented in reverse that means not skip (0), skip (1), skip (1), not skip (0) and finally skip (1). Since it is less than a byte, the remaining bits will be filled with 0's to avoid big values (line 12). Therefore, the final scatter-code is 0001 0110 or 0x16 (line 13). The algorithm from line 14 to 25 is described further.

**Example 1.** Let assume that the message is "MYLEG", and the message is encrypted as "@#$%!" with scatter-code 0x16. Go one byte backward (line 14). "M" replaced (scatter-code=0) the current DQT value, then skip (scatter-code=1) a byte backwards and then replaced the DQT value with "Y", skip (scatter-code=1) one-byte backwards and then replaced the DQT value with "L", replaced (scatter-code=0) the DQT value with "E", then skip (scatter-code=1) a byte backwards and replaced the DQT value with "G". The whole message hiding process is illustrated in Figure 2.

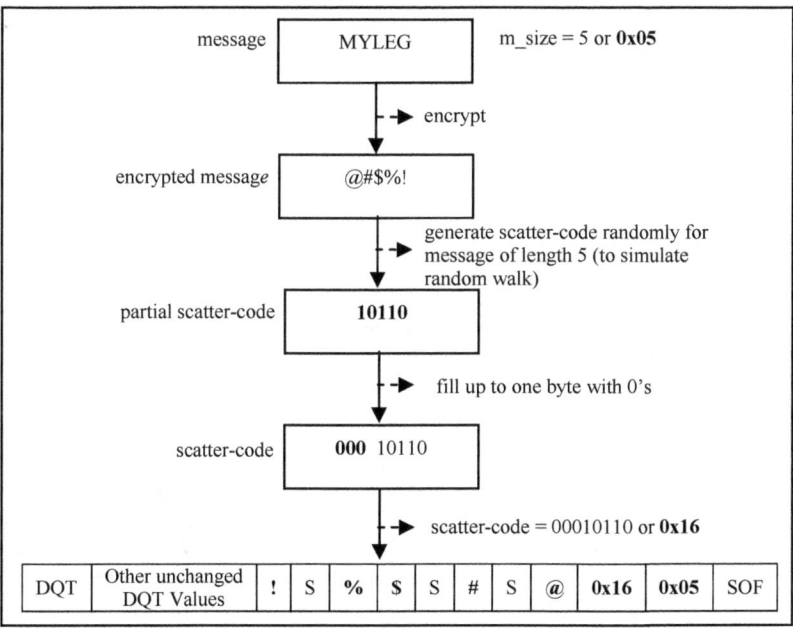

**Fig. 2.** in-DQT technique for message hiding

Encrypting and scattering help protects against unauthorized hidden message extraction [12]. By using good encryption and compression, more messages can be embedded into a DQT table. In summary, the message is stored on one byte basis. First the message size (1 byte) is stored in the last byte of the selected DQT table, then move backwards and store the scatter-code values to implement random walk storing pattern, finally store all the encrypted message bytes in reverse order according to the scatter-code value i.e. 0 means no skip and replace the current DQT value, and if scatter-code value is 1, thus skip a byte and then replace a byte of message.

Note that, the letter "S" in Figure 2 represents skips one byte, but in actual implementation the original DQT value at that address/location remained.

# 4  Experimentation

In-DQT algorithm is implemented into myHide stego tool using C language on Windows XP operating system with processor Intel® dual core 1.8 MHz and memory 2GB.

## 4.1  Embedding Message

These tests are done on various encrypted message size of 5, 10, 15, 20 and 24 bytes and concealed in the last DQT table prior to SOF. A simple encryption is used in these experiments, but the encryption process will not be discussed in this paper. The scatter-code and the message size used for the experiments are shown in Table 2. The scatter-code is purposely filled with 1's to maximize skip action during embedding the message and to test using bigger range of AC values in DQT table. For these tests, myHide (refer to Figure 3) is run 11 times and uses message sizes and scatter-codes values from Table 2. These scatter-code values are hard-coded into myHide instead of randomly generated for ease of experimentation. The results of these tests are illustrated in Table 3.

**Table 2.** List of scatter-code and message size used for experiment

| Message size (bytes) | Scatter-code size (bytes) | Scatter-code (binary) | Scatter-code (Hex) | Message size (Hex) |
|---|---|---|---|---|
| 5 | 1 | 0001 1111 | 0x1F | 0x05 |
| 10 | 2 | 0000 0011 1111 1111 | 0x03 FF | 0x0A |
| 15 | 2 | 0111 1111 1111 1111 | 0x7F FF | 0x0F |
| 20 | 3 | 0000 1111 1111 1111 1111 1111 | 0x0F FF FF | 0x14 |
| 24 | 3 | 1111 1111 1111 1111 1111 1111 | 0xFF FF FF | 0x18 |
| 25 | 4 | 0000 0001 1111 1111 1111 1111 1111 1111 | 0x01 FF FF FF | 0x19 |
| 26 | 4 | 0000 0011 1111 1111 1111 1111 1111 1111 | 0x03 FF FF FF | 0x1A |
| 27 | 4 | 0000 0111 1111 1111 1111 1111 1111 1111 | 0x07 FF FF FF | 0x1B |
| 28 | 4 | 0000 1111 1111 1111 1111 1111 1111 1111 | 0x0F FF FF FF | 0x1C |
| 29 | 4 | 0001 1111 1111 1111 1111 1111 1111 1111 | 0x1F FF FF FF | 0x1D |
| 30 | 4 | 0011 1111 1111 1111 1111 1111 1111 1111 | 0x3F FF FF FF | 0x1E |

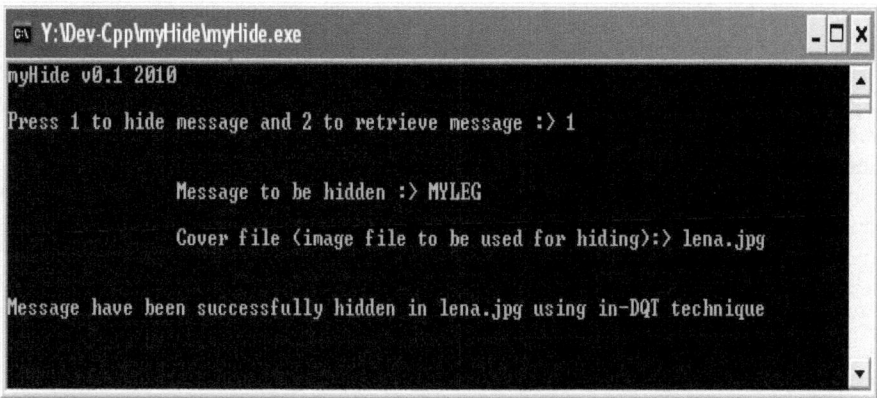

**Fig. 3.** A sample screen shot of myHide concealing message ("MYLEG") into a cover file (lena.jpg)

**Table 3.** JPEG images with messages of different sizes hidden within DQT table

| Message Size (Bytes) | Steganography Image (baboon.jpg) | Steganography Image (lena.jpg) |
|---|---|---|
| 5, 10, 15, 20, 24 | (no noticeable image distortion) | (no noticeable image distortion) |
| 25, 26, 27, 28, 29 | (slight visible image distortion) | (slight visible image distortion) |
| 30 | Image corrupted | Image corrupted |

## 4.2  Retrieving Message

myHide message retrieval is done right after each message is hidden into the cover image in section 4.1. Each messages retrieved by myHide can be verified by doing the reverse of the steps explained previously in Example 1. These messages can be manually figured out because scatter-code values are known (as listed in Table 2) and these messages are purposely not encrypted for ease of experimentations. The scatter-code can be viewed by using any hex editor such as HexAssistant (refer to Figure 5) commercial software [13] or free open source BinText software [14]. The sample screenshot of myHide message retrieval is shown in Figure 4.

To make the scatter-code hard to be decoded, it can be encrypted and then stored into a separate file to be used as a public key. Thus, this public key is needed during the message retrieval process.

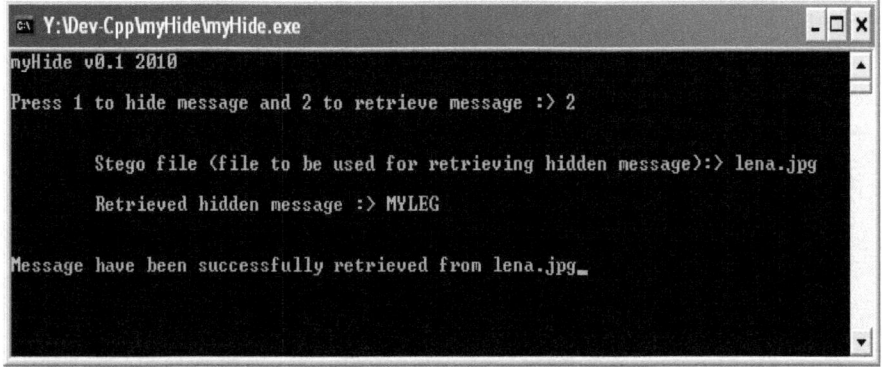

**Fig. 4.** A sample screenshot of myHide retrieving message ("MYLEG") from a cover file (lena.jpg)

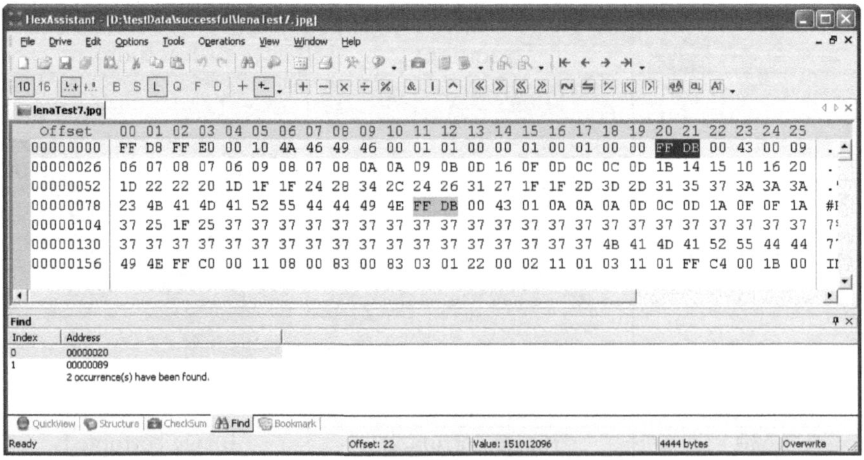

**Fig. 5.** A sample screenshot of an image opened using HexAssistant hex editor

### 4.3 Result and Discussion

From the results, it is shown that image quality degraded as the message capacity increased (refer to Table 3). The stego image cannot be viewed when the message size is 30 bytes. By focusing on the image quality, the proposed maximum message size for in-DQT (implemented in myHide) is 24 bytes with acceptable minimal image distortion. If the message size is 24, the scatter-code will be using 3 bytes of the AC values in DQT table. Suppose that the random scatter-code generated is all skips (all 1's), thus the scatter-code value would be 1111 1111 1111 1111 1111 1111 (24 bits or 3 bytes) or 0xFF 0xFF 0xFF. The results indicate that message up to 24 bytes of size can be concealed in the DQT table (the last DQT table prior to SOF) with acceptable minimal image distortion when opened with any standard JPEG image viewer software, e.g. Adobe Photoshop, Microsoft Office Picture Manager, ACDSee, Windows Picture and Fax Viewer.

Besides of being able to successfully embeds message up to 24 bytes with acceptable minimal image distortion, myHide also ables to retrieve message from a stego file that uses in-DQT technique to conceal the message.

Nevertheless, currently myHide is only using one DQT table for message concealment, even though a JPEG image can have up to 4 DQT tables. Each DQT table is made up of a $8 \times 8$ matrix consisting of 1 DC value and 63 AC values. However, the DC value will not be used for message hiding and will always remain unchanged. Only the AC values will be randomly replaced for embedding encrypted message according to scatter-code value.

## 5 Conclusion and Future Work

When using JPEG as a cover file, normally message is hidden in the AC values of quantized DCT coefficients. However, concealment of message in quantization table is yet to be done. A new technique to embed message in quantization table using bytewise insertion called in-DQT is introduced. This technique is implemented in myHide stego tool. myHide is also capable of retrieving message from a stego file that is concealed using in-DQT technique. The bytewise insertion method used in the technique, enables more messages to be hidden in a much smaller data space as compared to LSB insertion. This tool is able to hide message with a capacity of up to 24 bytes within 64 bytes of quantization table values with acceptable minimal image distortion.

The development of message integrity checker key (MIC-key) is underway. This would enable myHide to detect any unauthorized changes done to the hidden message prior to message retrieval.

Furthermore, myHide is currently using only one DQT table (the last DQT prior to SOF) for hiding message. In the future, we hope to increase myHide message capacity more than 24 bytes by using more than one DQT table.

## Acknowledgement

This work was supported by Universiti Tun Hussein Onn Malaysia.

# References

1. Brundick, F.S., Marvel, L.M.: Implementation of Spread Spectrum Image Steganography, Army Research Laboratory (March 2001),
   http://www.arl.army.mil/arlreports/2001/ARL-TR-2433.pdf
2. Jajodia, S., Johnson, N.F.: Exploring Steganography: Seeing the Unseen. Journal of IEEE Computer 31(2), 26–34 (1998)
3. File Carving, http://www.forensicswiki.org/wiki/File_Carving
4. Mohdavi, M., Samavi, S., Tavala, A., Malekiha, M.: Iterative Random Blocking for Steganography in JPEG Images. In: The Proceeding of 5th International Conference on Information Security and Cryptography, Tehran (October 2008)
5. Westfeld, A.: F5–a steganographic algorithm: High capacity despite better steganalysis. In: Moskowitz, I.S. (ed.) IH 2001. LNCS, vol. 2137, pp. 289–302. Springer, Heidelberg (2001)
6. Ping, W., Liu, F., Wang, G., Sun, Y., Gong, D.: Multi-class Steganalysis For JPEG Stego Algorithms. In: The Proceeding of 15th IEEE International Conference on Image Processing ICIP, pp. 2076–2079 (2008)
7. Silman, J.: Steganography and Steganalysis: An Overview, SANS Institute (2001)
8. Provos, N.: Defending against statistical steganalysis. In: The 10th USENIX Security Symposium, Washington DC (2001)
9. Fidrich, J., Goljan, M., Hogea, D.: Steganalysis of JPEG Images: Breaking the F5 Algorithm. In: Petitcolas, F.A.P. (ed.) IH 2002. LNCS, vol. 2578, pp. 310–323. Springer, Heidelberg (2003)
10. Provos, N., Honeyman, P.: Hide and Seek: An Introduction to Steganography. IEEE Security and Privacy Journal 1(3), 32–44 (2003)
11. Recommendation ITU-T.81: Information Technology-Digital Compression and Coding of Continuous-Tone Still Images-Requirements and Guidelines, International Telecommunications Union (1992)
12. Lee, Y., Chen, L.: Secure error-free steganography for JPEG images. International Journal of Pattern Recognition and Artificial Intelligence 17, 967–981 (2003)
13. HexAssistant Hex Editor, http://www.verytools.com
14. BinText Hex Editor,
    http://www.foundstone.com/us/resources/proddesc/bintext.htm

# An Analysis of Syndrome Coding

Md Amiruzzaman[1], M. Abdullah-Al-Wadud[2], and Yoojin Chung[3],*

[1] Department of Computer Science
Kent State University, Kent, Ohio 44242, USA
mamiruzz@cs.kent.edu
[2] Department of Industrial and Management Engineering,
Hankuk University of Foreign Studies,
Kyonggi, 449-791, South Korea
wadud@hufs.ac.kr
[3] Department of Computer Science,
Hankuk University of Foreign Studies,
Kyonggi, 449-791, South Korea
chungyj@hufs.ac.kr

**Abstract.** In this paper a detail analysis is presented based on BCH syndrome coding for covert channel data hiding methods. The experimented technique is nothing but a syndrome coding algorithm with a coset based approach, analyzed results are showing that the examined method has more flexibility to choose coset, also providing less modification distortion caused by data hiding. Analyzed method presented by clear mathematical way. As it is mathematical equation dependent, hence analyzed results are showing that the analyzed method has fast computation ability and find perfect roots for modification.

**Keywords:** Covert channel, BCH code, syndrome, hamming code.

## 1 Introduction

There are many different techniques are known for covert channel data hiding, among them steganography is one of the most popular [1]-[23]. The word *steganography* is often used to represent covert channel data hiding. The steganography concerns more about security than capacity. It is not so easy to conceal the existence of secret messages in digital image steganography. Researchers are trying to find concrete method for steganography which will have better resistance against steganalysis. Steganalysis is nothing but considered as a attacks to break steganographic methods. Finally, everyone came to a common decision that there is only two ways to develop a good steganographic method: one is reduce distortion and another is reduce the flip (modification). To find such a method which can reduce flip, matrix embedding method introduced by Westfiled [6], and less distortion introduced by Fridrich [13]. Combing less distortion and less modification a modified matrix embedding technique proposed [3]. Matrix embedding

---

* Corresponding author.

S.K. Bandyopadhyay et al. (Eds.): ISA 2010, CCIS 76, pp. 37–50, 2010.

technique is based on HC (Hamming code), where from a set of nonzero elements one or more elements modified to hide a fixed number of secret bits. In general ECC(Error Correction Code) is better also works same like HC. The BCH (Bose and Ray-Chaudhuri) coding is a ECC invented in 1960. For the first time, in [13], mentioned about the distortion by rounding operation in JPEG image processing. In their paper they gave a detail description of rounding errors. They also proposed an embedding technique by LSB modification with a modified matrix embedding.

In this analysis the discussed method has less distortion and less modification based on BCH syndrome coding. The main contributions of this paper is after analysis, it is suggesting the simplified BCH syndrome coding for steganography. At first the BCH coding was proposed in [21], and later modified for data embedding in a simplified way [22]. In [22], authors shown a search based technique for optimal roots for modification. However, their method is not perfectly simplified because their method can not find the best candidate roots for modification, and they only search form a part of total embedding place. This experimented method introduced equation based method to find best candidate roots for modification, this technique is faster than previous methods because this method is equation based.

The rest of this paper is organized as follows: In Section 2, existing methods are discussed. The analyzed method in Section 3. In Section 4, summarizes experimental results, and Section 5 concludes the paper.

## 2   Existing Methods

Sallee models the marginal distribution of DCT coefficients in JPEG-compressed images by the generalized Cauchy distribution (i.e., MBS1) [16]. Thus, the embedded message is adapted to the generalized Cauchy distribution using arithmetic coding. Arithmetic coding transforms unevenly distributed bit streams into shorter, uniform ones. One weak point of the MBS1 is that block artifact increases with growing size of the payload. MBS2 has presented a method to overcome this weakness [17]. The MBS2 embeds message in the same way as MBS1 does, but its embedding capacity is only half of that of MBS1. The other half of the nonzero DCT coefficients is reserved for de-blocking purpose. F5 steganographic method proposed by Westfeld [6], perhaps which is first method of data hiding with less modification. F5 algorithm based on matrix encoding technique, where among seven nonzero AC coefficients only one coefficient was modified to hide three bit of hidden message. The time when F5 algorithm was introduced, F5 was secure against existing steganalysis techniques. Still now, F5 is considering as a good steganographic method. However, F5 method has several limitations, such as F5 algorithm has no freedom to select position for modification (i.e., positions are coming from matrix). F5 is not modifying the LSB in a smart way, as a result number of zeros are increasing. Existing, F5 algorithm does not minimize the distortion. In [2], Provos kept the histogram shape of the DCT coefficients by compensating distortion of modified image (after data hiding). He has divided the set of the DCT coefficients into two disjoint subsets: first subset is used for data hiding, and second subset is used for compensating the modification distortions after data hiding to the first subset. As result, the histogram of the DCT coefficients after data hiding has the same shape as original histogram. Methods presented in [19] and [20] used similar approach. The F5 algorithm based on matrix encoding technique, where $a$ number of hidden message bit can be hide among $(2^a - 1)$ nonzero AC coefficients only changing by one nonzero coefficient. Like F4 algorithm, F5 also has shrinkage problem, which increases the number of zeros. Model based steganography is general framework for constructing steganographic systems that preserve a chosen *model* of the cover media [16], [17]. Suppose, the cover media is $C$, and $C$ is modeled as a random variable which is split in to 2 components $(C_i, C_e)$, where $C_i$ is invariant to embedding and $C_e$ is for modification during embedding.

## 3    Analyzed Method

After analyzing several BCH coding techniques, it is suggested to use the most recently developed BCH coding. However, in their paper the method did not show the extensive analysis and comparisons with other popular algorithms. This paper described the BCH syndrome coding which is mainly based on [23], in a simplest form. The technique is presented here in algorithmically rather than mathematically. This paper is presenting the simple way to find the equation based find roots for modification.

### 3.1    Coding Technique

(1) Let $f(x) = x^2 + ax + b$, now if $x_0$ is root of $f(x)$ then $x_0 + a$ is also root of $f(x)$. if $y_0$ is the root of $f(y) = y^2 + y + \frac{b}{a^2}$ then $x_0 = a * y_0$ is the root of $f(x) = x^2 + ax + b$ and create table index is $\frac{b}{a^2}$.

$$y_0 = table[\frac{b}{a^2}]$$

suppose, $x_1$, and $x_2$ is root of $f(x) = x^2 + ax + b$, then can be represented by The Equation (1)

$$\begin{cases} x_1 = a * y_0 \\ x_2 = a * y_0 + a \end{cases} \qquad (1)$$

(2) $f(x) = x^3 + (a^2 + b)x + ab + c$, now if $x_0$ is root of $f(x)$ then $x_0 + a$ is also root of $f(x) = x^3 + a^2x + bx + ab + c$.

(3) $p = a^2 + b$, $q = ab + c$ if $y_0$ is the root of $f(y) = y^3 + y + \frac{q}{p^{\frac{3}{2}}}$, then $x_0 = p^{\frac{1}{2}}y_0$ is the root of $f(x) = x^3 + px + q$ and create table index is $\frac{q}{p^{\frac{3}{2}}}$.

$y_i = table[\frac{q}{p^{\frac{3}{2}}}]$, where $i = 1, 2, 3, \cdots l$.

and the root of $f(x) = x^3 + a^2x + bx + ab + c$ is $x_i = p^{\frac{1}{2}}y_i + a$.

now, for $GF(2^k)$, table size will be $2^k \times 1$

$GF(2^k)$, table size will be $2^k \times 3$,

remove the row which does not have 3 roots, thus the table will be smaller size as, $d = \lceil \frac{C_n^3}{2^{2k}} \rceil$.

| $r$ | 31 | 63 | 127 | 255 | 512 |
|---|---|---|---|---|---|
| $k$ | 5 | 6 | 7 | 8 | 9 |
| $d$ | 5 | 10 | 21 | 42 | 85 |

then create new table with $d \times 3$, and record index of the row as $T_r$ with $d \times 1$.

### 3.2   Syndrome Coding to Hide Data

Any positive integers $k(k \geq 4)$, $t = 2$, $t$ is number of corrections.

Coefficient block length, $n = 2^k - 1$. Now let, $\alpha$ be a primitive element in $GF(2^k)$, then the parity-check matrix is

$$H = \begin{pmatrix} 1 & \alpha & \alpha^2 & \alpha^3 & \alpha^4 & \alpha^5 \cdots & \alpha^{n-4} & \alpha^{n-3} & \alpha^{n-2} & \alpha^{n-1} \\ 1 & \alpha^3 & \alpha^6 & \alpha^9 & \alpha^{12} & \alpha^{15} \cdots & \alpha^{3n-12} & \alpha^{3n-9} & \alpha^{3n-6} & \alpha^{3n-3} \end{pmatrix}$$

All nonzero coefficients are reshaped in $N$ blocks with length $n$, all secret message bits are also reshaped $N$ blocks with length $2^k$. Now, if such a block $b$ with $n$ nonzero coefficients is used to hide $2^k$ bits and the message is $m$, then for every block.

$S = m - H * b$ ($S$ is called syndrome), if $S = 0$ then no change in block $b$, otherwise, $\frac{S}{2} = \{s_1, s_3\}$

(1) If $s_3 + s_1^3 = 0$, then only one root $r_1$, and $r_1 = s_1$

(2) If $I_2 = \frac{s_3 + s_1^3}{s_1^3}$, if $T_2[I_2]$ is not empty then, let $y = T_2[I_2]$, where $T_2$ is the table for 2 degree roots, can be represented by The Equation (2)

$$\begin{cases} r_1 = s_1 y \\ r_2 = s_1 y + s_1 \end{cases} \tag{2}$$

(3) Let $z = 1 \cdots d$, $I_3 = (\frac{s_1^3 + s_3}{Tr[z]})^{\frac{1}{3}}$, if $T_3[I_3]$ is not empty then, let $y_i = T_3[I_3]$, and $r_i = I_3 y_i + s_1$, where $i = 1, 2, 3, \cdots l$, and $T_3$ is the table for 3 degree roots.

(4) Let $z = 1 \cdots d$, and $x = 1 \, ton$, $I_3 = (\frac{s_1^3 + s_1 x^2 + s_1^2 x + s_3}{Tr[z]})^{\frac{1}{3}}$, if $T_3[I_3]$ is not empty then, let $y_i = T_3[I_3]$ where $i = 1, 2, 3, \cdots l$, and can be represented by The Equation (3)

$$\begin{cases} r_i = I_3 y_i + s_1 + x \\ r_4 = x \end{cases} \tag{3}$$

(5) Let $z = 1 \cdots d$, and $x = 1ton$, $w = 1ton$, $I_2 = w$, $I_3 = (\frac{s^3 + s_1^3 + xs_1^2 + x^2 s_1 + x^3 w}{Tr[z]})^{\frac{1}{3}}$,

if $T_3[I_3]$ is not empty then, let $y_i = T_3[I_3]$, and

$r_1 = xy$, $r_2 = xy + x$, $r_i = I_3 y_i + s_1 + x$, where $i = 1, 2, 3, \cdots l$.

### 3.3   Message Decoding

The message decoding technique is very simple, decoding technique is also mathematical equation based. Let the output coefficient blocks are $r$, then extracted message $m$ can be obtain by Equation(4),

$$m = r.H \qquad (4)$$

## 4   Experimental Results

The analyzed method tested over 1173 gray scale images and successfully obtained better results (see Table 1, 2, 3). The analyzed method was tested with different JPEG compression QF (quality factor), such as 50, 75, 80, 95, and 100. As, different steganographic methods are working with different QF, thus it was important to perform the hiding operation of the analyzed method with different QF, for proper comparisons these results with other existing methods. during the experiment, this method hides 5%, 10%, 15%, and 20% secret message with respect to total embedding capacity. The embedding capacity was determined by counting all nonzero elements (each nonzero element was considered for hiding one bit of secret message). With 5%, and QF = 50, hiding capacity the analyzed method has achieved 46.55% error probability (Note: for the best situation the error probability is 50%). With same QF, 10%, 15%, and 20% hiding capacity the analyzed method has achieved 43.91%, 36.29%, and 26.49% error probability (see Table 1). With 5%, and QF = 75, hiding capacity the analyzed method has achieved 46.85% error probability. With same QF, 10%, 15%, and 20% hiding capacity the analyzed method has achieved 44.55%, 33.35%, and 23.30% error probability. Again, with 5%, and QF = 80, hiding capacity the analyzed method has achieved 46.55% error probability. With same QF, 10%, 15%, and 20% hiding capacity the analyzed method has achieved 41.78%, 29.98%, and 21.04% error probability. Similarly, with 5%, and QF = 95, hiding capacity the analyzed method has achieved 43.87% error probability. With same QF, 10%, 15%, and 20% hiding capacity the analyzed method has achieved 40.93%, 30.58%, and 20.27% error probability, and finally, with 5%, and QF = 100, hiding capacity the analyzed method has achieved 46.34% error probability. With same QF, 10%, 15%, and 20% hiding capacity the analyzed method has achieved 45.70%, 40.80%, and 34.41% error probability.

With 5%, and QF = 50, hiding capacity the analyzed method has achieved 1,506.43 numbers of mean modification. With same QF, 10%, 15%, and 20% hiding capacity the analyzed method has achieved 3,013.61, 4,521.41, and 6,025.20 numbers of mean modification (see Table 2). With 5%, and QF = 75, hiding

**Table 1.** Steganalysis Error probability of the analyzed method

| Steganalysis by Error Probability (EP) | | | |
|---|---|---|---|
| | 5% | 10% | 15% | 20% |
| QF = 50 | 46.55 | 43.91 | 36.29 | 26.49 |
| QF = 75 | 46.85 | 44.55 | 33.35 | 23.30 |
| QF = 80 | 46.55 | 41.78 | 29.98 | 21.04 |
| QF = 95 | 43.87 | 40.93 | 30.58 | 20.27 |
| QF = 100 | 46.34 | 45.70 | 40.80 | 34.41 |

capacity the analyzed method has achieved 2,250.51 numbers of mean modification. With same QF, 10%, 15%, and 20% hiding capacity the analyzed method has achieved 4,499.41, 6,751.40, and 9,003.64 numbers of mean modification. With 5%, and QF = 80, hiding capacity the analyzed method has achieved 2,544.20 numbers of mean modification. With same QF, 10%, 15%, and 20% hiding capacity the analyzed method has achieved 5,091.92, 13,978.63, and 18,633.97 numbers of mean modification. Similarly, with 5%, and QF = 95, hiding capacity the analyzed method has achieved 4,659.40 numbers of mean modification. With same QF, 10%, 15%, and 20% hiding capacity the analyzed method has achieved 9,316.98, 13,978.63, and 18,633.97 numbers of mean modification, and finally, with 5%, and QF = 100, hiding capacity the analyzed method has achieved 7,218.99 numbers of mean modification. With same QF, 10%, 15%, and 20% hiding capacity the analyzed method has achieved 14,428.94, 21,653.98, and 28,824.36 numbers of mean modification.

**Table 2.** Mean Modify of the analyzed method

| Steganalysis by Mean Modify (MM) | | | |
|---|---|---|---|
| | 5% | 10% | 15% | 20% |
| QF = 50 | 1,506.43 | 3,013.61 | 4,521.41 | 6,025.20 |
| QF = 75 | 2,250.51 | 4,499.41 | 6,751.40 | 9,003.64 |
| QF = 80 | 2,544.20 | 5,091.92 | 7,635.63 | 10,182.03 |
| QF = 95 | 4,659.40 | 9,316.98 | 13,978.63 | 18,633.97 |
| QF = 100 | 7,218.99 | 14,428.94 | 21,653.98 | 28,824.36 |

With 5%, and QF = 50, hiding capacity the analyzed method has achieved 60.04 numbers of mean distribution. With same QF, 10%, 15%, and 20% hiding capacity the analyzed method has achieved 234.49, 574.31, and 915.64 numbers of mean distribution (see Table 3). With 5%, and QF = 75, hiding capacity the analyzed method has achieved 91.92 numbers of mean distribution. With same QF, 10%, 15%, and 20% hiding capacity the analyzed method has achieved 358.00, 870.14, and 1,379.35 numbers of mean distribution (see Table 3). With 5%, and QF = 80, hiding capacity the analyzed method has achieved 104.86 numbers of mean distribution. With same QF, 10%, 15%, and 20% hiding capacity the analyzed method has achieved 409.20, 992.92, and 1,570.95 numbers of mean distribution. Similarly, with 5%, and QF = 95, hiding capacity the analyzed method has achieved 201.21 numbers of mean distribution. With same QF, 10%, 15%, and 20% hiding capacity the analyzed method has achieved 793.01, 1,911.09, and 3,001.78 numbers of mean distribution, and finally, with 5%, and QF = 100, hiding capacity the analyzed method has achieved 302.61 numbers of mean distribution. With same QF, 10%, 15%, and 20% hiding capacity the analyzed method has achieved 1,234.05, 2,990.06, and 4,681.87 numbers of mean distribution.

**Table 3.** Mean Distribution of the analyzed method

| Steganalysis by Mean Distribution (MD) | | | | |
|---|---|---|---|---|
| | 5% | 10% | 15% | 20% |
| QF = 50 | 60.04 | 234.49 | 574.31 | 915.64 |
| QF = 75 | 91.92 | 358.00 | 870.14 | 1,379.35 |
| QF = 80 | 104.86 | 409.20 | 992.92 | 1,570.95 |
| QF = 95 | 201.21 | 793.01 | 1,911.09 | 3,001.78 |
| QF = 100 | 302.61 | 1,234.05 | 2,990.06 | 4,681.87 |

### 4.1   Comparisons with Other Existing Methods

Finally this analyzed [23] method was tested for steganlysis method, which is analyzed by the method proposed in [14], and in [15]. Obtained results compared with other existing popular methods. During the comparisons, it was concerned that different methods was proposed for different JPEG quality factor. Because F5 method uses default quality factor 80, and OutGuess uses quality factor 75. Moreover, this method also tested with quality factor 50, 95 and 100. It is known to all that any method may be strong against stegnalysis, if that has less distortion and less modification. Less modification and less distortion results of the analyzed method also compared with other existing methods. Compare to other existing methods, the analyzed method has better performance. The analyzed method provides less distortion than other existing methods. Compare to other existing methods, the analyzed method has better performance. The analyzed method provides less mean modification than other existing methods. The summary is brought after performing an extensive analysis based on more than 1,000 JPEG images.

## 5   Conclusions

The analyzed methods are showing comparative results based on detection resistance by steganalysis. It is clear that better steganography means less detection and less modification. This paper also proved that error correction code is better than hamming code for steganography. A steganographic method with higher capacity and less resistance against detection technique can not be considered as a good method, however a technique with the higher detection resistance ability but less capacity will be considered as a good method. For faster computation a method needs to be mathematical equation based. The main advantage of the analyzed method is equation based roots finding approach, which is faster for computation.

## Acknowledgments

This work was supported by Hankuk University of Foreign Studies Research Fund of 2009.

## References

1. Upham, D.:
   `http://www.funet.fi/pub/crypt/stegangraphy/jpeg-jsteg-v4.diff.gz`
2. Provos, N.: Defending Against Statistical Steganalysis. In: Proc. 10th USENIX Security Symposium, Washington, DC (2001)
3. Kim, Y., Duric, Z., Richards, D.: Modified Matrix Encoding Technique for Minimal Distortion Steganography. In: Camenisch, J.L., Collberg, C.S., Johnson, N.F., Sallee, P. (eds.) IH 2006. LNCS, vol. 4437, pp. 314–327. Springer, Heidelberg (2007)
4. JP Hide&Seek, `http://linux01.gwdg.de/~alatham/stego.html`
5. Sachenv, V., Kim, H.J., Zhang, R., Choi, Y.S.: A Novel Approach for JPEG Steganography. In: Proc. of IWDW 2008, pp. 216–226 (2008)
6. Westfeld, A.: F5: A steganographic algorithm: High capacity despite better steganalysis. In: Moskowitz, I.S. (ed.) IH 2001. LNCS, vol. 2137, pp. 289–302. Springer, Heidelberg (2001)
7. Westfeld, A., Pfitzmann, A.: Attacks on Steganographic Systems. In: Pfitzmann, A. (ed.) IH 1999. LNCS, vol. 1768, pp. 61–76. Springer, Heidelberg (1999)
8. Provos, N., Honeyman, P.: Detecting Steganographic Content on the Internet, CITI Technical Report 01-11 (2001)
9. Westfeld, A.: Detecting Low Embedding Rates. In: Petitcolas, F.A.P. (ed.) IH 2002. LNCS, vol. 2578, pp. 324–339. Springer, Heidelberg (2000)
10. Fridrich, J., Goljan, M., Hogea, H.: Attacking the Out-Guess. In: Proc. of the ACM Workshop on Multimedia and Security, pp. 967–982 (2002)
11. Fridrich, J., Goljan, M., Hogea, H.: Steganalysis of JPEG image: Breaking the F5 algorithm. In: Petitcolas, F.A.P. (ed.) IH 2002. LNCS, vol. 2578, pp. 310–323. Springer, Heidelberg (2003)
12. Böhme, R., Westfeld, A.: Breaking Cauchy Model-Based JPEG Steganography with First Order Statistics. In: Samarati, P., Ryan, P.Y.A., Gollmann, D., Molva, R. (eds.) ESORICS 2004. LNCS, vol. 3193, pp. 125–140. Springer, Heidelberg (2004)
13. Fridrich, J., Goljan, M., Soukal, D.: Perturbed Quantization Steganography with Wet Paper Codes. In: Proc. ACM Multimedia Security Workshop, Magdeburg, Germany, September 20-21, pp. 4–15 (2004)
14. Fridrich, J.: Feature-based steganalysis for JPEG images and its implications for future design of steganographic schemes. In: Fridrich, J. (ed.) IH 2004. LNCS, vol. 3200, pp. 67–81. Springer, Heidelberg (2004)

15. Pevny, T., Fridrich, J.: Merging Markov and DCT Features for Multi-Class JPEG Steganalysis. In: Proc. of SPIE Electronic Imaging, Photonics West, pp. 03–04 (2007)
16. Sallee, P.: Model-based steganography. In: Kalker, T., Cox, I., Ro, Y.M. (eds.) IWDW 2003. LNCS, vol. 2939, pp. 154–167. Springer, Heidelberg (2004)
17. Sallee, P.: Model-based methods for steganography and steganalysis. International Journal of Image and Graphics 5(1), 167–190 (2005)
18. Solanki, K., Sarkar, A., Manjunath, B.S.: YASS: Yet another steganographic scheme that resists blind steganalysis. In: Furon, T., Cayre, F., Doërr, G., Bas, P. (eds.) IH 2007. LNCS, vol. 4567, pp. 16–31. Springer, Heidelberg (2007)
19. Eggers, J., Bauml, R., Girod, B.: A communications approach to steganography. In: SPIE, Electronic Imaging, Security, and Watermarking of Multimedia Contents, San Jose, CA (2002)
20. Noda, H., Niimi, M., Kawaguchi, E.: Application of QIM with dead zone for histogram preserving JPEG steganography. In: Processing ICIP, Genova, Italy (2005)
21. Schönfeld, D., Winkler, A.: Embedding with syndrome coding based on BCH codes. In: Proc. of the 8th workshop on Multimedia and security, pp. 214–223 (2006)
22. Schönfeld, D., Winkler, A.: Reducing the Complexity of Syndrome Coding for Embedding. In: Furon, T., Cayre, F., Doërr, G., Bas, P. (eds.) IH 2007. LNCS, vol. 4567, pp. 145–158. Springer, Heidelberg (2008)
23. Zhang, R., Sachnev, V., Kim, H.J.: Fast BCH Syndrome Coding for Steganography. In: Katzenbeisser, S., Sadeghi, A.-R. (eds.) IH 2009. LNCS, vol. 5806, pp. 48–58. Springer, Heidelberg (2009)

# Appendix

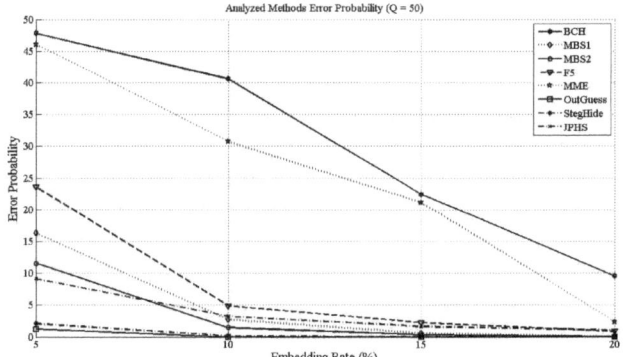

**Fig. 1.** Steganalysis comparison by Error Probability using support vector machine (SVM) with Quality Factor (QF) 50

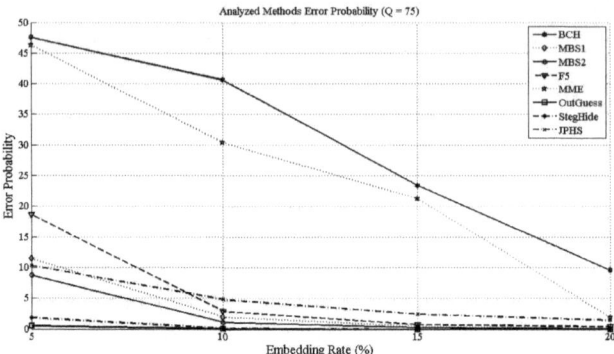

**Fig. 2.** Steganalysis comparison by Error Probability using support vector machine (SVM) with Quality Factor (QF) 75

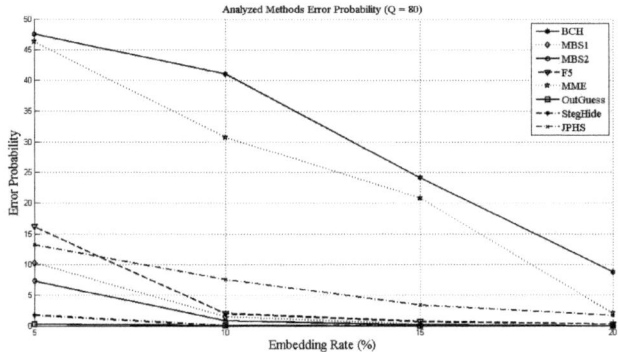

**Fig. 3.** Steganalysis comparison by Error Probability using support vector machine (SVM) with Quality Factor (QF) 80

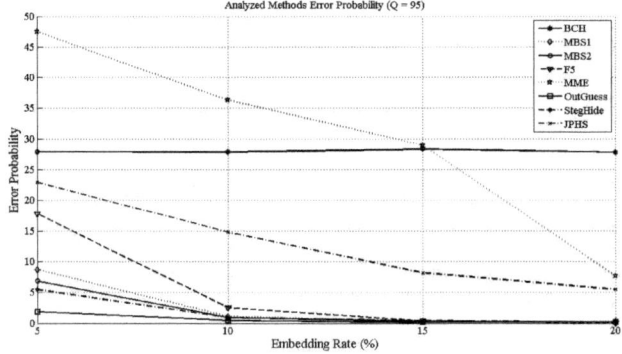

**Fig. 4.** Steganalysis comparison by Error Probability using support vector machine (SVM) with Quality Factor (QF) 95

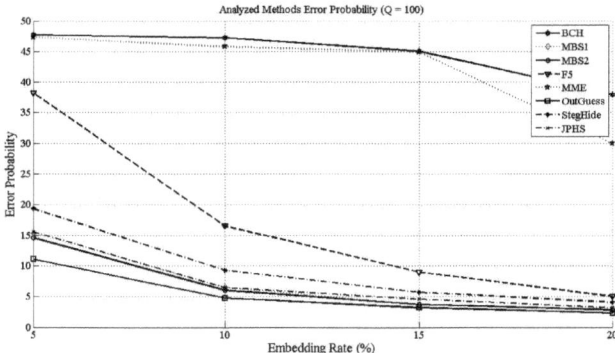

**Fig. 5.** Steganalysis comparison by Error Probability using support vector machine (SVM) with Quality Factor (QF) 100

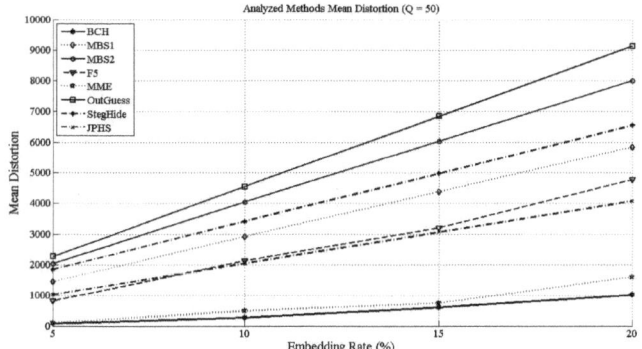

**Fig. 6.** Steganalysis comparisons by mean distortion using support vector machine (SVM) with quality factor 50

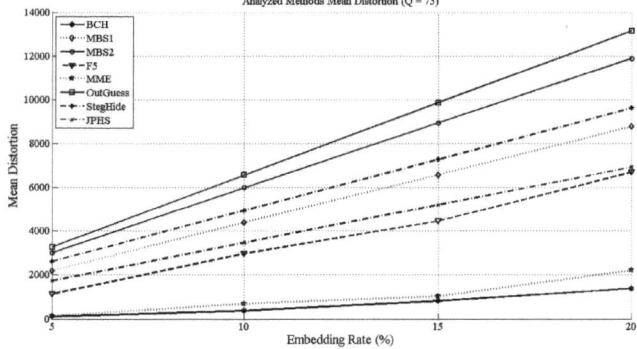

**Fig. 7.** Steganalysis comparisons by mean distortion using support vector machine (SVM) with quality factor 75

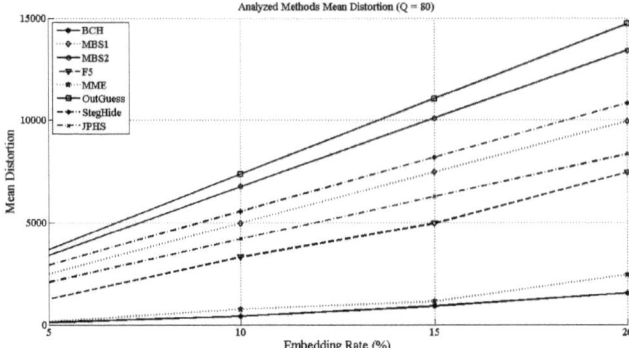

**Fig. 8.** Steganalysis comparisons by mean distortion using support vector machine (SVM) with quality factor 80

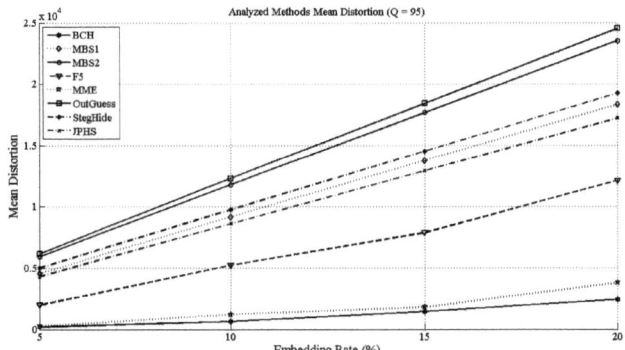

**Fig. 9.** Steganalysis comparisons by mean distortion using support vector machine (SVM) with quality factor 95

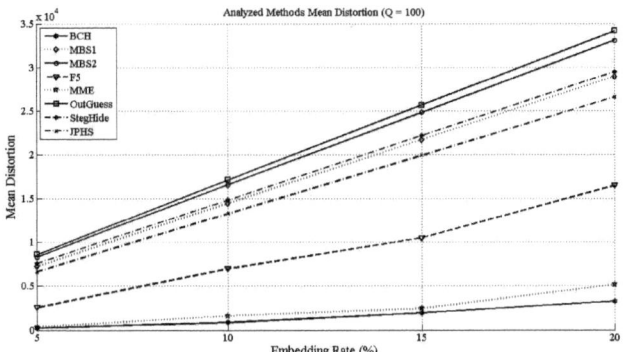

**Fig. 10.** Steganalysis comparisons by mean distortion using support vector machine (SVM) with quality factor 100

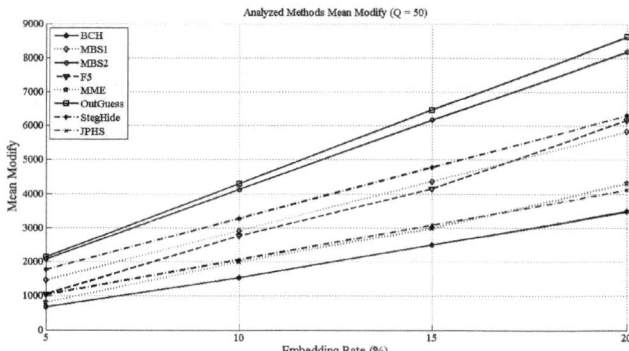

**Fig. 11.** Steganalysis comparisons by mean modification using support vector machine (SVM) with quality factor 50

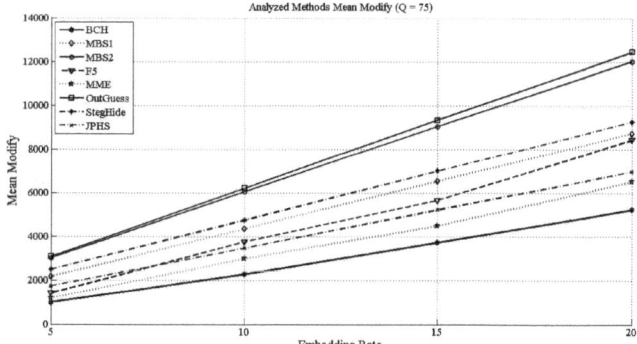

**Fig. 12.** Steganalysis comparisons by mean modification using support vector machine (SVM) with quality factor 75

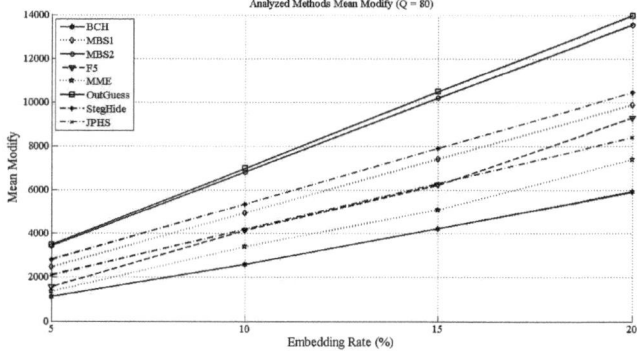

**Fig. 13.** Steganalysis comparisons by mean modification using support vector machine (SVM) with quality factor 80

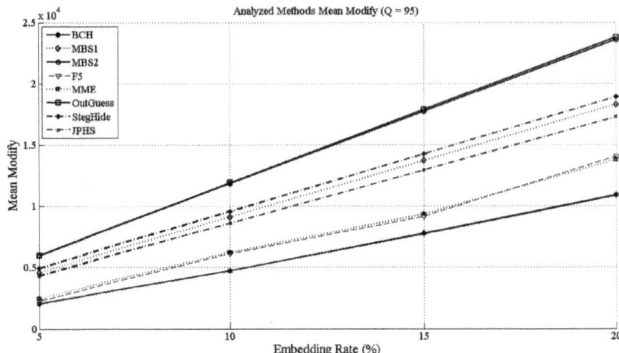

**Fig. 14.** Steganalysis comparisons by mean modification using support vector machine (SVM) with quality factor 95

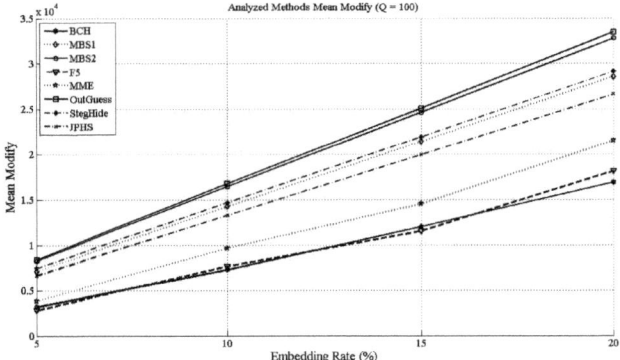

**Fig. 15.** Steganalysis comparisons by mean modification using support vector machine (SVM) with quality factor 100

# Intrusion Correlation Using Ontologies and Multi-agent Systems

Gustavo Isaza[1], Andrés Castillo[2], Marcelo López[1], Luis Castillo[3], and Manuel López[1]

[1] Systems and Informatics Department, University of Caldas, Street 65 # 26-10,
Manizales, Colombia
{gustavo.isaza,mlopez,felipe}@ucaldas.edu.co
[2] Language, Informatics Systems and Software Engineer Department,
Pontifical University of Salamanca, Campus Madrid, Paseo Juan XXIII, 3, Madrid, Spain
andres.castillo@upsam.net
[3] Industrial Engineer Department, National University, Street 64 # 27-60, Manizales, Colombia
lfcastilloo@unal.edu.co

**Abstract.** This paper proposes an ontology model for representing intrusion detection events and prevention rules, integrating multiagent systems based on unsupervised and supervised techniques for classification, correlation and pattern recognition. The semantic model describes attacks signatures, reaction tasks, axioms with alerts communication and correlation; nevertheless we have developed the prevention architecture integrated with another security tools. This article focuses on the approach to incorporate semantic operations that facilitate alerts correlation process and providing the inference and reasoning to the ontology model.

**Keywords:** Ontology, Intrusion Detection, Intrusion Prevention, Alert Correlation, Semantic IDS.

## 1 Introduction

Nowadays, existing taxonomies and standards for IDSs are insufficient to support optimal attacks identification, reasoning and predictive anomalous behaviour's definition. Ontologies describe objects, concepts and relationships in a knowledge domain, for our case, attack signatures resources, detection rules, reaction and prevention processes need to be semantically described in order to facilitate uniformity in the knowledge bases of the systems underlying and the possibility to providing a reasoning framework, intelligence and inference from these models onto-semantic.

The traditional intrusion detection architectures are weak in areas such as central console becoming a single point of failure, in such case; the network could go down without protection if this one fails, the scalability is limited, processing all the information in a node implies a limit in the network size that can monitor, reconfiguration

S.K. Bandyopadhyay et al. (Eds.): ISA 2010, CCIS 76, pp. 51–63, 2010.

difficulties and add capabilities to scale IDS signatures, the data analysis can be defective, the autonomous behaviour and learning capabilities are precarious. Multi-agent systems, ontologies and intelligence computing can help to minimize these problems incorporating distribution, intelligence capabilities, reactivity, proactive, autonomy and dynamic adaptation.

This paper presents the partial progress using a correlation model with ontological representation for intrusion detection and prevention over multi-agents architectures. The remainder of this paper is organized as follows: We present in the section 2 the relevant previous works in this area, in section 3 the ontological model used for attacks signatures and reaction rules to support the prevention system is presented and the correlation model; section 4 evidences the results achieved by integrating the ontology in the multiagent system, and the correlation tasks. Finally we summarize our research work and discuss the future contributions.

## 2 Previous Work

The standards for representation and ontologies in Intrusion Detection manifest a precarious effort, proposes as IDMEF (Intrusion Detection Message Exchange Format) and the CIDF (The Common Intrusion Detection Framework) [1] defined APIs and protocols for research projects in intrusion detection that can share information and resources, as well as components which can be refused by constructing a model of representation based on XML syntax. The research developed in [2] has defined a target centric ontology for intrusion detection, new approaches have proposed ontologies as a way to represent and uunderstand the attacks domain knowledge, expressing the intrusion detection system much more in terms of their domain and performing intelligent reasoning. These projects aim to define an ontology DAML-OIL (DARPA Agent Markup Language + Ontology Interface) target centric based on the traditional taxonomy classification  migrated to semantic model, the investigation done in [3] integrates ontology entities and interactions captured by means of an centric-attack ontology which provides agents with a common interpretation of the environment signatures which are matched through a data structure based on the internals of the Snort network intrusion detection tool.

A Security Ontology for DAML+OIL in order to control access and data integrity to Web resources was developed in [4] and [5]. More recent research as [6] proposes an ontology-based approach to instantiate security policies to map alerts into attack contexts to identify the policies to be applied in the network to solve threats. In addition, the project development by [7] describes the *Scyllarus* system, which performs IDS fusion, using Bayes nets and qualitative probability, and an extensive ontology for expressing the Intrusion Reference Model (IRM), which contains information about the configuration of the site to be protected, the site's security policies and objectives, and the intrusion events.

In the multi-agent systems field applied to IDSs, one of the most relevant research has been developed by the Research Center for Information Security at Purdue

University [8] which was developed an agent-based system for intrusion detection systems, known as AAFID (Autonomous Agents for Intrusion Detection) using a model with mobile agents and integrating data mining techniques to identify coordinated attacks from different subsystems. The research done by [9] presents a security platform based on agents as a strategy for an efficient and robust intrusion detection designed for high performance in high-speed networks. Other relevant research has combined different architectures based on agents [10], [11], [12], [13], [14].

## 3 Ontology for Intrusion Detection and Prevention

The Intrusion Detection Messages Exchange Format (IDMEF) [15] allows to incorporate interoperability between heterogeneous IDS (Intrusion Detection Systems) nodes, representing a specification for a standard alert format and a standard transport protocol. IDMEF use a hierarchal configuration with three main elements (sensors, managers and analyzers). IDMEF is based on XML in such sense it becomes a syntactic representation and not semantic, not allowing reasoning or inference processing. The problem presented in our model defines multiple concepts, relations and the meaning integration with other security technologies like firewalls and vulnerabilities scanner. Ontology can help to optimize the knowledge representation, reduce the messages size, decrease the redundancy and allow incorporating more intelligence in the information analysis. The ontological Engineering Group of the Polytechnic University of Madrid has developed a methodology [16] that allows to build ontologies in the knowledge level, has its roots in the activities identified by the software development process proposed by the IEEE and other knowledge engineering methodologies. Its main activities include the specification, conceptualization, formalization, implementation and maintenance. We have decided to use METHONTOLOGY as the methodology for developing the ontology, because in different studies is considered one of the most mature methodologies that seek to follow the life cycle of the software proposed in the IEEE 1074 standard, which is recommended by the Foundation for Intelligent Physical Agents (FIPA). In the specification phase, a set of competence questions (CQ) are proposed identified for the domain in question, for example:

- What is the events sequence that describes an attacks type?
- What kind of reaction must be assumed as a result of a possible attack?
- What impact does an attack on the underlying distributed environment?
- What kind of attacks requiring priority reactions (high, medium, low)?

Axioms and rules are describing the attack types by a total of 25 intrusion classifications obtained through the applied clustering algorithm (K-Means), described in [17] and near 4800 instances for our ontology. An example for a *SQL Injection Rule* that describes the intrusion state *(p)* directed to node *(z)*, with source host *(x)* is given in the following SWRL Rule.

```
(NetworkNode(?x) ∧ NetworkNode(?z)
    ∧ IntrusionState(?p) ∧
  GeneratedBY(?p, ?z) ∧
    SQLInjection(?p) ∧
  Directed_To(?p, ?z) →
SystemSQLInjectionState(?p, ?z)
```

For a Web Attack Rule, an example that allows generate an value attribute in the inference process, is showing in the following example, when a host state is defined as *True* under Web Attack given the axioms, sentences and conditions that meet the claim.

```
(NetworkNode(?x)∧
  IntrusionState(?y)∧
  GeneratedBY(?x,?y)∧
GeneratedBY(?x,?y)∧ WebAttack(?z) ∧
  AttackTypeOf(?y,?z)→
UnderWebAttack(?x, ?true)
```

To design and implement the ontology, OWL language was used, which allows formalisms and knowledge representations, some of the most important influences in the design of OWL are derived from its predecessor DAML + OIL logic of descriptive paradigm frameworks models and RDF / XML. The logic description and its interpretation has a strong influence on the design of OWL, particularly on the semantic formalization, the language constructors choice, and the data types integration and values, thus OWL DL and OWL Lite can be seen as expressions of the logic description. Some relevant characteristics of the logic is the inclusion of descriptive formalisms describing roles, concepts, individuals, formal terminological formalisms assertive and capabilities to infer new knowledge from reasoning techniques [18]. To define the rules we are using the Semantic Web Rule Language (SWRL), it is an expressive OWL-based rule language. SWRL allows writing rules expressed in OWL concepts providing reasoning capabilities. A SWRL rule contains an antecedent part to describe the *body*, and a consequent part, referring the *head*.

At the moment we have defined around 2200 attacks signatures and 1210 prevention rules instances in our ontology, in addition we described the events sequence that happen in real time. The Reaction Agent generates the Intrusion Prevention events sending rules messages to other network components reconfiguring dynamically the security environment. The predicates definition describes sequence attacks having input causes and possible consequences. An hybrid source data was used, having the input data was gathered via *tcpdump* and converted to the DARPA Data Sets Intrusion Detection Evaluation [19] format used in the clustered process, additionally the attacks were created with other testing tools, normal traffic captured using *JPCap* and *tcpdump* and processed in the multi-agent for IDS and IPS (*OntoIDPSMA* – Ontological Intrusion Detection and Prevention Multi-agent system). The raw data was converted to XML then processed to OWL instances; furthermore the ontology is updated via SPARQL sentences.

The ontology represents the signatures for known attacks and novel attacks, the intelligent behaviour uses the inference model and reasoning tools integrating neuronal networks in the multi-agent system; this implementation provides an ontological model for reaction rules creating the prevention system. A fragment of the ontology defined that implements the intrusion detection and prevention knowledge is depicted in Fig. 1 that presents a high level view. Otherwise, the behaviour for the Intrusion Detection and Prevention multi-agent has been designed using an ontological model integrated with the signature and reaction rule ontology. At the moment we have implemented a system based on agents fulfilling tasks as cooperation, autonomy and responsiveness, plus the integration of model and semantic ontological signatures to facilitate communication and interaction among agents Intrusion Detection.

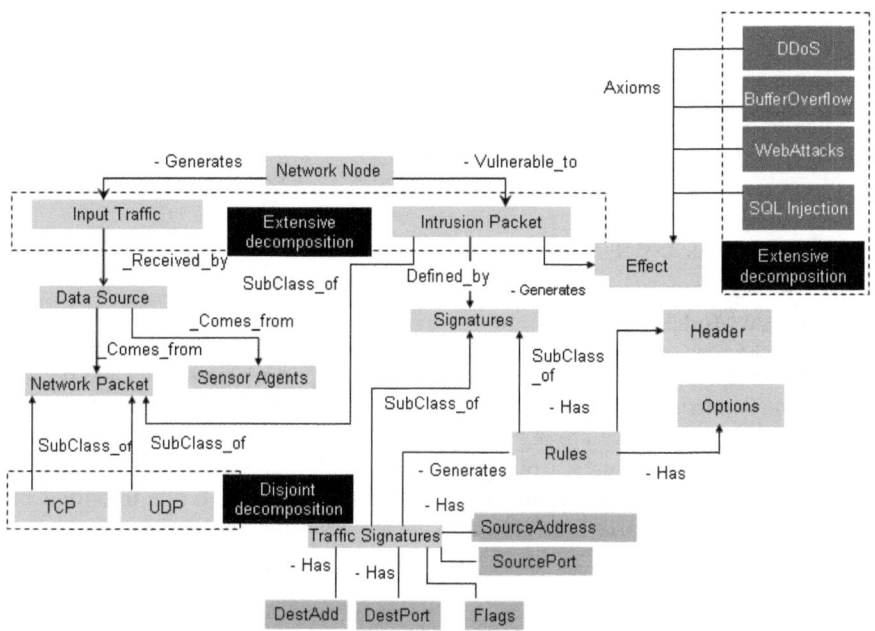

**Fig. 1.** Concept and Domain Model for the Intrusion Detection and Prevention Ontology

Fig. 2 presents the complete architecture for the proposed system (OntoIDPSMA) integrating the Ontology in the Intelligent Multiagent System, we have described this model in [17]. To improve the privacy, for communication between agents we are using an authentication mechanism, which assigns agents to a user, and provides a permission service method to give authorization for the Multi-Agent system. Each action is authenticated and can be permitted or denied according to a set of rules defined in ACL's (Access Control List). In addition we are integrating another component to ensure data integrity, confidentiality, bidirectional authenticated connections using JADE Containers having its Internal Message Transport Protocol (IMTP) over TLS/SSL [20]. This approach aims to provide a security and permission service for authentication, signature and encryption service for message signature and message encryption. In addition the Security agent layer includes a policy manager to control permissions to create or kill a Main Container, Agent Containers, among other agent's resources.

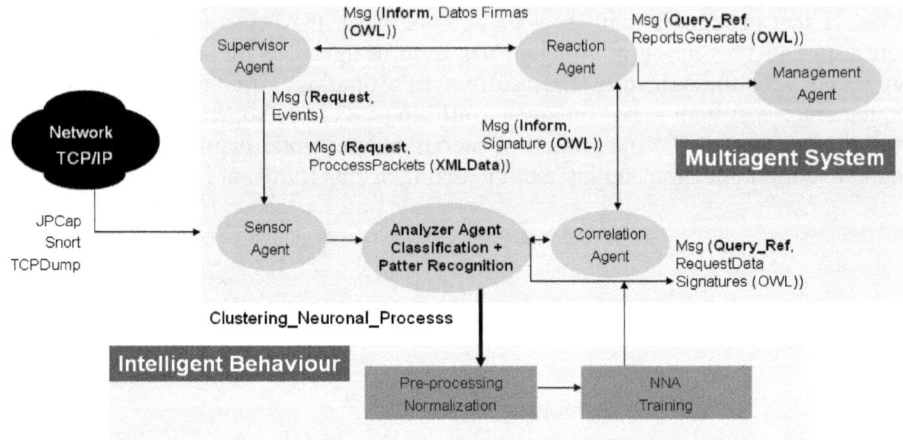

**Fig. 2.** Multiagent System Architecture *OntoIDPSMA*. [17]

## 3.1 Semantic Model

For this ontology we have defined rules that allow properties inferences and reasoning process. The *IntrusionState, WebAttack, SQLInjection, BufferOverflow, DoS, dDoS, PrivilegedAccess* properties among others, describe the anomaly behaviour, they are defined as ontology' attributes, from the captured and processed attack instance using the detection engine, identifying the *Type of Intrusion*. This value is imported in the Ontology through the format conversion sequence described in the Fig. 3.

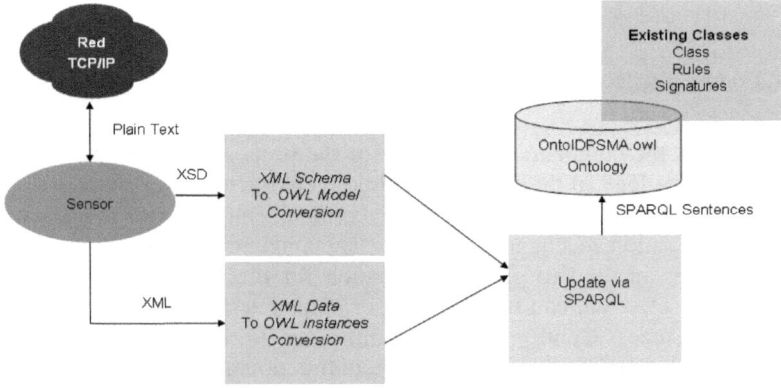

**Fig. 3.** Conversion XML Signatures, Anomalous and Traffic Data to OWL Instances

The description for the axiom that describes a *RootAccess* state is denoted as:

$$\text{RootAccess} \equiv \exists \, (\text{IntrusionState} \cap \text{InputTraffic} \cap \\ \text{NetworkNode}) \\ \cap \, \exists \, \text{Generated\_by}(\text{AnomalousSSH} \cup \\ \text{AnomalousFTP} \\ \cup \, \text{WebAttack} \cup \text{TelnetAccess}) \cap \\ \text{UID\_Try}(\text{UID\_0})$$

Using JESS as complement to incorporate reasoning and inference model, it's possible to give the semantic capabilities to the ontology. JESS is a rule engine and open source environment that allows to construct Java applications with reasoning using knowledge providing from declarative rules [21]. An example for an inferred axioms using JESS in our model is giving by:

```
SystemWebAccessState
        (http:/url/../OntoIDSSMA.owl#
        WebAttack_1,Nodo2)
SystemWebAccessState
        (http://url/../OntoIDSSMA.owl#
        WebAttack_2,Nodo1)
UnderSynFloodAttack
        (http://url/../OntoIDSSMA.owl#
        Nodo1,True)
UnderBufferOverflow
        (http://url/../OntoIDSSMA.owl#
        Nodo3,True)
```

And an inferred individual having SQL Injections and Denial of Services instances is represented as:

```
SQLInjection(SQL_Injecion_3)
        SQLInjection(SQL_Injecion_3)
        owl:Thing(SQL_Injection3)
        Consequences(SQL_Injection_3)
        IntrusionState(SQL_Injection_3)

DoS(DoS_6)owl:Thing(DoS_6)
        Consequences(DoS_6)
        IntrusionState(DoS_6)
```

## 3.2 Correlation

The intrusion correlation function purpose aims to integrate and correlate alerts to provide recognition and give information about attacks sequence to generate intruder intentions or to manifest possible implicit attacks not giving explicitly.

The correlation use depends of the multiple sources context, for our case, several *Sensor Agents* with the ontological representations knowledge. The alert verification and the fusion can minimize the total alerts in a distributed environment, without compromise the interpretation capability in each IDS node, and allowing to incorporate a more understandable and intelligent model for the management user.

The sequence for the correlation process integrated in our multiagent system in shown in Fig. 4.

The correlation model used combines alerts from different detection sources and applies a hybrid technique of similarity and statistical analysis from priority attributes. In our multiagent system, the correlation engine performs a lock on a suspicious sequence present within the network monitored by the sensors. These locks are propagated by all the reaction agents that are registered within the main container of the supervisor, regardless of the network to which they belong, in order to block possible attacks on these networks, even if such traffic has not been there. This ability of agents provides the framework prevent intrusions suggested model.

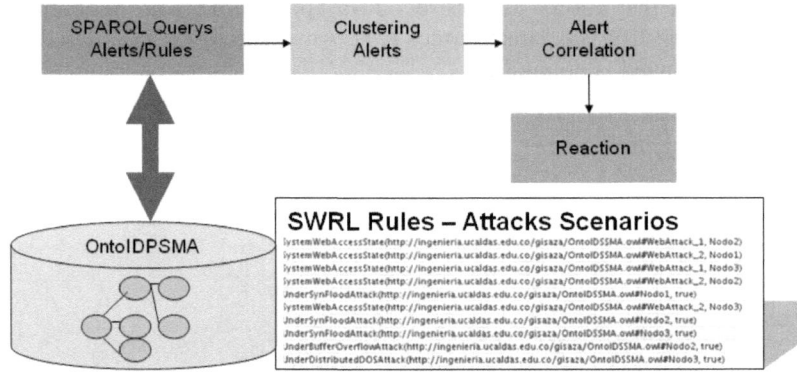

**Fig. 4.** Correlation Model for the OntoIDPSMA

The correlation engine has a *whitelist* or list of privileged directions that are in this list will not be blocked, regardless of what action should be taken when considering a warning that comes from a particular host. The implementation has five functional operational modes, each one has a qualification range *[0 ... 5]* or *[0 ... 10]*, using the *Supervisor Agent* is possible to select the minimal qualification to generate a block event. The 5 modes are described in Table 1.

**Table 1.** Operational Correlation Mode

| Mode | Description |
|---|---|
| Type 1. Direct Block | Any notification alert that arrives to the *Supervisor Agent* from any sensor is treated as a possible security problem. It is sent to all *Reaction Agents*, the request to conduct a lock for the IP that caused the alert by the time configured in the *Supervisor Agent* |
| Type 2. Active Block | Performs a lock if a notification arrives from a *Sensor Agent* with an asset value exceeding configured on the *Supervisor Agent*. Thus, each *Sensor Agent* is described by an asset value, which corresponds to the importance of the server and services in the run. The range of qualifying this option is 0 to 5. |

**Table 1.** (*continued*)

| Mode | Description |
|------|-------------|
| Type 3. Priority Block | The correlation engine takes the priority level of the alert generated. If the priority level is greater than the configured within the Supervisor Agent's interface, is sent to all registered *Reaction Agents*, the request to conduct a lock for the IP that caused the alert by the time configured in the agent supervisor. The qualified range is 0 to 5. |
| Type 4. Reliability | Refers to the frequency of alerts generated by a host. If that address has generated many alerts within those available in the correlation engine, the confidence level will increase. |
| Type 5. Risk | The calculation of the risk level, involving the three ways described above, a level parameter is calculated. |

Let *NA* the total alerts from one host and *TA* the total alerts, the qualification is in the range 0 to 10. The reliability *R* value is calculated as:

$$\text{Re}\,liability = \text{Round}(\frac{NA}{TA} \times 10) \tag{1}$$

Let *VA* the Active Value, *PS* Priority Sensor and *R* Reliability, the risk value is giving by:

$$Risk = \text{Round}(\frac{VA \times PS \times R}{10}) \tag{2}$$

In this approach the reliability level has more relevance, if a host is generating several alerts, independently of the active value where the sensors are executed and the same priority is probably that a major problem is affecting the environment. Any alert caused by the correlation engine, have a designated time block, configurable at the interface of the *Supervisor*. The *Supervisor Agent* has a behaviour that monitors the blocks list needed by the correlation engine locks looking for expired, and if it is found, it notifies to the *Reaction Agents* to perform the respective release.

In addition we are working to improve the model integrating a new correlation process based on predefined attacks scenarios using SWRL extensions. At the moment the correlation is generated using SPARQL queries to the ontology, making the similarity attributes tasks, classification and priority control using the correlation agent in the SMA architecture, but we consider it's possible to enhance the semantic performance integrating these capabilities in the ontology with language complements processing. For this purpose, we are using the model designed in [22] in the CRIM project.

The logic representation using OWL for a correlation instance definition is presented as:

```
<rdf :RDF
xmlns                                                          :
j.0="http://ingenieria.ucaldas.edu.co/gisaza/OntoIDPSMA.owl
#"
....
xmlns : rdf=
resource="Resource"/>
....
  "Ontology IDSPSMA">
        </owl:Ontology>
        <owl:class rdf:ID="PortScan">
        <rdfs:Subclass of>
        <owl class rdf:ID="Alert">
                <Name> Port Scanning </Name>
                <AlertType>R2L</AlertType>
                <Reaction>Inform</Reaction>
                <Protocol> tcp </Protocol>
                <Source> home_net </Source>
                <Destination>external_net</Destination>
                .
                .
                .
</rdf :RDF>"
```

From these representations, it's possible to construct attacks scenarios to define pre-conditions and post-conditions to determine for example that $A$ is a set of subclasses of relations between attacks $A_1$ where if an attack is an attack type $A_2$, then we say that $A_1$ is $A_2$ subclass of attack and the super-class of $A_1$ and if an attack has two states $S_1$ and $S_2$ prerequisites and there is an instance of $A$ with their respective bodies and $S_1$ and $S_2$ are prerequisites of a state, then to succeed. This SWRL representation is given by:

$$A(?p) \wedge S_1(?q) \wedge PreconditionIntrusionState(?p, ?q)$$
$$\wedge S_2(?z) \wedge PreconditionIntrusionState(?p, ?q)$$
$$\rightarrow State(?p, true)$$

## 4 Results

As we presented in [23] the complete model integrates de Multiagent System, the ontology and an hybrid intelligence computing technique using Clustering K-Means and Neuronal Networks for classification and pattern recognition. The comparison having and Standard IDS and our MAS model is detailed in Table 2. This table presents the detection rate and elapsed time for the packets selected in the previous phase (normal and anomalous clustered), the processing time of the answer aims to traces processed.

**Table 2.** Performance Multiagent System Comparison

| Data Processed | Standard IDS | OntoIDPSMA |
|---|---|---|
| Traffic and Packets | 92,1 % | 91,64 % |
|  | 60.375 | 58.847 |
| Anomalous Detected | 89,3 % | 96,4% |
| Detection Time | 44,54 sec | 33,21 sec |

The following table presents an example of the results generated after the correlated alerts process by *Type of Attack* integrated in the multiagent system using the *Correlation Agent*.

**Table 3.** Alert Correlated by Sensor

| Signature | Source IP | Destination IP | Sensor | Tag |
|---|---|---|---|---|
| Apache NIDS | 200.X.Y.31 | 201.21.X.Y | Sensor01 | Correlated |
| SQL Injection | 200.X.Y.36 | 201.21.X.Y | Sensor02 | Correlated |
| Buffer Overflow | 200.X.Y.41 | 201.21.X.Y | Sensor03 | Correlated |

Having multiple Sensors alerts, the Table 4 presents a summary of correlated alerts.

**Table 4.** Alerts Correlated using the SMA Architecture

| Sensor | General Alerts | Correlated Alerts |
|---|---|---|
| Sensor01 | 22114 | 125 |
| Sensor02 | 13431 | 3210 |
| Sensor03 | 8952 | 803 |

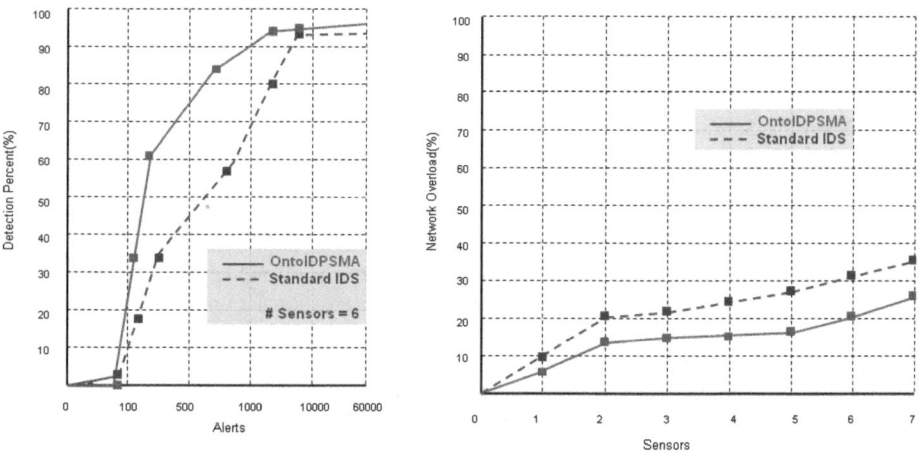

**Fig. 5.** (a) Detection Percent vs. Alerts Number (b) Network Overload

Fig. 5 (a) presents the detection rate percent comparing with other IDS having six (6) sensors; this performance may improve by the integration of pattern recognition, classification and inference model. Additionally, the network overhead is reduced using multi-agent system and incorporating OWL embedded in the ACL message for information exchange between agents as shown in Fig. 5(b).

## 5   Conclusions and Future Work

The ontological model over multi-agent systems increases the performance in tasks such as distribution, intelligence reasoning, knowledge representation, generating inferences, and adaptability, among others; in addition, to provide for our model prediction capabilities, we have used pattern recognition algorithms and clustering techniques. The semantic capabilities provided in our ontology facilitate the inference process and the correlation tasks embedded in the Multiagent architecture. As shown in Fig. 5 (b) the Ontology integration in the intrusion detection and prevention multiagent system shows better performance in terms of network overload based on the reduced message size and the optimization for knowledge interpretation based on the inference model, in addition, integrating intelligent techniques the detection rate increase as evidenced in Fig. 5 (a). However, the CPU usage at each node is greater due to interaction with multiple tools, virtual machines processing and ontological management. Our contribution to previous work is part of the integration semantic ontology integration in the multi-agent system, incorporating the reasoning and inference in real time and loading the traffic data captured on line. Additionally the correlation model provides scalability to the ontology providing a more semantic approach to the model. By the time the full system integration is still under development, we will continue testing and integrating new classification, reasoning and intelligence methods to optimize the intelligence behaviour, as well as the incorporation to the model the semantic inferences rules in the multi-agent system that provides a complete correlation behaviour using an extended ontology.

## References

1. Al-Mamory, S., Zhang, H.: Intrusion detection alarms reduction using root cause analysis and clustering, pp. 419–430. Butterworth-Heinemann, Butterworths (2009)
2. Undercoffer, J., Finin, T., Joshi, A., Pinkston, J.: A target centric ontology for intrusion detection: using DAML+OIL to classify intrusive behaviors. Knowledge Engineering Review - Special Issue on Ontologies for Distributed Systems, 2–22 (2005)
3. Mandujano, S., Galvan, A., Nolazco, J.: An ontology-based multiagent approach to outbound intrusion detection. In: The 3rd ACS/IEEE International Conference on Computer Systems and Applications, p. 94 (2005)
4. Denker, G., Kagal, L., Finin, T., Paolucci, M., et al.: Security for DAML Web Services: Annotation and Matchmaking. In: Fensel, D., Sycara, K., Mylopoulos, J. (eds.) ISWC 2003. LNCS, vol. 2870, pp. 335–350. Springer, Heidelberg (2003)
5. Raskin, V., Hempelmann, C.C.F., Triezenberg, K., Nirenburg, A.: Ontology in Information Security: A Useful Theoretical Foundation and Methodological Tool. In: Proceedings of the 2001 Workshop on New Security Paradigms (NSPW 2001), pp. 53–59 (2001)
6. Cuppens-Boulahia, N., Cuppens, F., Lopez de Vergara, J.E., Vazquez, E., et al.: An ontology-based approach to react to network attacks. In: Third International Conference on Risks and Security of Internet and Systems, CRiSIS 2008, pp. 27–35 (2008) (on Publication)
7. Goldman, R., Harp, S.: Model-based Intrusion Assessment in Common Lisp. In: International Lisp Conference, 2009. Association of Lisp Users and ACM SIGPLAN, Cambridge (2009)

8. Balasubramaniyan, J., Garcia-Fernandez, J., Spafford, E., Zamboni, D.: An Architecture for Intrusion Detection using Autonomous Agents. Department of Computer Sciences. Purdue University, West Lafayette (1998)
9. Krmicek, V., Celeda, P., Rehak, M., Pechoucek, M.: Agent-Based Network Intrusion Detection System. In: Proceedings of the 2007 IEEE/WIC/ACM International Conference on Intelligent Agent Technology. IEEE Computer Society, Los Alamitos (2007)
10. Orfila, A., Carbo, J., Ribagorda, A.: Autonomous decision on intrusion detection with trained BDI agents, pp. 1803–1813. Butterworth-Heinemann, Butterworths (2008)
11. Lips, R., El-Kadhi, N.: Intelligent Mobile Agent for Intrusion Detection System (IMAIDS), European Institute of Technology. rue Pasteur - 94270, Le Kremlin-France (2008)
12. Herrero, A., Corchado, E., Pellicer, M., Abraham, A.: Hybrid Multi Agent-Neural Network Intrusion Detection with Mobile Visualization. In: Corchado, E. (ed.) Innovations in Hybrid Intelligent Systems. ASC, vol. 44, pp. 320–328. Springer, Heidelberg (2008)
13. Sandhya, P., Ajith, A., Crina, G., Johnson, T.: Modeling intrusion detection system using hybrid intelligent systems, pp. 114–132. Academic Press Ltd., London (2007)
14. Zurutuza, U., Uribeetxeberria, R., Azketa, E., Gil, G., et al.: Combined Data Mining Approach for Intrusion Detection. In: International Conference on Security and Criptography, Barcelona, Spain (2008)
15. IETF-IDMEF. he Intrusion Detection Message Exchange Format (IDMEF) (2007), http://www.ietf.org/rfc/rfc4765.txt (Consulted: Febrero 2008)
16. Corcho, O., López, M., Gómez-Pérez, A., López-Cima, A.: Building Legal Ontologies with METHONTOLOGY and WebODE. In: Benjamins, V.R., Casanovas, P., Breuker, J., Gangemi, A. (eds.) Law and the Semantic Web. LNCS (LNAI), vol. 3369, pp. 142–157. Springer, Heidelberg (2005)
17. Isaza, G., Castillo, A., Lopez, M., Castillo, L.: Towards Ontology-based intelligent model for Intrusion Detection and Prevention. In: 2nd International Workshop on Computational Intelligence in Security for Information Systems, CISIS 2009, pp. 109–116. Springer, Heidelberg (2009)
18. Baader, F., Nutt, W.: Basic description logics. In: The description logic handbook: theory, implementation, and applications, pp. 43–95. Cambridge University Press, Cambridge (2003)
19. DARPA. DARPA Intrusion Detection Evaluation, The 1999 DARPA off-line intrusion detection evaluation, LINCOLN LABORATORY Massachusetts Institute of Technology, http://www.ll.mit.edu/IST/ideval/data/1999/1999_data_index.html (Consulted 2008)
20. Vila, X., Schustera, A., Riera, A.: Security for a Multi-Agent System based on JADE. Computers and Security. Science Direct 26(5), 391–400 (2007)
21. Friedman-Hill, E., Sandia, L.: Jess, The Rule Engine for Java Platform (2009), http://www.jessrules.com/jess/docs/index.shtml (Consulted 2009)
22. Cuppens, F., Miège, A.: Alert Correlation in a Cooperative Intrusion Detection Framework. In: IEEE Symposium on Security and Privacy, Oakland, May 12 - 15 (2002)
23. Isaza, G., Castillo, A., Duque, N.: An Intrusion Detection and Prevention Model Based on Intelligent Multi-Agent Systems, Signatures and Reaction Rules Ontologies. In: 7th International Conference on Practical Applications of Agents and Multi-Agent Systems (PAAMS 2009). AISC, vol. 55, pp. 237–245. Springer, Heidelberg (2009)

# Tag ID Subdivision Scheme for Efficient Authentication and Security-Enhancement of RFID System in USN*

Kijeong Lee, Byungjoo Park**, and Gil-Cheol Park

Department of Multimedia Engineering, Hannam Univ.,
133 Ojeong-dong, Daedeok-gu, Daejeon, Korea
{kijeong,bjpark,gcpark}@hnu.kr

**Abstract.** Radio frequency identification (RFID) is a generic term that is used to describe a system that transmits the identity (in the form of a unique serial number) of an object or person wirelessly, using radio waves. However, there are security threats in the RFID system related to its technical components. For example, illegal RFID tag readers can read tag ID and recognize most RFID Readers, a security threat that needs in-depth attention. Previous studies show some ideas on how to minimize these security threats like studying the security protocols between tag, reader and Back-end DB. In this research, the team proposes an RFID Tag ID Subdivision Scheme to authenticate the permitted tag only in USN (Ubiquitous Sensor Network). Using the proposed scheme, the Back-end DB authenticates selected tags only to minimize security threats like eavesdropping and decreasing traffic in Back-end DB.

**Keywords:** RFID System, Authentication, Tag ID Subdivision, Tag Group.

## 1 Introduction

Radio Frequency Identification/Ubiquitous Sensor Network (RFID/USN) is a key infrastructure component of technology-driven society. With boundless growth potential, it can bring changes to all industrial sectors as great as the Internet once did. This new technology is expected to lead a new information revolution, if it is applied to public and private sectors, including health, education, national defense, industrial logistics, living convenience, safety, dietary life, medical services, environment, and manufacturing. However, there are security threats in the RFID system because it uses radio frequency to communicate. To solve these security problems, RFID system uses light-weight security authentication protocols. Thus, the team proposes Tag ID Subdivision Scheme for efficient authentication and security-enhancement.

This paper proposes an efficient authentication scheme using tag ID subdivision for RFID system, which is composed of one Back-end DB and multiple readers in USN. If many of the readers are allowed to read a particular tag, the proposed scheme

---

* This work was supported by National Research Foundation of Korea Grant funded by the Korean Goverment (2009-0074117).
** Corresponding author.

S.K. Bandyopadhyay et al. (Eds.): ISA 2010, CCIS 76, pp. 64–71, 2010.

does not carry out duplicated authentication and reduces traffic of Back-end DB. Therefore, system efficiency can be increased and security threat problems minimized. This paper explains the outline of RFID systems. Chapter 1: Security threats in RFID and security authentication protocols; Chapter 2: Propose RFID Tag ID Subdivision Scheme; Chapter 3 & 4: RFID system authentication procedure using proposed scheme; and Chapter 5: Conclusion.

## 2  Related Work

### 2.1  RFID System

RFID system recognizes tag attached to product/object through RF wireless signal by non-contact method. RFID system is composed of tag, reader that reads tag ID and Back-end DB which stores information of tags and objects/products attached to tags.[1] Reader sends query message via RF wireless signal to tag then tag responses its ID to reader via RF wireless signal. After receiving the tag ID, the reader sends it to the Back-end DB server. The Back-end DB server performs authentication procedure using security protocol. After authenticating the tag ID, the RFID system transport tag's information. Figure 1 illustrates the five methods on how RFID system works [2].

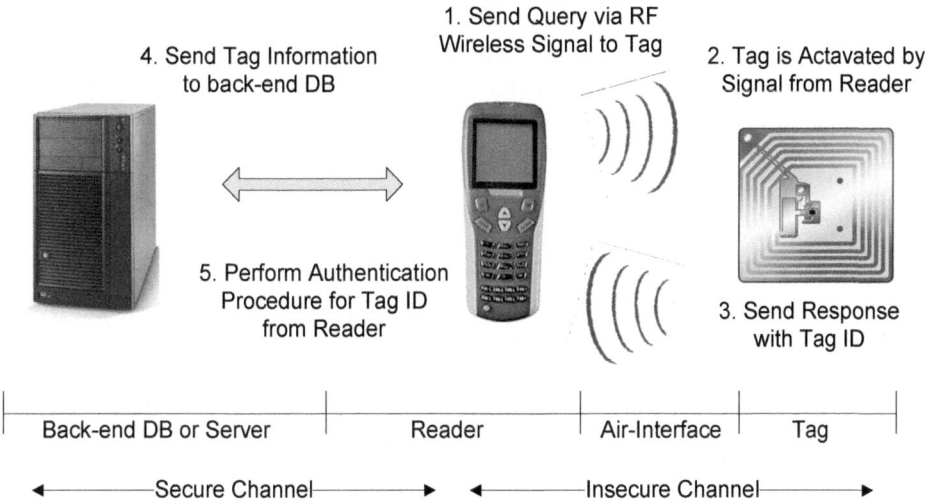

**Fig. 1.** Methods on How RFID Tag Works

The RFID system has two types of tags: Active RFID tags, and Passive RFID tags. Active RFID tags are equipped with battery, so it can send information actively. Passive RFID tags are batteryless and obtain the power necessary to operate from the query signal itself. Active RFID tags have long-range signal transmission, but they have time constraints because they use batteries. Passive RFID tags can be used for longer time periods because they are battery-less, but they have short-range signal transmission [3].

## 2.2  Security Threats of RFID System

The RFID system uses light-weight hash function protocols for security authentication because RFID readers and tags have limited resources to calculate. Despite using these protocols, RFID systems are exposed to security threats [4]. Eavesdropping is the act of secretly listening to the private data between reader and tag. It occurs primarily in the wireless sector. The solution is applying security protocol to block by exposing tag information or by using exposed tag information to access Back-end DB server.

Replay Attack stores the intercepted message between tag and reader while they are communicating and retransmitting this message to trick server/reader/tag in believing that it is a legal message.

Spoofing Attack is a malicious attacker disguised as a legitimate user then passes through the authentication or occurs as a wrong authentication.

## 2.3  Existing Authentication Protocol for RFID Security

RFID system uses hash function based light-weight mutual authentication protocol to solve security threat problems that should occur in wireless communication sector between reader and tag. First, hash-lock method creates temporary metaID for authentication.[5][6] In hash-lock method, only hash function is realized in the tag. When the reader sends a query to get a tag ID, the tag responses with the fake ID, or a metaID. This method uses hash function for only one time. Therefore, it is more feasible to use cheap RFID tags because it can block exposing the real ID. It also  uses hash value of random key (meataID=$h$(key)). Figure 2 illustrates the methods on how hash-lock works.

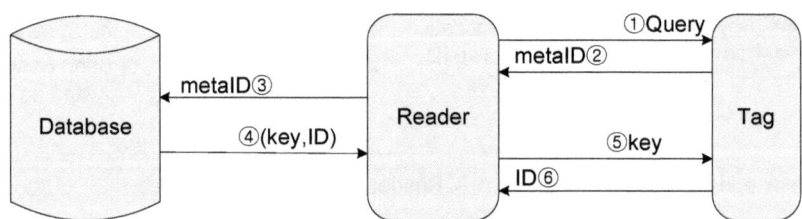

**Fig. 2.** Hash-Lock Protocol

However, hash-lock method can be tracked because the metaID is fixed. Eavesdropping is easy because data is transmitted without encryption. In the final part of authentication, the tag transmits its real ID to the reader, exposing its real ID. A randomized hash-lock method is proposed to improve using fixed metaID in hash-lock method. In randomized hash-lock method, the tag creates random number R and responses randomly. Therefore, randomized hash-lock method can solve location tracking problem, but there are some problems, wherein a malicious reader can perform replay attack after getting value of R and $h(ID_k\|R)$.

## 3   Tag ID Subdivision Scheme

In this chapter, a Tag ID Subdivision Scheme is proposed for improving authentication efficiency and minimizing security threats such as eavesdropping and location tracking when each sensor is distinguished using RFID system in USN Environment. Figure 3 illustrates the RFID system environment, which has one Back-end DB or Server with multiple readers. In this environment, the reader must read only permitted tags. However, in the existing RFID system, every reader reads all the tags and the Back-end DB performs duplicated authentication procedure based on number of the tags that was read.

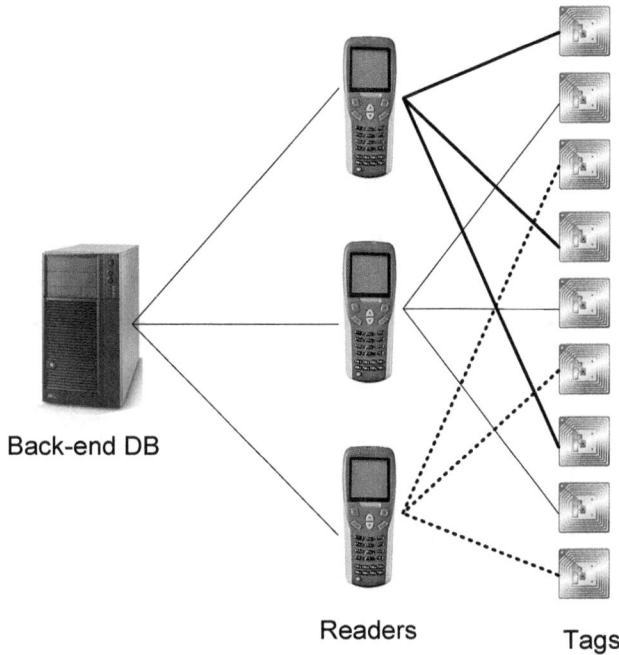

Back-end DB

Readers          Tags

**Fig. 3.** RFID System Environment for apply Tag ID Subdivision Scheme

If the RFID reader reads the tags allowed in RFID system that has one Back-end DB server and multiple readers, the proposed scheme makes the reader perform authentication procedure for only allowed tags through subdivided tag group information. In this scheme, if the reader reads the prohibited tags then Back-end DB does not perform authentication procedure. Traffic can be reduced for duplicated authentication procedure. Consequently, the authentication efficiency can be improved in RFID system. In this system, it is assumed that the RFID system applied to the proposed scheme is designed based on stable multiple reader networks and there is no interference problem among readers.

## 3.1 Classifying RFID Tag Using Tag ID Subdivision Scheme

RFID tag ID has uniqueness to distinguish each tag. In the proposed scheme, the tag's own ID is changed to string and sort all tag's IDs, which is further changed to string in ascending order from the first tag's ID to the ID of the last tag. It then performs a string comparison from the first character of each of the ID string, comparing the first character of the first ID string and second ID string whether it is the same or not. After string comparison, if the first character of all tag ID strings is the same, then the second character of all tag ID strings are compared. If different characters are found during the comparison characters in this manner, then memorize sequence number of tag ID and sequence number of tag ID string. After subdividing tags and classifies it into different characters, it is possible to classify tags into several groups.

Table 1 shows the process of subdivision and the result of subdivided tags using proposed scheme. Based on the table below, every first character to tenth character in the tag 1 to tag 10 is the same. Tags cannot be classified into several groups when comparing from first character to tenth character of tag ID string. However, the eleventh character of tag 7 and tag 8 are different. The eleventh character of tag ID string

**Table 1.** Tag ID Subdivision by Comparing Character of Tag ID String

| Group (EA) | 1 | 1 | 1 | 1 | 1 | 1 | 1 | 1 | 1 | 1 | **2** | 2 | 2 | **5** | **8** | **9** | **10** |
|---|---|---|---|---|---|---|---|---|---|---|---|---|---|---|---|---|---|
| No | 1 | 2 | 3 | 4 | 5 | 6 | 7 | 8 | 9 | 10 | 11 | 12 | 13 | 14 | 15 | 16 | 17 |
| Tag 1 | E | 0 | 0 | 4 | 0 | 1 | 0 | 0 | 0 | 0 | 7 | 7 | 8 | 8 | F | C | 2 |
| Tag 2 | E | 0 | 0 | 4 | 0 | 1 | 0 | 0 | 0 | 0 | 7 | 7 | 8 | 7 | 4 | 4 | 5 |
| Tag 3 | E | 0 | 0 | 4 | 0 | 1 | 0 | 0 | 0 | 0 | 7 | 7 | 8 | A | 3 | D | 9 |
| Tag 4 | E | 0 | 0 | 4 | 0 | 1 | 0 | 0 | 0 | 0 | 7 | 7 | 8 | A | 4 | 8 | 4 |
| Tag 5 | E | 0 | 0 | 4 | 0 | 1 | 0 | 0 | 0 | 0 | 7 | 7 | 8 | B | 4 | A | 2 |
| Tag 6 | E | 0 | 0 | 4 | 0 | 1 | 0 | 0 | 0 | 0 | 7 | 7 | 8 | B | 4 | 6 | 3 |
| Tag 7 | E | 0 | 0 | 4 | 0 | 1 | 0 | 0 | 0 | 0 | 7 | 7 | 8 | B | 5 | F | 4 |
| Tag 8 | E | 0 | 0 | 4 | 0 | 1 | 0 | 0 | 0 | 0 | 9 | A | C | D | B | E | D |
| Tag 9 | E | 0 | 0 | 4 | 0 | 1 | 0 | 0 | 0 | 0 | 9 | A | C | D | B | E | 0 |
| Tag 10 | E | 0 | 0 | 4 | 0 | 1 | 0 | 0 | 0 | 0 | 9 | A | C | D | D | 5 | 4 |

in tag 1 to tag 7 is "7", but tag 8 to tag 10 is "9". Therefore, it is possible to classify tags into 2 groups. The number located on top of the table indicates the number of groups which are the sequence numbers of characters. If one wants to classify tags into subdivided groups, continue comparing the tag ID strings. Table 1, determines that it is possible to classify tags into 2 groups at the eleventh character, 5 groups at the fourteenth character, 8 groups at the fifteenth character, 9 groups at the sixteenth character, and 10 groups at the seventeenth character.

### 3.2   Storing Subdivided RFID Tag ID Information

After classifying the tag into groups using the proposed scheme, subdivided tag ID group stores the information in Back-end DB and adds the reader's information to tag group information to give permission to each group. The reader's own ID or S/N was used as reader's information to distinguish itself from other readers. When reader reads the tag ID and sends it to Back-end DB, the reader sends its ID or S/N to Back-end DB at the same time.

## 4   RFID Tag Authentication Procedure Using Tag ID Subdivision Scheme

Figure 4 shows the authentication procedure that the reader reads tag ID and sends it to Back-end DB to process authentication in RFID system that proposed scheme is applied. Because each tag is already classified into subdivided groups and Back-end DB stores these groups' information. The reader can be determined to allow the subdivided tag group. Back-end DB accepts the authentication request for certain groups of tags which are allowed by the reader. The RFID tag authentication procedure applied tag ID subdivision scheme is indicated in Figure 4.

The proposed scheme is applied to RFID system wherein there is one Back-end DB server with multiple readers. The Back-end DB server must accept the authentication for tag ID, which is sent by permitted reader. First, select one reader and read the tags, the tag that receives query from reader will transmit its tag ID value to the reader. After receiving the value of tag ID from the tag, reader sends it to Back-end DB with reader's own ID or S/N. Then Back-end DB loads tag data stored in database using tag ID, which is received from reader. After loading the tag data, Back-end DB compares the subdivided tag group information that is loaded from database and reader's ID that was received from reader. If the result of comparing reader's ID that is sent by reader and subdivided tag group information that is loaded from database using tag ID which is received from reader is allowed, then Back-end DB performs authentication procedure.

Authentication procedure performs security protocol that the system adapted. If the result of comparing reader's ID and subdivided tag information is not allowed then, Back-end DB does not perform authentication procedure and prepares to receive next tag's information.

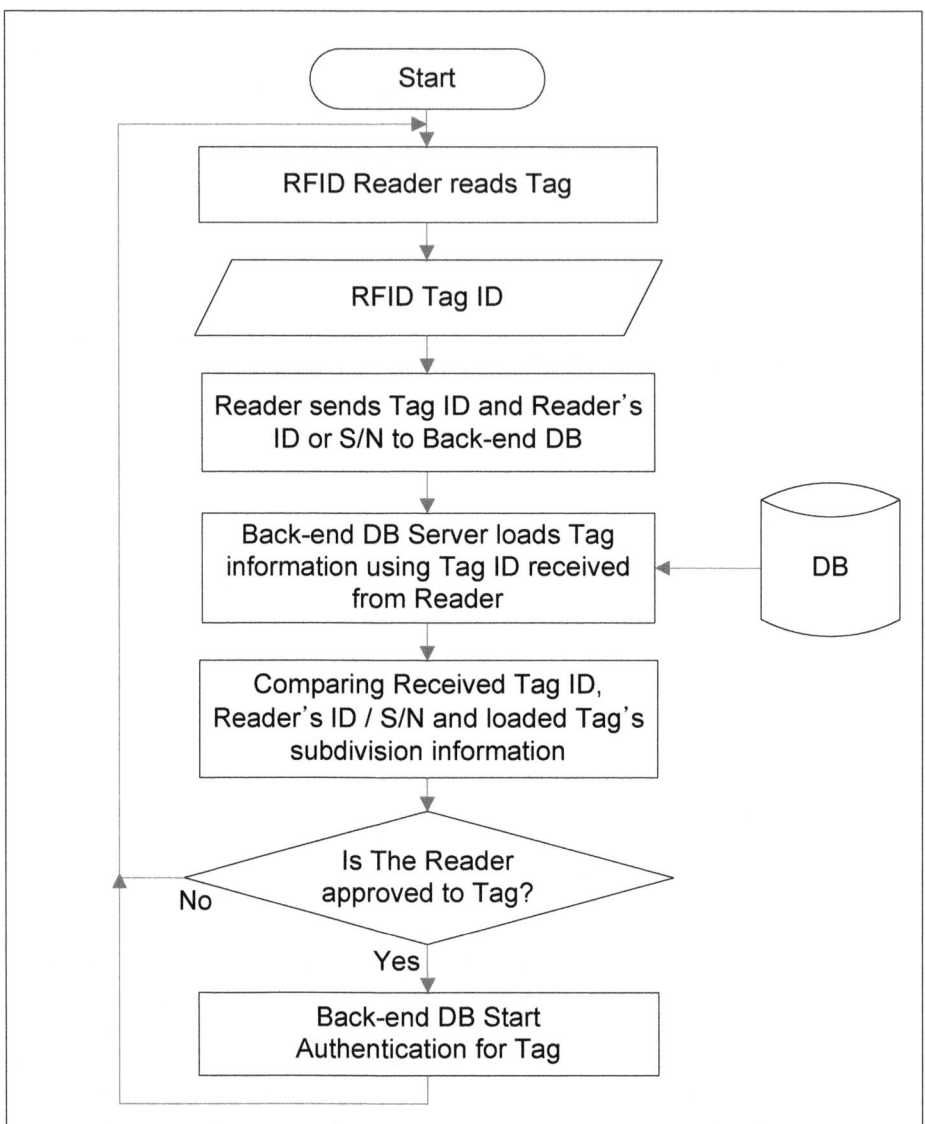

**Fig. 4.** RFID Tag Authentication Procedure using Tag ID Subdivision Scheme

The RFID system that is applied to the proposed scheme does not carry out dupli-cated authentication procedure because the Back-end DB performs authentication procedure for tag ID sent by only allowed reader. Therefore, Back-end DB can reduce its traffic due to duplicated authentication procedure. Also, RFID system can mini-mize security threats such as eavesdropping, spoofing attack among tag, reader and Back-end DB server's authentication procedure.

# 5  Conclusion

RFID system became an important technology to recognize objects in USN Environment. In this research the proposed Tag ID Subdivision Scheme reduces Back-end DB traffic and minimizes the security threats in RFID system which has one Back-end DB server with multiple readers. This study introduced a new RFID tag authentication procedure that was applied to the proposed scheme. The RFID system applied Tag ID Subdivision Scheme can reduce Back-end DB traffic and minimize security threats and consequently, improve authentication efficiency and enhance security.

# References

1. Klaus, F.: RFID handbook, 2nd edn. John Wiley & Sons, Chichester (2003)
2. Choi, G.Y., Seong, N.S., Mo, H.S., Park, C.W., Quan, S.H.: Trends in RFID Technology and Standardization. ETRI Analysis of Electronic Telecommunication Trends 22(3), 30 (2007)
3. Auto-ID Center: 860MHz-960MHz Class 1 Radio Frequency Identification Tag Radio Frequency & Logical communication Interface Specification Proposed Recommendation Version 1.0.0. Technical Report MIT-AUTOID-TR-007 (November 2002)
4. Juels, A.: FID Security and Privacy: A Research Survey. IEEE Journal 24(2), 381–394 (2006)
5. Sarma, S., Weis, S., Engels, D.: RFID Systems and Security and Privacy Implications. In: Kaliski Jr., B.S., Koç, Ç.K., Paar, C. (eds.) CHES 2002. LNCS, vol. 2523, pp. 454–469. Springer, Heidelberg (2002)
6. Weis, S.: Security and Privacy in Radio-Frequency Identification Devices. Master Thesis, 2003(5) (2003)

# Fault Attacks against the Miller's Algorithm in Edwards Coordinates

Nadia El Mrabet

GREYC − LMNO, University of Caen, France
nadia.el_mrabet@info.unicaen.fr
ANR Pairing and Advances for Cryptology and Ecash*

**Abstract.** Initially, the use of pairings did not involve any secret entry. However in an Identity Based Cryptographic protocol, one of the two entries of the pairing is secret, so fault attack can be applied to Pairing Based Cryptography to find it. In [18], the author shows that Pairing Based Cryptography in Weierstrass coordinates is vulnerable to a fault attack. The addition law in Edwards coordinates is such that the exponentiation in Edwards coordinates is naturally protected to Side Channel attacks. We study here if this property protects Pairing Based Cryptography in Edwards coordinates against fault attacks.

**Keywords:** Pairing Based Cryptography, Edwards coordinates, fault attack.

## 1 Introduction

Originally, pairings were used in a destructive way. Pairings convert the discrete logarithm problem from an elliptic curve subgroup to the discrete logarithm problem in a finite field. This property was used in the MOV [29] and Frey Ruck attack [19]. This pairing property permits the construction of new protocols. The first constructive use of pairings was the tripartite key exchange of A. Joux [22]. It was followed by original protocols like Identity Based Cryptography (IBC), which was introduced by D. Boneh and M. Franklin in 2001 [10], or short signature schemes [20].

The use of pairings in IBC involves a secret entry during the pairing calculation. Several pairing implementations exist, for example [32] and [5]. Side Channel Attacks (SCA) against Pairing Based Cryptography were first developed three years ago ([30], [33] and [24]).

In [30], D. Page and F. Vercauteren introduce a fault attack against the particular case of the Duursma and Lee algorithm. The fault attack consists in modifying the number of iterations of the algorithm. This idea was completed in [18] in application to the Miller's algorithm in Weierstrass coordinates. In [33] the authors conclude that if the secret is used as the first argument of the pairing computation, then it cannot be found. This countermeasure is not one,

---

* https://pace.rd.francetelecom.com/welcome-to-france-telecom-r-d-pace/view?

S.K. Bandyopadhyay et al. (Eds.): ISA 2010, CCIS 76, pp. 72–85, 2010.
© Springer-Verlag Berlin Heidelberg 2010

as concluded in [18]. These three articles consider the case of Weierstrass coordinates. Recently, Edwards coordinates were introduced for pairings computation [6,8,23,3].

Edwards curves became interesting for elliptic curve cryptography when it was proved by Bernstein and Lange in [7] that they provide addition and doubling formulas faster than all addition formulas known at that time. The advantage of Edwards coordinates is that the addition law can be complete and thus the exponentiation in Edwards coordinates is naturally protected against Side Channel Attacks.

Our contribution is to find out if Pairing Based Cryptography in Edwards coordinates is protected against fault attacks. We show that a fault attack against the Miller's algorithm in Edwards coordinates can be done through the resolution of a non linear system.

The outline of this article is as follow.

First we give a short introduction to pairings in Section 2. After that we recall the background of Edwards coordinates and to pairing in Edwards coordinates in Section 3 and to Pairing Based Cryptography in Section 4. Section 5 presents our fault attacks against Pairing Based Cryptography in Edwards coordinates, and we conclude, we conclude in Section 6.

## 2 Pairings and the Miller's Algorithm

First, before introducing the properties of Edwards curves and Pairing Based Cryptography over Edwards curves, we recall the definition and properties of pairings.

### 2.1 A Short Introduction to Pairings

In this section we give a brief overview of the definition of pairings on elliptic curves and of Miller's algorithm [28] used in pairing computation. Let $q$ be a prime power not divisible by 2, $E$ an elliptic curve over $\mathbb{F}_q$ and $r$ a prime factor of $\#(E(\mathbb{F}_q))$. Suppose $r^2$ does not divide $\#(E(\mathbb{F}_q))$ and $k$ be the *embedding degree* with respect to $r$, i.e. the smallest integer such that $r$ divides $q^k - 1$. We denote $\mathcal{O}$ the point at infinity of the elliptic curve.

**Definition 1.** *A pairing is a bilinear and non degenerate function:*

$$e : \mathbb{G}_1 \times \mathbb{G}_2 \to \mathbb{G}_3$$
$$(P, Q) \to e(P, Q)$$

where $\mathbb{G}_1$ and $\mathbb{G}_2$ are subgroups of order $r$ on the elliptic curve and $\mathbb{G}_3$ is generally $\mu_r$, the subgroup of the $r$-th roots of unity in $\mathbb{F}_{q^k}$. In general we take $\mathbb{G}_1 = E(\mathbb{F}_q)[r]$ and $\mathbb{G}_2 \subset E(\mathbb{F}_{q^k})[r]$, where we denote by $E(K)[r]$ the subgroup of $K$-rational points of order $r$ of the elliptic curve $E$. We also denote $E[r]$ the subgroup of points of order $r$ defined over the algebraic closure of $\mathbb{F}_q$.

Let $P \in \mathbb{G}_1$, $Q \in \mathbb{G}_2$. The goal of Miller's algorithm is to construct a rational function $f_{s,P}$ associated to the point $P$ and some integer $s$, and to evaluate this function at the point $Q$ (in fact at a divisor associated to this point). The function $f_{s,P}$ is such that the divisor associated to it is:

$$\text{div}(f_{s,P}) = s(P) - (sP) - (s-1)(\mathcal{O}).$$

Suppose we want to compute the sum of $iP$ and $jP$. Take $h_1$ the line going through $iP$ and $jP$ and $h_2$ the vertical line through $(i+j)P$. Miller's idea was to make use of the following relation

$$f_{i+j,P} = f_{i,P} f_{j,P} \frac{h_1}{h_2}, \tag{1}$$

in order to compute $f_{s,P}$ iteratively. Moreover, Miller's algorithm uses the double-and-add method to compute $f_{s,P}$ in $\log_2(s)$ operations [28].

**The reduced Tate pairing**

The reduced Tate pairing, denoted $\widehat{e}_{Tate}$, is defined by:

$$\mathbb{G}_1 \times \mathbb{G}_2 \mapsto \mathbb{G}_3$$
$$(P,Q) \mapsto \widehat{e}_{Tate}(P,Q) = f_{r,P}(Q)^{\frac{p^k-1}{r}}.$$

## 3    Background on Edwards Curves

**Definition and properties.** Edwards showed in [16] that every elliptic curve $E$ defined over an algebraic number field is birationally equivalent over some extension of that field to a curve given by the equation:

$$x^2 + y^2 = c^2(1 + x^2 y^2). \tag{2}$$

In this paper, we use the notion of Twisted Edwards curves denoted $E_{a,d}$ and defined over a field $\mathbb{F}_q$, where $q$ is a power of prime different from 2:

$$E_{a,d} := \left\{ (x,y) \in \mathbb{F}_q^2 \text{ such that } ax^2 + y^2 = 1 + dx^2 y^2 \right\}$$

They were introduced by Bernstein et al in [8] as a generalization of Edwards curves.

On a twisted Edwards curve, we consider the following addition law:

$$(x_1, y_1), (x_2, y_2) \rightarrow \left( \frac{x_1 y_2 + y_1 x_2}{1 + dx_1 x_2 y_1 y_2}, \frac{y_1 y_2 - a x_1 x_2}{1 - dx_1 x_2 y_1 y_2} \right). \tag{3}$$

The neutral element of this addition law is $O = (0,1)$. For every point $P = (x,y)$ the opposite element is $-P = (-x,y)$.

In [7], it was shown that this addition law is *complete* when $d$ is not a square. This means that it is defined for all pairs of input points on the Edwards curve with no exception for doubling, neutral element and others.

In the following sections we use projective coordinates. A projective point $(X,Y,Z)$ satisfying $(aX^2 + Y^2)Z^2 = Z^4 + dX^2 Y^2$ and $Z \neq 0$ corresponds to the affine point $(X/Z, Y/Z)$ on the curve $ax^2 + y^2 = 1 + dx^2 y^2$. The Edwards curve has two points at infinity $(0:1:0)$ and $(1:0:0)$. The fastest formulas for computing pairings over Edwards curves are given in [3].

## 3.1    Pairings over Edwards Curves

For efficiency reasons, we restrict the domain of the Tate pairing to a product of cyclic subgroups of order $r$ on the elliptic curve. In general, the point $P$ can be chosen such that $\langle P \rangle$ is the unique subgroup of order $r$ in $E(\mathbb{F}_q)$. In order to get a non-degenerate pairing, we take $Q$ a point of order $r$, $Q \in E(\mathbb{F}_{q^k}) \backslash E(\mathbb{F}_q)$. Moreover, if the embedding degree is even, it was shown that the subgroup $\langle Q \rangle \subset E(\mathbb{F}_{q^k})$ can be taken so that the $x$-coordinates of all its points lie in $\mathbb{F}_{q^{k/2}}$ and the $y$-coordinates are products of elements of $\mathbb{F}_{q^{k/2}}$ with $\sqrt{\alpha}$, where $\alpha$ is a non square in $\mathbb{F}_{q^{k/2}}$ and $\sqrt{\alpha}$ is in $\mathbb{F}_{q^k}$ (see [25,3] for details).

The same kind of considerations apply to Edwards curves and Twisted Edwards curves [3]. Using the trick of [25] the point $Q \in E(\mathbb{F}_{q^k})$ is written $(X_Q \sqrt{\alpha}; Y_Q; Z_Q)$ using a twist of degree 2. The element $X_Q$, $Y_Q$, $Z_Q$ and $\alpha$ are in $\mathbb{F}_{q^{k/2}}$ and $\sqrt{\alpha} \in \mathbb{F}_{q^k}$. The point $P$ is written $(X, Y, Z)$ with $X$, $Y$ and $Z \in \mathbb{F}_q$. In the following algorithm we used the denominator elimination trick [25].

---

**Algorithm 1.** Miller $(P, Q, s)$

---

**Data**: $s = (s_n \ldots s_0)$(binary decomposition), $P \in \mathbb{G}_1$ $Q \in \mathbb{G}_2$;
**Result**: $f_{s,P}(Q) \in \mathbb{G}_3$;
$T \leftarrow P$, $f \leftarrow 1$,
**for** $i = n - 1$ **to** $0$ **do**
    $T \leftarrow [2]T$ and $f \longleftarrow f^2 \times g_d(Q)$
    **if** $s_i = 1$ **then**
      | $T \leftarrow T + P$ and $f \longleftarrow f \times g_a(Q)$
    **end**
**end**
**return** $f = f_{s,P}(Q) \in \mathbb{F}_{q^k}^*$

---

Fig. 1. Miller's algorithm

The equation of functions $g_d$ and $g_a$ are described in the following sections.

**Doubling step.** We now take a look into the details of the computation of a Miller iteration. The doubling step is done for each iteration of the Miller's algorithm. We note $T = (X_1, Y_1, Z_1)$. Following [3], the doubling formulas for $2T = (X_3, Y_3, Z_3)$ are:

$$X_3 = (2X_1 Y_1)(2Z_1^2 - aX_1^2 - Y_1^2),$$
$$Y_3 = Y_1^4 - a^2 X_1^4,$$
$$Z_3 = (aA_1^2 + Y_1^2)(2Z_1^2 - aA_1^2 - Y_1^2).$$

The function $g_d$ has the following equation:

$$g_d(Q) = c_{Z^2} \eta' \sqrt{\alpha} + c_{XY} y_0 + c_{XZ},$$

where

$$\eta' = \frac{Z_Q + Y_Q}{X_Q} \text{ and } y_0 = \frac{Y_Q}{Z_Q},$$
$$c_{Z^2} = X_1(2Y_1^2 - 2Y_1Z_1),$$
$$c_{XY} = 2Z_1(Z_1^2 - aX_1^2 - Y_1Z_1),$$
$$c_{XZ} = Y_1(2aX_1^2 - 2Y_1Z_1).$$

**Addition step.** This step is done only when the current bit of $s$ is equal to 1. We note $T = (X_1, Y_1, Z_1)$ and $P = (X_P, Y_P, Z_P)$. Following [3], the addition formulas for $T + P = (X_3, Y_3, Z_3)$ in extended Edwards form are:

$$T_1 = \frac{X_1Y_1}{Z_1} \text{ and } T_P = \frac{X_PY_P}{Z_P},$$
$$X_3 = (T_1Z_P + T_PZ_1)(X_1Y_P - X_PY_1),$$
$$Y_3 = (T_1Z_P + T_PZ_1)(Y_1Y_P + aX_1X_P),$$
$$Z_3 = (X_1Y_P - X_PY_1)(Y_1Y_P + aX_1X_P).$$

The function $g_a$ has the following equation:

$$g_a(Q) = c_{Z^2}\eta'\sqrt{\alpha} + c_{XY}y_0 + c_{XZ},$$

where

$$\eta' = \frac{Z_Q + Y_Q}{X_Q} \text{ and } y_0 = \frac{Y_Q}{Z_Q},$$
$$c_{Z^2} = X_1X_P(Y_1Z_P - Y_PZ_1),$$
$$c_{XY} = Z_1Z_P(X_1Z_P - Z_1X_P + X_1Y_P - Y_1X_P)$$
$$c_{XZ} = X_PY_PZ_1^2 - X_1Y_1Z_P^2 + Y_1Y_P(X_PZ_1 - X_1Z_P).$$

## 4   Identity Based Cryptography

The aim of identity based encryption is that the users public key are their identity, and a trusted authority sends them their private key. This trusted authority creates all the private keys related to an identity based protocol. The general scheme of identity based encryption is described in [10].

The most useful property in Pairing Based Cryptography is bilinearity:

$$\forall (n, m) \in \mathbb{Z}^2, \ e([n]P, [m]Q) = e(P, Q)^{nm}.$$

Pairings permit several protocol simplifications and original scheme creation, for example Identity Based Cryptography (IBC) protocols. A nice survey of protocols using pairings is done in [15]. A recent book [17] is dedicated to IBC.

The general scheme of an identity based encryption is described in [10], we briefly recall it. We also describe an exchange between Alice and Bob using the Boneh and Franklin scheme [10].

The public data are an elliptic curve $E$ defined over $\mathbb{F}_q$, for $q$ a power of a prime $p$, $\mathbb{G}_1$ a subgroup of $E$ and $\mathbb{G}_3$ a subgroup of $\mathbb{F}_{q^k}$, where $k$ is the embedding degree of $E$ relatively to $r = \#\mathbb{G}_1$, a pairing $e : \mathbb{G}_1 \times \mathbb{G}_1 \to \mathbb{G}_3$, and $P_{pub}$ a generator of $\mathbb{G}_1$. Let $H_1 : \{0,1\}^{*} \to \mathbb{G}_1$, $H_2 : \mathbb{G}_1 \to \{0,1\}^n$, be two hash functions, with $n$ the bitlength of the message.

The public key of Bob is $Q_B = H_1(Id_B) \in \mathbb{G}_1$, where $Id_B$ is the identity of Bob. His private key is constructed by a trusted authority denoted $T_A$. $T_A$ chooses an integer $s$ kept secret and computes $K_{pub} = [s]P_{pub} \in \mathbb{G}_1$ the public key of the protocol, and the private key of Bob by $P_B = [s]Q_B \in \mathbb{G}_1$.

With the public data Alice can compute $Q_B = H_1(Id_B)$, and the pairing $g_B = e(Q_B, K_{pub})$.

She chooses an integer $m$ and sends to Bob $C = \langle [m]P_{pub}, M \oplus H_2(g_B^m) \rangle$, which we denote $C = \langle U, V \rangle$.

To decipher the message $C$, Bob recovers his private key and computes $V \oplus H_2(e(P_B, U))$.

Considering the property of bilinearity:

$$ e(P_B, U) = e([s]Q_B, [m]P_{pub}) = e(Q_B, [s]P)^m = e(Q_B, K_{pub})^m = g_B^m. $$

Consequently, Bob can read the message by computing $V \oplus H_2(g_B^m)$.

The important point is that to decipher a message using an Identity Based Protocol, a computation of a pairing involving the private key and the message is done. Side Channel Attacks can therefore be applied to find this secret. The particularity of Identity Based Protocol is that an attacker can know the algorithm used, the number of iterations and the exponent. The secret is only one of the arguments of the pairing. The secret key influences neither the execution time nor the number of iterations of the algorithm.

## 5    Fault Attack against Pairing Based Cryptography

The goal of a fault injection attack is to provoke mistakes during the calculation of an algorithm, for example by modifying the internal memory, in order to reveal sensitive data. This attack needs very precise timing, position and expensive apparatus to be performed. Nevertheless, new technologies could allow this attack [21].

### 5.1    Description of the Fault Attack

We follow the scheme of attack described in [30] and completed in [18]. We assume that the pairing is used during an Identity Based Protocol, the secret point is introduced in a smart card or an electronic device and is a parameter of the pairing. In order to find the secret, we modify the number of iterations in the Miller's algorithm by the following way.

First of all, we have to find the flip-flops belonging to the counter of the number of iterations (i.e. $\log_2(s)$) in the Miller's algorithm. This step can be done by using reverse engineering procedures. Once we found it, we provoke disturbances in order to modify it and consequently the number of iterations of the Miller's algorithm. For example, the disturbance can be induced by a laser [2]. Lasers are nowadays thin enough to make this attack realistic [21]. Counting the clock cycles, we are able to know how many iterations the Miller's loop has done. Each time, we record the value of the Miller's loop and the number of iterations we made. The aim is to obtain a couple $(\tau, \tau + 1)$ of two consecutive values, corresponding to $\tau$ and $\tau + 1$ iterations during the Miller's algorithm.

We denote the two results by $F_{\tau,P}(Q)$ and $F_{\tau+1,P}(Q)$. To conclude the attack, we consider the ratio $\frac{F_{\tau+1,P}(Q)}{F_{\tau,P}(Q)^2}$. By identification in the basis of $\mathbb{F}_{q^k}$, we are lead to a system which can reveal the secret point, which is described in Section 5.4.

The probability for obtaining two consecutive numbers is sufficiently large to make the attack possible [18]. In fact, for an 8-bits architecture only 15 tests are needed to obtain a probability larger than one half, $P(15, 2^8) = 0.56$, and only 28 for a probability larger than 0.9.

## 5.2   The $\tau^{th}$ Step

We execute the Miller's algorithm several times. For each execution we provoke disturbance in order to modify the value of $\log_2(s)$, until we find the result of the algorithm execution for two consecutive iterations, the $\tau^{th}$ and $(\tau + 1)^{th}$ iterations of algorithm 1. We denote the two results by $F_{\tau,P}(Q)$ and $F_{\tau+1,P}(Q)$. After $\tau$ iterations, the algorithm 1 will have calculated $[j]P$. During the $(\tau+1)^{th}$ iteration, it calculates $[2j]P$ and considering the value of the $(\tau + 1)^{th}$ bit of $\log_2(s)$, it either stops at this moment, or it calculates $[2j + 1]P$. In order to simplify the equations, we consider $k = 4$, but the method described can be generalized for $k \geq 4$. We denote $B = \{1, \gamma, \sqrt{\alpha}, \gamma\sqrt{\alpha}\}$ the basis used for writting the elements of $\mathbb{F}_{q^k}$. This basis is constructed by a tower extensions [4].

## 5.3   Finding $j$

We know $\log_2(s)$, the order of the point $Q$, (as $P$ and $Q$ have the same order). By counting the number of clock cycles during the pairing calculation, we can find the number $\tau$ of iterations. Then reading the binary decomposition of $\log_2(s)$ gives us directly $j$. We consider that at the beginning $j = 1$, if $s_{n-1} = 0$ then $j \leftarrow 2j$, else $j \leftarrow 2j+1$, and we go on, until we arrive to the $(n-1-\tau)^{th}$ bit of $s$. For example, let $s = 1000010000101$ in basis 2, and $\tau = 5$, at the first iteration we compute $[2]P$, at the second, as $s_{n-1} = 0$ we only make the doubling, so we calculate $[4]P$. It is the same thing for the second, third and fourth steps so we have $[32]P$ in $T$.

At the fifth iteration, $s_{n-6} = 1$, then we make the doubling and the addition, so $j = 2 \times 32 + 1$, i.e. $j = 65$.

## 5.4   Curve and Equations

In [30,34,18], only the affine coordinates case is treated. In [30,34], a simple identification of the element in the basis of $\mathbb{F}_{q^k}$ gives the result. Here, the difference between these cases and Edwards coordinates is that we solve a nonlinear system.

Using the equation of the pairing calculation proposed in Section 3.1, we find a nonlinear system of $k$ equations using the equality $g(Q) = R$, where $g(Q)$ defines the equation of update of $f$ during the Miller's algorithm. This system is solvable with the resultant method. To solve the system in Edwards coordinates we need $k$ to be greater than 2.

**The embedding degree.** In order to simplify the equations, we consider case $k = 4$. As the important point of the method is the identification of the decomposition in the basis of $\mathbb{F}_{q^k}$, it is easily applicable when $k$ is larger than 2.

We denote $B = \{1, \gamma, \sqrt{\alpha}, \gamma\sqrt{\alpha}\}$ the basis of $\mathbb{F}_{q^k}$, constructed by a tower extensions. The point $P \in E(\mathbb{F}_q)$ is given in Jacobian coordinates, $P = (X_P, Y_P, Z_P)$ and the point $Q \in E(\mathbb{F}_{q^k})$ also. As $k$ is even, we can use a classical optimization in Pairing Based Cryptography which consists in using the twisted elliptic curve to write $Q = (X_Q\sqrt{\alpha}; Y_Q; Z_Q)$, with $X_Q$, $Y_Q$, $Z_Q$ and $\alpha \in \mathbb{F}_{q^2}$ and $\sqrt{\alpha} \in \mathbb{F}_{q^4}$, as described in Section 3.1.

**Case 1: $s_{\tau+1} = 0$.**   We know the results of the $\tau^{th}$ and $(\tau + 1)^{th}$ iterations of the Miller's algorithm, $F_{\tau,P}(Q)$ and $F_{\tau+1,P}(Q)$. We examine what happens during the $(\tau + 1)^{th}$ iteration.

The doubling step gives:

$$F_{\tau+1,P}(Q) = (F_{\tau,P}(Q))^2 \times g_d(Q).$$

As we suppose that $s_{\tau+1} = 0$, the additional step is not done. The return result of the Miller's algorithm is $F_{\tau+1,P}(Q) = (F_{\tau,P}(Q))^2 g_d(Q)$. We dispose of $F_{\tau,P}(Q)$, $F_{\tau+1,P}(Q)$ and the point $Q = (X_Q\sqrt{\alpha}; Y_Q; Z_Q)$, with $X_Q$, $Y_Q$ and $Z_Q \in \mathbb{F}_{q^2}$. Recall that the coordinates of $Q$ can be freely chosen and that we describe the attack for $k = 4$. This can easily be generalized for $k > 4$.

We can calculate the value $R \in \mathbb{F}_{q^k}^*$ of the ratio $\frac{F_{\tau+1,P}(Q)}{(F_{\tau,P}(Q))^2}$,

$$R = R_3\gamma\sqrt{\alpha} + R_2\sqrt{\alpha} + R_1\gamma + R_0,$$

where $R_3$, $R_2$, $R_1$, $R_0 \in \mathbb{F}_q$.

Moreover, we know the theoretical form of $R$ in the basis $B = \{1, \gamma, \sqrt{\alpha}, \gamma\sqrt{\alpha}\}$ which depends on coordinates of $jP$ and $Q$:

$$R = g_d(Q) = c_{Z^2}\eta'\sqrt{\alpha} + c_{XY}y_0 + c_{XZ},$$

where the $c_{Z^2}$, $C_{XY}$, $c_{XZ}$ are in $\mathbb{F}_q$ and $\eta'$, $y_0 \in \mathbb{F}_{q^2}$.

**When the secret is the first argument**

This position was presented as a countermeasure to SCA in [33]. We know the point $Q$, thus the values of $\eta'$ and $y_0 \in \mathbb{F}_{q^2}$ and their decomposition in $\mathbb{F}_{q^2}$, $\eta' = \eta'_0 + \eta'_1\gamma$, $y_0 = y_{00} + y_{01}\gamma$, where $(1, \gamma)$ defines the basis of $\mathbb{F}_{q^2}$. The elements $c_{Z^2}$, $c_{XY}$ and $c_{XZ}$ are in $\mathbb{F}_q$. Using the equality:

$$c_{Z^2}(\eta'_0 + \eta'_1\gamma)\sqrt{\alpha} + c_{XY}(y_{00} + y_{01}\gamma) + c_{XZ} = R_0 + R_1\gamma + R_2\sqrt{\alpha} + R_3\gamma\sqrt{\alpha},$$

by identification in the basis of $\mathbb{F}_{q^k}$, we obtain, after simplification, the following system of equations in $\mathbb{F}_q$:

$$\begin{cases} c_{XZ} = \lambda_2 \\ c_{XY} = \lambda_1 \\ c_{Z^2} = \lambda_0 \end{cases}$$

The value $\lambda_0$, $\lambda_1$ and $\lambda_2$ are known. With the resultant method we recover the coordinates of the secret point $P$. An example is given in the appendix.

**When the secret is the second argument**

We know the point $P$, thus the values of $c_{Z^2}$, $c_{XY}$ and $c_{XZ} \in \mathbb{F}_q$. Using the equality:

$$c_{Z^2}(\eta'_0 + \eta'_1\gamma)\sqrt{\alpha} + c_{XY}(y_{00} + y_{01}\gamma) + c_{XZ} = R_0 + R_1\gamma + R_2\sqrt{\alpha} + R_3\gamma\sqrt{\alpha}.$$

By identification in the basis of $\mathbb{F}_{q^k}$, we can recover the values $\eta'$ and $y_0$, and thus the coordinates of the point $Q$.

$$\begin{cases} \eta'_0 = \frac{R_2}{c_{Z^2}} \text{ and } \eta'_1 = \frac{R_3}{c_{Z^2}}, \\ y_{00} = \frac{R_0 - c_{XZ}}{c_{XY}} \text{ and } y_{01} = \frac{R_1}{c_{XY}} \end{cases}$$

Indeed, once we have $y_0 \left(= \frac{Y_Q}{Z_Q}\right)$, using the elliptic curve we can find the values of $x_0 \left(= \frac{X_Q}{Z_Q}\right)$, and the coordinates of the point $Q$.

**Case 2: $s_{\tau+1} = 1$.**  In this case, the $(\tau + 1)^{th}$ iteration involves the addition in the Miller's algorithm.

Thus, at the $(\tau + 1)^{th}$ iteration, Miller's algorithm computes $F_{\tau+1,P}(Q) = (F_{\tau,P}(Q))^2 g_d(Q)g_a(Q)$. We could repeat the scheme of the previous case, and thanks to the resolution of a non linear system, we can recover the secret point, whatever its position is. To obtain the system, we just have to develop the product $g_d(Q)g_a(Q)$. Using the polynomial reduction for the base of $\mathbb{F}_{p^{k/2}}$ and $\mathbb{F}_{p^k}$, we find the system by identification in this basis.

## 6    Conclusion

We have studied if the Miller's algorithm in Edwards coordinates is vulnerable to a fault attack. We demonstrated that it is the case, whatever is the position of the secret. Consequently, the property of Edwards curves does not protect Pairing Based Cryptography in Edwards coordinates towards fault attack. A discussion about weakness to this fault attack of pairings based on this algorithm was done in [18]. The authors show that the Weil pairing is directly sensitive to the fault attack described, and some methods to override the final exponentiation are given; and then, for a motivated attacker, the final exponentiation will no longer be a natural countermeasure for the Tate and Ate pairings [12]. Thus implementation of Pairing Based Cryptography in Edwards coordinates must be protected. A possible protection could be to use an asynchrone clock to confuse the attack and physical shield to protect the counter.

# References

1. Abraham, D.G., Dolan, G.M., Double, G.P., Stevens, J.V.: Transaction Security System. IBM Systems Journal 30, 206–229 (1991)
2. Anderson, R., Kuhn, M.: Tamper Resistance – a Cautionary Note. In: The Second USENIX Workshop on Electronic Commerce Proceedings, Okland, California, pp. 1–11 (1996)
3. Arène, C., Lange, T., Naehrig, M., Ritzenhaler, C.: Faster Pairing Computation of the Tate pairing, Cryptology ePrint Archive, Report 2009/155 (2009), http://eprint.iacr.org/2009/155
4. Bajard, J.C., El Mrabet, N.: Pairing in cryptography: an arithmetic point de view. In: Advanced Signal Processing Algorithms, Architectures, and Implementations XVI, part of SPIE (August 2007)
5. Bertoni, G.M., Chen, L., Fragneto, P., Harrison, K.A., Pelosi, G.: Computing Tate pairing on smartcards. In: Proceedings of Ches 2005, Workshop on Cryptographic Hardware and Embedded Systems 2005 (CHES 2005), Edinburgh, Scotland (2005)
6. Bernstein, D.J., Lange, T.: Performance evaluation of a new side channel resistant coordinate system for elliptic curves (2007), http://cr.yp.to/antiforgery/newelliptic-20070410.pdf
7. Bernstein, D.J., Lange, T.: Faster additions and doubling on elliptic curves. In: Kurosawa, K. (ed.) ASIACRYPT 2007. LNCS, vol. 4833, pp. 29–50. Springer, Heidelberg (2007)
8. Bernstein, D.J., Birkner, P., Joye, M., Lange, T., Peters, C.: Twisted Edwards curves. In: Vaudenay, S. (ed.) AFRICACRYPT 2008. LNCS, vol. 5023, pp. 389–405. Springer, Heidelberg (2008)
9. Ionica, S., Joux, A.: Another Approach to Pairing Computation in Edwards Coordinates. In: Chowdhury, D.R., Rijmen, V., Das, A. (eds.) INDOCRYPT 2008. LNCS, vol. 5365, pp. 400–413. Springer, Heidelberg (2008)
10. Boneh, D., Franklin, M.: Identity-based encryption from the Weil pairing. In: Kilian, J. (ed.) CRYPTO 2001. LNCS, vol. 2139, pp. 213–229. Springer, Heidelberg (2001)
11. Brier, E., Joye, M.: Point multiplication on elliptic curves through isogenies. In: Fossorier, M.P.C., Høholdt, T., Poli, A. (eds.) AAECC 2003. LNCS, vol. 2643, pp. 43–50. Springer, Heidelberg (2003)
12. Boneh, D., DeMillo, R., Lipton, R.: On the importance of checking cryptographic protocols faults. In: Fumy, W. (ed.) EUROCRYPT 1997. LNCS, vol. 1233, pp. 37–51. Springer, Heidelberg (1997)

13. Cohen, H., Frey, G. (eds.): Handbook of elliptic and hyperelliptic curve cryptography. Chapman & Hall/CRC, Boca Raton (2006)
14. Yang, B., Wu, K., Karri, R.: Scan Based Side Channel Attack on Dedicated Hardware Implementation of Data Encryption Standard. In: Test Conference 2004, Proceedings ITC 2004, pp. 339–344 (2004)
15. Dutta, R., Barua, R., Sarkar, P.: Pairing-Based Cryptographic Protocols: A Survey. Cryptology ePrint Archive, Report 2004/064 (2004)
16. Edwards, H.: A normal Form for Elliptic Curve. Bulletin of the American Mathematical Society 44(3) (July 2007)
17. Joye, M., Neven, G.: Identity-Based Cryptography. Cryptology and Information Security Series, vol. 2. IOS Press, Amsterdam
18. El Mrabet, N.: What about Vulnerability to a Fault Attack of the Miller's Algorithm During an Identity Based Protocol? In: Park, J.H., Chen, H.-H., Atiquzzaman, M., Lee, C., Kim, T.-h., Yeo, S.-S. (eds.) ISA 2009. LNCS, vol. 5576, pp. 122–134. Springer, Heidelberg (2009)
19. Frey, G., Müller, M., Rück, H.G.: The Tate Pairing and the Discrete Logarithm Applied to Elliptic Curve Cryptosystems. IEEE Transactions Inf. Theory 45, 1717–1719 (1999)
20. Galbraith, S., Paterson, K.G.: Pairings, Chapter IX. In: Blake, F., Seroussi, G., Smart, N. (eds.) Advances in Elliptic Curve Cryptography. London Mathematical Society Lecture Note Series, vol. 317. Cambridge University Press, Cambridge (2005)
21. Habing, D.H.: The Use of Lasers to Simulate Radiation-Induced Transients in Semiconductor Devices and Circuits. IEEE Transactions on Nuclear Science 39, 1647–1653 (1992)
22. Joux, A.: One round protocol for tripartite Diffie-Hellman. In: Bosma, W. (ed.) ANTS 2000. LNCS, vol. 1838, pp. 385–393. Springer, Heidelberg (2000); Full version: Journal of Cryptology 17, 263–276 (2004)
23. Ionica, S., Joux, A.: Faster Pairing Computation on Edwards Curves. Presented at the C2 conference (pre-print), http://c2-2008.inria.fr/C2/
24. Kim, T.H., Takagi, T., Han, D.-G., Kim, H.W., Lim, J.: Side Channel Attacks and Countermesures on Pairing based Cryptosystems over Binary Fields. In: Pointcheval, D., Mu, Y., Chen, K. (eds.) CANS 2006. LNCS, vol. 4301, pp. 168–181. Springer, Heidelberg (2006)
25. Koblitz, N., Menezes, A.J.: Pairing-based cryptography at high security levels. In: Smart, N.P. (ed.) Cryptography and Coding 2005. LNCS, vol. 3796, pp. 13–36. Springer, Heidelberg (2005)
26. Macwilliams, F.J., Sloane, N.J.A.: The Theory of Error-Correcting Codes II. North-Holland Mathematical Library, vol. 16. North-Holland, Amsterdam (1998)
27. Menezes, A.: An introduction to pairing-based cryptography. Notes from lectures given in Santander, Spain (2005),
    http://www.cacr.math.uwaterloo.ca/~ajmeneze/publications/pairings.pdf
28. Miller, V.: The Weil pairing and its efficient calculation. J. Cryptology 17, 235–261 (2004)
29. Menezes, A., Okamoto, T., Vanstone, S.A.: Reducing Elliptic Curve Logarithms to Logarithms in a Finite Field. IEEE Trans. Inf. Theory 39(5), 1639–1646 (1993)
30. Dan, P., Frederik, V.: Fault and Side Channel Attacks on Pairing Based Cryptography. IEEE Transactions on Computers 55(9), 1075–1080 (2006)
31. PARI/GP, version 2.1.7, Bordeaux (2005), http://pari.math.u-bordeaux.fr/
32. Scott, M.: Computing the Tate Pairing. In: Menezes, A. (ed.) CT-RSA 2005. LNCS, vol. 3376, pp. 293–304. Springer, Heidelberg (2005)

33. Whelan, C., Scott, M.: Side Channel Analysis of Practical Pairing Implementation: Which Path is More Secure? In: Nguyên, P.Q. (ed.) VIETCRYPT 2006. LNCS, vol. 4341, pp. 99–114. Springer, Heidelberg (2006)
34. Whelan, C., Scott, M.: The Importance of the Final exponentiation in Pairings when considering Fault Attacks. In: Takagi, T., Okamoto, T., Okamoto, E., Okamoto, T. (eds.) Pairing 2007. LNCS, vol. 4575, pp. 225–246. Springer, Heidelberg (2007)

# Appendix

## A   The Probability for the Fault Attack

The important point of this fault attack is that we can obtain two consecutive couples of iterations, after a realistic number of tests. The number of picks with two consecutive numbers is the complementary of the number of picks with no consecutive numbers. The number $B(n, N)$ of possible picks of $n$ numbers among $N$ integers with no consecutive number is given by the following recurrence formula:

$$
\begin{cases}
N \leq 0, n > 0, B(n, N) = 0, \\
\forall N, n = 0 B(n, N) = 1 \\
\quad B(n, N) = \sum_{j=1}^{N} \sum_{k=1}^{n} B(n - k, j - 2).
\end{cases}
$$

With this formula, we can compute the probability to obtain two consecutive numbers after $n$ picks among $N$ integers. This probability $P(n, N)$ is

$$
P(n, N) = 1 - \frac{B(n, N)}{C_{n+N}^{n}}.
$$

## B   Example of Resolution of a System

We consider the Edwards elliptic curves given in [6]: $E_{1,-1}$ over $\mathbb{F}_q$ with $q = 2^5 20 + 2^3 63 - 2^3 60 - 1$.

We consider that after a differential attack, we obtain the following values for $c_{Z^2}$ and $c_{XY}$:

$$
\begin{cases}
c_{Z^2} = 34048376154121925359113429375521510393131211202148147144793425 \\
\quad 34029342793292985388461167229695405257330782051548185233985909 \\
\quad 7790323384550119208941089386681807, \\
c_{XY} = 17520806845701679087874508433242642859361996080064213725858540 \\
\quad 91707452190313544768238501361334785917437694094417592638973798 \\
\quad 59991288038826511945916794250369 8
\end{cases}
$$

To solve the system

$$
\begin{cases}
X(2Y^2 - 2YZ) = c_{Z^2}, \\
2Z(Z^2 - aX^2 - YZ) = c_{XZ}, \\
(aX^2 + Y^2)Z^2 = Z^4 + dX^2Y^2,
\end{cases}
$$

we use the following Pari-GP [31] code:

```
q = 2^520 + 2^363 - 2^360 - 1;

a=Mod(1,q);

d=Mod(-1,q);

cZZ = 3404837615412192535911342937552151039313121120214814714479342 5\
      3402934279329298538846116722969540525733078205154818523398590 9\
      779032338455011920894108938681807;

cXY = 1752080684570167908787450843324264285936199608006421372585854 0\
      9170745219031354476823850136133478591743769409441759263897379 8\
      5999128803882651194591679425036 98;
```

We construct the polynomial corresponding to each line of the system:

```
x = X*(2*Y^2-2*Y*Z) - cZZ;

y = - cXY + 2*Z*(Z^2-a*X^2-Y*Z);

z = (a*X^2+Y^2)*Z^2 - Z^4 - d*X^2*Y^2;
```

We apply the resultant method to obtain one equation in one unknown value:

```
Z1 = polresultant(x,y,X);

Z2 = polresultant(x,z,X);

Z3 = polresultant(Z1,Z2,Y);
```

$Z3$ is the final equation in $Z$, it is an equation of degree 16. We can find the solution of this equation:

```
polrootsmod(Z3,p)
```

We find 4 solutions in $Z$.

We are looking for points on the elliptic curve, thus $Z$ must be different from 0. So we have 3 possible values.

```
[Mod(0, q),
Mod(901525105405827680078932099881135208347014760557116161414786496\
6898087582081014331390758210475534342660764975515278975723117752716\
43438166345974764910619 13,q),
Mod(943029634660650213489325189263739902235878374981732742513043934\
8268937376183411243681855740333148594089845464209933234063573499498\
8690964171008230410163313 2,q),
Mod(239921668486407187599373200028884318556413779905064814412212597\
7692123342437202117570816442035015313748006996320319779030774725627\
0529614366357152861883783 62, q)]~
```

To each of the 3 non zero value, using equation $Z2$ we find one value for $Y$:

```
Z = Mod(9015251054058276800789320998811352083470147605571161614147864\
   96689808758208101433139075821047553434266076497551527897572311775271\
   6434381663459747649061913,q)
```

```
Y = [Mod(2616647236923767714125198006192101918016786492107325345575050\
   999892174925093897971705778547452808016256451379938199954909912375542\
   916450574500329476293105973,q)]~
```

```
Z = Mod(9430296346606502134893251892637399022358783749817327425130439\
   34826893737618341124368185574033314859408984546420993323406357349949\
   8869096417100823041016333132,q)
Y = [Mod(56777,q)]~
```

```
Z = Mod(2399216684864071875993732000288843185564137799050648144122125\
   97769212334243720211757081644203501531374800699632031977903077472562\
   7052961436635715286188378362, q)]
```

```
Y = Mod(8157515931415371433657523933485946906179311579807671572015975\
   622958230307824554135471310507202775003271478125582659372844508775611\
   87764320480065590487910657,q)
```

Using these 3 couples of values, we find 6 triplets and an exhaustive research gives us the correct secret point.

# A Cryptosystem for Encryption and Decryption of Long Confidential Messages

Debasis Giri[1], Prithayan Barua[2], P.D. Srivastava[3], and Biswapati Jana[4]

[1] Department of Computer Science and Engineering
Haldia Institute of Technology, Haldia 721657, India
debasis_giri@hotmail.com
[2] Department of Computer Science and Automation
Indian Institute of Science, Bangalore 560012, India
prithayan_09@yahoo.co.in
[3] Department of Mathematics
Indian Institute of Technology, Kharagpur 721 302, India
pds@maths.iitkgp.ernet.in
[4] Department of Computer Science
Vidyasagar University, Midnapore, West-Bengal 721102 , India
biswapatijana@vidyasagar.ac.in

**Abstract.** In this paper, we propose a cryptosystem which can encrypt and decrypt long (text) messages in efficient manner. The proposed cryptosystem is a combination of symmetric-key and asymmetric-key cryptography, where asymmetric-key cryptography is used to transmit the secret key to an intended receiver and the sender/receiver encrypts/decrypts messages using that secret key. In 2002, Hwang et al. proposed a scheme for encrypting long messages. The main drawback of their scheme is that it requires more computational overhead. Our proposed scheme is more efficient from the computational point of view compared to that of their scheme. Our scheme is a block cipher, long messages are broken into fixed length plaintext blocks for encryption. It supports parallel computation, since encryption/decryption of all the blocks of plaintext/plaintext are independent and thus can be carried out simultaneously. In addition, our scheme retains the same security level as their scheme.

**Keywords:** Encryption, Decryption, Security, Public key, long Messages, Hash function.

## 1 Introduction

Existing techniques for encryption of messages can be classified as symmetric and asymmetric. Symmetric cryptosystem tends to be more efficient than asymmetric, because asymmetric-key cryptography commonly deals with numbers greater than 1024 bits for security consideration. The overhead of dealing with such large numbers is time consuming due to some exponentiation operations. As a result asymmetric techniques require more time to encrypt large messages. On the other hand, symmetric-key cryptography incurs the overhead of management of a large number of secret keys. It requires a shared secret key between two parties. If there is a group of $N$ entities,

S.K. Bandyopadhyay et al. (Eds.): ISA 2010, CCIS 76, pp. 86–96, 2010.

every entity needs $N$ different keys to communicate with each other, which makes a total of $N(N-1)/2$ keys, if the same key is used for both directions. Another problem with symmetric cryptosystem is the distribution of secret keys. Communication of so many secrets is another overhead of the system. For efficient encryption and decryption of large confidential messages a combination of the symmetric and asymmetric cryptosystem can be used. We propose such a scheme which combines both symmetric-key (where a symmetric-key is generated using cryptographic one-way hash function and the shared secret master key between sender and receiver) and and asymmetric-key cryptography. We use asymmetric cryptosystem for exchanging a master key, then using the shared secret master key the long message is encrypted. In our scheme, the *Diffie-Hellman* [1] like key exchange protocol is used to exchange a shared secret master key. We then use the one-time pad (OTP) encryption algorithm in which the plaintext is combined with a secret random key or pad, which is used only once for encrypting each message block. A one time pad is the only currently known unconditionally secure encryption system. In our proposed scheme, a block of message will be exclusive-ored($\oplus$) with some message digest values of a Hash function, where for each block of message digest values are different. However, we have shown that our scheme is more efficient than that of Hwang et al.'s scheme [2].

The remainder of this paper is organized as follows. Section 2 gives a brief overview of Hwang et al.'s scheme. In Section 3, we introduce our proposed scheme for encrypting a long confidential message. In Section 4, we analyze the security and the time complexity of our scheme. Section 5 deals with the implementation of our scheme. In Section 6, our scheme is compared with the Hwang et al.'s scheme. Finally, Section 7 concludes the paper.

## 2    Brief Review of Hwang et al.'s Cryptosystem

In this section, we briefly review Hwang et al.'s [2] cryptosystem.

The Hwang et al. scheme is based on ElGamal cryptosystem [3], which works with a public modulus $p$ and a public generator $g \in \mathbb{Z}_p^*$. Suppose there is a user $u_l$. The key pair of the user $u_l$ is $(x_l, y_l)$, where $y_l = g^{x_l} \bmod p$ and $x_l$ is the secret key and $y_l$ the public key of $u_l$. To encrypt a long message $M$, the sender breaks up the message $M$ into $t$ blocks $M_1, M_2, \ldots, M_t$, such that bit length of each $M_i$ $(i = 1, 2, \ldots, t)$ is less than that of $p$. First, the encryption algorithm picks up two random numbers $r_1, r_2 \in \mathbb{Z}_p^*$, and then it computes $b_1 = g^{r_1} \bmod p$ and $b_2 = g^{r_2} \bmod p$. For $j = 1, 2, \ldots, t$, the encryption algorithm computes $C_j = M_j \cdot (y_l^{r_1} \oplus (y_l^{r_2})^{2^j}) \bmod p$, where $\oplus$ denotes the bitwise exclusive-OR operator. The ciphertext that is to be sent by the sender to the receiver is $C = (b_1, b_2, \langle C_1, C_2, \ldots, C_t \rangle)$. To decrypt a ciphertext $C = (b_1, b_2, \langle C_1, C_2, \ldots, C_t \rangle)$, the receiver computes $M_j = C_j \cdot (y_l^{r_1} \oplus (y_l^{r_2})^{2^j})^{-1} \bmod p$, $1 \le j \le t$.

## 3    Proposed Cryptosystem

In this section, we introduce an improved cryptosystem for encrypting as well as decrypting long confidential messages. The improved cryptosystem consists of following phases.

**Key Generation.** We use Diffie-Hellman [1] like protocol for exchanging the master key between a sender and a receiver. The master key is a symmetric key which will be used by both the sender and receiver for encryption and decryption respectively. Any user, who wants to *receive* a confidential message, generates a pair of secret key and public key. Before establishing the keys, two primes $p$ and $q$, such that $p$ is of $k$ bits and $p = 2q + 1$, where $k$ is at least 1024 are chosen. A primitive element $g$ such that $g \in \mathbb{Z}_p^*$ which is of order $q$ over modulo $p$ (where $p$, $q$ and $g$ are public parameters) is also chosen. We use the hash algorithm *SHA-256* [4] as the non invertible function (which is denoted as $H$), where the output of *SHA-256* is a 256-bit message digest.

Each user can execute the following for generating their public and private key (secret key) pairs:

1. Each user selects a secret random number $secret\_key$, such that $1 < secret\_key < q - 1$.
2. The corresponding public key is calculated as $public\_key = g^{secret\_key} \bmod p$
3. $public\_key$ is public, while $secret\_key$ is a secret information.

Suppose $U_a$ be a user. $U_a$ randomly chooses $secret\_key_a$ ($1 < secret\_key_a < q - 1$) as secret key and computes the corresponding $public\_key_a = g^{secret\_key_a} \bmod p$ as public key.

**Encryption.** Suppose a user wants to transmit a long confidential message $M$ of length, say $L$ bits, to another authorized user $U_a$. To encrypt a long message it is to be broken into several blocks each of length $k$ bits. So it is necessary to make the length of the message a multiple of $k$ bits by padding. We have broken the message into blocks of length 1024 bits, that is $k = 1024$, so 11 bits are enough to represent the number of padding bits. There are three possible cases of padding which are listed as follows.

1. If $L + 11 = 0 \bmod k$ then sender composes a message of total length $L + 11$ bits in which the first $L$ most significant bits are the original message bits while 11 least significant bits represent the number of padding bits. In this case, 11 least significant bits of the composed message contain binary representation of 11.
2. Sender computes the least residue $r = L \bmod k$ and checks whether $k - r > 11$. If it is true, then sender composes a message of length $L + k - r$ bits which consists of $L$ most significant bits as original message, next $k - r - 11$ bits as zero bits and 11 least significant bits contain the binary representation of the number of padding bits i.e. binary representation of $k - r$.
   **Note:** In this case, we can have $r = 0$.
3. Sender computes the least residue $r = L \bmod k$ and checks whether $r \neq 0$ and $k - r < 11$. If both are true then sender composes a message of length $L + 2k - r$ bits which consists of $L$ most significant bits as original message, next $2k - r - 11$ bits as zero bits and 11 least significant bits contain the binary representation of the number of padding bits i.e. binary representation of $2k - r$.

**Note:** The number of padding bits cannot exceed $2^{11} - 1$. As a result, 11 least significant bits are sufficient to store the number of padding bits. Clearly, total length of message is multiple of $k$, i.e., multiple of 1024 after padding some bits.

**Remark 1.** *We consider that the message has been broken in $t$ blocks each of length $k$ bits.* ∎

In order to encrypt a long message $M$, we use the above steps to get a final message, say, $M'$ of $k \cdot t$ bits after padding some bits with $M$. Of course, the step will be chosen according to the length of the message $M$. Now, sender first breaks up the message $M'$ into $t$ blocks of equal length k bits, say, $M_1$, $M_2$, ..., $M_t$, where $M' = M_1||M_2 \dots ||M_t$. Then the sender executes the following steps.

1. The long message is broken into $t$ number of blocks (shown above) each of 1024 bits.
2. Randomly choose $r$ such that $1 < r < q - 1$ and compute $X = (public\_key_a)^r \bmod p$.
3. Compute $K = g^r \bmod p$ as a master key between the sender and the receiver.
4. Compute
   $MD_i = H(K||4i) \parallel H(K||\overline{4i+1}) \parallel H(K||\overline{4i+2}) \parallel H(K||\overline{4i+3})$, for $i = 1, 2, \dots, t$, where $\parallel$ is the concatenation operator.
   **Note:** $H$ denotes *SHA-256* hash function, whose output is a 256-bit message digest. Thus after concatenation bit length of $MD_i$ is 1024-bit which is same as the block length of each message block.
5. Finally the cipher text corresponding to $i$th block message $M_i$ is computed as:

$$C_i = M_i \oplus MD_i,$$

for $i = 1, 2, \dots, t$.
   **Note:** One can consider it as OTP encryption.
6. Send $C = (X, \langle C_i : i = 1, 2, \dots, t \rangle)$ to the receiver via public channel.

**Decryption.** To recover the original plaintext $M$ corresponding to the received ciphertext $C$, receiver $U_a$ executes the following
   1. Compute the master secret-key $K$ as

$$K = X^{secret\_key_a^{-1} \bmod q} \bmod p$$

2. Compute
   $MD_i = H(K||4i) \parallel H(K||\overline{4i+1}) \parallel H(K||\overline{4i+2}) \parallel H(K||\overline{4i+3})$,
   for $i = 1, 2, \dots, t$, where $\parallel$ is the concatenation operator.
3. Recover the plaintext $M_i$ using $M_i = C_i \oplus MD_i$, for $i = 1, 2, \dots, t$.
4. Recover the message $M'$ as $M' = M_1||M_2 \dots ||M_t$. To recover the original plaintext message $M$, the receiver discards the lower ordered padding bits from $M'$, the number of padding bits is the number stored in the 11 least significant bits of $M'$.

**Correctness.** Suppose $C = (X, \langle C_i : 1, 2, \ldots, t \rangle)$ is a ciphertext of $M'$ which is constructed after padding some lower-order bits with the original message $M$. Let $M_i$ be the $k$ bit $i$th block of $M'$ (where bit length of $M'$ is $k \cdot t$) and $C_i$ be the corresponding ciphertext (encrypted message) block. Now, we consider only the $i$th ciphertext block $C_i$ from $C = (X, \langle C_i : 1, 2, \ldots, t \rangle)$. The receiver recovers the $i$th block $M_i$ of $M'$ as shown below.

Since, $C_i = M_i \oplus MD_i$ is the $i$th ciphertext block, so in order to recover $i$th plaintext block $M_i$, the receiver has to perform operation $M_i = C_i \oplus MD_i$ with the knowledge of $X$ and his/her secret key $secret\_key_a$. Because, $public\_key_a = g^{secret\_key_a} \bmod p$ and $X = public\_key_a^r \bmod p$, so $K = X^{secret\_key_a^{-1} \bmod q} \bmod p$ ($= public\_key_a^{r \cdot secret\_key_a^{-1} \bmod q} \bmod p = g^{secret\_key_a \cdot r \cdot secret\_key_a^{-1} \bmod q} \bmod p = g^r \bmod p$). Hence, $MD_i$ can be computed. Hence, using $X$ and his/her secret key $secret\_key_a$, receiver $U_a$ recovers $M_i$ as $M_i = C_i \oplus MD_i$. In the similar fashion, receiver can recover all $M_i$ for $i = 1, 2, \ldots, t$ from $C = (X, \langle C_i : 1, 2, \ldots, t \rangle)$. As a result, receiver recovers $M' = M_1 || M_2 || \ldots, || M_t$. To recover the original plaintext message $M$, the receiver discards the padding bits from $M'$. Hence, receiver can decrypt the encrypted long confidential message.

## 4 Analysis

### 4.1 Security Analysis

We analyze the security of our proposed scheme.

We now define the HDH assumption [5] with public information.

**Hash Diffie-Hellman (HDH) Assumptions with public information:** When a cryptographic one-way hash function $H(\cdot)$ applied on $g^{uv} \bmod p$ with some public information $PI$ and some other parameters, it yields a hard-core bits as well as produces a pseudo random number. This assumption is referred as Hash Diffie-Hellman assumptions with public information.

Now, the corresponding security of the above assumption is as follows.

Let $l$ be the message digest length of $H(\cdot)$, $PI$ a public information and $\mathcal{A}$ an adversary. Consider the experiments $Exp_{H(\cdot),PI,\mathcal{A}}^{HDH-real}$ (see Algorithm 1) and $Exp_{H(\cdot),PI,\mathcal{A}}^{HDH-rand}$ (see Algorithm 2).

---

**Algorithm 1.** Experiment $\boldsymbol{Exp_{H(\cdot),PI,\mathcal{A}}^{HDH-real}}$

---

$u \xleftarrow{R} \mathbb{Z}_q^* - \{1, q-1\}; U \leftarrow g^u \bmod p;$
$v \xleftarrow{R} \mathbb{Z}_p^* - \{1, q-1\}; V \leftarrow g^v \bmod p;$
$W \leftarrow H(g^{uv} \bmod p || PI);$
$b \leftarrow \mathcal{A}(U, V, W);$
Return $b$;

---

**Algorithm 2.** Experiment $Exp_{H(\cdot),PI,\mathcal{A}}^{HDH-rand}$

---

$u \stackrel{R}{\leftarrow} \mathbb{Z}_p^* - \{1, q-1\}; U \leftarrow g^u \bmod p;$
$v \stackrel{R}{\leftarrow} \mathbb{Z}_p^* - \{1, q-1\}; V \leftarrow g^v \bmod p;$
$W \leftarrow \{0,1\}^l;$
$b \leftarrow \mathcal{A}(U, V, W);$
Return $b$;

---

Now, the advantage of $\mathcal{A}$ is defined as

$$Adv_{H(\cdot),\mathcal{A}}^{HDH} = Pr[Exp_{H(\cdot),PI,\mathcal{A}}^{HDH-real} = 1] - Pr[Exp_{H(\cdot),PI,\mathcal{A}}^{HDH-rand} = 1], \qquad (1)$$

where $Pr[X]$ denotes the probability of occurrence of the event $X$.

HDH will be secure in the sense of indistinctively if for any probabilistic polynomial time adversary $\mathcal{A}$, the $Adv_{H(\cdot),\mathcal{A}}^{HDH}$ is negligible.

**Definition 1** *(Message authentication codes (MACs)). A $MAC$ is a tuple $\langle Key(\cdot),$ $Tag_k(\cdot), Ver_k(\cdot, \cdot) \rangle$ of polynomial time algorithms, where*

**$Key(\cdot)$** *is a randomized key generation algorithm that that takes an input $1^l$, where $l$ is a security parameter and $1^l$ is the unary representation of $l$, and returns a key $k$.*
**$Tag_k(\cdot)$** *is a randomized algorithm that takes a message $m \in \{0,1\}^*$ and the key $k$ as inputs and produce an output tag $t$.*
**$Ver_k(\cdot, \cdot)$** *is a verification algorithm that takes $m, k, t$ as inputs and produces a bit value $b \in \{0,1\}$. If $t = Tag_k(m)$ then $Ver_k(m, Tag_k(m))$ returns $b = 1$; otherwise it returns $b = 0$.* ∎

In the following, security of the $MAC$ is as follows.

Let $MAC = (Key(\cdot), Tag_k(\cdot), Ver_k(\cdot, \cdot))$ be a message authentication scheme and $\mathcal{A}$ an adversary. Consider the experiment $Exp_{MAC,\mathcal{A}}^{suf-cma}$ (where suf-cma represents strong unforgeability against a chosen message attack) is shown in Algorithm 3.

---

**Algorithm 3.** Experiment $Exp_{MAC,\mathcal{A}}^{suf-cma}$

---

1: $k \leftarrow Key(i^l)$;
2: $(m^*, t^*) \leftarrow \mathcal{A}^{Tag_k(\cdot),Ver_k(\cdot,\cdot)}$;
3: **if** $Ver_k(m^*, t^*) = 1$ and $t^*$ is not returned by $Tag_k(\cdot)$ with input $m^*$ **then**
4:    $b \leftarrow 1$;
5: **else**
6:    $b \leftarrow 0$;
7: **end if**
8: Return b;

---

Now, we define the suf-cma-advantage of $\mathcal{A}$ against $MAC$ as follows: $Adv_{MAC,\mathcal{A}}^{suf-cma}$ $= Pr[Exp_{MAC,\mathcal{A}}^{suf-cma} = 1]$ and define the suf-cma-insecurity-measure of $MAC$ as

$Adv_{MAC}^{suf-cma}(t, q_t, \mu_t, q_v, \mu_v) = Max_{\mathcal{A}}\{Adv_{MAC,\mathcal{A}}^{suf-cma} : \mathcal{A}$ runs with time-complexity $t$, the tag oracle at most $q_t$ queries the sum of whose lengths is at most $\mu_t$ bits and the verification oracle at most $q_v$ queries the sum of whose lengths is at most $\mu_v$ bits$\}$.

We can informally say that $MAC$ is secure if the suf-cma-insecurity-measure $Adv_{MAC}^{suf-cma}(t, q_t, \mu_t, q_v, \mu_v)$, is sufficiently small for practical values of $t$, $q_t$, $\mu_t$, $q_v$, $\mu_v$. However, a meaningful notion of security requires a limit on the number of queries. This leads to the assumption of $MAC$ security as follows.

**Assumption of secured MAC:** A $MAC$ is $\varepsilon$-secure after $q$ oracle queries if $Pr[Tag_k(m) = t|t_1 = Tag_k(m_1), t_2 = Tag_k(m_2), \ldots, t_q = Tag_k(m_q)] < \varepsilon$ for all adversaries $\mathcal{A}$ with key $k$, where $q = q_t = q_v$, $m$ is different from all $m_i$ for $i = 1, 2, \ldots, q$ and $m$ is not asked to the oracle $Tag_k(\cdot)$.

It is very difficult for an attacker to compute the shared secret master key $K$ from public information. Our key-distribution scheme is based on the Diffie-Hellman like protocol. $public\_key$, $p$, $g$, and $X$ are known to all, because they are all public information. Due to the discrete logarithm problem, it is computationally infeasible to compute the $secret\_key$ from $public\_key = g^{secret\_key} \bmod p$, where $public\_key, g, p$ are public to all.

If an attacker has a *ciphertext and plaintext block* pair, the $MD_i$ can be computed as:

$$MD_i = M_i \oplus C_i$$

But $MD_i = H(K\|4i) \| H(K\|\overline{4i+1}) \| H(K\|\overline{4i+2}) \| H(K\|\overline{4i+3})$. Hash algorithms have the property of *preimage resistance*, so it is extremely difficult to find the key (on which the hashing was done) from the message digest (the output of the hash). For computation of $MD_i$, for two different $i$, the argument to the hash function are different. Hence, our scheme is therefore *secure against chosen plaintext attack*.

Patterns of the plaintext are not preserved in the ciphertext. Moreover the hash function has the property to produce random output (see HDH assumption). So the ciphertext produced by the exclusive-OR operation is also random. Thus an important property of the *ciphertext produced by our scheme is that it is random*. This makes it difficult to implement statistical attack on our scheme.

**Proposition 1.** *Given $p, q, g$, $X$ (where $X = public\_key^r \bmod p$), $public\_key$ (where $public\_key = g^{secret\_key} \bmod p$) and $H(K\|PI_1)$, $H(K\|PI_2)$, ..., $H(K\|PI_n)$, where the session key $K = g^r \bmod p$, it is computationally hard to compute $H(K\|PI)$ without knowing either $r$ or $secret\_key$, where $PI$ is different from the public information $PI_i$ for $i = 1, 2, \ldots, n$.*

*Proof.* If either $r$ or $secret\_key$ is known, we can easily compute the master secret key $K$. Hence, we can compute $H(K\|PI)$ in polynomial time. But, in case of given $X$ and $H(K\|PI_i)$ for $i = 1, 2, \ldots, n$, it is computationally hard to compute $H(K\|PI)$ due to discrete logarithm problem (DLP). Hence, establish the proposition. $\square$

**Remark 2.** *Our scheme is based on a variant of Diffie-Hellman protocol [1] and one-way hash function [6]. Whereas, Diffie-Hellman key distribution protocol is based on the DLP. Therefore, it is difficult for an illegal user (adversary) to compute the secret* *key secret_key of the user u from public_key* $= g^{secret\_key}$ mod p. *It is also diffi-cult task for an adversary to compute K (which is equal to $g^r$ mod p) from the given knowledge public_key* $= g^{secret\_key}$ mod p *and* $X = public\_key^r$ mod p, *because it is computationally infeasible to solve the DLP over a finite field [3].* ∎

**Proposition 2.** *In our proposed scheme, it is computationally hard to retrieve the orig-inal ith plaintext block from t ciphertext blocks (of a long plaintext) even if other $t-1$ plaintext blocks corresponding to that ciphertext is known by an adversary. In other words, knowing $t-1$ blocks, say, $M_1$, $M_2$, ..., $M_{i-1}$, $M_{i+1}$, ..., $M_t$ of a long mes-sage $M'$ (after padding some lower-order bits with the original message M) and the ciphertext C, it is computationally hard to to retrieve the original ith plaintext block $M_i$ by an adversary.*

*Proof.* The adversary $\mathcal{A}$ can only derive $MD_j = H(K||4j)||\ H(K||\overline{4j+1})||\ H(K||\overline{4j+2})||\ H(K||\overline{4j+3})$ using $C_j$ and $M_j$, where $C_j = MD_j \oplus M_j$ for $1 \le j \le t$, $j \ne i$. Let us assume $\mathcal{A}$ can compute $M_i$ from the given knowledge. Therefor $\mathcal{A}$ can easily compute $MD_i$ as $MD_i = M_i \oplus C_i$, which implies that $\mathcal{A}$ solves the HDH hardness (see Proposition 1). Therefore, our assumption is wrong. Hence, it is computationally hard for the adversary to compute $M_i$ from $M_1$, $M_2$, ..., $M_{i-1}$, $M_{i+1}$, ..., $M_t$ and $C = (X, \langle C_i : i = 1, 2, ..., n \rangle)$, where $X = public\_key^r$ mod p and $public\_key = g^{secret\_key}$ mod p and $secret\_key$ is the secret key of the receiver. □

### 4.2 Computational Complexity

In our scheme, for each block of plaintext two operations are required to be done, the Hash and an exclusive-OR operation. There are four Hash *SHA2* operations and one exclusive-or operation. It has been seen that the *SHA2* function takes approximately half the time taken in a 1024 bits modular multiplication. Thus four *SHA2* can be con-sidered equivalent to two multiplications. So to encrypt $t$ blocks of plaintext, $2t$ mul-tiplications, $t$ exclusive-or operations and two exponentiation operations are required. The two exponentiation operations are required for calculating the master secret, which can be pre-computed.

***Possible Improvement***
It is possible to reduce the computationally complexity of our proposed encryption algorithm. We have used *SHA2* as the Hashing algorithm. *SHA2* has a 256-bit message digest. But since a block of message is of length 1024 bits, the *SHA2* operation has to be repeated four times to get a concatenated output of 1024 bits. Thus if we can use a Hash Function with message digest size of 1024 bits or even 512 bits (for SHA-512 [4])we can reduce the time considerably.

## 5  Implementation

The proposed algorithm has been implemented in C++. The cryptosystem involves ma-nipulation of 1024 bits numbers and Hashing-(*SHA2*) function. We have used *NTL*, the Number Theory Library for manipulation of large 1024 bits integers, and generation of cryptographically strong random numbers. The *cryptlib* library has been used to implement the hashing function. The *cryptlib* library supports only SHA1 and SHA2 algorithms. *cryptlib* library is a very strong security toolkit, it provides implementation of many other cryptographic algorithms and various encryption and authentication functionalities. We use only the *SHA2* implementation from this library.

*NTL:* *NTL* is a high-performance, portable C++ library providing data structures and algorithms for arbitrary length integers; for vectors, matrices, and polynomials over integers and over finite fields; and for arbitrary precision floating point arithmetic. We have used the class $ZZ$ of this library to represent signed, arbitrary length integers. It has routines for all of the basic arithmetic operations, as well as for some more advanced operations such as modular arithmetic, primality testing and prime number generation. Another class $ZZ\_p$ is used to represent integers modulo $p$. Objects of the class $ZZ\_p$ are represented as a $ZZ$ in the range $0...p - 1$.

*Development Software:* Microsoft Visual C++, MSVC++ V6 has been used to develop the program.

## 6  Comparison

Now we will compare our scheme with Hwang et al.'s scheme [2]. In Hwang et al.'s scheme, computational requirements are four times exponentiation operation, $t$ times exclusive-OR operations, $t$ times multiplication operations and $t$ times square operations. Furthermore the multiplication and square operations are modulo a prime, thus a division is also implied in each operation. If we compare the number of operations it is evident that our scheme is more efficient than this scheme. We have implemented our scheme and Hwang et al.'s scheme in C++. Then we used both the programs to encrypt and decrypt large text files (of size of a few thousand Mega Bytes) and recorded the time taken.

**Table 1.** Time taken to encrypt and decrypt by both schemes

| Size | Our Scheme | | Hwang et al.'s scheme | |
|------|------------|------------|------------|------------|
| of file | Encryption | Decryption | Encryption | Decryption |
| 1987 KB | 2 sec | 2 sec | 23 sec | 15 sec |
| 2711 KB | 2 sec | 3 sec | 33 sec | 23 sec |
| 3957 KB | 4 sec | 4 sec | 47 sec | 33 sec |
| 4813 KB | 4 sec | 5 sec | 58 sec | 40 sec |
| 5773 KB | 6 sec | 6 sec | 69 sec | 48 sec |
| 6698 KB | 6 sec | 7 sec | 80 sec | 55 sec |

Table 1 shows the time taken by both the schemes to encrypt and decrypt text files. The graphs plotted with the data in Table 1 are shown in Figure 1 and Figure 2. The graphs shows that our scheme takes lesser time to encrypt and decrypt large text files

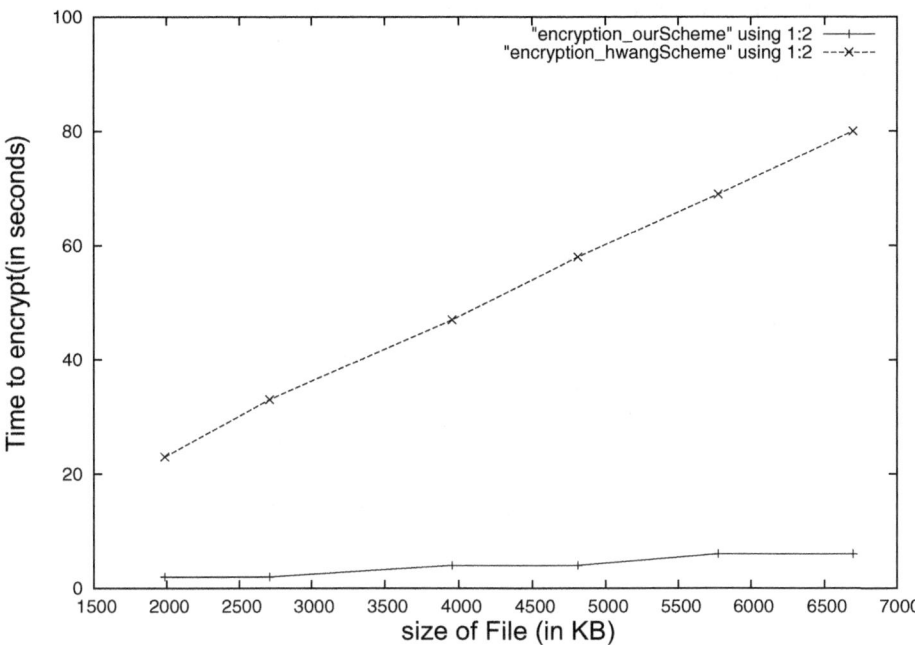

**Fig. 1.** Comparison of time taken to encrypt

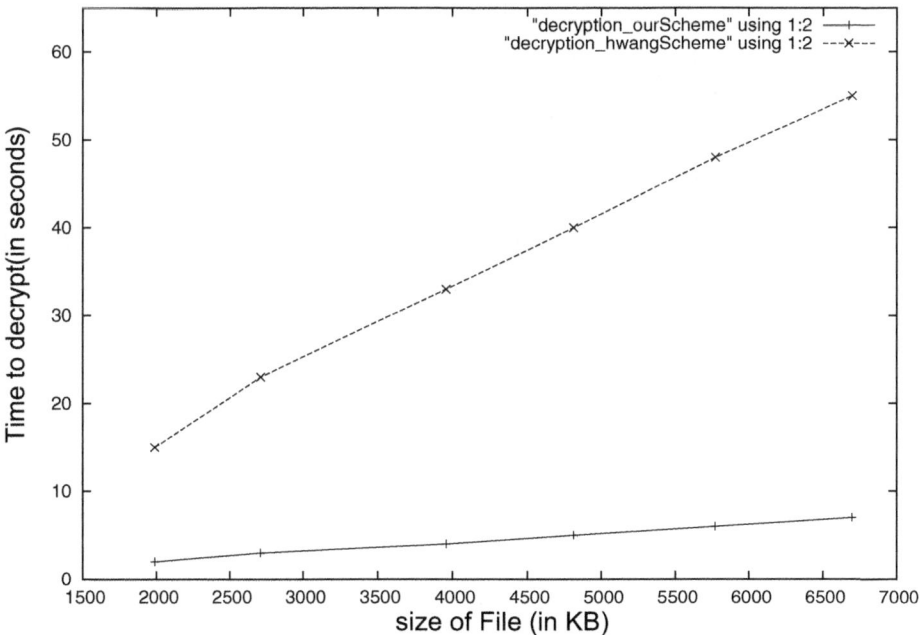

**Fig. 2.** Comparison of time taken to decrypt

compared to those of Hwang et al.'s scheme. The results of the implementation can be used to prove that our scheme is an efficient cryptosystem for exchanging large confidential messages.

## 7   Conclusion

In this paper, we have proposed a scheme for encryption of long messages in an efficient and secure manner. The computational complexity has been shown to be comparably lesser. Actually our scheme just uses the exclusive-OR and the *SHA2* operations on each block of message. Modular arithmetic on large integers is limited to calculation of the shared secret key. Security analysis also shows that our scheme is secure from the cryptographic point of view. The use of secure Hash functions adds to the security of our scheme. All the properties of Hash function strengthens the security of our scheme. Furthermore, our scheme supports parallel computation, that is all the blocks of a message/ciphertext can be encrypted/decrypted simultaneously.We have even implemented the proposed scheme in C++, and compared the actual time taken to encrypt large text files with existing schemes and proved the efficiency. We have used efficient libraries like *cryptlib* and *NTL* for the implementation.

## References

1. Diffie, W., Hellman, M.: New directions in cryptography. IEEE Transactions on Information Theory 22(6), 644–654 (1976)
2. Hwang, M.-S., Chang, C.C., Hwang, K.F.: An elgamal-like cryptosystem for enciphering large messages. IEEE Transactions on Knowledge and Data Engineering 14(2), 445–446 (2002)
3. El Gamal, T.: A public key cryptosystem and a signature scheme based on discrete logarithms. IEEE Transactions on Information Theory 31(4), 469–472 (1985)
4. NIST, U.S. Department of Commerce, Secure hash standard, U.S. Federal Information Processing Standard (FIPS) 180-2 (August 2002)
5. Abdalla, M., Bellare, M., Rogaway, P.: The oracle Diffie-Hellman assumptions and an analysis of DHIES. In: Naccache, D. (ed.) CT-RSA 2001. LNCS, vol. 2020, pp. 143–158. Springer, Heidelberg (2001)
6. Schneier, B.: Applied Cryptography, 2nd edn. John Wiley & Sons Inc., Chichester (1996)

# Lane Design for Speed Optimization

Debnath Bhattacharyya[1], Arijit Chakraborty[2], Feruza Sattarova[1], Young-hun Lee[3],
and Tai-hoon Kim[1,*]

[1] Multimedia Department, Hannam University,
Daejeon, Republic of Korea
debnathb@gmail.com, mymail6585@gmail.com, taihoonn@empal.com
[2] Computer Science and Engineering Department
Heritage Institute of Technology
Kolkata-700007, India
arijit_chakraborty2004@rediffmail.com
[3] Dept. of Electronic Engineering, Hannam University,
Daejeon, Republic of Korea
yhlee@hnu.kr

**Abstract.** Lane Design for Speed Optimization (LDSO) presents a new critical lane analysis as a guide for designing speed optimization to serve rush-hour traffic demands. Physical design and speed optimization are identified, and methods for evaluation are provided. The Lane Design for Speed optimization (LDSO) analysis technique is applied to the proposed design and speed optimization plan. Lane Design for Speed Optimization can robustly boost the speed management and operations. Therefore how to increase the Speed optimization of the Lane is widely concerting issue. There has been a limited research effort on the optimization of the LDSO systems.

**Keywords:** LDSO (Lane Design for Speed Optimization), Lane, Crossover.

## 1 Introduction

The identical challenges of the lane design system are to move traffic safely and efficiently. Although highways and motor vehicles are designed to operate safely at speed. The existing methodology for the traffic systems often replies on the speed optimization analytical model. It is open to discussion due to the facts as follows:

(1) The established tactic often ignores driving behaviors (e.g., Car following, Lane Switching,Speed Optimization). However, these "trivial" driving behaviors turned out to be critical in many cases.
(2) Many traditional Speed optimization algorithms were designed to optimize deterministic problems and therefore they cannot tackle the inherent randomness in the traffic systems.

---

* Corresponding author.

S.K. Bandyopadhyay et al. (Eds.): ISA 2010, CCIS 76, pp. 97–107, 2010.
© Springer-Verlag Berlin Heidelberg 2010

(3) The solutions suggested by the traditional Speed optimization algorithms cannot answer such questions as "how robust is the optimal solution to avoid congesition?" or "How much probability will the optimal solution fail if something unexpected occurs?".

The purpose of this article is to address these two issues by introducing the showing approximation technique into the optimal LDSO design. We structure this paper into 2 parts:

(a) in the first part, we analyze the major issues residing in the latest practice of the speed optimization of traffic systems;
(b) in the last part, we discuss the possible applications of this new technique with probabilistic study and new algorithm.

## 2 Previous Works

Elizabeth Alicandri and Davey L. Warren, January/February 2003 – vol. 66. No .4, proposed a new The twin challenges of the transportation system are to move traffic safely and efficiently. Although highways and motor vehicles are designed to operate safely at speeds traveled by most motorists, almost one in every three traffic fatalities in the United States is related to speeding, either involving exceeding the posted speed limit or driving too fast for conditions. In 2000, more than 12,000 lives were lost in speeding-related crashes, and more than 700,000 people were injured. The National Highway Transportation Safety Administration (NHTSA) estimates that speeding-related crashes cost society $28 billion annually. That's $53,243 per minute, or almost $900 per second. Because speeding is a complex problem involving many factors—personal behavior, vehicle performance, roadway characteristics, and enforcement strategies—the U.S. Department of Transportation (USDOT) organized a multidisciplinary, multiagency team to tackle the problem. The USDOT Speed Management Team includes personnel from the Federal Highway Administration (FHWA), the Federal Motor Carrier Safety Administration (FMCSA), and NHTSA, representing backgrounds ranging from traffic engineering and enforcement to psychology and marketing [1].

H Ludvigsen, Danish Road Directorate, DK; J Mertner, COWI A/S, DK, 2006, published, Differentiated speed limits allowing higher speed at certain road sections whilst maintaining the safety standards are presently being applied in Denmark. The typical odds that higher speed limits will increase the number of accidents must thus be beaten by the project. The Danish Road Directorate has been asked by the Ministry of Energy and Transport based on a request from parliamentarians to suggest an approach to assess the potential for introduction of differentiated speed limits on the Danish state road network. A pilot project was carried in late 2006 and the entire state network will be assessed during the first half of 2007 - first of all to identify where speed limits may be raised. The paper will present the methodology and findings of a project carried out by the Danish Road Direc-torate and COWI aimed at identifying potential sections where the speed limit could be increased from 80 km/h to 90 km/h without jeopardising road safety and where only minor and cheaper measures are necessary. Thus it will be described how to systematically assess the road network when the speed limit is to be increased [2].

In the Operation and Safety of Right-Turn Lane Designs's objectives of this research by the Texas Department of Transportation were to determine the variables that affect the speeds of free-flow turning vehicles in an exclusive right-turn lane and explore the safety experience of different right-turn lane designs. The evaluations found that the variables affecting the turning speed at an exclusive right-turn lane include type of channelization present (either lane line or raised island), lane length, and corner radius. Variables that affect the turning speed at an exclusive right-turn lane with island design include : (a) radius, lane length, and island size at the beginning of the turn and (b) corner radius, lane length, and turning-roadway width near the middle of the turn. Researchers for a Georgia study concluded that treatments that had the highest number of crashes were right-turn lanes with raised islands. This type of intersection had the second highest number of crashes of the treatments evaluated in Texas. In both studies, the "shared through with right lane combination" had the lowest number of crashes. These findings need to be verified through use of a larger, more comprehensive study that includes right-turning volume [3].

C.J. Messer and D.B. Fambro, 1977, presents a new critical lane analysis as a guide for designing signalized intersections to serve rush-hour traffic demands. Physical design and signalization alternatives are identified, and methods for evaluation are provided. The procedures used to convert traffic volume data for the design year into equivalent turning movement volumes are described, and all volumes are then converted into equivalent through-automobile volumes. The critical lane analysis technique is applied to the proposed design and signalization plan. The resulting sum of critical lane volumes is then checked against established maximum values for each level of service (A, B, C, D, E) to determine the acceptability of the design. We provide quidelines, a sample problem, and operation performance characteristics to assist the engineer in determining satisfactory design alternatives for an intersection [4].

## 3  Our Work

Lane Design for Speed Optimization (LDSO) – finding methods in other literature are a family of optimization algorithms which incorporate level of traffic services in the algorithms. There are two major issues, in the first part , we analyze the major issues residing in the latest practice of the speed optimization of traffic systems; in the last part, we discuss the possible applications of this new technique with probabilistic study and new algorithm.

Let $A = \{a1, a2, \ldots\ldots\ldots, an\}$, $B = \{b1, b2, \ldots\ldots\ldots, bn\}$, $C = \{c1, c2, \ldots\ldots\ldots, cn\}$ be three mutually exclusive set, The 3 x N points are to be disbursed in two or more lane, such that the following :

  i)   That every element ai, bi, ci, $1 <= i <= N$ where ai, bi, ci belongs to three set A, B, C the property speed/cost/efficiency or symbolic value say $Va(ai) > Va(aj)$ where $i >= j$.,

  ii)  This technique is applicable for all node and all lane. $1 <= j <= i <= N$.

iii) The speed/cost/efficiency or symbolic value is given on the basis of probability that a(2|3) lane of n nodes having r nodes at any given time, p is the probability of accident and $q=1-p$, ${}^{n}c_{r} p^{r} q^{n-r}$.

## 4 Result

Our work aimed to design "Lane Design for Speed Optimization" in an open unplanned area, so as to increase traffic movement in rush hours and to minimize collision using the concept of Cross Over between adjacent Lanes.

Following, Fig. 1, States three vertical lanes that are unidirectional, and A = {a1,a2,......,an}, B = {b1,b2,......bn}, C = {c1,c2,....,cn}, with the property of the three lanes.

The randoms distribution of entities in an open area to lanes is taken care as far as possible.

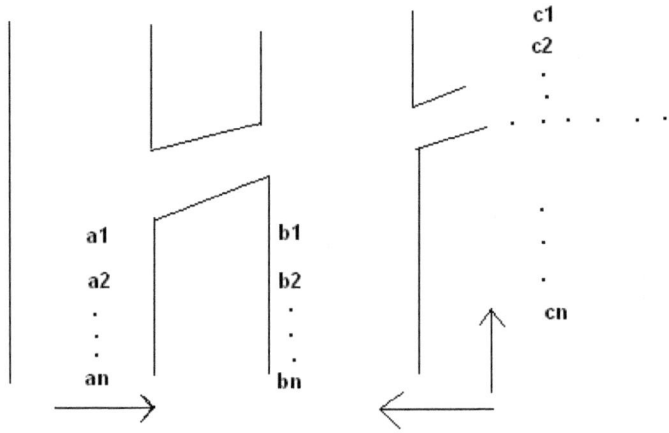

**Fig. 1.** Vertical lanes that are unidirectional and with the property of the three lane

**Algorithm**

Step 1: Insert a node say ai,bi,ci 1<=i<=N.
Step 2: Repeat step 3 to step 5 for I=1, 2, 3 ......N.
Step 3: if Va(ai) < Va(aj) then
       Step 3.1 if Va(aj) < Vb(bi) then
              3.1.1 if Va(aj) < Vc(ci) then
                     PUSH(Tansition1,aj);
                     Endif
          Endif
     Endif
Step 4: if Vb(bj) > Vb(bi) then
       4.1 if Vb(bj) > Vc(ci) then
            PUSH(Transition2,bj);

```
              Else
                      If Vb(bj) > Va(ai) then
                              PUSH(Transition1,bj);
                          Endif
                      Endif
              Endif
Siep 5: if  Vc(cj) > Vc(ci) then
          5.1 if Vc(cj) > Vb(bi) then
                  PUSH(Transition2,cj);
              Else
                      5.1.1 if Vc(cj) > Va(ai) then
                                  PUSH(Transition1,cj);
                                  Endif
                          Endif
                  Endif
[End of Loop]
Step 6: Exit
```

## Analysis:

- The above algorithm is a 3 lane design implemented on open unplanned area.
- The objective will follow linear queue as long as speed/value/cost of proceeding to greater than the immediate next.
- Transiotion/Cross over are used and they again follow appropriate data structure in order to maintain the preceding step rule.
- Here we assume the lanes are narrow enough to limit the bidirectional approach.
- Here we also maintain optimize speed for each lane.

## Simulation Code:

```c
#include<stdio.h>
#include<conio.h>
#include<stdlib.h>
#define SIZE 10
int a[SIZE],b[SIZE],c[SIZE];  //to store speed of cars for lane a,b and c
static int count=0;
void set_abc();          //to random initialization of speed of all cars in all lanes
void show_abc();         //to show speed of all cars in all lanes at a single point
void PUSH(int,char,int,int); //to show actual transition
void main()
{        int i,j;
         clrscr();
         set_abc();
         show_abc();
for(i=0;i<SIZE;i++)
{  for(j=0;j<SIZE;j++)
                 { if(a[i]<a[j])
```

```
                        if(a[j]<b[i])
                                if(a[j]<c[i])
                                        PUSH(1,'a',j,a[j]);
                if(b[j]>b[i])
                { if(b[j]>c[i])
                        PUSH(2,'b',j,b[j]);
            else
                if(b[j]>a[i])
                        PUSH(1,'b',j,b[j]);
                }
                if(c[j]>c[i])
                { if(c[j]>b[i])
                                PUSH(2,'c',j,c[j]);
                Else
                        if(c[j]>a[i])
                                        PUSH(1,'c',j,c[j]);
                }
            }
        }
        printf("\n\n\nTotal transition=%d",count);
        getch();
}
void set_abc()
{               int i;
                for(i=0;i<SIZE;i++)
                {       a[i]=rand()%100;
                        b[i]=rand()%100;
                        c[i]=rand()%100;
                }
}
void show_abc()
{       int i;
        printf("\nCar no. \t Lane a \t Lane b \t Lane c \n\n");
        for(i=0;i<SIZE;i++)
        printf("\n%d \t\t %d \t\t %d \t\t %d",i+1,a[i],b[i],c[i]);
}
void PUSH(int trans,char lane, int pos,int speed)
{       ++count;
        printf("\n\nTransition%d -> Lane ->%c Car Position ->%d  Car speed -
        >%d",trans,lane,pos+1,speed);
  if(count%15==0)
        { getch();
        clrscr();
        show_abc();
        }
}
```

## Simulated Results

Above simulated code generate the following results which is depicted in fig. 2-6, which has some different states.

## State 1:

```
Car no.              Lane a              Lane b              Lane c

1                    46                  30                  82
2                    90                  56                  17
3                    95                  15                  48
4                    26                  4                   58
5                    71                  79                  92
6                    60                  12                  21
7                    63                  47                  19
8                    41                  90                  85
9                    14                  9                   52
10                   71                  79                  16

Transition1 -> Lane ->b Car Position ->2   Car speed ->56

Transition1 -> Lane ->b Car Position ->5   Car speed ->79

Transition2 -> Lane ->c Car Position ->5   Car speed ->92

Transition1 -> Lane ->b Car Position ->7   Car speed ->47

Transition2 -> Lane ->b Car Position ->8   Car speed ->90

Transition2 -> Lane ->c Car Position ->8   Car speed ->85

Transition1 -> Lane ->b Car Position ->10  Car speed ->79

Transition2 -> Lane ->c Car Position ->1   Car speed ->82

Transition2 -> Lane ->c Car Position ->4   Car speed ->58

Transition2 -> Lane ->b Car Position ->5   Car speed ->79

Transition2 -> Lane ->c Car Position ->5   Car speed ->92

Transition2 -> Lane ->b Car Position ->8   Car speed ->90

Transition2 -> Lane ->c Car Position ->8   Car speed ->85

Transition2 -> Lane ->b Car Position ->10  Car speed ->79

Transition2 -> Lane ->c Car Position ->1   Car speed ->82_
```

**Fig. 2.** Result state 1

**State 2:**

```
Car no.              Lane a              Lane b              Lane c

1                    46                  30                  82
2                    90                  56                  17
3                    95                  15                  48
4                    26                  4                   58
5                    71                  79                  92
6                    60                  12                  21
7                    63                  47                  19
8                    41                  90                  85
9                    14                  9                   52
10                   71                  79                  16

Transition2 -> Lane ->b Car Position ->2  Car speed ->56

Transition2 -> Lane ->c Car Position ->4  Car speed ->58

Transition2 -> Lane ->b Car Position ->5  Car speed ->79

Transition2 -> Lane ->c Car Position ->5  Car speed ->92

Transition2 -> Lane ->b Car Position ->8  Car speed ->90

Transition2 -> Lane ->c Car Position ->8  Car speed ->85

Transition2 -> Lane ->c Car Position ->9  Car speed ->52

Transition2 -> Lane ->b Car Position ->10  Car speed ->79

Transition1 -> Lane ->b Car Position ->1  Car speed ->30

Transition2 -> Lane ->c Car Position ->1  Car speed ->82

Transition1 -> Lane ->b Car Position ->2  Car speed ->56

Transition2 -> Lane ->b Car Position ->5  Car speed ->79

Transition2 -> Lane ->c Car Position ->5  Car speed ->92

Transition1 -> Lane ->b Car Position ->7  Car speed ->47

Transition2 -> Lane ->b Car Position ->8  Car speed ->90
```

**Fig. 3.** Result state 2

**State 3:**

```
Car no.           Lane a            Lane b            Lane c

1                 46                30                82
2                 90                56                17
3                 95                15                48
4                 26                4                 58
5                 71                79                92
6                 60                12                21
7                 63                47                19
8                 41                90                85
9                 14                9                 52
10                71                79                16
Transition2 -> Lane ->c Car Position ->8   Car speed ->85

Transition2 -> Lane ->b Car Position ->10  Car speed ->79

Transition1 -> Lane ->b Car Position ->8   Car speed ->90

Transition2 -> Lane ->b Car Position ->1   Car speed ->30

Transition2 -> Lane ->c Car Position ->1   Car speed ->82

Transition2 -> Lane ->b Car Position ->2   Car speed ->56

Transition2 -> Lane ->c Car Position ->3   Car speed ->48

Transition2 -> Lane ->c Car Position ->4   Car speed ->58

Transition2 -> Lane ->b Car Position ->5   Car speed ->79

Transition2 -> Lane ->c Car Position ->5   Car speed ->92

Transition2 -> Lane ->b Car Position ->7   Car speed ->47

Transition2 -> Lane ->b Car Position ->8   Car speed ->90

Transition2 -> Lane ->c Car Position ->8   Car speed ->85

Transition2 -> Lane ->c Car Position ->9   Car speed ->52

Transition2 -> Lane ->b Car Position ->10  Car speed ->79
```

**Fig. 4.** Result state 3

**State 4:**

```
Car no.            Lane a            Lane b            Lane c

1                  46                30                82
2                  90                56                17
3                  95                15                48
4                  26                4                 58
5                  71                79                92
6                  60                12                21
7                  63                47                19
8                  41                90                85
9                  14                9                 52
10                 71                79                16

Transition2 -> Lane ->c Car Position ->1   Car speed ->82

Transition2 -> Lane ->b Car Position ->2   Car speed ->56

Transition2 -> Lane ->c Car Position ->3   Car speed ->48

Transition2 -> Lane ->c Car Position ->4   Car speed ->58

Transition2 -> Lane ->b Car Position ->5   Car speed ->79

Transition2 -> Lane ->c Car Position ->5   Car speed ->92

Transition2 -> Lane ->b Car Position ->8   Car speed ->90

Transition2 -> Lane ->c Car Position ->8   Car speed ->85

Transition2 -> Lane ->c Car Position ->9   Car speed ->52

Transition2 -> Lane ->b Car Position ->10  Car speed ->79

Transition1 -> Lane ->a Car Position ->1   Car speed ->46

Transition1 -> Lane ->a Car Position ->5   Car speed ->71

Transition2 -> Lane ->c Car Position ->5   Car speed ->92

Transition1 -> Lane ->a Car Position ->6   Car speed ->60

Transition1 -> Lane ->a Car Position ->7   Car speed ->63
```

**Fig. 5.** Result state 4

**State 5:**

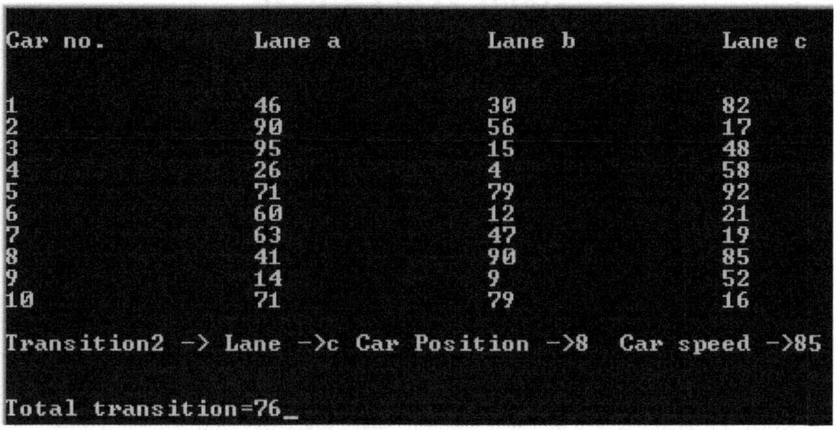

```
Car no.            Lane a              Lane b              Lane c

1                   46                  30                  82
2                   90                  56                  17
3                   95                  15                  48
4                   26                  4                   58
5                   71                  79                  92
6                   60                  12                  21
7                   63                  47                  19
8                   41                  90                  85
9                   14                  9                   52
10                  71                  79                  16

Transition2 -> Lane ->c Car Position ->8  Car speed ->85

Total transition=76_
```

**Fig. 6.** Result state 5

## 5  Conclusion

The main limitation of the approach is that vertical Bi-Directional movements are not taken care off. Our future effort will certainly be on that direction.

Here in this work, we have tried to optimize the speed of the vehicles, in a secured collision manner.

## References

1. Alicandri, E., Warren, D.L.: Managing Speed, United States Department of Tranportation Federal Highway Administration, vol. 66(4) (January/February 2003),
   http://www.tfhrc.gov/safety/ihsdm
   (ManagingSpeed, January-February 2003 PublicRoads.htm)
2. Differentiated speed limits. In: European Transport Conference Differentiated speed limits (2007)
3. Fitzpatrick, K.: Operation and Safety of Right-Turn Lane Designs, Schneider IV, William Henry, Park, Eun Sug, Texas Transportation Institute,
   http://dx.doi.org/10.3141/1961-07
4. Messer, C.J., Fambro, D.B.: Critical Lane Analysis For Intersection Design
5. Transportation Research Record No. 644, pp. 26–35 (1977)

# Biometric Authentication Using Infrared Imaging of Hand Vein Patterns

Debnath Bhattacharyya[1], A. Shrotri[2], S.C. Rethrekar[2], M.H. Patil[2],
Farkhod A. Alisherov[1], and Tai-hoon Kim[1,*]

[1] Department of Multimedia Division
Hannam University, Republic of Korea
debnathb@gmail.com, sntdvl@yahoo.com, taihoonn@empal.com
[2] Department of Electronics
Walchand College of Engineering, Sangli, India
{Shrotri.aditya,rethrekar.2.11,mhpatilyashwant}@gmail.com

**Abstract.** Hand vein patterns are unique and universal. Vein pattern is used as biometric feature in recent years. But, it is not very much popular biometric system as compared to other systems like fingerprint, iris etc, because of the higher cost. For conventional algorithm, it is necessary to use high quality images, which demand high-priced collection devices. There are two approaches for vein authentication, these are hand dorsa and hand ventral. Currently we are working on hand dorsa vein patterns. Here we are putting forward the new approach for low cost hand dorsa vein pattern acquisition using low cost device and proposing a algorithm to extract features from these low quality images.

**Keywords:** vein pattern, hand-dorsa, NIR- webcam.

## 1 Introduction

A reliable biometric system, which is essentially a pattern-recognition that recognizes a person based on physiological or behavioral characteristic, is an indispensable element in several areas, including ecommerce(e.g. online banking), various forms of access control security (e.g. PC login), and so on. Nowadays, security has been important for privacy protection and country in many situations, and the biometric technology is becoming the base approach to solve the increasing crime [1].

As the significant advances in computer processing, the automated authentication techniques using various biometric features have become available over the last few decades. Biometric characteristics include fingerprint, face, hand/finger geometry, iris, retina, signature, gait, voice, hand vein, odor or the DNA information, while fingerprint, face, iris and signature are considered as traditional ones.

Due to each biometric technology has its merits and shortcoming, it is difficult to make a comparison directly. Jain[1] et al. have identified seven factors, which are (1) universality, (2) uniqueness, (3) permanence, (4) measurability, (5) performance, (6) acceptability, (7) circumvention, to determine the suitability of a trait to be used in

---

\* Corresponding author.

S.K. Bandyopadhyay et al. (Eds.): ISA 2010, CCIS 76, pp. 108–115, 2010.
© Springer-Verlag Berlin Heidelberg 2010

a biometric application. Vein pattern is the network of blood vessels beneath person's skin. The idea using vein patterns as a form of biometric technology was first proposed in 1992, while researchers only paid attentions to vein authentication in last ten years [8]. Vein patterns are sufficiently different across individuals, and they are stable unaffected by ageing and no significant changed in adults by observing. It is believed that the patterns of blood vein are unique to every individual, even among twins.

Contrasting with other biometric traits, such as face or fingerprint, vein patterns provide a really specific that they are hidden inside of human body distinguishing them from other forms, which are captured externally. Veins are internal, thus this characteristic makes the systems highly secure, and they are not been affected by the situation of the outer skin (e.g. dirty hand).

## 2 Features of Vein Pattern

Vein based authentication uses the vascular patterns of an individual's hand as personal identification data. Compared with finger , the back of a hand or a palm has a broader and more complicated vascular pattern and thus contains a wealth of differentiating features for personal identification. The features of vein pattern are enlisted as below

- Unique and universal.
- Carry deoxidized blood towards the heart except umbilical & pulmonary veins.
- Palm & digits have collaterals of ulnar vein & palmer digital veins
- Developed before birth and persist throughout the life, well into old age.
- Differ even between identical twins.
- Internal trait protected by the skin.
- Less susceptible to damage.

### 2.1 Principle

When hand is exposed to NIR light, then the deoxidized hemoglobin in the vein vessels absorbs light having a wave length of about 760 nm within the near infrared area. When the infrared ray image captured, only the blood vessel pattern containing the deoxidized hemoglobin is visible as a series of dark lines.

In vein authentication based on this principle, the region used for authentication is photographed with near-infrared light, and the vein pattern is extracted by image processing and registered. The vein pattern of the person being authenticated is then verified against the preregistered pattern.

## 3 Previous Works

Vein pattern recognition technology appeared in 1990s, but it is not attracted much attention in that decade. From 2000, more papers on this topic appeared. However, up to now, there is no vein pattern database. So, each researcher has to design his own hardware setup.

Toshiyuki Tanaka, Naohiko Kubo[8], 2004 used 2 infrared LED arrays (Sanyo SLR931A), CCD camera (Cv-15H) and video card (IO-DATA GV-VCP3/PCI) and adopted phase only correlation and template matching for authentication.

L.Wang, G Leedham, S-y Cho[10] used NEC Thermo Tracer TS 7302 for FIR imaging Wang Lingyu and G.Leedham used Hitachi KP-F2A infrared CCD camera for NIR imaging.

C.Laxmi, A.Kandaswamy[9] used WAT902H near IR camera. Some researchers have worked on Fujistu palm vein sensor for vein pattern acquisition.

## 4  Our Work

From previous work, it is clear that former researchers used high cost devices to obtain high quality images which can be easily processed. In our research, we want to reduce cost of system considerably to make device "cheap". So, we have used webcam for this purpose. First, the webcam is made sensitive to IR region and used to obtain vein images.

Our webcam (Logitech Pro 2000) costs about 25$ which is much cheaper than IR cameras used by others. This can reduce device price by at least 10 times. This is significant cost reduction and if we could extract vein structure from these low cost devices, as good as others, then we do a very meaningful wok. In the following, we will discuss hardware setup and propose an algorithm for vein pattern analysis.

## 5  How to Make Webcam Sensitive to IR Region?

Webcams are actually sensitive to both visible spectrum of light as well as IR spectrum of light. But, internal IR filter blocks IR light and passes only visible light to camera. This filter is fitted either near to lens or on the casing of chip. If this filter is removed and replaced by another filter to block light in visible spectrum, then webcam becomes sensitive to only IR light. Special care has to be taken while removing IR filter on chip case, because it may damage webcam permanently.

Frames captured from IR sensitive webcam are shown below in Fig. 1 and 2. We can see that IR illumination by single LED used in TV remote can provide sufficient illumination.

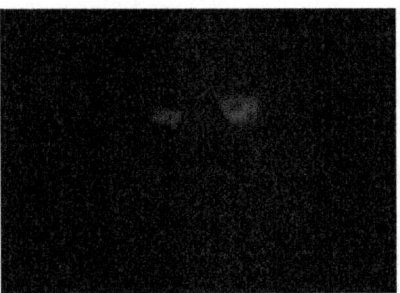     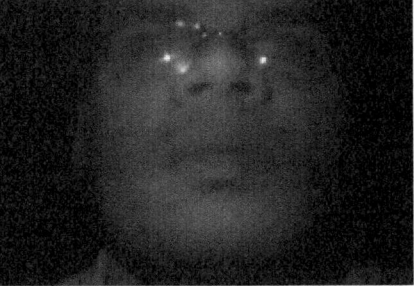

**Fig. 1.** IR Frame          **Fig. 2.** IR Frame

# 6  Hardware Setup

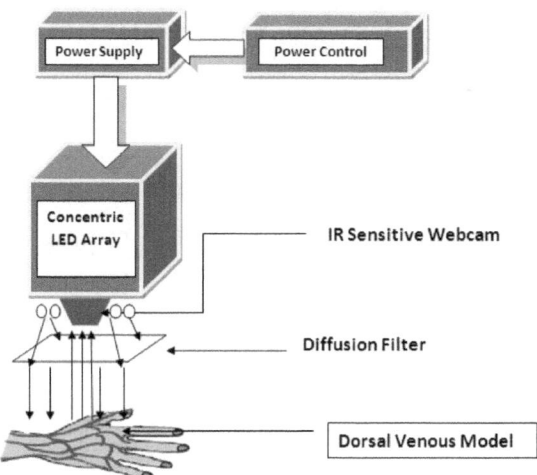

**Fig. 3.** Hardware Setup

As mentioned in the introduction, the hardware setup (Fig. 3) has a crucial role in the acquisition of vein images. Two aspects can be underlined here:

- The actual camera used for taking the snapshot has only one important parameter, the response to near infrared radiation. Spatial resolution and frame rate are of lower importance since for the acquisition of a vein pattern a still image is required and the details are easily seen even at a lower resolution.
- The design of the lighting system is one of the most important aspects of the image acquisition process. A good lighting system will provide accurate contrast between the veins and the surrounding tissue while keeping the illuminations errors to a minimum.

For lighting system, we have used IR LEDs as it provides high contrast and also it is cheap and easily available. But, LED array formed using IR LEDs do not give uniform illumination.

Various matrix arrangements of LEDs will modify illumination. LEDs can be arranged as 2D single or double array or rectangular array or concentric arrays. Among these, concentric LED array arrangement gives better distribution of light with single or more concentric LED arrays and camera lens at centre can acquire image with good contrast.

Contrast of image can be controlled by controlling power supplied to LEDs. Some trials by controlling power can give required contrast. High power to light source will decrease contrast due to high intensity. Polarizing filters can also be used to increase contrast by reducing specular reflection of skin.

With reference to above discussion, we have designed IR light source arranged in concentric fashion Fig.4 and Fig.5 shows IR illumination sensed by IR sensitive webcam.

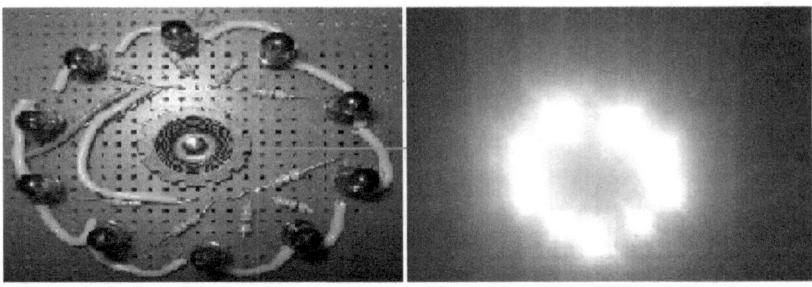

**Fig. 4.** IR illumination          **Fig. 5.** IR illumination

Fig. 6 & 7 show ventral and dorsal veins respectively captured by IR sensitive webcam and IR light source (Fig.4).

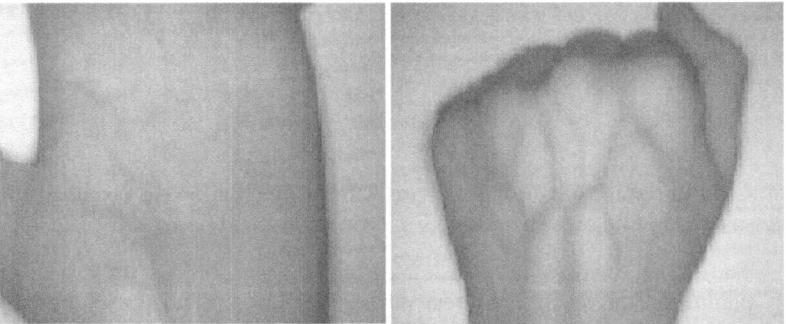

**Fig. 6.** Ventral veins          **Fig. 7.** Dorsal veins

The limitation of our hardware setup is, the images obtained are of low quality. So, we now propose an algorithm to extract the features from these images.

## 7  Vascular Pattern Analysis

As we are doing image enhancement in spatial domain, the steps in processing of image are as follows:

- a. Image acquisition in NIR region
- b. Pre-processing
- c. Finding region of interest
- d. Gray scaling
- e. Thresholding
- f. Edge Detection
- g. Removal of small unwanted objects
- h. Thinning

## 7.1 Algorithm

Here we are proposing a vascular pattern analysis algorithm which we are going to implement in the future.

a.  Open Near-Infrared Palm Image File in input mode
b.  Convert the Loaded Image into PlanarImage
c.  Set the Horizontal and Vertical kernels (3 x 3).
d.  Generated image is passed through kernel.
e.  Then image is stored into grayscale image file.
f.  Close all Image file(s).
g.  Open resultant Grayscale Image File, in input mode
h.  Open Binary Image File in output mode
i.  While not End of File
j.  Loop
k.  Read pixel intensity value
l.  If pixel intensity value lies above 'y', then
m.  Convert the intensity value to 0 (white)
n.  Elseif
o.  If pixel intensity value lies below 'x', then
p.  Convert the intensity value to 255 (black)
q.  Else
r.  If neighbouring pixel is edge pixel then make current pixel 0 (white)
s.  End if
t.  Write the intensity value to Binary Image
u.  End Loop
v.  Close all Image Files

**Note:** 'x' and 'y' are lower and upper thresholds respectively for canny edge detection.

Thresholding is an image processing technique for converting a grayscale image to a binary image based upon a threshold value. If a pixel in the image has an intensity value less than the threshold value, the corresponding pixel in the resultant image is set to black. Otherwise, if the pixel intensity value is greater than or equal to the threshold intensity, the resulting pixel is set to white. Thus, creating a binarized image, or an image with only 2 colors, black (0) and white (255). Image thresholding is very useful for keeping the significant part of an image and getting rid of the unimportant part or noise. This holds true under the assumption that a reasonable threshold value is chosen. In our case the threshold range is taken 10 to 70.

We have done image processing using OpenCV1.*1 (Open Computer Vision Library)* on the platform of Microsoft Visual C++ 2003 Edition. We used a computer with processor Pentium Core2duo with frequency 2.3GHz.

Results after the implementation of above algorithm are shown below. The Fig.8 below shows the gray level palm vein image and edge detected image.

We can see by adjusting the lower and upper thresholds, we can get successful edge detection (Fig. 9 & 10).

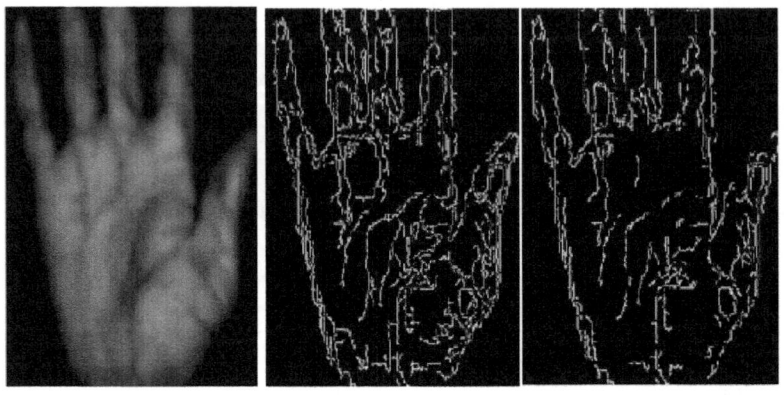

**Fig. 8.** Gray Image      **Fig. 9.** Detected edges      **Fig. 10.** Detected edges

## 8   Applications

  a.   Log in Control PC –Access System
  b.   Security systems: physical admission into secured areas
  c.   Healthcare: ID verification for medical equipment
  d.   Electronic Record Management
  e.   Banking and financial services: access to ATM, kiosks, vault

## 9   Discussion

Due to the unavailability of Palm Vein Image Database, we have considered images on which different people have already worked. You can see images captured by other people and images captured by us using our IR-sensitive webcam with which we are going to proceed further. Here we have proposed an algorithm and a way of low cost vein pattern authentication using low quality images.

## 10   Future Work

We are planning to do verification and matching part based on our low quality image based authentication system. We are aiming to implement it as a secured smart card and hand vein based person authentication system and we have already started work in that direction.

# References

1. Jain, A.K., Ross, A., Prabhakar, S.: An Introduction to Biometric Recognition. IEEE Transactions on Circuits and Systems for Video Technology 14(1), 4–20 (2004)
2. Crisan, S., Tarnovan, I.G.: Vein pattern recognition. Image enhancement and feature extraction algorithms
3. Cui, F.-y., Zou, L.-j.: Edge Feature Extraction Based on Digital Image Processing Techniques
4. Hao, Y., Sun, Z., Tan, T., Ren, C.: Multispectral Palm Image Fusion for Accurate Contact-free Palmprint Recognition
5. Jeyaprakash, R., Lee, J., Biswas, S., Kim, J.M.: Secured Smart Card Using Palm Vein Biometric On-Card-Process
6. Wang, J.-G., Yau, W.-Y., Suwandy, A.: Fusion of Palmprint and Palm Vein Images for Person Recognition Based on "Laplacianpalm" Feature
7. Wang, J.-G., Yau, W.-Y., Suwandy, A.: Feature-Level Fusion of Palmprint And Palm Vein For Person Identification Based on A "Junction Point" Representation
8. Tanaka, T., Kubo, N.: Biometric Authentication by Hand Vein Patterns. In: SICE Annual Conference, Sapporo, August 4-6, pp. 249–253 (2004)
9. Lakshmi Deepika, C., Kandaswamy, A.: An Algorithm for Improved Accuracy in Unimodal Biometric Systems through Fusion of Multiple Feature Sets. ICGST-GVIP Journal 9(III) (June 2009) ISSN 1687-398X
10. Wang, L., Leedham, G., Cho, S.-Y.: Infrared imaging of hand vein patterns for biometric purposes. IET Comput. Vis. 1(3-4) (2007)

# IPV6 Mobile Network Protocol Weaknesses and a Cryptosystem Approach

Maricel Balitanas and Tai-hoon Kim[*]

Multimedia Engineering Department, Hannam University,
133 Ojeong-dong, Daeduk-gu, Daejeon, Korea
jhe-c1756@yahoo.com, taihoonn@hnu.kr

**Abstract.** This paper reviews some of the improvements associated with the new Internet protocol version 6, an emphasis on its security-related functionality particularly in its authentication and concludes with a hybrid cryptosystem for its authentication issue. Since new generation of Internet protocol is on its way to solve the growth of IP address depletion. It is in a process that may take several years to complete. Thus, as a step to effective solution and efficient implementation this review has been made.

**Keywords:** Authentication, Advance Encryption Standard, Mobile IPv6, Elliptic Curve Cryptographic.

## 1 Introduction

The problem which Mobile IPv6 advocates have run into so far is that individual businesses don't see the logic in investing time and money in Mobile IPv6 deployment during a recession where they have far more pressing and immediate needs and issues to consider. However, despite it is consider as the next generation's internet protocol Mobile Pv6 could pose major security problems for business' networks even if they had not yet deployed the new internet layer protocol. This is because operating systems such as Vista and Linux [1] are already Mobile IPv6 capable and thus any networks that use these operating systems might be handling Mobile IPv6 traffic without their operator's knowledge.

Mobile IPv6 intends to enable IPv6 nodes to move from one IP subnet to another. This means that while a mobile node is away from home it can send information about its current location to a home agent and the home agent intercepts packets addressed to the mobile node and tunnels them to the mobile node's present location. This protocol is on its way to solve growth of IP address depletion under the current Internet layer protocol, IPv4 [1].

One method through which Mobile IPv6 addresses connect to each other over IPv4 networks is through encapsulating Mobile IPv6 data in IPv4 packets and then "tunneling" through the older network. But, because firewall is unable to unwrap IPv4 capsules to inspect the traffic inside, they could be a way for hackers to break into the

---

[*] Corresponding author.

S.K. Bandyopadhyay et al. (Eds.): ISA 2010, CCIS 76, pp. 116–127, 2010.

networks. Firewalls do not look closely enough at encapsulated packets because the typical firewall has no opening capsule capability. Creating dual-stack transition networks that run IPv4 and Mobile IPv6 traffic can create vulnerabilities. Thus, securing the network perimeter first, hardening network devices and building the Mobile IPv6 network first from the core and then out to the edge is the main objective of this paper.

## 1.1 Mobile IPv6

Mobile IPv6 is not a superset of IPv4 but an entirely new suite of protocols. The following are list of Mobile IPv6 interesting features [2] [3]

- Larger address space: IPv4 provides only as many as 232 addresses1. On the other hand, Mobile IPv6 provides for as many as 2128 addresses.
- Hierarchical addressing: in Mobile IPv6 there are three major types of addresses: unicast, multicast, and anycast addresses. Unicast addresses are assigned to a single Mobile IPv6 node. Multicast addresses are assigned to multiples nodes within a single multicast group. Packets sent to a multicast address must be delivered to all members of the same multicast group. On the other hand, although anycast addresses are also assigned to groups of nodes, they do not need to be delivered to all members of the group—it is sufficient that one node receives the packets. Additionally, Mobile IPv6 defines a new routing infrastructure that provides for more efficient and smaller routing tables.
- Stateless and stateful address configuration: Mobile IPv6 allows hosts to acquire IP addresses either in a stateless or autonomous way or through a controlled mechanism such as DHCPv6.
- Quality-of-service: the Mobile IPv6 packet header contains fields that facilitate the support for QoS for both differentiated and integrated services
- Better performance: Mobile IPv6 provides for significant improvements such as better handling of packet fragmentation, hierarchical addressing, and provisions for header chaining that reduce routing table size and processing time.
- Built-in security: although IPSec is also available for IPv4 implementations, it is not mandated but optional. Support for IPSec in Mobile IPv6 implementations is not an option but a requirement.
- Extensibility: despite the fact that Mobile IPv6 addresses are four times larger than IPv4 addresses, the new Mobile IPv6 header is just twice the size of the IPv4 header (i.e., two times 20 bytes = 40 bytes). As shown in Fig 1, the new Mobile IPv6 header does not include any optional fields. It does not include a checksum either. Optional fields can be added as extension headers up to the size of the Mobile IPv6 packet. This feature does not only provide for better extensibility but also for reducing the time a router process Mobile IPv6 header options, increasing the network overall performance.
- Mobility: Mobile IPv6 provides mechanisms that allow mobile nodes to change their locations and addresses without losing the existing connections through which those nodes are communicating. This service is supported at the Internet level and therefore is fully transparent to Upper-layer protocols.

## 1.2  Improvements in Mobile IPv6

The following sub-sections summarize the Mobile IPv6's improvements that provide better network security.

IPSec consists of a set of cryptographic protocols that provide for securing data communication and key exchange. IPSec uses two wire-level protocols, Authentication Header (AH) and Encapsulating Security Payload (ESP). The first protocol provides for authentication and data integrity. The Second protocol provides for Authentication, data integrity and confidentiality [5]. In Mobile IPv6 networks both the AH header and the ESP header are defined as extension headers. Additionally, IPSec provides for a third suite of protocols for protocol negotiation and key exchange management known as the Internet Key Exchange (IKE). This protocol suite provides the initial functionality needed to establish and negotiating security parameters between endpoints. In addition to that, it keeps track of this information to guarantee that communication continues to be secure up to the end.

IPSec cryptographic component technologies use Data Encryption Standard (DES ) Encryption. However DES is considered to be insecure for many applications [11]. This is chiefly due to the 56-bit key size being too small. . Table 1 depicts the comparison outlining the basics for the most popular ciphers. [12] Clearly, Rijndael is the most secure cipher out there and for most vendors of WPA implementation use AES (Advance Encryption Standard). The standard comprises three block ciphers, AES - 128, AES-192 and AES-256, adopted from a larger collection originally published as Rijndael. In this paper we are going consider the algorithm of AES in WPA PSK mode cross with the asymmetric algorithm of Elliptic curve cryptography.

**Table 1.** Comparison of the most popular ciphers

| Algorithm | Created by | Key size | Algorithm Structure | Existing Crack |
|-----------|-----------|----------|---------------------|----------------|
| Rijndael | Joan Daemon & Vincent Rijmen 1998 | 128 bits, 192 bits or 256 bits | Substitution permutation Network | Side Chanel attacks |
| Twofish | Bruce Schneir 1993 | 128 bits, 192 bits or 256 bits | Feisel Network | Truncated differential cryptanalysis |
| Blowfish | Bruce Schneier | 32-448 bits in steps of the 8 bits 128 bits by default | | Second-order differential attack |
| RC4 | Ron Rivest 1987 | Variable | Stream | Distinguishers based on weak key schedule |
| RC2 | Ron Rivest 1987 | 8-128 bits in steps of 8 bits 64 bits by default | Source-Heavy Feistel Network | Related-Key attack |

**Authentication Header:** Prevents IP packets from being tampered or altered. In a typical IPv4 packets, the AH is part of the payload. Figure 1 depicts an example of an IPv4 packet with an AH as payload [6][7]. When the AH protocol was implemented, there was some concern about how to integrate it to the new IPv6 packet format. The problem centered on the fact that IPv6 extension headers can change in transit as information they contain is updated through the network. To solve this problem, IPv6

AH was designed with flexibility in mind—the protocol authenticates and do integrity check only on those fields in the IPv6 packet header that do not change in transit. Also, in IPv6 packets, the AH is intelligently located at the end of the header chain—but ahead of any ESP extension header or any higher level protocol such as TCP/UDP [8].

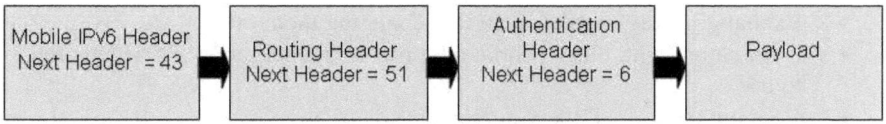

**Fig. 1.** Extension headers order

AH header protocol also provides optional protection against replay attacks. The protocol uses its sequence number field as part of a sliding window mechanism that prevents arbitrary packet delays and malicious replay [8].

**Encapsulating Security Payloads:** To provides the same functionality, the AH protocol provides – authentication, data integrity and replay protection –ESP also provides confidentiality. In the ESP extension header, the security parameter index (SPI) field identifies what group of security parameters the sender is using to secure communication. Figure 2 below shows the ESP header Specification.

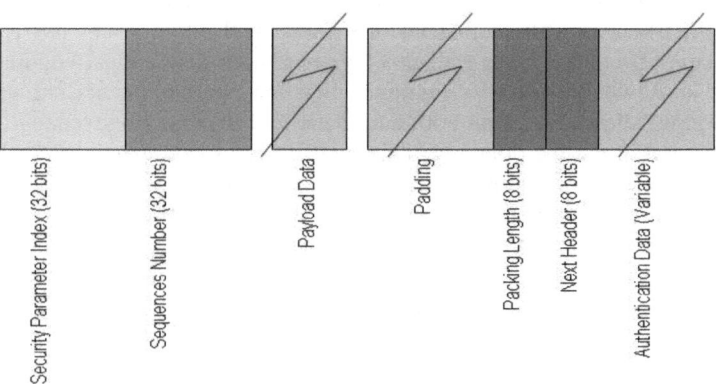

**Fig. 2.** ESP headers Specification

ESP supports any number of encryption mechanisms. However the protocol specifies DES-CBC as its default. Also, ESP does not provide the same level of authentication available with AH. While AH authenticates the whole IP header, ESP authenticates only the information the follows it [7] ESP provides data integrity by implementing an integrity check value (ICV) that is part of the ESP header trailer – the authentication field. The ICV is computed one any encryption is complete and it includes the whole ESP header/trailer - except for the authentication field, of course. The ICV uses *hash message authentication code* (HMAC) with SHA-1 and MD5 as the recommended cryptographic hash functions [7].

**Protocol Negotiation and Key Exchange management:** IPSec also specify additional functionality for protocol negotiation and key exchange management [10] IP Sec encryption capabilities depend on the ability to negotiate and exchange encryption keys between parties. To accomplish this task, IPSec specifies an Internet key exchange (IKE) protocol. IKE provides the following functionality:

- Exchanging keys easily, including changing them often
- Negotiating with other people the protocols, encryption algorithm, and keys, to use
- Keeping track of all these agreements

All the protocol and encryption algorithm agreements, IPSec uses the SP field in both AH and ESP headers to keep track. This field is an arbitrary 32-bit number that represents a security association (SA). When communication is negotiated, the receiver node assigns an available SPI which is not in use, and preferably on that has not been used in a while. It then communicates this SPI to this communication partner establishing a security association. From then until that SA expires, whenever a node wishes to communicate with the other using the same SA, it must use the same SPI to specify it. The other node, on receipt, would look at the SPI to determine which SA it needs to use. Then it authenticates and/or decrypts the packet according to the rules of that SA, using the agreed-upon keys and algorithms the SA specifies. The node then uses the same agree-upon information to verify that the data really does come from the node it claims. Also, the node uses the same information to verify that the data has not been modified as well as that no one between the two nodes has read the exchanged data. Of course, before all this happens, both nodes must negotiate a set of keys. The keys will be used to guarantee that the SA parameters are securely exchanged. IPSec allows for using both automatic and manual key exchange. However, because manual exchange does not scale well, IPSec recommends using IKE. IPSec IKE offers a robust mechanism to authenticate communication parties based on a *public key infrastructure* (PKI). Encryption keys are generated with a Diffie-Hellman algorithm based on each node's public and private key pairs [8]. This mechanism offers perfect forward secrecy (generating keys that are not reliant on previously generated key values) as well as reasonable scalability.

### 1.3 Mobile IPv6 Authentication

Authentication process starts with access request that is generated by mobile client. This request is encrypted on the service object side along with inserted unique token tag and returned to mobile client. New message passes from mobile client through telecom communication infrastructure and is received and processed by access provider, which then accepts or rejects the request according to the implemented algorithm. The algorithm itself represented behavior of the specific usage and can vary from case to case. Access provider can give only two specific responses: mobile client can get authentication, or it cannot get authentication.

In telecommunication industry, two distinct types of client accounts: prepaid and postpaid are identified. They differ in the way the customers pay for their wireless services, data and voice traffic. Prepaid clients pay their services in advance by purchasing a coupon or a voucher which can be used during a specific period of time. On the other hand, postpaid clients are charged after they have consumed the telecommunication's service. Authentication can fails due to four reasons which are shown in the following table.

**Table 2.** Use-case Authentication Failure

| Client Account Type | Description |
| --- | --- |
| Prepaid | There are not enough funds on the client account |
| | Mobile client has no access privileges to ACO (Access Controlled Object) |
| Postpaid | The service cannot be charged the account is closed or error in the telecommunication's infrastructure |
| | Mobile client has no access privileges to ACO (Access Controlled Object) |

## 2 Mobile IPv6 Security Weaknesses

Mobile IPv6 protocol stack represents a considerable advance in relation to the old IPv4 stack. However, despite its numerable virtues, IPv6 still continues to be by far vulnerable. In this section some of the IPv6 issues are discussed:

### 2.1 Header Manipulation Issues

The *extension headers* and IPSec can deter some common sources of attack based on header manipulation. However, the fact that EH must be processed by all stacks can be a source of trouble—a long chain of EH or some considerably large-size could be used to overwhelm certain nodes (e.g., firewalls) or masquerade an attack. Best practices recommend to filter out traffic with unsupported services [3].

Spoofing continues to be a possibility in IPv6 networks [4]. However, because of ND, spoofing is only possible by nodes on the same network segment. The same does not apply to 6to4 transition networks. Although one approach to 6to4 transition is using some form of dual-stack functionality, another approach is using some type of tunneling. Because tunneling requires that a protocol is encapsulated in another, its use could be a source of security problems such as address spoofing—in this case if the spoofed address is used to masquerade an external packet as one that was originated from the inside network [4].

### 2.2 Flooding Issues

Scanning for valid host addresses and services is considerably more difficult in IPv6 networks than it is in IPv4 networks. As mentioned above, to effectively scan a whole IPv6 segment may take up to 580 billion years— because the address space uses 64 bits.

However, the larger addressing space does not mean that IPv6 is totally invulnerable to this type of attack. Nor the lack of broadcast addresses makes IPv6 more secure. New features such as multicast addresses continue to be source of problems [5]. Smurf-type attacks are still possible on multicast traffic. Again, filtering out unnecessary traffic is the recommended best practice [2].

## 2.3 Mobility

Mobility is a totally new feature of IPv6 that was not available in its predecessor. Mobility is a very complex function that raises a considerable amount of concern when considering security. Mobility uses two types of addresses, the real address and the mobile address. The first is a typical IPv6 address contained in an *extension header*. The second is a temporary address contained in the IP header. Because of the characteristics of this networks (something more complicated if we consider wireless mobility), the temporary component of a mobile node address could be exposed to spoofing attacks on the home agent. Mobility requires special security measures and network administrators must be fully aware of them [3] [4] [10].

# 3    Crossed Cryptosystem Algorithm for the Mobile IPv6 Authentication

The most recent physical security protocol, Wi-Fi Protected Access (WPA) and the emerging 802.11i standard, both specify 802.1 x securities as a framework for strong wireless security. 802.1x use authentication, it requires user to provide credentials to security server before getting access to the network. The credentials can be in the form of user name and password, certificate, token or biometric. The security server authenticates the user's credentials to verify that the user is who he or she claims to be and is authorized to access the network. The security server also verifies that the access point is a valid part of the network. This is done to protect the user from connecting to an authorized access point that may have been set ups to fraudulently capture network data.

## 3.1 ECC as Asymmetric

RSA (Rivest, Shamir and Adleman) is widely used public key stream. It is an asymmetric key system, which uses variable key sizes. 512-bit, 1024-bit and 2048-bit RSA are the most common. Its security lies in the difficulty of factoring large composite integers. Although RSA is the most popular Asymmetric cryptography, ECC offers a smaller key sizes, faster computation, as well as memory, energy and bandwidth savings and is thus better suited for small devices. Thus, in this paper we have prioritized using ECC over RSA.

## 3.2 AES in Pre-shared Key Mode

Pre-shared key mode is one of the operation modes of WPA it is also known as Personal mode. It is designed for home and small office networks that don't require complexity of 802.11i authentication server. Each wireless network device encrypts the network traffic using a 256 bit key. This key may be entered either as a string of 64 hexadecimal digits, or as a passphrases of 8 to 63 printable ASCII characters. Shared-key WPA is vulnerable to password cracking attacks if a weak passphrase is used. To protect against brute force attack, a 13 character truly random passphrase is sufficient [2].

### 3.3 Hybrid Cryptosystem

From the two major types of encryptions we can conclude that Asymmetric encryption provides more functionality than symmetric encryption, at the expense of speed and hardware cost.

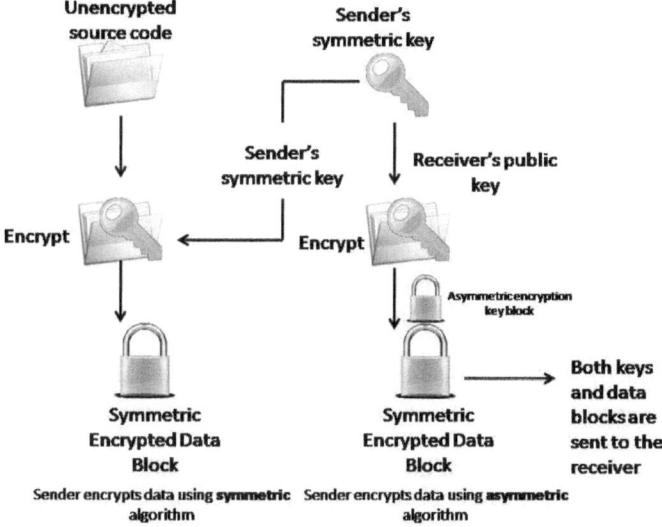

**Fig. 3.** Hybrid crypto-scheme

On the other hand symmetric encryption provides cost-effective and efficient methods of securing data without compromising security and should be considered as the correct and most appropriate security solution for many applications. In some instances, the best possible solution may be the complementary use of both symmetric and asymmetric encryption. Diagram of a hybrid crypto-scheme is shown in Figure 3.

The algorithm presented here combines the best features of both the symmetric and asymmetric encryption techniques. The plain text data is to be transmitted in encrypted using the AES algorithm. Further details on AES can be taken from [8]. The AES key which is used to encrypt the data is encrypted using ECC. The cipher text of the message and the cipher text of the key are then sent to the receiver. The message digest by this process would also be encrypted using ECC techniques. The cipher text of the message digest is decrypted using ECC technique to obtain the message digest sent by the sender. This value is compared with the computed message digest. If both of them are equal, the message is accepted otherwise it is rejected.

# 4 Implementation

In this research off-the-shelve technologies are used and applied in the previous research prototype designed the vaccination planner [13]. The goal was to create a flexible system that can be easily altered and redesigned throughout the project development process.

The proposed system can be implemented virtually with any contemporary mobile technology. Mobile client can be any modern mobile phone that supports Java 2 Micro Edition (J2ME). Today all middle- or high-end cellular phones fulfill this request, even a lot of more affordable, and available, low-end models can execute custom J2ME and Symbian applications. This provides a wide base of potential client that can use in this system for accessing restricted objects and services.

The same range of choices applies to selection of Access Controlled Object. ACO can be any industry-grade PC computer, bare-bone PC, or process computer with support for Bluetooth, GSM/GPRS/UMTS and serial networking. depending on the specific software running on ACO, it doesn't have to have a high processing power. Software running on Java or Microsoft .NET are also conceivable. The most important requirement on ACO is embedded support for Personal Area Networks (PAN) and Wide Area Networks (WAN). Serial networking is required to communicate with the physical device such, e.g. doors, gates, vaults, elevators, which are access controlled and are part of ACO. With telecom infrastructure component there are different Business-to-Business (B2B) interfaces to choose from which can be used to transfer data and information to and from the whole telecom infrastructure. This part of the system is the least defined because it greatly depends on specific implementation which varies from one to other telecom company. But since there are only a few global standards such as XML Web Services and CORBA which are always available, one can be safe to say that the problem of communicating with telecom infrastructure is always easily solvable.

Access provider is any computer system with support for B2B and high processing power that enables it to respond quickly, preferably in real-time, to all requests coming from mobile client. Access provider can be made of one or more servers, and it can be 1- or n-tier system. There are no strict limitations on access provider component as long as it provides fast, constant and reliable service.

This approach enabled to test all involved technologies which was of the highest importance since all individual technologies are completely clear and well-defined, but the collection of these technologies in a single project is a challenge. The test system was designed around PocketPC platform and Microsoft .NET CF framework. As a mobile client we have used simulator Pocket PC in figure 4 with Windows Mobile 2003 SE operating system, Bluetooth, IrDA and Wi-Fi connectivity.

Mobile client used Bluetooth to communicate with access controlled object, or Wi-Fi to gain access to the Internet and ask service provider for access key. ACO was an ordinary PC with Windows XP operating system and Bluetooth support. This PC emulated a door that could be opened and responded to Bluetooth messages from the mobile client. The PC had a fixed IP address. Communication with access provider, i.e. the server, was routed through LAN which emulated Internet connectivity via public GSM/GPRS networks. Therefore authentic telecom infrastructure was avoided by special software layers developed in ACO and access provider that emulated real B2B data transfer and different messages received from the telecom.

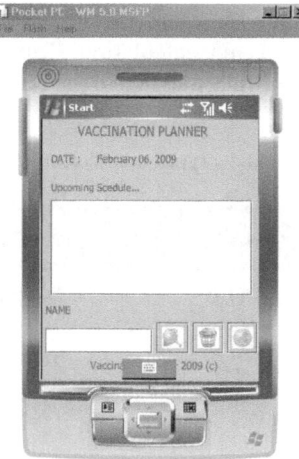

**Fig. 4.** Simulator Pocket PC[16]

Access provider was a server that listened and responded to messages from mobile client and ACO nearly in real-time. All messages were put in a queue and waited their execution. Access provider also had a fixed IP address so it could be contacted by any other three objects in the action diagram. Our experience shows that with existing technologies this system easily can be made robust and reliable. Our intention is to move to other information platforms including those that are open-source like Linux or Linux RT operating systems and Apache web server. We will also port the mobile client's software to Symbian OS and Java 2 Micro Edition (J2ME). This will enable the system to be used on a whole range of different mobile devices not just Pock-etPCs. We would also like to extend GSM/GPRS communication capabilities to SMS text messages so mobile clients can use text messages to request  authentication tokens and to access controlled objects. The text message would have to be of a specific predefined format and directed to the mobile telephone number of ACO or access provider. SMS messaging is a very popular form of wireless communication so by using it instead of just wireless Internet access the system could  become even more appealing to the general public.

The classes for these implementation are available in the Java package of java.security, javax, crypto, javax.crypto.spec. More details in [14]. The code uses these packages and the header files are the following

```
import java.security.*;
import javax.crypto.*;
import javax.crypto.spec.*;
import java.io.*;
```

Generation point in java elliptic curved developed, both the private and public key generation and encryption and decryption was based using EIG method. Further the java class of BigInteger to handle large integers and the method of ISProbablePrime to determine whether the large integer is prime or not.

Testing the crossed algorithm on a test data of various sizes. Table 3 provides details for encryption, decryption and calculation. Table 4 depicts an encryption and decryption of 128 bit AES and MDS message digest using ECC.

**Table 3.** AES encryption and decryption and calculation of MD5 message digest

| File Size | 128 bit AES Encryption | 128 bit AES Decryption | MD5 Message |
|-----------|------------------------|------------------------|-------------|
| 50        | 1903                   | 1986                   | 1365        |
| 100       | 2274                   | 2544                   | 1504        |

**Table 4.** Encryption & Decryption of 128 bit AES key and MD5 message digest using ECC

|                      | Encryption | Decryption |
|----------------------|------------|------------|
| 128 bit AES key      | 30         | 34         |
| MID5 Message digest  | 33         | 35         |

With the presented cryptosystem dealing with 128 bit key the total number of combination is $2^{128}$. Stallings [15] states that the computational omplexity for breaking the elliptic-curve cryptosystem, for an elliptic curve key size of 150 bit is $3.8 \times 10^{10}$ MIPS (Million Instructions Per Second years).

## 5 Conclusion

This algorithm is presented to be implemented in a Mobile IPv6 device application through which recent technologies are geared. The study was are conducted to anticipate potential breaches of security. In this paper, researchers have presented the improvements over IPv4, the vulnerabilities and possible solution in the authentication issue through the algorithm suggested. A design and implementation of combined algorithm was done in java and have presented results of various testing for different sizes of files. To ensure integrity of the data, in this research MD5 hash alg.

**Acknowledgement.** This work was supported by the Security Engineering Research Center, granted by the Korean Ministry of Knowledge Economy.

# References

1. http://www.cio.com/article/492101
2. Davies, J.: Understanding IPv6. Microsoft Press, Redmond (2003)
3. Popoviciu, C., Levy-Avegnoli, E., Grossetete, P.: Deploying IPv6 Networks. Cisco Press, Indianapolis (2006)
4. Szigeti, S., Risztics, P.: Will IPv6 bring better security? In: Proceedings 30th Euromicro Conference, August 31- September 3, pp. 532–537 (2004)
5. Kent, S., Seo, K.: Security Architecture for the Internet Protocol. RFC 4301 (December 2005), http://tools.ietf.org/html/4301
6. Karve, A.: IP Security. IT Architect (January 1998),
   http://www.itarchitect.com/shared/article/
   showArticle.jhtml?articleId=17600993
7. Friedl, S.: An illustrated Guide to IPSec, Unixwiz.net (August 2005),
   http://www.unixwiz.net/techtips/iguide-ipsec.html
8. Davies, J.: Understanding IPv6. Microsoft Press, Redmond (2003)
9. Vives, A., Palet, J.: IPv6 Distributed Security: Problem Statement. In: The 2005 Symposium on Applications and the Internet Workshops. Saint Workshops 2005, December 31-January 04, pp. 18–21 (2005)
10. Sierra, J.M., Ribagorda, A., Munoz, A., Jayaram, N.: Security protocols in the Internet new framework. In: Proceedings IEEE 33rd Annual 1999 International Carnahan Conference on Security Technology, pp. 311–317 (1999)
11. http://en.wikipedia.org/wiki/Data_Encryption_Standard
12. 802.11mb Issues List v12 (excel). CID 98, The use of TKIP is deprecated. The TKIP algorithm is unsuitable for the purposes of this standard, January 20 (2009)
    https://mentor.ieee.org/802.11/file/08/
    11-08-1127-12-000m-tgmb-issues-list.xls
13. Balitanas, M., et al.: Security Threats in Auto Vaccination Architecture Implemented in Handheld Device. In: Proceedings of the KAIS Spring Conference 2009 (2009)
14. http://java.sun.com/j2se/1.3/docs/guide/
    security/CryptoSpec.html
15. Stallings, W.: Cryptography and Network Security, 2nd edn. Prentice Hall, Upper Saddle River (1999)
16. Balitanas, M., Robles, R.J., Kim, N., Kim, T.: Crossed Crypto-scheme in WPA PSK Mode. In: Proceedings of BLISS 2009, Edinburgh, GB. IEEE CS, Los Alamitos (2009) ISBN 978-0-7695-3754

# Fuzzy-Based Detection of Injected False Data in Wireless Sensor Networks*

Hae Young Lee[1], Tae Ho Cho[2], and Hyung-Jong Kim[3]

[1] ETRI, Daejeon 305-700 Republic of Korea
haelee@etri.re.kr
[2] Sungkyunkwan University, Suwon 440-746 Republic of Korea
taecho@ece.skku.ac.kr
[3] Seoul Women's University, Seoul 139-774 Republic of Korea
hkim@swu.ac.kr

**Abstract.** Wireless sensor networks are vulnerable to false data injection attacks in which an adversary injects fabricated reports into the network with the goal of deceiving the base station or of draining the energy resources. Several security solutions against the attacks have been proposed by researchers. Most of them, however, make nodes to involve additional computation and communication overhead in the report generation and forwarding processes, which may result in extra energy consumption. This paper presents a false data detection method that exploits a fuzzy rule-based system to verify the authenticity of sensing reports in sensor networks. Three parameters computed based on the collected reports in the base station are used for the verification. Compared to the existing crisp-based detection solutions, the method can reduce errors in the detection, thanks to approximate reasoning provided by fuzzy logic. Compared to the en-route filtering solutions, extra energy can be also conserved since it involves neither complex report generation nor en-route verification.

**Keywords:** Wireless sensor networks, false data injection attack, attack detection, fuzzy logic, network security.

## 1 Introduction

A wireless sensor network (WSN) consists of a large number of small sensor nodes that report surrounding events (e.g., the appearance of enemy vehicles) on the field and a few base stations (BSs) that collect the nodes' reports [1]. In most applications, WSNs are vulnerable to physical attacks since they are deployed on hostile environments and unattended during their operations [2]. An adversary could physically compromise some sensor nodes and use them to launch *false data injection attacks* (FDIAs) in which the adversary inject false reports containing nonexistent events into the network (Fig. 1) [3]. False reports could drain the limited energy resources of the network while they are being delivered to the BSs over multiple hops [4]. Moreover,

---

* This work was supported by National Research Foundation of Korea Grant funded by the Korean Government(2009-0068361).

S.K. Bandyopadhyay et al. (Eds.): ISA 2010, CCIS 76, pp. 128–137, 2010.

they cause false alarms that could waste real-world response efforts [5] (e.g., dispatching some response taskforces based on false reports). Thus, to minimize the energy draining and false alarms caused by injected false reports, they should be identified and discarded as soon as possible [6].

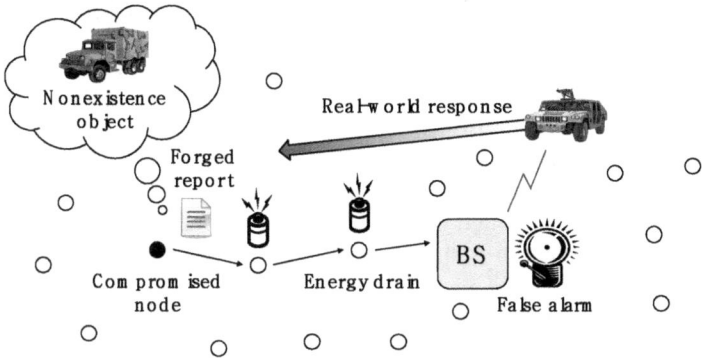

**Fig. 1.** False data injection attacks (FDIAs)

Researchers have recently proposed several en-route filtering solutions, such as the statistical en-route filtering scheme (SEF) [3], the interleaved hop-by-hop authentication scheme (IHA) [5] and the key inheritance-based filtering scheme (KIF) [6]. Each of these solutions can prevent reporting of non-existent events and save a large amount of energy resources since it can filter false reports out during its forwarding process. However, all they are inefficient in terms of energy savings when FDIAs do not actually occur [7]. They usually involve extra communication and computation overhead; every report must carry additional information (communication overhead), such as key indices, and are verified by some forwarding nodes based on a secure hash or encryption algorithm (computation overhead). To conserve energy resource in normal situation, a few detection-based solutions [7,8] have been recently proposed. Each of them uses a production system to distinguish false reports from the reports collected in the BS. However, there would be uncertainties in its inference processes and in data used within the inference, while they are based on crisp set.

In this paper, we propose a fuzzy-based FDIAs detection method for WSNs. The fuzzy rule-based system verifies the authenticity of each object reported by sensing reports, based on the correctness of the reports, the number of the reports and the fluctuation in the number of the reports. Thanks to approximate reasoning provided by fuzzy logic, the proposed method can reduce errors in FDIAs detection, compared to the existing crisp-based detection solutions. The method involves neither complex report generation process nor en-route verification process. Thus, it can conserve more energy resources than the en-route filtering solutions. The performance of the proposed method is shown with the simulation results.

The remainder of the paper is organized as follows: Section 2 briefly describes security solutions against FDIAs. Section 3 describes the proposed method in detail. Section 4 reviews the simulation results. Finally, conclusions and future work are discussed in Section 5.

## 2   Security Solutions against FDIAs

In order to defend against FDIAs, several en-route filtering solutions have been proposed, such as SEF [3], IHA [5] and KIF [6]. These solutions can detect false sensing reports during the forwarding process before the number of compromised nodes reaches a pre-defined security value. Their basic idea is similar: Every node possesses some symmetric keys shared with some other nodes. When an event of interest, such as appearances/disappearance of vehicles, occurs, nearby nodes detect the event and collaboratively generate a report on the event. The report is endorsed by attaching multiple votes generated by all of them using their keys. As the report is forwarded towards the BS over multiple hops, each forwarding node verifies the correctness of some votes carried in the report using its keys. If the verification fails, the node drops the report immediately. Although their idea is similar, their energy consumption characteristics differ [9]. Other en-route filtering solutions against FDIAs can be found in [4,10-12].

While such filtering-based solutions are energy-efficient against FDIAs, they consume more energy resource in normal situation [7]. As stated the above, they require some complex report generation and en-route verification processes, which bring about additional computation and communication overhead. To prevent extra energy consumption due to such processes, a few detection-based solutions [7,8] have been recently proposed. Each of them uses a production system (a rule-based system) to determine whether an event is legitimate or forged. Since the detection process is done within the BS, based on the reports just collected in the BS, they can save energy resource in normal situation. However, they all are based on crisp set, while there are some uncertainties in their inference processes in the data they use. For example, the data collected from sensor nodes would not be precise due to their misbehavior [13]. Approximate reasoning could increase the performance of the detection-based solutions.

## 3   Fuzzy-Based False Data Detection

This section presents the proposed method in detail.

### 3.1   Network Model

We consider a dense WSN comprised of a large number of sensor nodes and a single BS. Every moving object, such as a vehicle, is continuously moving on the field (Fig. 2(a)) and detected by multiple sensor nodes (Fig. 2(b)). Sensor nodes are similar to the current generation of sensor nodes, such as Crossbow IRIS [14], in their computation and communication capability and power resources. Every node has a single key shared with the BS, used to generate message authentication codes (MACs) for sensing reports. Due to cost constraints, the node is not equipped with tamper-resistant hardware. Thus, the node can be physically compromised by a malicious adversary. When a node senses an appearance or disappearance of a moving object, the node produces a report for the object. Each report typically contains the identifier of the source node, the type of the object, and the timestamp on the report. The node then attaches a MAC, generated by its key over the report, onto the report (Fig. 2(c)). Finally, the node forwards the report toward the BS. We assume that the BS cannot be compromised. We also assume that the BS can know or estimate the location of each node on the field.

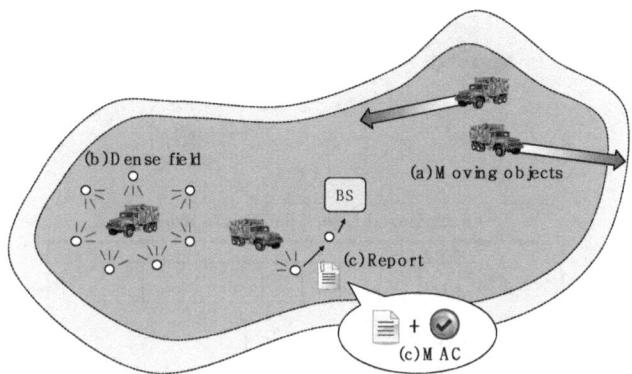

**Fig. 2.** Network model

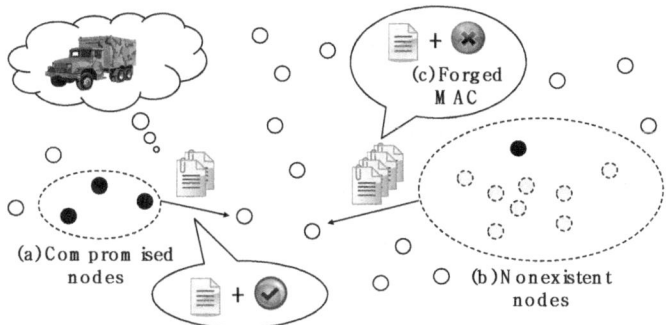

**Fig. 3.** Adversary model

## 3.2  Adversary Model and Design Goal

The adversary can compromise a few sensor nodes on the field. It would be very difficult or impossible to compromise a large number of nodes without being detected. The adversary can use the compromised nodes to launch FIDAs, as shown in Fig. 3(a). The adversary would generate legitimate MACs using the nodes' keys and attach the MACs into false reports. The adversary can also inject false reports into the network without compromise of nodes, as shown in Fig. 3(b). However, the adversary needs to forge MACs for the reports (Fig. 3(c)).

Our primary goal is to design a method that can detect such false data without additional computation or communication operations in sensor nodes. Thus, the detection of false data should be done using only the data collected in the BS. That is, the method should consume just the BS's resources. The second goal is to design a method that can detect false data without the deployment or equipment of additional hardware. That is, any deployment of monitoring- or verification-purpose nodes should be avoided.

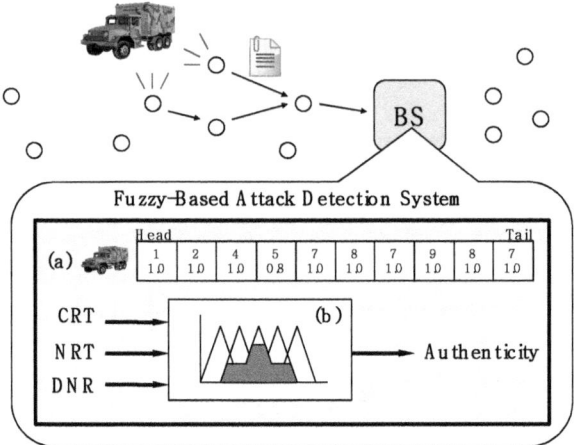

**Fig. 4.** Basic structure

### 3.3  Basic Structure and Procedure

The proposed method is usually loaded on BS. The method consists of FIFO queues to temporarily store objects' data and a fuzzy rule-based system to verify the authenticity of reported objects. For each object on the field, the number of and the correctness of reports informing the object for a period of time is periodically added in the tail of one of the queues. The correctness of reports is computed by the BS based on the MACs carried in the reports. Fig. 4(a) shows an example of a queue for a truck on the field. For the recent period of time, the truck has informed by 7 reports. The correctness of the seven reports is 1.0. That is, all the MACs carried in the reports are legitimate. For each object, the fuzzy rule-based system verifies the authenticity of the object based on the data in the corresponding queue (Fig. 4(b)). The average correctness of the reports, the number of the reports and the fluctuation in the number of the reports are used for the authenticity verification. If the fuzzy system concludes that an object is legitimate, the propose method stops the examination on the object; it stops storing the corresponding data and frees the corresponding queue. If an object is identified as false by the system, the method issues an alarm. To actually counter FDIAs after the detection of them, we can use the adaptive countering scheme [7] in which a countermeasure is activated based on the conclusions of an attack detection system. For example, SEF [3] can be activated when FDIAs have just been detected.

## 3.4  Parameters for Authenticity Verification

In order to verify the authenticity of an event informed by sensing reports, the correctness of the reports for a given period of time (CRT) should be considered. Since every sensor node has a key shared with the BS, the BS can verify the legitimacy of the MACs attached in the reports generated by the node. If the MAC attached in a report is legitimate, the correctness of the report is 1.0. The correctness is 0.0 if not. CRT for an actual object would be almost 1.0. For example, CRT for the truck in Fig. 4 is 57/58≈0.98. Due to possible misbehavior of nodes [13], we cannot guarantee that it will be always 1.0 for actual objects. On the other hand, CRT for a non-existent object fabricated by the adversary without the use of compromised nodes would be nearly 0.0 since the adversary should forge a MAC for each injected report. However, for a fake object, CRT could be 1.0 if the event is fabricated using compromised nodes' keys.

The number of the reports for the given period of time (NRT) should be also considered to verify the authenticity of a reported object. Since every object is moving on the dense sensor field, it would be detected by multiple sensor nodes for the period. Thus, for an actual object, NRT would be large enough. For example, NRT for the truck in Fig. 4 is 1+2+4+5+7+8+7+9+8+7=58. On the other hand, NRT would be relatively small for a non-existent object if a few compromised nodes are used to fabricate the object. However, NRT for a forged object could be also large enough when the adversary injects false reports without the use of compromised data. But CRT for the object would be nearly 0.0.

Even NRT for an actual object could not be large enough when the object has just entered into or left from the field. Thus, to verify the authenticity, we should consider the difference between the number of the reports for the last half of the period and the number for the first half of the period (DNR). A large positive value in DNR for an object would indicate that the object is appearing on the field, while a disappearing object would result in a large negative value in DNR. For example, DNR for the truck in Fig. 4 is 39–19=20. That is, the truck is probably appearing on the field. If NRT for an object is still small when DNR for it becomes negative, the object would be false one.

There are much more factors that can improve the performance in the authenticity determination. However, additional equipments or nodes are often required to acquire such factors [9,15,16]. One of the design goals of the proposed method is to detect FDIAs without the deployment of or equipment of additional hardware. Thus, such factors have been excluded in the proposed method.

## 3.5  Fuzzy System Design

The proposed method exploits a fuzzy rule-based system to verify the authenticity of every report since fuzzy rule-based systems can be used for approximate reasoning [17]. It is particularly important when there is uncertainty in reasoning processes and/or in data. The proposed method detects FDIAs based on the data from sensor nodes, which may misbehave [13]. Thus, it needs to use approximate reasoning to handle such fuzzy data.

The membership functions of three input parameters – CRT, NRT and DNR – of the fuzzy rule-based system are shown in Fig. 5(a), (b) and (c). The labels in the fuzzy variables are presented as follows.

— CRT = {L (Low), M (Medium), H (High)},
— NRT = {VS (Very Small), S, M, L (Large), VL},
— DNR = {LN (Large Negative), N, Z (Zero), P (Positive), LP}.

The output parameter of the fuzzy system is Authenticity = {F (False), S (Suspicious), U (Unknown), C (Convincing), L (Legitimate)}, which is represented by the membership functions as shown in Fig. 5(d). The membership functions of the fuzzy system are manually determined based on the simulation results. To apply the proposed method on other WSN, the membership functions should be optimized for the network.

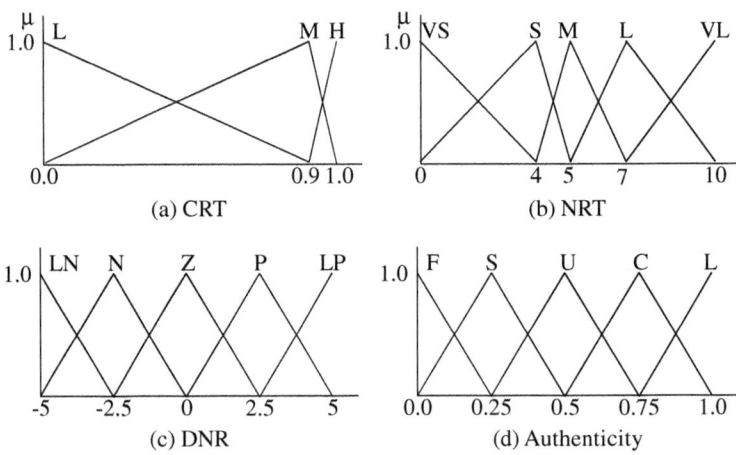

**Fig. 5.** Fuzzy membership functions

The output parameter of the fuzzy system is Authenticity = {F (False), S (Suspicious), U (Unknown), C (Convincing), L (Legitimate)}, which is represented by the membership functions as shown in Fig. 5(d).

If CRT is H (High) and NRT is VL (Very Large) and DNR is LP (Large Positive), Authenticity is L (Legitimate); the corresponding object would be legitimate since it has been informed by a large number of legitimate sensing reports and NRT is still increasing. The method concludes an object as legitimate (or false) if the defuzzified output value exceeds a pre-defined threshold value. Some of the rules are shown below.

— Rule 1: IF CRT is H and NRT is VL and DNR is LP      THEN Authenticity is L
— Rule 2: IF CRT is M and NRT is VL and DNR is LP      THEN Authenticity is S
— Rule 3: IF CRT is L and NRT is VL and DNR is LP      THEN Authenticity is F
— Rule 4: IF CRT is H and NRT is L and DNR is LP      THEN Authenticity is C
— Rule 5: IF CRT is M and NRT is L and DNR is LP      THEN Authenticity is S
— Rule 6: IF CRT is L and NRT is L and DNR is LP      THEN Authenticity is F

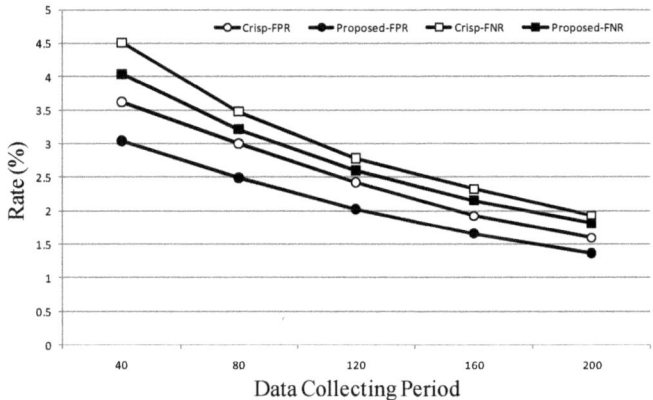

**Fig. 6.** Detection performance

# 4 Simulation Results

In order to show the performance of the proposed method, we have compared the method with the existing solutions. A field size of 1,000×100 m² is used and the BS is located at the end of the field. Each node takes 16.25, 12.5µJ to transmit/receive a byte, and each MAC generation consumes 15µJ [3]. The size of an original report is 24 bytes. The size of a MAC is 8 bytes. The false positive rate and false negative rate were first measured for the performance indexes in the simulation. The false positive rate (FPR) is the rate of legitimate objects among the objects concluded as false by a detection system. The false negative rate (FNR) is the rate of false objects undetected by a detection system among the objects concluded as legitimate. Thus, FNR is in inverse proportion to the detection performance of a detection system. Fig. 6 shows FPR (circles) and FNR (rectangles) in the detection of FDIAs. As shown in the figures, both rates are reduced as the data collection period. Since the proposed method detects FDIAs based on the collected data, its detection performance improves as more data are available. However, an extension would also increase the detection time and space complexity. Both the existing crisp-based FDIAs detection solution [7] (empty ones) and the proposed method (filled ones) use almost the same data to detect FDIAs. However, thanks to approximate reasoning, the proposed method can reduce errors in the detection, compared to the existing one.

We also used simulations to show the energy-efficiency of the proposed method. The average energy consumption was measured for the performance indexes in the simulation. Energy is considered as the most important resource in WSNs due to the limitations of battery power of nodes. Fig. 7 shows the average energy consumption per report delivery in normal situation. As shown in the figure, the proposed method (filled rectangles) was much more efficient than the existing solutions (SEF, IHA and KIF) in terms of energy savings under normal situation (i.e., when false traffic rate is 0%) since the complex report generation and en-route verification processes do not occur in the method. However, the proposed method cannot intercept false traffic during the forwarding process since it just 'detects' FDIAs. Therefore, the energy consumption does not vary with false traffic. In order to intercept such traffic, a FI-DAs countermeasure should be activated after the detection of the traffic.

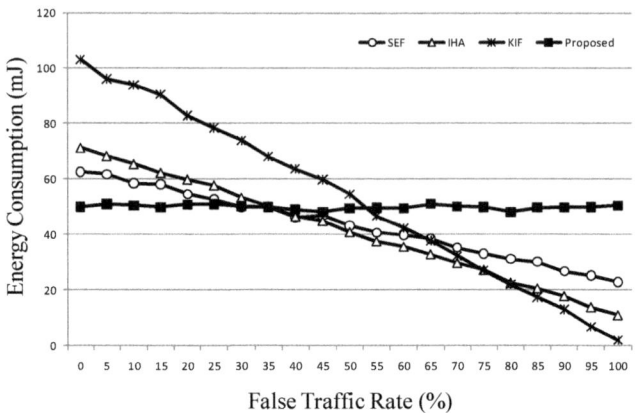

**Fig. 7.** Energy efficiency

## 5 Conclusions and Future Work

A FDIAs detection method for WSNs was presented. The proposed method exploits a fuzzy rule-based system to verify the authenticity of each reported object. The fuzzy system uses CRT, NRT and DNR for the authenticity verification. The method can reduce errors in FDIAs detection, compared to the existing crisp-based detection solutions. It can also conserve more energy resources than the en-route filtering solutions since it does not involve the complex report generation process or en-route verification process. The performance of the proposed method was shown with the simulation results.

To enhance the detection performance of the proposed method, we will study the fuzzy membership functions optimization techniques for the method. Additional simulation runs will be also done with other input parameters not covered in this work. Also, we are planning to apply the adaptive countering scheme [7] on the proposed method in order to deal with the detected FDIAs.

## References

1. Buttyan, L., Dora, L., Vajda, I.: Statistical Wormhole Detection in Sensor Networks. In: Molva, R., Tsudik, G., Westhoff, D. (eds.) ESAS 2005. LNCS, vol. 3813, pp. 128–141. Springer, Heidelberg (2005)
2. Przydatek, B., Song, D., Perrig, A.: SIA: Secure Information Aggregation in Sensor Networks. In: Proc. SenSys, pp. 255–265 (2003)
3. Ye, F., Luo, H., Lu, S.: Statistical En-Route Filtering of Injected False Data in Sensor Networks. IEEE J. Sel. Area Comm. 23, 839–850 (2005)

4. Yang, H., Lu, S.: Commutative Cipher Based En-Route Filtering in Wireless Sensor Networks. In: Proc. VTC, pp. 1223–1227 (2004)

5. Zhu, S., Setia, S., Jajodia, S., Ning, P.: Interleaved Hop-by-Hop Authentication against False Data Injection Attacks in Sensor Networks. ACM Transactions on Sensor Networks 3 (2007)

6. Lee, H.Y., Cho, T.H.: Key Inheritance-Based False Data Filtering Scheme in Wireless Sensor Networks. In: Madria, S.K., Claypool, K.T., Kannan, R., Uppuluri, P., Gore, M.M. (eds.) ICDCIT 2006. LNCS, vol. 4317, pp. 116–127. Springer, Heidelberg (2006)

7. Lee, H.Y.: Adaptive Selection of Secure-Routing Protocols in Wireless Sensor Networks. Ph.D. Dissertation, Sungkyunkwan University (2008)

8. Lee, H.Y., Lee, S.J., Cho, T.H.: Detection of False Positive Attacks in Ubiquitous Sensor Networks. Journal of the Korea Society for Simulation 18, 83–90 (2009)

9. Lee, H.Y., Cho, T.H.: Fuzzy Adaptive Selection of Filtering Schemes for Energy Saving in Sensor Networks. IEICE Trans. Commun. E90-B, 3346–3353 (2007)

10. Yuan, T., Zhang, S., Zhong, Y., Ma, J.: KAEF: An En-Route Scheme of Filtering False Data in Wireless Sensor Networks. In: Proc. IPCCC (2008)

11. Yu, L., Li, J.: Grouping-Based Resilient Statistical En-Route Filtering for Sensor Networks. In: Proc. INFOCOM (2009)

12. Yu, C.M., Lu, C.S., Kuo, S.Y.: A DoS-Resilient En-Route Filtering Scheme for Sensor Networks. In: Proc. MobiHoc, pp. 343–344 (2009)

13. Marti, S., Giuli, T.K., Lai, K., Baker, M.: Mitigating Routing Misbehavior in Mobile Ad hoc Networks. In: Proc. MobiCom, pp. 255–265 (2000)

14. Crossbow Technology, http://www.xbow.com/

15. Silva, A.P.R., Martins, M.H.T., Rocha, B.P.S., Loureiro, A.A.F., Ruiz, L.B., Wong, H.C.: Decentralized Intrusion Detection in Wireless Sensor Networks. In: Proc. Q2SWinet, pp. 16–23 (2005)

16. Mitrokotsa, A., Karygiannis, A.: Intrusion Detection Techniques in Sensor Networks. In: Wireless Sensor Network Security. IOS Press, Amsterdam (2008)

17. Serrano, N., Seraji, H.: Landing Site Selection using Fuzzy Rule-Based Reasoning. In: Proc. ICRA, pp. 4899–4904 (2007)

# Pattern Recognition Using Artificial Neural Network: A Review

Tai-hoon Kim[*]

Multimedia Engineering Department
Hannam University
Daejeon, Korea
taihoonn@empal.com

**Abstract.** Among the various frameworks in which pattern recognition has been traditionally formulated, the statistical approach has been most intensively studied and used in practice. More recently, artificial neural network techniques theory have been receiving increasing attention. The design of a recognition system requires careful attention to the following issues: definition of pattern classes, sensing environment, pattern representation, feature extraction and selection, cluster analysis, classifier design and learning, selection of training and test samples, and performance evaluation. In spite of almost 50 years of research and development in this field, the general problem of recognizing complex patterns with arbitrary orientation, location, and scale remains unsolved. New and emerging applications, such as data mining, web searching, retrieval of multimedia data, face recognition, and cursive handwriting recognition, require robust and efficient pattern recognition techniques. The objective of this review paper is to summarize and compare some of the well-known methods used in various stages of a pattern recognition system using ANN and identify research topics and applications which are at the forefront of this exciting and challenging field.

**Keywords:** Pattern Recognition, correlation, Neural Network.

## 1 Introduction

Pattern recognition is the study of how machines can observe the environment, learn to distinguish patterns of interest from their background, and make sound and reasonable decisions about the categories of the patterns. In spite of almost 50 years of research, design of a general purpose machine pattern recognizer remains an elusive goal. The best pattern recognizers in most instances are humans, yet we do not understand how humans recognize patterns. Ross [1] emphasizes the work of Nobel Laureate Herbert Simon whose central finding was that pattern recognition is critical in most human decision making tasks: "The more relevant patterns at your disposal, the better your decisions will be. This is hopeful news to proponents of artificial intelligence, since computers can surely be taught to recognize patterns. Indeed, successful

---

[*] Corresponding author.

S.K. Bandyopadhyay et al. (Eds.): ISA 2010, CCIS 76, pp. 138–148, 2010.
© Springer-Verlag Berlin Heidelberg 2010

computer programs that help banks score credit applicants, help doctors diagnose disease and help pilots land airplanes depend in some way on pattern recognition... We need to pay much more explicit attention to teaching pattern recognition". Our goal here is to introduce pattern recognition using artificial neural network as the best possible way of utilizing available sensors, processors, and domain knowledge to make decisions automatically.

## 2  Pattern Recognition

Automatic (machine) recognition, description, classification, and grouping of patterns are important problems in a variety of engineering and scientific disciplines such as biology, psychology, medicine, marketing, computer vision, artificial intelligence, and remote sensing. A pattern could be a fingerprint image, a handwritten cursive word, a human face, or a speech signal. Given a pattern, its recognition/classification may consist of one of the following two tasks: 1) supervised classification (e.g., discriminant analysis) in which the input pattern is identified as a member of a predefined class, 2) unsupervised classification (e.g., clustering) in which the pattern is assigned to a hitherto unknown class. The recognition problem here is being posed as a classification or categorization task, where the classes are either defined by the system designer (in supervised classification) or are learned based on the similarity of patterns (in unsupervised classification).These applications include data mining (identifying a "pattern", e.g., correlation, or an outlier in millions of multidimensional patterns), document classification (efficiently searching text documents), financial forecasting, organization and retrieval of multimedia databases, and biometrics. The rapidly growing and available computing power, while enabling faster processing of huge data sets, has also facilitated the use of elaborate and diverse methods for data analysis and classification. At the same time, demands on automatic pattern recognition systems are rising enormously due to the availability of large databases and stringent performance requirements (speed, accuracy, and cost). The design of a pattern recognition system essentially involves the following three aspects: 1) data acquisition and preprocessing, 2) data representation, and 3) decision making. The problem domain dictates the choice of sensor(s), preprocessing technique, representation scheme, and the decision making model. It is generally agreed that a well-defined and sufficiently constrained recognition problem (small intraclass variations and large interclass variations) will lead to a compact pattern representation and a simple decision making strategy. Learning from a set of examples (training set) is an important and desired attribute of most pattern recognition systems. The four best known approaches for pattern recognition are: 1) template matching, 2) statistical classification, 3) syntactic or structural matching, and 4) neural networks.

## 3  Artificial Neural Networks

The main characteristics of neural networks are that they have the ability to learn complex nonlinear input-output relationships, use sequential training procedures, and adapt themselves to the data. The most commonly used family of neural networks for pattern classification tasks [2] is the feed-forward network, which includes multilayer perceptron and Radial-Basis Function (RBF) networks. Another popular network is the Self-Organizing Map (SOM), or Kohonen-Network [3], which is mainly used for data clustering and feature mapping. The learning process involves updating network architecture and connection weights so that a network can efficiently perform a specific classification/clustering task. The increasing popularity of neural network models to solve pattern recognition problems has been primarily due to their seemingly low dependence on domain-specific knowledge and due to the availability of efficient learning algorithms for practitioners to use. Artificial neural networks (ANNs) provide a new suite of nonlinear algorithms for feature extraction (using hidden layers) and classification (e.g., multilayer perceptrons). In addition, existing feature extraction and classification algorithms can also be mapped on neural network architectures for efficient (hardware) implementation. An ANN is an information processing paradigm that is inspired by the way biological nervous systems, such as the brain, process information. The key element of this paradigm is the novel structure of the information processing system. It is composed of a large number of highly interconnected processing elements (neurons) working in unison to solve specific problems. An ANN is configured for a specific application, such as pattern recognition or data classification, through a learning process. Learning in biological systems involves adjustments to the synaptic connections that exist between the neurons.

## 4 Works Done

In 1989, P. M. Grant [4] applied the concept of linear matched filtering, which is widely applied for the detection of communications and radar signals. It then explored the similarities and differences between matched filters and one type of artificial neural network, the 'associative memory', which was widely applied to pattern recognition and recall applications. Subsequently, a more promising approach based on 'multilayer perceptrons' is investigated for the design of nonlinear filters and its application is examined for the filtering of distorted data from communications channels to equalize and reduce the distortion prior to a binary decision process. It was well recognized that the optimal filter for detecting a signal contaminated by white Gaussian noise is the matched filter. For a coded signal waveform the matched-filter function is achieved by correlating the received signal against a reference waveform to give the correlated output. This is achieved by multiplying together the two time series waveforms and performing the time integration. Two basic realizations of the receiver are possible: the active correlator and the linear matched filter. For a filtering or pattern recognition operation where the form of the input data is known in advance, linear matched filters or correlators are optimized signal detectors. In other situations, where time-varying or non-stationary signal or channel characteristics occur, it is appropriate to consider applying artificial neural-network approaches.

Young-Sang Han, Seong-Sik Min, Won-Ho Choi and Kyu-Bock Cho (1992) [5] implemented ANN for fault detection of induction motor (IM). It was a learning pattern recognition system which cans prognose and diagnoses faults as well as aging conditions of the IM. For the diagnosis, this system uses frequency spectrum analysis method based on vibration conditions of the rotating machine. In ANN, inputs are several vibration frequencies. Outputs of artificial neural networks provide the information on the fault condition of motor. The PDP model, namely multi-layer perceptron model with an error back propagation learning algorithm is used for this diagnostic system. As the induction motor (IM) has merits such as easy maintenance, robustness and low cost, IM is the most widely used motor in industry applications. For the reason, it becomes very important to diagnose operating conditions, and to detect the faults of the machine for the improvement of its security and the reliability of the whole system. Although a motor is carefully constructed, it has inherent possibilities of faults which result from stress involved in energy conversion. Hence, it becomes very important to diagnose (incipient) faults and to prolong the life assessment of the IM for the reliability of the system. Conventional researches have been only concentrated on estimating machine parameters that can indicate the conditions of the machine. In those approaches, one fatal drawback is that its accurate dynamics should be known. An ANN based incipient fault detector has two parts of artificial neural networks. One part is a disturbance and noise filter. The other part is a high order incipient fault detector. It detects faults of turn to turn isolation and bearing wear only. Vibration Frequency by faults of major faults of the IM are unbalanced rotor, air gap variation, and unbalanced magnetic attraction force of slot, defect of ball, inner and outer race of bearing. Then a fault occurred in the motor, the symptom of the fault is directly shown through vibration. Therefore, it is very reasonable to analyze problems by means of vibration. Thus, the frequency spectrum of vibration is employed as inputs and the outputs correspond to the information on the defect of IM. For pattern recognition, a multi-layer perceptron model was chosen. It optimizes connection weights by means of error back propagation learning method; the back propagation algorithm uses an objective function, which is defined as the summation of square errors between the desired outputs and the network outputs. It then employs a steepest-descent search algorithm to find the minimum of tie objective function. If a motor is in operation, the capability of an expert system for these kinds of problems is normally limited because the user must be a skilled person to reach such decision making in diagnostic system. On the other hand, the proposed method can be easily utilized by a non-expert. Detection method of this paper will be appropriate for condition monitoring diagnostic problem concerning optimal maintainability and availability of existing machine, or assurance of production quality control of motors.

In 1997, Nallasamy Mani and Bala Srinivasan [6] applied artificial neural network approach for optical character recognition (OCR). That was a simple pattern recognition system using artificial neural network to simulate character recognition. A simple feed-forward neural network model has been trained with different set of noisy data. The back-propagation method was used for learning in neural network. The range of applications includes postal code recognition, automatic data entry into large administrative systems, banking, automatic cartography and reading devices for blind. Here the image processing time was significantly reduced while maintaining efficiency and versatility at the same time. But the complete system which encompassed all the features of a practical OCR system was yet to be realized. The key factors involved in the implementation are: an optimal selection of features which categorically defines the details of the characters, the number of features and a low image processing time. The character from the scanned image has been normalized from 60 X 60 pixel into 32 X 32. The horizontal and vertical vectors (Vh and Vv respectively) are added together to form the input vector of the neural network. Finally, an input vector that contains 64 (horizontal + vertical) unique features of the character is evaluated. Histogram techniques have been used here for automatic processing of lines, words and characters extraction in the sequence. The erosion and dilation operations make the object smaller and larger respectively. Erosion makes an object smaller by removing or eroding away the pixel on its edges. Dilation makes an object larger by adding pixel around its edges. Dilation technique is used for extracting a word from the original image (gray scale). Image dilation is applied to make the characters in a word thicker until they join together. The image erosion techniques have been used for extracting each character from a word. The pattern editor is very useful in creating the training data files. The advantage is to train the network with user defined character sets, numerals and even with other languages. Once the network is trained it would create: an associated weight of the particular training file. The experiment had shown the recognition rate as 70% for noisy data to up to 99%. The main demerit of this work was that the experiment failed for multiple font and size characters and hand written character recognition.

A rain attenuation model based on artificial neural network was proposed by Hongwei Yang, Chen He, Wentao Song, Hongwen Zhu in 2000 [7]. Based on analyzing several of factors affecting rain attenuation, a rain attenuation model with artificial neural network was founded after training and verifying many different neural network topologies. The results had shown that applying the artificial neural network to predict rain attenuation of high frequency wave is a good approach and decreases the mean prediction error by 0.59dB and the root of mean square error by 0.69dB. The work in this paper shows that it's a new and effective way to predict rain attenuation with artificial neural network. To predict rain attenuation from known rain rate is therefore essential for design reliability and validity of communication system. The prediction of rain attenuation is a very complex and difficult task. Generally, the prediction models can be either theoretical (also called deterministic), or empirical (also called statistic), or a combination of these two. The deterministic models are based on the principles of physics and therefore, can be applied in different conditions without affecting the accuracy but their implementation usually requires a great database of radio meteorology characteristics such as atmospheric pressure, atmospheric temperature and so on, which is nearly impossible to obtain. Due to that the implementation of the deterministic models is usually restricted to the special area where radio meteorology data can be available. In the empirical models, nearly all influences are taken into account regardless of whether or not they can be separately recognized. This is the main advantage of these models. However, the accuracy of these models depends on the accuracy of the measurements, similarities between the conditions where the rain attenuation is analyzed, the conditions where the measurements are carried out. Proper factors affecting rain attenuation are considered as inputs of neural network and enough data used for neural network are selected. After training and verifying many different neural network topologies, an applied rain attenuation model is finally founded. Under the consideration of the factors affecting rain attenuation, 8 inputs have been selected. One group of the inputs has been chosen to take into account the effects of radio parameters on the rain attenuation. These inputs include frequency (in GHz), elevation angle (in degree) and polarization angle (in degree). The second group of inputs contains latitude (in degree), longitude (in degree), altitude (in km) and height (in km) of the earth station, which are intended for taking into account the terrain effects on the attenuation due to rain. The last group of inputs is rainfall rate (in mm/hour) which is the main meteorological factor affecting rain attenuation. When defining the prediction error as the difference between the measured and the predicted attenuation value at the same condition, the prediction error distribution of the ANN model and a conventional model ( such as CCIR model ) has been computed. The ANN model obtained mean prediction error 1.39 dB, RMS error 2.01dB and maximum prediction error 4.7dB over the range of the validation set, more accurate than mean prediction 1.98dB, RMS error 2.7048 and maximum prediction error 7.4 dB of CIRR model. It is easy to see that the ANN model showed satisfactory, even very good accuracy with nearly 0.6 dB increasing in average.

In 2006, ANN method was used for Electrocardiogram (ECG) pattern recognition by Lin He, Wensheng Hou, Xiaolin Zhen and Chenglin Peng [8]. Four types of ECG patterns were chosen from the MIT-BIH database to be recognized, including normal sinus rhythm (N), premature ventricular contraction (PVC), and atrial premature beat (A) and left bundle branch block beat (L). ECG morphology and R-R interval features were performed as the characteristic representation of the original ECG signals to be fed into the neural network models. Three types of artificial neural network models, SOM, BP and LVQ networks were separately trained and tested for ECG pattern recognition and the experimental results of the different models have been compared. The SOM network exhibited the best performance and reached an overall accuracy of 95.5%, and the BP and LVQ network reached 92.5% and 91.5%. A typical ECG waveform contains P wave, QRS complex and T wave in each heart beat. Recognizing an ECG pattern is essentially the process of extracting and classifying ECG feature parameters, which may be obtained either from the time domain or transform domain. The features being frequently used for ECG analysis in time domain include the wave shape, amplitude, duration, areas, and R-R intervals. The basic problem of automatic ECG analysis occurs from the non-linearity in ECG signals and the large variation in ECG morphologies of different patients. And in most cases, ECG signals are contaminated by background noises, such as electrode motion artifact and electromyogram-induced noise, which also add to the difficulty of automatic ECG pattern recognition. Compared with the traditional clustering methods, the artificial neural network models have good adaptive ability to environmental changes and new patterns, and the recognition speed of neural network is fast, owing to its parallel processing capability. Therefore, artificial neural network models for ECG pattern recognition have been used here. The performance of artificial neural network to recognize ECG patterns may be lowered by noise corrupted ECG signals. Even though the neural network has some degree of fault tolerance, it is desirable that clean ECG signals are provided. Three different neural network models, which are SOM, BP and LVQ networks, were employed to recognize the ECG patterns. The ECG records of 4 different types of patterns were obtained from 11 patients. 200 ECG segments were chosen for each of the pattern, which produces a dataset with a total number of 800 ECG records, each containing a QRS complex. The four types of patterns are respectively designated as N, A, L and V. The training strategy of the neural network was as follows, the whole dataset was divided into four groups of equal size with equal number of the 4 patterns in each group, and every neural network model is tested by a different data group, while the other three is used for training. The performance of the neural networks was evaluated by the recognition sensitivities, the overall recognition accuracy and the neurons number needed. The overall accuracy is defined as the ratio of the total number of beats recognized correctly to the total number of beats in the test phase. It is observed that the performance of the SOM network is relatively better than BP network; while the SOM network needs a longer time for training. The error of BP network was defined as the mean difference of the ideal output and the real output which was 0.0459 in the training phase and 0.1041 in the testing phase. While the error of SOM network and LVQ network was not considered.

Shahrin Azuan Nazeer, Nazaruddin Omar, Khairol Faisal Jumari and Marzuki Khalid (2007) [9] used ANN approach in face recognition. They evaluated the performance of the system by applying two photometric normalization techniques: histogram equalization and homomorphic filtering, and comparing with Euclidean Distance, and Normalized Correlation classifiers. The system produced promising results for face verification and face recognition. Over here the face recognition system consists of face verification, and face recognition tasks. In verification task, the system knows a priori the identity of the user, and has to verify this identity, that is, the system has to decide whether the a priori user is an impostor or not. In face recognition, the a priori identity is not known: the system has to decide which of the images stored in a database resembles the most to the image to recognize. The primary goal of this work was to present the performance evaluation carried out using artificial neural network for face verification and recognition. It composed of several modules which are Image Acquisition, Face Detection, Training, Recognition and Verification. In enrollment phase the image is acquired using a web camera and stored in a database. Next, the face image is detected and trained. During training, the face image is preprocessed using geometric and photometric normalization. The features of the face image are extracted using several feature extraction techniques. The features data is then stored together with the user identity in a database. In recognition/verification phase a user's face biometric data is once again acquired and the system uses this to either identify who the user is, or verify the claimed identity of the user. While identification involves comparing the acquired biometric information against templates corresponding to all users in the database, verification involves comparison with only those templates corresponding to claimed identity. Thus, identification and verification are two distinct problems having their own inherent complexities. The recognition/verification phase comprises of several modules which are image acquisition, face detection, and face recognition /verification. In image acquisition/face detection module face detection is used to detect face and to extract the pertinent information related to facial features. In this module, the background or the scenes unrelated to face will be eliminated. The system can detect a face in real-time. The face detection system is also robust against illumination variance and works well with different skin color and occlusions such as beards, moustache and with head cover. The face recognition module comprised of preprocessing, feature extraction, and classification sub-modules. The input to the face recognition/verification module is the face image, which is derived from two sources: from the camera and from the database. From these sources, each image is preprocessed to get the geometric and photometric normalized form of the face image. During feature extraction, the normalized image is represented as feature vectors. The result of the classification for the recognition purpose is determined by matching the client index with the client identity in the database. Multilayer Feed-forward Neural Networks (MFNNs) is an ideal means of tackling a whole range of difficult tasks in pattern recognition and regression because of its highly adaptable non-linear structure. Result of the experiment presented a face recognition system using artificial neural networks in the context of face verification and face recognition using photometric normalization for comparison. The classification techniques used here was Artificial Neural Network (NN), Euclidean Distance(ED) and Normalized Correlation (NC).The experimental results show that N.N. is superior to the Euclidean distance and normalized correlation decision rules using both PCA and LDA for overall performance for verification. However, for recognition, E.D. classifier gives the highest accuracy using the original face image.

In order to improve the precision of electric power system short term load forecasting, a new load forecasting model was put forward in 2007 by Wenjin Dai, ping Wang [10]. This paper presents a short-term load forecasting method using pattern recognition which obtains input sets belong to multi-layered fed-forward neural network, and artificial neural network in which BP learning algorithm is used to train samples. Load forecasting has become one of the major areas of research in electrical engineering in recent years. The artificial neural network used in short-time load forecasting can grasp interior rule in factors and complete complex mathematic mapping. Therefore, it is worldwide applied effectively for power system short-term load forecasting. Short-term load forecasting has been useful in safe and economical planning operation of an electrical power system. It has been also used in start-up and shutdown schedules of generating units, overhaul planning and load management. One of the characteristics of electric power is that it can't be stockpiled, that is, the power energy is generated, transmitted, distributed and consumed at the same time. In normal working condition, system generating capacity should meet load requirement anytime. If the system generating capacity is not enough, essential measure should be taken such as adding generating units or importing some power from the neighboring network. On the other hand, if the system generating capacity is of surplus, essential measure should be taken too, such as shutting-down some generating units, or outputting some power to neighboring network. Load variation trend and feature forecasting are essential for power dispatch, layout and design department of power system. Artificial Neural Network and Expert System methods belong to quantitative forecasting methods. In this approach, the ANN traces previous load patterns and predicts a load pattern using recent load data. It also can use weather information for modeling. The ANN is able to perform non-linear modeling and adaptation. It does not need assumption of any functional relationship between load and weather variables in advance. The ability to outperform experiential qualitative forecasting methods especially during rapidly changing weather conditions and the short time required to their development, have made ANN based load forecasting models very attractive for on line implementation in energy control centers. Therefore, it is worldwide applied effectively for the power system short-term load forecasting. The Back propagation algorithm has been used in the experiment. The proposed method does not require heavy computational time and that the patterns considered for training the ANNs also have an impact on forecasting accuracy.

Currently, there are mainly two kinds of stock price pattern recognition algorithms: the algorithm based on rule-matching and the algorithm based on template-matching.

However, both of the two algorithms highly require the participation of domain experts, as well as their lacks of the learning ability. To solve these problems, Xinyu Guo, Xun Liang & Xiang Li [11] proposed a stock price pattern recognition approach based upon the artificial neural network. The experiment shows that the neural network can effectively learn the characteristics of the patterns, and accurately recognize the patterns. As an approach for stock investment, technical analysis has been widely-scrutinized by research communities, and the technical pattern analysis is regarded as one of the most important technical analysis approaches. In the long-term stock analysis experience, stock analysts summarized many technical patterns beneficial for the investment decision-making, which can be classified into two categories: the continuation pattern and the reversal pattern. Continuation pattern indicates that the stock price is going to keep its current movement trend; while the reversal pattern indicates that the stock price will move to the opposite trend. In this paper, 18 typical technical patterns are chosen as the research target, including 10 continuation patterns and 8 reversal patterns. The technical pattern recognition algorithm can mainly be classified into two categories, one is the rule-based algorithm, and the other is template-based algorithm. In this work, an approach relying on neural network has been proposed, whereas the most noticeable difference lies in that the inputs of the network do not cover every time point in the series. On the contrary, a segmentation process is adopted in this work to first transform the original time series into a sequence of trend segments and corresponding features, with each of the features calculated in terms of the price at the last time point within the segment. Eventually, this sequence of features, instead of the whole time series, is designated as part of the inputs of the network, which not only reduce the calculation expense but also enable the alteration of time granularity for stock patterns by adjusting the length of the segments. Here, 18 kinds of typical technical patterns have been examined. A three-layer feed forward neural network is typically composed of one input layer, one output layer and one hidden layers. In the input layer, each neuron corresponds to a feature; while in the output layer, each neuron corresponds to a predefined pattern. The best situation is that once a certain sample is input into the network, the output will be a vector with all elements as zero only except the one corresponding to the pattern that the sample belongs to. Nonetheless, due to the existence of classification errors and the fact that some testing samples don't belong to any of the 18 predefined patterns; some samples can not get exactly the expected output. 2029 samples out of 508 stocks from Stock Exchange were taken, which include 593 continuation patterns and 1436 reversal patterns, as training samples. At the mean time, 4937 samples as the testing samples out of 155 stocks were extracted from another Stock Exchange within the same time-interval. There are 54 continuation patterns, 270 reversal patterns and 4613 belong to neither of the two.

Interactive Voice Response (IVR) with pattern recognition based on Neural Networks was proposed by Syed Ayaz Ali Shah, Azzam ul Asar and S.F. Shaukat [12] for the first time in 2009. In this case, after entering the correct password the user is asked to input his voice sample which is used to verify his identity. The addition of voice pattern recognition in the authentication process can potentially further enhance the security level. The developed system is fully compliant with landline phone system. The results are promising based on false accept and false reject criteria offering quick response time. It can potentially play an effective role in the existing authentication techniques used for identity verification to access secured services through telephone or similar media. Over here speaker specific features are extracted using Mel Frequency Cepstral Coefficient (MFCC) while Multi Layer Perceptron (MLP) is used for feature matching. Our model is based on 8 kHz, 8 bit format using Pulse Code Modulation (PCM). At highest level, all speaker recognition systems contain two modules: Feature Extraction and Feature Matching. Similarly they operate in two modes: Training and Recognition/Testing modes. Both training and recognition modes include Feature Extraction and Feature Matching. In training mode speaker models are created for database. This is also called enrollment mode in which speakers are enrolled in the database. In this mode, useful features from speech signal are extracted and model is trained. The objective of the model is generalization of the speaker's voice beyond the training material so that any unknown speech signal can be classified as intended speaker or imposter. In recognition mode, system makes decision about the unknown speaker's identity claim. In this mode features are extracted from the speech signal of the unknown speaker using the same technique as in the training mode. And then the speaker model from the database is used to calculate the similarity score. Finally decision is made based on the similarity score. For speaker verification, the decision is either accepted or rejected for the identity claim. Two types of errors occur in speaker verification system- False Reject (FR) and False Accept (FA). When a true speaker is rejected by the speaker recognition system, it is called FR. Similarly FA occurs when imposter is recognized as a true speaker. Neural networks learn complex mappings between inputs and outputs and are particularly useful when the underlying statistics of the considered tasks are not well understood. Neural Networks being relatively new approach is investigated in this proposed solution. In this technique, a feed forward back propagation network is used for classification of speakers. The network is trained with the training sets extracted from the input speech by using MFCC technique of feature extraction. The model developed is a text-independent speaker verification system which can identify only a specific speaker based on his voice and rejects the claim of any other speaker. Multilayer Perceptron (MLP) having four layers comprising of one input layer, two hidden layers and one output layer has been used. The input layer has nineteen (19) neurons (as there are nineteen feature vectors from MFCC processor) and uses linear transfer function. The output layer has one neuron (as binary decision is to be made) and uses linear transfer function. It is trained using back propagation algorithm. The network is trained by using a built in train function .This function trains the network on training data (Supervised Learning). The training algorithm used for this network is Gradient Descent (GD). In testing phase, 10% tolerance is present for the intended speaker i.e. if the output of the network is 10% less or greater than 10%, still the speaker is recognized as the intended speaker otherwise rejected. The test data consists of fifty (50) speech samples (other than those used for training the neural network) of the speaker for whom network is trained and 125 samples of imposter speech. The imposter speech data was collected from 13 persons (male). Out of 50 samples of the intended speaker 41 was recognized. So false reject is only 18%. Similarly for imposter data out of 125 trials only 17 were falsely accepted. Thus false accept is about 14%.

# 5  Conclusions

While investigating the works chronologically we have noticed that though there are some merits and demerits of each individual work the application of ANN in each pattern recognition case always performed better result than that of without implementing ANN. The accuracy level of forecasting on the basis of present data set (experience) was always better.

# References

1. Ross, P.E.: Flash of Genius. Forbes, 98–104 (November 1998)
2. Jain, A.K., Mao, J., Mohiuddin, K.M.: Artificial Neural Networks: A Tutorial. Computer, 31–44 (March 1996)
3. Kohonen, T.: Self-Organizing Maps. Springer Series in Information Sciences, Berlin, vol. 30 (1995)
4. Grant, P.M.: Artificial neural network and conventional approaches to filtering and pattern recognition. Electronics & Communications Engineering Journal, 225 (1989)
5. Han, Y.-S., Min, S.-S., Choi, W.-H., Cho, K.-B.: A Learning Pattern Recognition System using Neural Network for Diagnosis and Monitoring of Aging of Electrical Motor. In: International Conference, November 9-13 (1992)
6. Mani, N., Srinivasan, B.: Application of Artificial Neural Network Model for Optical Character Recognition. In: IEEE international conference, October 12-15 (1997)
7. Yang, H., He, C., Song, W., Zhu, H.: Using Artificial Neural Network approach to predict rain attenuation on earth-space path. In: Antennas and Propagation Society International Symposium, IEEE, vol. 02 (2000)
8. He, L., Hou, W., Zhen, X., Peng, C.: Recognition of ECG Patterns Using Artificial Neural Network. In: Sixth International Conference on Intelligent Systems Design and Applications, vol. 02 (2006)
9. Nazeer, S.A., Omar, N., Jumari, K.F., Khalid, M.: Face detecting using Artificial Neural Networks Approach. In: First Asia International Conference on Modelling & Simulation (2007)
10. Dai, W., Wang, P.: Application of Pattern Recognition and Artificial Neural Network to Load Forecasting in Electric Power System. In: Third International Conference on Natural Computation, vol. 01 (2007)
11. Guo, X., Liang, X., Li, X.: A Stock Pattern Recognition Algorithm Based on Neural Networks. In: Third International Conference on Natural Computation, vol. 02 (2007)
12. Ali Shah, S.A., ul Asar, A., Shaukat, S.F.: Neural Network Solution for Secure Interactive Voice Response. World Applied Sciences Journal 6(9), 1264–1269 (2009)

# PeerReview Analysis and Re-evaluation for Accountability in Distributed Systems or Networks

Zhifeng Xiao and Yang Xiao[*]

Department of Computer Science
The University of Alabama
Tuscaloosa, AL 35487-0290
zxiao1@ua.edu, yangxiao@ieee.org

**Abstract.** Accountability implies that any entity should be held responsible for its own specific action or behavior so that the entity is part of a larger chain of accountability. PeerReview [1] is designed as a practical system that provides accountability for distributed systems. A key assumption in PeerReview is that a message sent from one correct node to another will be eventually received. In the real world, however, message loss is commonplace and unavoidable due to the dynamics and uncertainties of the current Internet, and it prevents a message from always reaching its destination. Beginning with this point, we have comprehensively analyzed the behavior of PeerReview with the assumption that, eventually, a message will probably be lost. We have shown that PeerReview would be unable to maintain its completeness and accuracy under such a circumstance. We present six possible errors and the causes from which they originate. We re-evaluated PeerReview with two newly defined metrics, Node Accountability and System Accountability, which are employed to assess the degree of system accountability. Simulation results show that message loss decreases the performance of PeerReview in terms of both metrics.

**Keywords:** Accountability, distributed systems, Internet, wireless Internet.

## 1 Introduction

Accountability has been a longstanding concern of trustworthy computer systems [21], and it has recently been elevated to a first class design principle for dependable networked systems [2] [15]. Accountability implies that any entity should be held responsible for its own specific action or behavior so that the entity is part of a larger chain of accountability [22].

Some work [1, 3-5, 10-14, 22-23] has been done to determine how an accountable system could be designed. In this paper, we focus on PeerReview [1], which is designed as a software library capable of providing accountability for distributed systems that suffer general Byzantine faults. PeerReview ensures that Byzantine faults whose effects are observed by a correct node will eventually be detected and irrefutably linked to a faulty node. Meanwhile, a correct node can always defend itself against

---

[*] Corresponding author.

S.K. Bandyopadhyay et al. (Eds.): ISA 2010, CCIS 76, pp. 149–162, 2010.
© Springer-Verlag Berlin Heidelberg 2010

false accusations. In systems with multiple trust domains, the features provided by PeerReview are particularly important in detecting faults and assigning responsibilities.

PeerReview relies on message exchange/track to make a faulty node detectable and observable. A strong assumption is that a message sent from one correct node to another will eventually be received. To prevent messages from being lost, great efforts have been made by PeerReview, e.g., retransmission of lost messages and the use of witness nodes to forward missed messages indirectly. These efforts aim at increasing the probability that a message will eventually arrive at its destination.

Regarding the complexity and dynamics of the current Internet, however, message loss is commonplace [8] and cannot be rooted out. In addition, wireless networks have already been integrated with the Internet, whereas a wireless channel can be in a very bad condition, making communication links lossy, unstable, and asymmetric. The physical link failure is not the only aspect, though. In the Internet, there are thousands of hosts, routers/switches, and servers that are up and down every second; some of them suffer hardware/software malfunctioning; some are attacked and crashed. Messages might be intercepted by malicious hosts while both the sender and receiver do not even know what happens. Furthermore, since PeerReview is implemented in the application layer, some attacks operated in lower layers cannot be managed by Peer-Review. Therefore, we claim that in a complex network with multiple lossy links and diverse attacks, a message might never arrive at its destination; no matter how many times the message is re-transmitted.

In this paper, we adopt a more realistic assumption that a message might eventually be lost. Under this assumption, a message may never reach its destination. This will bring serious consequences for PeerReview. We have re-visited the protocols in PeerReview and analyzed each of them in detail. Our analysis shows that two key properties of PeerReview, *completeness* and *accuracy*, are proven to no longer hold since there is a chance that correct nodes could be treated as bad ones and faulty nodes could avoid detection. According to the combination of indications and node statuses, we have defined six error types and found out the causes for each of them.

To verify our analysis, we have defined two metrics, node accountability and system accountability, to evaluate system performance. The simulation results show that message loss would decrease the performance of PeerReview in terms of both metrics.

The rest of this paper is organized as follows. Related work is discussed in Section 2. Some PeerReview basics are introduced in section 3. Taking message loss into account, we re-visit the protocols and properties of PeerReview in Section 4. We re-evaluate PeerReview in Section 5. The conclusion is drawn in Section 6.

## 2   Related Work

Recent advances have explored the application of accountability in various network contexts. Yumerefendi *et al.* present CATS [14], a network storage service with strong accountability properties. AudIt [13] is described as an accountability interface to determine which unit is responsible for dropping or delaying the traffic. The authors in [3] and [4] present accountable IP (AIP), which improves the current IP layer by using a hierarchy of self-certifying addresses. Mirkovic *et al.* propose to jointly use the source signature, packet tickets, and a reputation system to build strong accountability into future Internet [5]. PeerReview [1] is designed as an accountable system for deterministic environment; CSAR [10] extends PeerReview's work to make randomized systems accountable. Keller *et al.* [11] have discussed the issue of accountability in hosted virtual networks and examined two possible approaches. The authors in [12] have presented a layered trust management framework to help email receivers eliminate their unwitting trust and to provide them with accountability support. Re-ECN [16-17] allows accurate congestion monitoring throughout the network, thus enabling the upstream party at any trust boundary in the internetwork to be held responsible for the congestion that they cause or allow to be caused.

Some accountable systems [1,10,14] have already been experimented. Nevertheless, regarding performance evaluation, they are more concerned about general system cost metrics like message overhead, throughput, response time, etc.

No prior work has experimentally answered the question that how accountable the system is. In this paper, we explore an approach to evaluate PeerReview in terms of the degree of accountability.

## 3   PeerReview Preliminaries

In this section, we provide a short review for PeerReview [1], which ensures that

- Byzantine faults whose effects are observed by a correct node are eventually detected and irrefutably linked to a faulty node;
- A correct node can always defend itself against false accusations.

Some critical assumptions in PeerReview are listed below [1]:

- The application that each node runs is deterministic, meaning that a certain input will generate a unique output. To check the correctness of other nodes, a reference implementation is employed; for a specific input, only the output produced by the reference implementation is correct.
- A message sent from one correct node to another is eventually received, if retransmitted sufficiently often.
- Each node has a public/private key pair bound to a unique node identifier, and thus no identity is forgeable.
- Each node is indicated as one of {'trusted', 'suspected', or 'exposed'}.
- Each node $k$ has a witness set $w(k)$, which will monitor $k$'s behavior and announce other nodes if $k$ becomes faulty.

PeerReview consists of six components, each of which is responsible for a specific function: tamper-evident logs, commitment protocol, consistency protocol, audit protocol, challenge/response protocol, and evidence transfer protocol [1].

**Tamper-evident logs** [1]: PeerReview requires that each node maintains a secure log to faithfully record all events that happen within the node. A log is append-only. Each log entry is defined as $e_k = (s_k, t_k, c_k)$, where $s_k$ is the sequence (seq) number, $t_k$ is the message (msg) type, and $c_k$ is the content. Also, each entry $e_k$ includes a recursively defined hash value $h_k = H(h_{k-1} \| s_k \| t_k \| H(c_k))$. An authenticator [ $\alpha_k^i = \sigma_i(s_k, h_k)$ ] is a signed statement by node $i$ that its log entry $e_k$ has a hash value $h_k$. The resultant hash chain, along with a set of authenticators, makes the log tamper-evident.

**Commitment protocol** [1]: When node $i$ sends a message $m$ to node $j$, node $i$ must commit to having sent the message $m$, and node $j$ must commit to having received message $m$. To this end, node $j$ will obtain the authenticator attached with message $m$; meanwhile, node $i$ is supposed to receive the authenticator attached with the ACK($m$) returned from node $j$. Therefore, a node cannot invent log entries for messages that it never received. If there is no response from node $j$, node $i$ will create a challenge and send it to the witness of node $j$; then the challenge/response protocol will be involved.

**Consistency protocol** [1]: A faulty node can attempt to escape detection by keeping more than one log or a log with multiple branches. To avoid this attack, PeerReview enables a node to produce a connecting log segment for each pair of authenticators that it has ever signed if and only if it maintains a single, linear log.

If a node $i$ receives authenticators from another node $j$, it must eventually forward these authenticators to the witness set $w(j)$. Thus, the witnesses obtain verifiable evidence of every message that node $j$ has sent or received. Periodically, each witness, $w \in w(j)$, picks the authenticators with the lowest and the highest sequence number and challenges node $j$ to return all log entries in this range. If node $j$ is correct, these log entries form a linear hash chain that contains the hash values in all of the other authenticators. If they do not, the witness set $w(j)$ has obtained verifiable evidence that node $j$ is faulty.

Finally, each $w \in w(j)$ uses the log entries to extract all of the authenticators that node $j$ has received from other nodes and sends them to the corresponding witness sets. This is necessary because node $j$ could be acting as a faulty accomplice of some node $k$ and it could forward node $k$'s messages without sending the authenticators to $w(k)$.

**Audit protocol** [1]: Node $i$ 's witness set $w(i)$ will periodically look up its most recent authenticator from node $i$ (denoted as $\alpha_k^i$) and then challenge node $i$ to return all log entries since its last audit, up to and including $e_k$. By replaying the logs and comparing the outputs with the reference implementation, a witness is able to check the correctness of the node that it is witnessing.

**Challenge/response protocol** [1]: There are two types of challenges defined in Peer-Review: send challenge (*chal*) and audit challenge. The *send chal* is created in the commitment protocol. If node $j$ does not respond to node $i$, then node $i$ will send a challenge to node $j$'s witness, which will later forward the challenge to node $j$ to push it to reply to node $i$. The audit protocol employs the audit challenge to retrieve log segments from the node that it is witnessing.

**Evidence transfer protocol** [1]: PeerReview allows every node $i$ to periodically fetch the challenges collected by the witnesses of every other node $j$. By doing so, all correct nodes eventually output a failure indication for each faulty node.

# 4  When PeerReview Suffers Message Loss

The goal is to determine how PeerReview will be affected if messages are eventually lost. To assist with the analysis, we formally described the PeerReview system model and defined six error types. For convenience and consistency, all notations and conventions will be consistent with PeerReview in [1].

## 4.1  System Model and Error Type

Let $G(V,)$ denote the a PeerReview-enabled system, where $V$ is the node set of system. Also, let $V_c$ denote the correct node set. We define a status set $O = \{$Correct (C), Faulty (F), and Ignorant (I)$\}$. Let $o_v$ represent the status of node $v$. For $\forall v \in V$, $o_v \in O$. An *ignorant* node is loosely defined as a node that ignores all incoming messages, with no response to any node. A *faulty* node is a node that suffers general Byzantine fault, and thus its behavior becomes arbitrary and unpredictable. Strictly, an ignorant node is also one type of faulty nodes, but the system itself is unable to tell the difference between an ignorant node and a node suffering bad message loss. Therefore, no evidence could be provided to expose an ignorant node. A correct node complies with the application protocol faithfully and always responds as desired.

An indication of node $i$ is that how node $i$ will be judged by other nodes. In Peer-Review, an indication set is defined as $U = \{T, E, S\}$, where $T$, $E$, and $S$ stand for 'trusted', 'exposed', and 'suspected', respectively. For $\forall v \in V$, an indication table $\Gamma_v = \{< i, u_{i,v} > | i \in V, u_{i,v} \in U\}$ is maintained in node $v$, where $u_{i,v}$ is an indication of node $i$ generated by node $v$ before further actions are performed. If $u_{i,v} = T$, node $v$ will consider node $i$ as a trusted node and interact with node $i$ in normal procedure. In particular, we have $u_{v,v} \equiv T$, i.e., node $v$ always considers itself to be a trusted node. If $u_{i,v} = E$, node $v$ will consider node $i$ as an exposed node and stop communicating with node $i$ so that node $v$ is thus protected from being fooled. If $u_{i,v} = S$, node $v$ will consider node $i$ to be a suspected node. In the initial state, we let $\Gamma_v = \{< i, u_{i,v} > | i \in V, u_{i,v} = T\}$. In other words, node $v$ will treat every other node $i$ as a trusted node at the beginning. When the system is running, $\Gamma_v$ will be updated in real time.

According to our definitions, we have three types of indications corresponding to three statuses. Let $u_{i,v} | o_i$ denote the indication of node $i$ generated by node $v$, given that node $i$ is in status $o_i$. For instance, $(u_{i,v} = T) | (o_i = C) = T | C$ means that node $i$ is 'Trusted' by node $v$ when node $i$ is a correct node. For $\forall v, i \in V$, obviously, there are nine cases, i.e, *T|C, E|F, S|I, E|C, S|C, T|F, S|F, T|I,* and *E|I,* of how node $v$ would indicate node $i$ of any possible status.

There are three out of nine cases, i.e., *T|C, E|F,* and *S|I,* that node $v$ would accurately indicate the status of node $i$, and the remaining six cases are errors (i.e., being inaccurate).

In this paper, message loss is considered to be the only cause of errors. If message loss never happens, the network is error free and completely accountable. PeerReview allows message loss but it requires that a temporarily lost message would eventually arrive at the destination; hence errors could happen in a short term but would ultimately be resolved. Under such situation, PeerReview eventually achieves 100 percent accountability.

Based on the primitives of PeerReview, $E|I$ will not happen because a correct node has no means with which to provide any evidence to expose a totally irresponsive node. Under our assumption that messages may eventually be lost, the situation of $E|I$ will also not happen.

### 4.2 Tamper-Evident Log Protocol

In this protocol, message loss might happen during either transmissions of authenticators or the inspection process.

We first consider the case of transmissions of authenticators. After sending $\alpha_k^i = \sigma_i(s_k, h_k)$ (attached with the message $m_k$) to node $j$, node $i$ commits to having logged $e_k = (s_k, t_k, c_k)$ and all entries before $e_k$, where $s_k$ is the sequence number, $t_k$ is the message (msg) type, $c_k$ is the content, $\alpha_k^i = \sigma_i(s_k, h_k)$ is a signed statement by node $i$ that its log entry $e_k$ has a hash value $h_k$, $h_k = H(h_{k-1} \parallel s_k \parallel t_k \parallel H(c_k))$, and $H$ is the hush function. Since $\alpha_k^i$ is attached to the message $m_k$, for all messages from node $i$ to node $j$, both node $i$ and node $j$ are supposed to maintain a complete and continuous copy of an authenticator set. However, $m_k$ will probably be lost; hence node $i$ will not receive the ACK($m_k$) from node $j$. In this case, node $i$ will suspect node $j$ so that a temp error $u_{j,i} | o_j = S | C$ is triggered, and node $i$ sends a challenge to node $j$'s witnesses; node $i$ also stops sending any following messages to node $j$ until the challenge is answered. Since all messages before $m_k$ (i.e., from $m_0$ to $m_{k-1}$) were received successfully, the authenticators attached tp these messages (i.e., from $\alpha_0^i$ to $\alpha_{k-1}^i$) would also be completely stored in node $j$. Similarly, node $i$ would receive all ACK messages before ACK($m_k$) and all authenticators attached to them. If ACK($m_k$) arrives at node $i$ at a later time, the authenticator sets will keep growing continuously on both sides, and $u_{j,i} | o_j = S | C$ will switch back to $u_{j,i} | o_j = T | C$. If $m_k$ is eventually lost, the error $S | C$ will never be resolved. However, the existing authenticators and logs before $e_k$ and $h_k$ can still be used as verifiable evidence to check node $i$'s behavior (good or bad) before $e_k$.

We then consider the case of the inspection process. Any node can use $\alpha_k^j$ to inspect $e_k$ and the entries preceding it in node $j$'s log. For example, to inspect $x$ entries, node $i$ challenges node $j$ to return $e_{k-(x-1)}$, ..., $e_k$ and $h_{k-x}$; if node $j$ responds, based on the information returned by node $j$, node $i$ is able to re-calculate the hash value $\tilde{h}_k$

and compare it with $h_k$ in $\alpha_k^j$. However, in transmissions, these $x$ entries might be loaded into multiple packets, some of which could probably be lost due to network problems. For example, if $e_l$, where $k-(x-1)<l<k$, is eventually lost, then entries after $e_l$ cannot be checked correctly since $h_l$, $h_{l+1}$ up to $h_k$ fail to be calculated. In this case, node $i$ is unable to distinguish between message loss and compromised log data; node $i$ will probably then 'expose' node $j$ mistakenly; thus an error $u_{j,i} \mid o_j = E \mid C$ occurs.

In summary, when a packet could eventually be lost, the log is still tamper-evident; but it will probably cause $S \mid C$ and $E \mid C$.

## 4.3 Commitment Protocol

For any message $m_k$ that node $i$ sends to node $j$, node $j$ is assumed to return an ACK($m_k$); both $m_k$ and ACK($m_k$) contain authenticators. Message loss will not affect the function of the commitment protocol. For instance, if node $i$ does not receive ACK($m_k$), there are two cases: 1) $m_k$ is lost; 2) $m_k$ is received by node $j$, but ACK($m_k$) is lost. No matter which case happens, node $i$ will believe that node $j$ does not receive and log $m_k$ and then create a challenge, which will be handled according to the challenge/response protocol.

In summary, message loss will not influence the commitment protocol.

## 4.4 Consistency Protocol

The purpose of consistency protocol is to detect whether a node keeps more than one log or a log with multiple branches. We will analyze this protocol in three steps as follows.

- **Step 1:** A node $i$ will periodically forward all authenticators received from node $j$ to the witness set $\omega(j)$. If any of these authenticators eventually is lost in transmission, the witnesses in $\omega(j)$ might not obtain a full copy of node $j$'s authenticators, which will probably incur some difficulty in the following checking process. As an example, if $k \in \omega(j)$ and node $k$ fails to obtain a full copy of node $j$'s authenticators, node $k$ is supposed to provide $seq_x$ and $seq_y$ in order to check the log segment between $e_x$ and $e_y$ ($x<y$); however, if $\alpha_y^j$ is lost, node $k$ has to give up this checking round, or re-schedule the checking range.
- **Step 2:** Even if $seq_x$ and $seq_y$ are prepared and sent out as a challenge to node $j$, message loss will cause problems similar to the inspection process in the tamper-evident protocol;

- **Step 3:** Then, each $w \in \omega(j)$ uses the log entries to extract all of the authenticators that node $j$ has received from other nodes and sends them to the corresponding witness sets in order to provide information to discover faulty accomplices. This transmission of authenticators is similar to step 1.

In summary, eventual message loss makes it difficult for a node to provide a pair of authenticators as required. In the long run, nodes can seldom obtain full copies of authenticators of other nodes. This problem will spread to the network as time passes.

## 4.5  Audit Protocol

The witnesses of node $i$ will periodically check whether node $i$'s behavior conforms to its reference implementation. To achieve this, each $w \in \omega(i)$ is required to challenge node $i$ to return the log segment since the last audit and then replay it and compare the outputs. The replay procedure concerns the 'input' and 'output' messages, which might be lost. If some inputs are lost, the replay point will jump to the next input; if some outputs are lost, the checking process fails because the outputs do not match those expected by the reference implementation; either will crash the functionality of the audit and trigger the error $u_{i,w} \mid o_i = E \mid C$ .

In summary, in the audit protocol, eventual message loss will cause the error $E \mid C$ , and this causes the witness to be untrustworthy.

## 4.6  Challenge/Response Protocol

This protocol aims at handling the unresponsive nodes to determine whether a node is ignorant or if it just suffers from network problems. This is a remedial approach that drives the system working normally with less impact of message loss. However, even with this protocol, packets can eventually be lost. There are two kinds of challenges defined in Peer Review.

1)  *Audit challenge.* We have already discussed the audit challenge in the last section.
2)  *Send challenge.* When node $i$ learns that node $j$ does not respond, node $i$ begins to 'suspect' node $j$ and creates a *send chal* message; node $i$ then sends the challenge to node $j$'s witnesses, which forward it to node $j$. Message loss might happen
   a)  from node $i$ to $\omega(j)$ when delivering the *send chal,*
   b)  from node $k$ ( $k \in \omega(j)$ ) to node $j$, and
   c)  from node $j$ to node $i$ when transmitting an ACK, if *send chal* arrives at node $j$.
   Thus a message might eventually be lost and node $j$ will continue to be 'suspected' by node $i$. Therefore, error $u_{j,i} \mid o_j = S \mid C$ is triggered.

In summary, eventual message loss will ruin the challenge/response protocol, incurring both $S \mid C$ and $E \mid C$ .

## 4.7  Evidence Transfer Protocol

The goal of this protocol is to ensure that all correct nodes eventually output the same indication for each faulty node. To indicate a certain node $j$, every node $i$ is required to periodically retrieve evidence from $\omega(j)$.

During evidence transfer, the nodes in the whole network expect to retrieve evidence from $\omega(j)$, which is a huge task; evidence probably is lost in transmission, causing some nodes to keep 'trusting' a faulty or ignorant node and to be easily compromised. Thus $u_{j,i} \mid o_j = T \mid F$ and $u_{j,i} \mid o_j = T \mid I$ might occur.

In summary, eventual message loss will prevent the expected effect of the evidence transfer protocol; additionally, it is likely to bring inconsistency of judgment to the system. Nodes not receiving expected evidence would still 'trust' those faulty or ignorant nodes and therefore trigger $T \mid F$ and $T \mid I$.

## 4.8  Revisiting the Theorems of PeerReview

Each node $v$ maintains an evidence set $\varepsilon_{i,v}$ for every other node $i$. Peer Review assumes that if nodes $v$ and $k$ are correct nodes, then $\varepsilon_{i,v}$ and $\varepsilon_{i,k}$ are eventually consistent. However, we will not rule out the possibility that message eventual loss happens in the transmission of evidence; hence $\varepsilon_{i,v}$ might not be consistent with $\varepsilon_{i,k}$; thus, unlike PeerReview, we do not use $\varepsilon_i$ to uniformly represent the evidence set of node $i$ in other nodes.

*1) One Theorem*
In PeerReview [1], one *Theorem* states that: *Eventually, every detectably ignorant node is suspected forever by every correct node.*

Our analysis is stated as follows. If a node $j$ is detectably ignorant, then any other nodes that attempt to communicate with it will not receive ACK's from it. We assume that node $i$ has sent a message $m$ to node $j$ but there is no response, and then node $i$ will add the *chal (send, m)* challenge to $\varepsilon_{j,i}$, which will be forwarded to other correct nodes; however, due to message loss, some nodes do not receive the challenge and still trust node $j$. Moreover, if *chal (send, m)* is answered at a later time, the answer *resp* might be lost, causing some nodes to continue suspecting node $i$.

Our conclusions for the above theorem are stated as follows. 1) Due to the loss of challenges, every node that was detectably ignorant might still be trusted by some nodes. 2) Due to the loss of responses, every node that was suspected in some time might keep being suspected even if it answers all challenges related to it.

*2) Another Theorem*
In PeerReview [1], another *Theorem* states that: *No correct node is forever suspected by a correct node.*

Our analysis is stated as follows. If node $j$ is suspected by node $i$ at time $t_1$, then $\varepsilon_{j,i}$ must have contained some valid challenge $c$. We assume that node $j$ is actually correct, whenever it receives $c$ and that it will generate a valid response $r$ and send it back. Still, if $r$ is eventually lost, any node $k$ whose $\varepsilon_{j,k}$ includes $c$ will keep a pending status and node $j$ will continue to be suspected by these nodes.

Our conclusion for the above theorem is stated as follows. A correct node might be suspected by other correct nodes in the lifetime of the system.

*3) Another Theorem*

In PeerReview [1], another *Theorem* states that: *No correct node is ever exposed by a correct node.*

Our analysis is stated as follows. The case that a correct node $j$ is exposed by another node $i$ will happen in the audit process, causing node $i$ to generate a *proof* and add it to $\varepsilon_{j,i}$. The problem occurs in the transmission of log segments, as we mentioned before, when the loss of either the 'input' or 'output' message will trigger a mismatch. Thus, error $u_{j,i} | o_j = E | C$ is triggered.

Our conclusion for the above theorem is stated as follows. A correct node will potentially be exposed by some other nodes.

## 5   Evaluation

In this section, we present simulation results for both PeerReview and MLT-PR. The original PeerReview library ensures that a message will never eventually be lost. In our simulation, each message has a probability of being lost; also the number of retransmissions is limited. Our objective is twofold: 1) to determine how message loss would affect the degree of accountability; 2) to compare PeerReview and MLT-PR in terms of the degree of accountability. We defined two metrics to assess the system.

**Definition 1. Node Accountability** $A_i^*$: For a correct node $i \in V$, $A_i^*$ is defined as the ratio of the number of accurate indications and the number of all indications;

$$A_i^* = \frac{\#\text{Accurate Indications}}{\#\text{All Indications}} = \frac{|\{T \mid C\}| + |\{E \mid F\}| + |\{S \mid I\}|}{|V|} \tag{2}$$

**Definition 2. System accountability** $A^*(G)$: Given a PeerReview-enabled system G, the system accountability $A^*(G)$ is defined as the mean node accountability of all correct nodes, i.e.,

$$A^*(G) = \frac{\sum_{\forall i \in V} A_i^*}{|V_c|} \tag{3}$$

The parameters specified in the simulations are listed in Table 3. For each set of parameters, we obtained the average results based on 20 experimental trails.

**Table 1.** Simulation Parameters

| Parameter | Value |
|---|---|
| $p_0$ – E2E message loss probability | 0.0, 0.1, 0.2 up to 1.0 |
| $N$ – node # in total | [50, 100, 250, 500] |
| $\varphi$ - initial faulty nodes rate | [0.0, 0.05, 0.1, 0.2] |
| $w$ – witness size | [2, 4, 6, 8] |

Fig. 1 shows the percentage of each indication type when $p_0$ equals to 0.2 (left), 0.4 (middle), and 0.8(right). Each sector in the pie represents the ratio of an indication type. We plot six kinds of indications, i.e., accurate indications and 5 error types. Since error $E|I$ never happens, we did not plot it. Evidently, with $p_0$ going up from 0.2 to 0.8, the accurate indications decrease by 49.3%; meanwhile, the number of each error rises. Also, we observe that for the five errors, $E|C$, $T|F$, and $T|I$ rarely happen. $E|C$ is triggered if and only if messages are lost in Audit protocol, and thus a witness is unable to produce the expected output; usually, a node has more than one witness, and this will remain consistent among them; hence a temp $E|C$ could happen but it would probably go back to the right indication later. The reason for $T|F$ and $T|I$ is that evidence packets are lost in evidence transfer protocol. Additionally, $S|C$ and $S|F$ occur quite often since they are readily triggered once a message or its ACK is lost. Some of these two errors would be resolved due to the effect of challenge/response protocol, and the rest, however, would make the system less accountable.

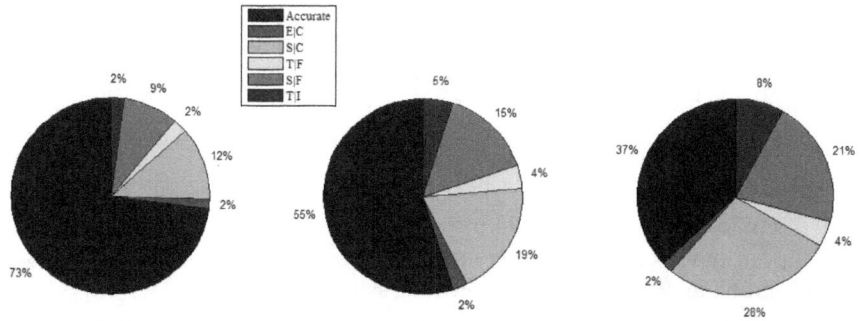

**Fig. 1.** Percentage of indication types when $p_0 = 0.2$ (left), 0.4 (middle), and 0.8(right)

Fig. 2 depicts how end-to-end (E2E) message loss affects system accountability. When message loss probability increases from 0 to 1, system accountability decreases. The witness size is regarded as a key parameter in our simulation, since one major function of witness is to decrease the eventual message loss probability. We compare two sets of experiment result, with $w = 2$ and $w = 6$. It turns out that when each node has more witnesses, the degree of system accountability will increase.

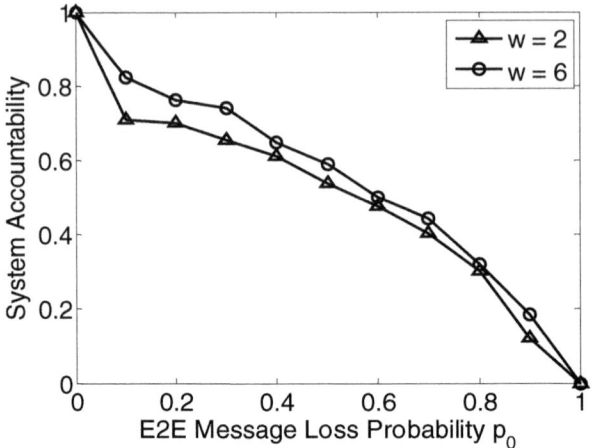

**Fig. 2.** E2E message loss probability and System Accountability

## 6  Conclusions

In this paper, we revisited PeerReview with the assumption that a message sent from the source might never arrive at its destination. The assumption implies that PeerReview is no longer error free. Also, two key properties, completeness and accuracy, that were supported by PeerReview are no longer valid.

We presented six kinds of errors and defined two metrics, node accountability and system accountability, to study the degree of system accountability in different granularities. We re-evaluated PeerReview through simulation; results showed message loss would decrease the performance of PeerReview in terms of the degree of system accountability.

Some example discoveries under eventual message loss are summarized as follows:

- The log is still tamper-evident; but it will probably cause errors $S \mid C$ and $E \mid C$.
- Difficulties occur for a node to provide a pair of authenticators as required. In the long run, node can seldom obtain full copies of authenticators for other nodes. This problem will spread to the network as time passing by.
- In the audit protocol, error $E \mid C$ occurs, and this prevents the witness from being trusted.
- The challenge/response protocol is ruined, incurring both $S \mid C$ and $E \mid C$.
- The expected effect of the evidence transfer protocol will fail; additionally, it is likely to bring inconsistency of judgment to the system. Nodes that do not receive expected evidence would still 'trust' those faulty or ignorant nodes and therefore trigger $T \mid F$ and $T \mid I$.
- Some of the theorems in PeerReview are not longer hold.
    - o  Due to the loss of challenges, every node that was detectably ignorant might still be trusted by some nodes.

    o   Due to the loss of responses, every node that was suspected at some time might keep being suspected even if it answers all challenges related to it.

    o   A correct node might be suspected by other correct nodes in the lifetime of the system.

    o   A correct node will potentially be exposed by some other nodes.

## Acknowledgment

This work was supported in part by the US National Science Foundation (NSF) under grants CNS-0716211, CNS-0737325, and CCF-0829827. In addition, the authors would like to thank the PeerReview research group to offer the software library.

## References

1. Haeberlen, A., Kouznetsov, P., Druschel, P.: PeerReview: Practical accountability for distributed systems. In: Proceedings of twenty-first ACM SIGOPS symposium on Operating systems principles, pp. 175–188. ACM, New York (2007)
2. Yumerefendi, A.R., Chase, J.S.: The role of accountability in dependable distributed systems. In: Proceedings of HotDep (2005)
3. Andersen, D., Balakrishnan, H., Feamster, N., Koponen, T., Moon, D., Shenker, S.: Holding the Internet accountable. In: ACM HotNets-VI (2007)
4. Andersen, D.G., Feamster, N., Koponen, T., Moon, D., Shenker, S.: Accountable internet protocol (AIP). In: Proceedings of the ACM SIGCOMM 2008 conference on Data communication, pp. 339–350. ACM, New York (2008)
5. Mirkovic, J., Reiher, P.: Building accountability into the future Internet. In: 4th Workshop on Secure Network Protocols, NPSec 2008, pp. 45–51 (2008)
6. http://peerreview.mpi-sws.org
7. Lamport, L., Shostak, R., Pease, M.: The Byzantine generals problem. ACM Transactions on Programming Languages and Systems (TOPLAS) 4, 382–401 (1982)
8. Paxson, V.: End-to-end Internet packet dynamics. SIGCOMM Comput. Commun. Rev. 27, 139–152 (1997)
9. Castro, M., Liskov, B.: Practical Byzantine fault tolerance and proactive recovery. ACM Trans. Comput. Syst. 20, 398–461 (2002)
10. Backes, M., Druschel, P., Haeberlen, A., Unruh, D.: CSAR: A practical and provable technique to make randomized systems accountable. In: Proceedings of the 16th Annual Network & Distributed System Security Symposium (NDSS 2009), San Diego, CA (February 2009)
11. Keller, E., Lee, R., Rexford, J.: Accountability in hosted virtual networks. In: Proc. ACM SIGCOMM Workshop on Virtualized Infrastructure Systems and Architectures (VISA) (August 2009)
12. Liu, W., Aggarwal, S., Duan, Z.: Incorporating accountability into internet email. In: Proceedings of the 2009 ACM symposium on Applied Computing, pp. 875–882 (2009)
13. Argyraki, K., Maniatis, P., Irzak, O., Ashish, S., Shenker, S., Epfl, L.: Loss and delay accountability for the Internet. In: IEEE International Conference on Network Protocols, ICNP 2007, pp. 194–205 (2007)
14. Yumerefendi, A.R., Chase, J.S.: Strong accountability for network storage. ACM Transactions on Storage 3 (2007)

15. Yumerefendi, A.R., Chase, J.S.: Trust but verify: accountability for network services. In: Proceedings of the 11th workshop on ACM SIGOPS European workshop, p. 37. ACM, Leuven (2004)
16. Re-ECN: Adding Accountability for Causing Congestion to TCP/IP, Bob Briscoe (BT & UCL), Arnaud Jacquet, Toby Moncaster and Alan Smith (BT), IETF Internet-Draft <draft-briscoe-tsvwg-re-ecn-tcp-07.txt> (March 2009)
17. Re-ECN: The Motivation for Adding Accountability for Causing Congestion to TCP/IP, Bob Briscoe (BT & UCL), Arnaud Jacquet, Toby Moncaster and Alan Smith (BT), IETF Internet-Draft <draft-briscoe-tsvwg-re-ecn-tcp-motivation-00.txt> (March 2009)
18. Madan, B.B., Goseva-Popstojanova, K., Vaidyanathan, K., Trivedi, K.S.: A method for modeling and quantifying the security attributes of intrusion tolerant systems. Performance Evaluation 56, 167–186 (2004)
19. Breu, R., Innerhofer-Oberperfler, F., Yautsiukhin, A.: Quantitative assessment of enterprise security system. In: Third International Conference on Availability, Reliability and Security, ARES 2008, pp. 921–928 (2008)
20. Sallhammar, K., Helvik, B., Knapskog, S.: A Game-Theoretic Approach to Stochastic Security and Dependability Evaluation. In: 2nd IEEE International Symposium on Dependable, Autonomic and Secure Computing, pp. 61–68 (2006)
21. Department of Defense. Trusted Computer System Evaluation Criteria. Technical Report 5200.28-STD, Department of Defense (1985)
22. Xiao, Y.: Flow-Net Methodology for Accountability in Wireless Networks. IEEE Network 23(5), 30–37 (2009)
23. Xiao, Y.: Accountability for Wireless LANs, Ad Hoc Networks, and Wireless Mesh Networks. IEEE Communication Magazine 46(4), 116–126 (2008)

# Tracing Potential School Shooters in the Digital Sphere

Jari Veijalainen, Alexander Semenov, and Jorma Kyppö

Univ. of Jyväskylä, Dept. of Computer Science and Information Systems,
P.O. Box 35 FIN-40014 Univ. of Jyväskylä
{Jari.Veijalainen,Alexander.Semenov,Jorma.kyppo}@jyu.fi

**Abstract.** There are over 300 known school shooting cases in the world and over ten known cases where the perpetrator(s) have been prohibited to perform the attack at the last moment or earlier. Interesting from our point of view is that in many cases the perpetrators have expressed their views in social media or on their web page well in advance, and often also left suicide messages in blogs and other forums before their attack, along the planned date and place. This has become more common towards the end of this decennium. In some cases this has made it possible to prevent the attack. In this paper we will look at the possibilities to find commonalities of the perpetrators, beyond the fact that they are all males from eleven to roughly 25 years old, and possibilities to follow their traces in the digital sphere in order to cut the dangerous development towards an attack. Should this not be possible, then an attack should be averted before it happens. We are especially interested in the multimedia data mining methods and social network mining and analysis that can be used to detect the possible perpetrators in time. We also present in this paper a probabilistic model that can be used to evaluate the success/failure rate of the detection of the possible perpetrators.

**Keywords:** School shootings, social media, multimedia data mining.

## 1 Introduction

Various educational institutions play an important role in the developed countries. Almost every individual spends at least nine years at school and majority of them continue their studies two to ten years more in vocational schools, high schools and universities. Thus, the time spent in these institutions has a big impact for the lives of the individuals both mentally and professionally. Success or failure at various stages in education can have a profound effect for the future of individuals.

Schools have existed several hundred years, but only since the 19th century they have become a mass institution that offers education for the entire population. There have been violent incidents at schools since the 19th century, but they were almost solely performed by adults. Since 1970'ies a new phenomenon can be observed; such attacks that are performed by the students that visit the educational institution at the time of the attack or have recently visited it. The target of the attack can be the institution itself, or the social order among peers. Often it is the goal to kill as many as

S.K. Bandyopadhyay et al. (Eds.): ISA 2010, CCIS 76, pp. 163–178, 2010.
© Springer-Verlag Berlin Heidelberg 2010

possible people randomly, but in some cases there can be also a list of people that should be at least killed. The attack has been in most cases performed by fire arms, although also explosive devices, Molotov cocktails, and knives and swords have been used alone or in combination with fire arms. This trend started in USA in the 1970'ies and has spread since then to Europe and to some extent to other countries, like Japan and Middle-East.

In this paper we first shortly review the history of attacks that have been performed against or at schools. After that we will present a mathematical model that predicts what the capture rate of the potential school shooters is during the planning phase or just before they are able to launch the attack. We then present an architecture for a system that is meant to crawl the "interesting" multimedia material in Internet and evaluate it from the perspective of the potential dangerous developments. Conclusions close the paper.

## 2 Historical Notes about School Shootings

The only global public source about school shootings seems to be Wikipedia [1, 2]. In USA there is an authority called National School Safety Center that collects statistics and publishes reports on the issues [5]. In Finland a working group has been set up in 2009 that has produced an intermediary report on school safety issues [7] and has published its final report in February 2010. In Germany, three incidents have happened during 2009 and the German experts have collected a list of 83 actions against such cases [8].

The Wikipedia page [1] reports 18 school shootings or other lethal incidences in or at elementary schools in various parts of the world before the year 1974 (since 18th century), where the perpetrators have been civilian adults, organized military forces or adult terrorists. The first incidence performed by a school kid is from January 17, 1974, when a 14-years old boy named Steven Guy shot the principal and wounded three others with a pistol and revolver at Clara W. Barton Elementary School in Chicago, USA. The reason seems to have been that it was decided that he would be transferred to a social adjustment center. The next similar case is from January 29, 1979, when 16 years old Brenda Ann Spencer killed 2 adults, and wounded eight children and one police officer. The reason for the shootings according to her "I don't like Mondays. This livens up the day". In addition to her, there are currently only two further known female perpetrators, one in USA and one in Germany (the latter from May 2009, see above).

The list of incidents is considerably longer for the secondary schools. The first incident of the current style seems to have happened in Vilnius on May 6, 1925, where two-three students have attacked the board of examiners and other students during final exam with revolvers and hand grenades killing 5-10 people including themselves. Since then there were some cases per each decennium, almost all reported from USA. The frequency of incidents begins to grow during 1960'ies, although during 1958-1966 there are no reported incidents but about six towards the end of the decennium. The first reported cases from Canada are from 1975. In both cases the perpetrators used guns and killed themselves after the shoot out. There are already ten cases during 1970'ies.

During 1980'ies the number of incidents begins to grow, reaching seventeen cases in total. The first incident reported from France is from the year 1984. The student killed his teacher and subsequently himself. The first incident from Finland is from the year 1989, when a 14-year old student killed two fellow students and tried to kill the third one. He used the pistol of his father. Most cases during 1980's are from USA. During 1990'ies the number of listed cases explodes to roughly 70. Most of the cases are from USA, but also two cases in Austria, one in Netherlands, one in UK, and one in Canada are recorded. In addition, there were a few military operations against schools in developing countries.

Since 1999 there have been almost 100 incidents at secondary schools. During the last ten years there have been almost ten incidents in Germany and several in Netherlands and in South-Africa and at least one in Brazil and Finland (in Jokela on Nov. 7, 2007). Perhaps the most known is Columbine High School  incident in Colorado, USA, performed by two students of the school, Eric Harris and Dylan Klebold on April 20, 1999. Although they also committed suicide after their rampage, they had left a lot of planning and other literary material, as well as video material behind. Since the release of the material to the public space by the police in 2006, several books have appeared on the case [3, 4]. On March 26, 2001 In Kenya, two students burned down a dormitory and 67 students were killed, 19 wounded. The reported reason for the arson was that the results of the exam were nullified by the university.  The pattern seems to be in most cases similar, as concerns the way of performing the attack. In North-America and Europe hand guns are mostly used as weapons. In some rare cases also inflammable liquids like gasoline or explosive devices are used. In Far-East knives have almost solely been used.

The list of incidents on university/college campuses also contains over hundred entries. The first is from the year 1908. The incidents are of private nature (grudge against a particular individual, love affairs within the college faculty etc.) until the case of Charles Whitman, 25, killed 14 people and wounded 32 in 1966,. After this the incidents perpetrated by students usually require one or at most few casualties, until Dec. 6, 1989 incident in Canada, Montreal. During this rampage Marc Lepine, 25, killed 15 and injured 14.  He also committed suicide.  During nineties the highest death toll in this category was six in 1991 In USA and six in 1997 in Russia.

The last ten years has meant increasing number of incidents in this category. Most of the cases required 1-3 victims. The worst case was the Virginia Tech massacre on April 16, 2007, performed by Seung-Hui Cho, 23. His shoot out left 33 dead and 25 injured. He also committed suicide. The next worst shoot out happened on April 30, 2009 in Baku, Azerbaijan, where Farda Gadirov, 29, shot 13 and injured 10 persons at the Azerbaijan State Oil Academy. He also committed suicide after his shootout. The third worst case has been the Kauhajoki shooting in Finland on September 23, 2008 performed by Matti Saari, 22, who also shot himself after the rampage. The trial against the police officer that had granted the gun license and did not confiscate the weapon of Saari on the previous day, Sept. 22nd, after an interview, has been started on Dec. 3, 2009 [14]. According to media reports the police officer was aware of the two videos that Saari had posted to YouTube where he was shooting with his gun on a shooting range.

There are about ten cases reported in [1] where the perpetrator or perpetrators have been discovered before they been able to launch the attack. Since 2006 all the cases are such that various Internet resources have played a role in foiling the case, because the perpetrators have left there clear enough signals for the planned attack.

## 3   Background of the Modeling and Related Work

Our basic view is that a baby is not predestined to become a school shooter. Rather, during the millions of interactions with the surrounding world his mental state, ideological and political views develop towards such a potential. Out of those with such a potential some individuals then begin to plan an attack and some of them really perform such an attack, before it is disclosed and prohibited. A school shooter goes through a particular mental process before he begins to plan an attack and finally performs it. During this process he very often engages in certain kind of behavioral patters that should be interpreted in a suitable way while assessing the violence potential.

This result was established in the US report [12] that was based on 37 incidents with 41 perpetrators during years 1974-2000 in USA. Ten detained perpetrators were also interviewed. The same idea is used in Germany [11,13]. According to the findings of [12] 1) school shootings are a special variant among the youth violence that is seldom characterized by excessive alcohol or drug consumption, bad school results, or breaking of common norms. 2) The perpetrators are often introvert and solitaire, 3) the perpetrators were often depressive and had even attempted suicide 4) many of the perpetrators had hinted about their plans in advance 5) just before the attack some negative things happened to the perpetrator or a stabilizing factor was lost from his life.

The German sample in [13] is rather small but covers all the school shooting cases in 1999-2006. In many ways the patterns are similar to those in USA. All the perpetrators came from stable family circumstances, six of them still lived at home. The families were middle class and no family problems were known in the neighborhood. All perpetrators except one had access to fire arms at home. Three had had incidents with police earlier and one was waiting for a trial. All had threatened to bring weapons to school and kill somebody.  In some cases the perpetrator had threatened to kill certain teacher or a peer. All seem to have narcissistic treats in their characters and low self-esteem. All had had recently problem in their life with school or a grandparent had just died (in two cases).

From our point of view interestingly, in all seven cases the perpetrators had leaked their intentions to attack to the environment. The last one in 2006 used Internet to do it, others communicated orally with their peers. The authors think, though, that Internet will gain fast more importance in this respect, i.e. leakage might happens more through Internet. This seems to be the case, but it would require more analysis to be more exact about this.

It has been observed in majority of the cases [15] that all school shooters have at least some kind of a plan before they start it. All phases take time, e.g. the detailed planning takes time. Finally, the school shooters often leave a message to the world before they perform the attack and they leak their plans openly or less openly. Nowadays this often happens in social media forums (YouTube, Twitter, private web pages, blogs, etc.). Thus, there is window of opportunity to capture the perpetrator or to protect the target before the perpetrator is able to launch the attack. But could the earlier signs emitted to the inter-subjective space be interpreted correctly?

In general, there is a lot of information about individuals in every society. Before a child is born, there is no information about him or her (well, perhaps in the dreams of the mother and father, though). After the pregnancy has been confirmed the parents and in many countries also authorities will create pieces of information about the unborn child.  After the birth information about the child further grows. In the technically developed states this information is often encoded into the digital sphere either by people themselves, other individuals or by authorities. But even in the most developed countries a large amount of information about individuals remains in the consciousness of the other people – and of the person him- or herself. A part of the information will exist in inter-subjective but analog form, on pieces of paper as text, drawings, as photographs, or entire books, etc. These kinds of pieces of information can be very valuable when somebody tries to estimate the potential of a person to attack a school, as the case in Columbine has been shown [3,4]. Unfortunately, the information about a student is often scattered around and nobody has a complete view on it [17, pp. 83-85]. This is partially deliberate and aims at protecting the privacy of the individuals, but partially this follows from the scattered nature of the control and support systems.

The overall situation concerning the information about an individual is depicted in Fig. 1. All digitally encoded public information is roughly information that can be accessed from a usual desktop everywhere in the world, if the user just knows how to search for it. This mostly contains pieces of information the person him- or herself has created and put into a blog, electronic discussion group or other social media platforms, or then somebody from the social of the person network has created and published it. The public digital information can also contain pieces of information collected and released by authorities, such as car ownership, taxation details, or school performance. Finally, some companies might publish some information about their customers. The widest set of digital information contains all the public and private records about a person, as well as information collected by the authorities (complete identity, driving and gun licenses, medical records, criminal record, drug incidents, domicile, etc.) and companies (customer profile, pseudonyms at a site, purchase history, credit card #, phone #, etc.). In Europe it is currently required by a directive [6] that the context information of every phone call, Internet (TCP/IP) connection, or SMS must be stored for 6 to 24 months into a database of an operator. The access to this information is naturally restricted only to authorities and only to cases where police suspects that the person is involved in criminal activities.

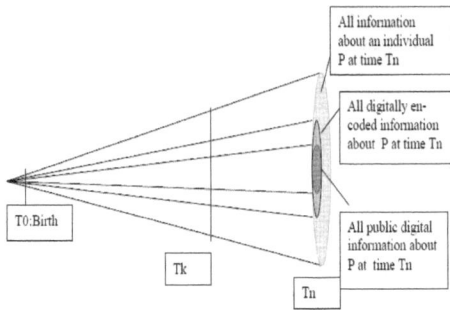

**Fig. 1.** Information about an individual over time

We apply the idea that any child goes through a certain development path while becoming an adult. In fact, there are extremely many possible paths. The totality of development paths is still given by the genes of the person. For instance, the maximum height of the person, his or her physical appearance, the potential to be brilliant or less brilliant in learning and using languages or mathematics is determined genetically. And trivially, only women have the potential to become a biological mother and men the biological father. (This potential does not, however, become real for about 19 % of the women in the contemporary USA, according to Wikipedia). During the millions of interactions with the outside world, especially with the social environment, certain potentially possible developments are chosen and others possibly prohibited. A very simple example is the question what languages can the person speak when he or she is 20 years old. If the school did not offer studies in Chinese and English is spoken at home, it is extremely improbable that the kid would understand Chinese when he or she becomes 20. On the other hand, if Chinese was offered at school then he or she might be rather fluent in speaking, writing and reading that language, instead of German or Spanish that he or she might have also learned. That is to say, he or she might have the genetic and mental potential to learn Chinese, but it requires certain conditions in the environment to be realized. Further, if one studies certain languages in the school, it is usually hard afterwards to enhance the language skills. This is because the ability learn new languages becomes worse with the growing age but more importantly, people do not have time any more to study when they have family and work. Thus, choosing certain languages at school prohibits certain others to be ever learned. In many countries with common liability to military service all males are taught to use weapons during the military training, but there is no reason why not almost every female would learn how to use them. Still in many countries this does not happen, because female persons are not given military training and for cultural and other reasons women are not allowed to learn these skills in civil life. Thus, majority of women in the world do not have shooting skills in practice.

Now the above said, are there people that would not become school shooters on any possible individual development path spanned by the genes, i.e. no matter how the life would treat him or her, the kid would not become a school shooter during his or her life. The answer is that with very high probability there are such kids, because we know that there are kids who were treated very badly, but did not organize a rampage. Further, female students hardly ever go on rampage. We can also pose the opposite question, are the people that will become school shooters no matter how their life would treat them? That would mean that they would be predestined by their genes to become school shooters. Here the answer is with extremely high probability no. This is because this way or reacting is given historically and different circumstances and external interventions can prohibit the development. The idea that it is question of development during childhood and adolescence has been elaborated e.g. in [15-18] and in many other sources. Newman's book [18] and [15] argue that these kinds of reactions are culturally determined, and it is the way the young (white) men in suburban and rural communities have begun to solve their problems with regard to social status – and psychological problems that are in some cases caused by the family and further social situation. According to [4] a part of the perpetrators are psychopaths (e.g. Eric Harris, Columbine), some are deeply traumatized (Mitchell Johnson, Arkansas massacre), and some are psychotic (e.g. Dylan Klebold, Columbine). Evidently, such people have gone to the schools also earlier, but they did not organize a massacre. The circumstances in the society have changed in order for this to become an option for individuals.

Now, the model would contain all possible developments the individual would have based on the genes. The concrete interactions with other people and physical environment then enable some of these and at the same time prohibit some of these. This is depicted in Fig. 2. A path in the tree models crucial possible development paths of an individual. The nodes model the crucial changes in external and internal circumstances of the individual. E.g. a divorce of the parents might be such an event, or relocation of the family – or beginning of a series of traumatic events, such as molestation or bullying. How many paths in this tree of possible developments are such that contain the possibility of school shooting? And if the development takes a certain course, does it stay on that course irrespective of the other influences from the environment. The larger the set of different circumstances that cannot misguide the development from the paths that lead to "normal life", the more resilient is the person against troubles in life. And vice versa, the less circumstances and paths lead to "normal life", the more there are risk potential for such an individual. At which phases of the individual development, and with what means, is it possible to keep the development on such paths that does not lead to these kinds of attacks - or any kind of violent attacks within the society? The problem is that – against a common belief – the "middle-class normality" in life would automatically lead to a development towards a "normal life".

How to determine, on which path the individual development is? If some external actor had all possible information about an individual, especially about his feelings and thoughts and the information the person is seeking in the digital sphere and elsewhere, this would be easy. This actor would know when the person started to feel bad, why is this so in his opinion, who and what he hates, when he starts to make plans for an attack, why, how, with whom. But in reality there is no such actor, although the person himself has of course the sufficient information in his consciousness. The path should be determined from the inter-subjective information emitted by a person to other people – or computer programs.

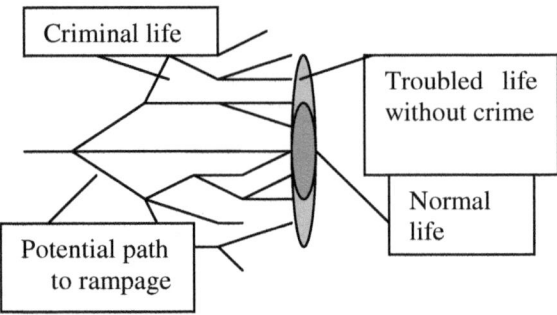

**Fig. 2.** Potential development paths of an individual

The latter can be used at least in two ways. The first is to design an expert system that is being used by the professionals. The expert system contains the typical characteristics of a path that might lead to a school shooting, especially towards the end of the path. These have been extracted from the past cases and general psychological and criminalist knowledge. The system poses questions that the user should answer concerning the case. The system responds with risk potential analysis. This approach is followed in Dyrias [9,10].

Another approach is to evaluate the public and possibly non-public digital information accessible in the digital sphere and try to find individuals that might be on a path leading to a rampage. This can be done automatically or semi-automatically. What is the information that should be sought? Where? In which relation is this information in the digital sphere to the information known by the peers and other people in the local social environment? Can we draw some conclusions about the path youngsters are on based on the public information? These are questions that we cannot answer at this stage of the research. Rather, we first design a general probabilistic model that should be able to measure the success and failure rates of discovering the dangerous development. It is the matter of further study to estimate the probabilities.

## 4   The Analytical Model

Based on the above considerations we can design a model that predicts how well it is possible to grasp the development of a person towards a school shooter. We will use a probabilistic approach. The main reason is that there is not a known set of sufficient conditions detectable in the person's life history that would predict with certainty an attack of this type. Also the set of five necessary conditions established e.g. in [18] can be challenged, at least as concerns the access to fire arms. The attack performed by Georg. R in Ansbach [19], Germany was performed without fire arms and several attacks in Far-East have happened with knives. As is known now [3], in the Columbine attack on April 20, 1999 the main weapons were explosive devices, the fire arms were just a backup. Still, in USA it is probably wise to keep the access to fire arms on the list of necessary conditions, because the culture is so gun oriented.

Another reason for using a probabilistic model is that it seems to be the only way try to measure the correctness of the reactions of the environment to various information. E.g. in the Kauhajoki shooting case the local police knew about the shooting videos in YouTube several days before the school shooting , but the decision of a senior police officer on Sept. 22nd, 2008 was that Saari (shooter) can keep his weapon, because the videos are harmless and because Saari seems to be "normal young man". He evidently [20] ignored the text in Saari's YouTube profile, next to the videos. It first speaks about forgotten war that returns, about dead children and how mothers screamed when war came and killed their children in fire, for revenge. It ends "... Whole life is war and whole life is pain; and you will fight alone in your personal war; War; This is war." Beneath are his hobbies: computers, guns, sex and beers. Movies he likes Saw1-3, and further horror movies. Can there be a clearer hint that the person is in a private war and that he will use his gun in it? Still, a study counselor at his school stated that it was impossible to detect any problems in his behavior [20]. This is one of the false negative cases whose probabilities should also be included into the model.

An essential assumption behind the model is that the more information the environment has about the person, his real thoughts and plans, the more probable it is that the correct interpretation of the path is possible. And vice versa. These are two independent events in our model. We model separately the phase of the individual's development until the point where he decides to perform an attack, and the development after that. We assume that it would be possible to redirect the person's development towards normal or at least in the first phase with a certain probability, assuming that the information about him is correctly interpreted. In the other phase he is already on a path leading to the rampage during which the attack is being planned and perhaps also other peers recruited into the plot or informed (cf. the German cases in [14]). In this phase the environment should try to interpret the possible signals correctly and prevent the attack. We distinguish between analog information and digital information in this respect, because the digital information can be mined later and automatic tools can perhaps be used to determine the path. Of course, the person's development can hardly be redirected by remote people, only by local community the person lives in. An attack plan can be disclosed by remote people, perhaps helped by software, but schools or other possible targets can only be protected by local people.

The set of people we primarily target in our model (person i) are the male's currently roughly 10 to 25 years old and having access to Internet. The "other people" that might take preventive actions or influence the development are potentially the entire mankind, but in practice a small group of mostly local people.

For each of those cases we define the following probabilities:

$P_i^{dana}$ = probability that a person i discloses information in an analog form (face-to-face, on a piece of paper, during a phone call) to other people that are relevant to determine that he is on a path that might lead to a rampage (up to a possible attack planning)

$P_i^{ddig}$ = probability that a person i discloses information in the digital sphere (social network sites, www pages, emails, text messages, chat rooms, etc) that are relevant to determine that he is on a path that might lead to a rampage (up to attack planning)

$P_i^{iana}$ = probability that another person j or group of people correctly interprets the analog information and determines the dangerous path the person i is on correctly

$P_i^{idig}$ = probability that another person or a group of them correctly interprets the digital information and determines the dangerous path person i is on correctly

$P_i^{iattack}$ = probability that the potential perpetrator i releases the attack plan including the schedule and perhaps suicide message before attack in an analog form to other people

$P_i^{dattack}$ = probability that the potential perpetrator i releases the attack plan including the schedule and possibly a suicide message before the attack in a digital form either on a social network site or similar or stores it into his computer.

[r,a] = time interval between the release of the attack plan information or exposure of the attack (e.g. weapons missing, perpetrator with weapon sighted) and the planned start of the attack.

$P_i^{avert}(t)$ = probability that police or other people in the community or outside it can avert the attack of i t seconds after they get the information that it is going to happen or is exposed

$P_i^{redirect}$ = probability that the potential perpetrator i is moved to a "normal path" in his life before attack by other people, after his being on the dangerous path has been identified by the local or remote community.

It is clear that the shorter the interval [r,a], the more difficult it is to prohibit the attack. It is also true that t < a-r must hold for averted cases. The probability to avert a planned attack is shown at (1).

$$P_{i,r,a}^{avert} = P_i^{avert}(t) \mid P_i(t < a - r) \qquad (1)$$

$P_{i,r,a}(t < a - r)$ = probability that the time between the exposure of deliberate disclosure of the plans and the planned start of the attack of perpetrator i is t seconds.

We also conjecture that if the person is moved from a possible development path that might lead to a rampage to a path leading only to "normal life", the probability of a rampage organized by this person becomes zero. Thus, rampage can only follow in the model, if redirection attempts did not take place at all or failed. In the model, the latter can only be attempted, if suitable signals emitted by person i were observable and were interpreted correctly. Thus, we get an overall measuring function (2).

$$P_i^{noharmtoothers} =$$
$$(P_i^{dana} \cdot (P_i^{iana} \mid P_i^{dana}) + P_i^{ddig} \cdot (P_i^{idig} \mid P_i^{ddig}) \cdot P_i^{redirect} + P_i^{redirect}) \times \qquad (2)$$
$$\times P_i^{iattack} \cdot (P_i^{avert} \mid P_i^{iattack} + P_i^{dattack} \cdot (P_i^{avert}(t) \mid P_i^{dattack}))$$

It is our goal to assess the above probabilities based on the existing cases. The function f is already loosely based on real cases. If the attack plan is published on a web site e.g. 5 minutes before the attack begins, there is no much chance the attack could be prevented by authorities. It is almost as probable as foiling the attack when the perpetrator tries to access the school and weapons are discovered at the gate or at the door.

The Kauhajoki case is an example of the false negative interpretation of the available information (see above). It seems that it was done in order to avoid false positive. Matti Saari was interpreted by the senior police officer to be on a normal enough path and he thought that he would just make the life of Saari more difficult, if he confiscated the weapon. Avoiding both false positives (3) and negatives (4) should be the goal. Our model must be slightly enhanced to capture these.

$P_i^{dnana}$ = probability that a person i discloses information in an analog form (face-to-face, on a piece of paper, during a phone call) to other people that are relevant to determine that he is on a normal path or at least not going to organize a school shooting

$P_i^{dndig}$ = probability that a person i discloses information in the digital sphere (social network sites, www pages, emails, text messages, chat rooms, etc) that are relevant to determine that he is on a normal path or at least not going to organize a school shooting

$P_i^{wnana}$ = probability that another person j or group of people wrongly interprets the analog information and concludes that person i is on a path leading perhaps to a rampage although he is not

$P_i^{wndig}$ = probability that another person or a group of them wrongly interprets the digital information about i and concludes that person i is on path leading perhaps to rampage although he is not

Now,

$$P_i^{false\ positive} = (P_i^{wnana} \mid P_i^{dnana}) + (P_i^{wndig} \mid P_i^{dndig}) \qquad (3)$$

$$P_i^{false\ negaitive} = P_i^{dana} \cdot \left(1 - P_i^{iana} \mid P_i^{dana}\right) + P_i^{ddig} \cdot \left(1 - P_i^{idig} \mid P_i^{ddig}\right) \qquad (4)$$

It is for further study, what is the exact relationship of the false negatives and false positives. Intuitively, the weaker the external signals of the potential problems in the development of an individual, the bigger the error towards false negative. But what kind of signals make the environment to err towards false positive? And what are the consequences for an individual in this case? Several cases have been lately reported in Finland, where the peers have revealed a student to police that has then taken him to custody and questioned him. It turned out that in one case this was a way of bullying the boy that did not quite fit into the class.

In order to assess the model and find ways of increasing the probabilities of detecting those who are on a path to become a school shooter or who have already determined to launch an attack, we must evidently look at old cases. What were the signals that should have been noticed? While going through the past school shooting cases, it would be tempting to collect as much information as possible concerning the perpetrators, including the medical history, social networks, relationships with opposite sex, social status of the family, complete history of the actions in the social media, etc. This is unfortunately impossible in most cases, especially for the cases lying back tens of years. Gathering even all the available information from the sources mentioned in [2] is as such a big task. Further, we are especially interested in foiled cases, because they make it possible to assess the probabilities with which the attack plans fail. Unfortunately, media coverage is not extensive in these cases, and following the development path of an individual backwards to a point where he turned towards a rampage is difficult due to a lack of available public information.

Many of the interesting pieces of information are such that we cannot capture them in the digital sphere at all or not without breach of privacy, but the more the people disclose information about themselves in the digital sphere the more we can find it and take action.

## 5   Technologies to Increase Detection Probabilities

The basic idea of using technology is to try to find the signals in the digital sphere that would help the environment to find out which path a young person is on. As it has turned out that the persons closest to the troubled individuals are not able to recognize the signs or interpret them correctly, and because latter sometimes leave clear information about their behavior into digital sphere, we will look into these signs. The first step would be implementing an ontology that captures relevant issues from the above studies.

We as researchers that can only use the public information have roughly four problems:

1) to compile an ontology that would capture the behavior patterns of possible perpetrators;
2) to filter out of hundreds of millions users at various social media sites those persons that might be on path to a rampage;
3) to evaluate closer the cases based on the information gathered;
4) to report towards the local communities if a person has announced targeted threats or a concrete attack plan.

At first it is necessary to compile the profile of potential perpetrator, including the keywords, video patterns and so on and make the set of the inference rules for the ontology system. Then, based on the ontology, system should capture the information from the most versatile web-sites for youth communication and add it to our storage.

The second problem is solved by a web crawler that accesses suitable sites and attempts to gather "interesting contents", i.e. such contents that contain signals about a person that might launch a rampage. The gathered multimedia content is stored in a database along the meta information that corresponds to the ontology above.

The social network information is also gathered and stored into a social network analyzer. The idea is to investigate, whether the people have connections to earlier perpetrators or to persons that had.

The third issue is basically solved by evaluating the multimedia material, such as videos, audio, text from blogs, etc. that is, multimedia data mining. For instance, finding shooting videos should be rather easy based on the sound of shots. Threatening contents is already a more complicated thing and requires further techniques. We will elaborate these issues below.

Below is presented a basic view on the architecture of the envisioned prototype system, without splitting it to different tiers.

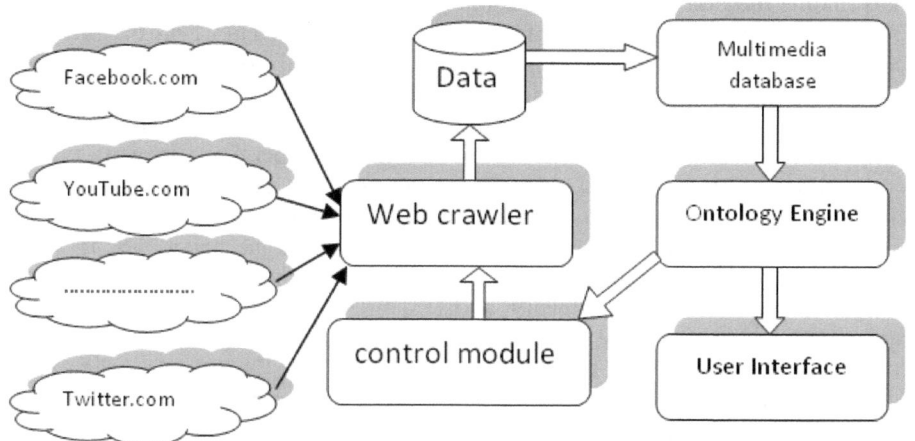

**Fig. 3.** Potential architecture of the detection and evaluation system

Information is going to be collected from the web with help of *web-crawler* that could fetch the data from public web-pages (like blogs) and protected areas (deep-web). For example, Facebook pages are closed to unregistered persons. Crawler should properly handle these situations. Crawler could be written using PHP or Python, also it is possible to use 3rd party software, like mnoGoSearch [21] or ASPSeek[22].

Fetched information should be stored into a multimedia database[23,26], in this case PostgreSQL will be used. Audio stream should be extracted from video and stored into a separate field of the table.

Data should be mined from multimedia database, using natural language processing, image and video data mining, speech recognition, mood and emotion detection (speech emotion detection, face emotion detection [24,31]), social network analysis (in case we have fetched social network to the database), face recognition techniques, authorship analysis. The latter can be used to find e.g. the texts of the same person at different online resources.

Rules for the data-mining and web-crawling should be contained in ontology referred to above. It can be described using suitable ontology languages (e.g. *OWL*). We can also consider using an expert system like CLIPS [25] for making set of the rules for describing and controlling the mining process.

After disclosing the information to another people in analog form it becomes possible that these people could disclose that information in digital form, for instance, in their blogs [27] (or at least their opinion about the intentions or advices to potential perpetrator). Natural language analysis, emotion detection and social network analysis could increase the probability of fetching such information. Authorship analysis could be useful, if the perpetrators or other people describe the event on some anonymous forums (or under pseudonyms). In the few cases that occurred during the last weeks we observed that people used the same pseudonym on different sites. That makes finding their traces in the digital sphere easy. Just use search engines.

After person has released the information about his intentions on the web it is becoming possible to analyze it using natural language analysis or emotion detection. Basically, it is possible to crawl some web-sites, containing video data (YouTube, Facebook, …), collect the videos into multimedia database, then use multimedia data mining for detecting harassment videos: containing shooting, screams, school shooting descriptions, bomb making process and so on, and analyze the commentators with the help of emotion detection and natural language processing. If a video commentator is positive about such contents, one could argue that P(ddig,i) >0 for that commentator. System should evaluate the contents by various means, comparing to the profile (offending video contents, texts, pictures contents analysis), using expert systems [25], natural language processing, authorship analysis (generating writeprint) [30], social network analysis, sentiment and affect analysis [28,29], image and video analysis [32,33], speech analysis. Finally, human expert should analyze the automatically mined information and change the rule-set of the system.

## 6   Conclusions

This article discusses basic issues in the rather new social phenomenon of school shootings. We first present a short history of the phenomenon and some recent foiled cases, where information in the web was crucial. We argue that it is possible to use ICT technologies to detect potential perpetrators, at least some of them, based on the traces they leave on various sites in Internet. We present in the paper a basic analysis and categorization of the information about individuals that can be used in general to detect certain behavioral patterns. We also present a mathematical model that can be used to evaluate the probability with which the possible perpetrator would be identified and his attack prohibited, if he advances to that point. The real values of the probabilities must be evaluated from the past cases and are for further study. Finally, we present prototype system architecture. The idea is that we will begin to search in the web such material, guided by an ontology, and evaluate it based on multimedia data mining techniques and social network analysis.

Further research requires a lot of work. One issue is to test the ontology against real cases, and modify it. Further, we will try to deduce upper bounds for the probabilities of finding the potential perpetrators by semiautomatic means and by local community actions. We will also investigate, what are the real values for the false positive and false negative cases.

# References

1. Wikipedia, School shooting,
   `http://en.wikipedia.org/w/`
   `index.php?title=School_shooting&oldid=350266831`
2. Wikipedia, listed attacks on schools,
   `http://en.wikipedia.org/w/index.php?title=`
   `List_of_school-related_attacks&oldid=350247039`
3. Cullen, D.: Columbine. Old Street Publishing Ltd., UK (2009)
4. Langman, P.: Why Kids Kill; Inside the minds of school shooters. Palgrave-MacMillan, USA/UK (2009)
5. National School Safety Center, `http://www.schoolsafety.us`
6. DIRECTIVE 2006/24/EC. Official Journal of the European Union, April 13 (2006),
   `http://eur-lex.europa.eu/LexUriServ/`
   `LexUriServ.do?Uri=CELEX:32006L0024:EN:HTML`
7. School safety working group in Finland, intermediary report (Oppilaitosten turvallisuustyöryhmä: väliraportti September 14 (2009),
   `http://www.intermin.fi/intermin/images.nsf/www/`
   `oppilaitosten_turvallisuus/$file/`
   `oppilaitosten_turvallisuustr_muisto_140909.pdf`
8. Spiegel online: 83 recommendations against school attacks (83 Empfehlungen gegen Amokläufe),
   `http://www.spiegel.de/schulspiegel/wissen/0,1518,652315,00.html`
9. Dyrias (Dynamisches Risiko Analyse System). Institut Psychologie und Bedrohungsmanagement (2009),
   `http://www.institut-psychologie-bedrohungsmanagement.de/`
   `index.php`
10. Lea, W.: School shootings: Software for early detection (Amoklauf; Software zur Früherkennung). Stern Magazine (March 15, 2009),
    `http://www.stern.de/wissen/mensch/`
    `amoklauf-software-zur-frueherkennung-657867.html`
11. Elstermann, H., Buchwald, P.: School shootings and severe violence in German schools – state of the art (Amokläufe und schwere Gewalt an deutschen Schulen –Stand der Dinge). Bergische Universität Wuppertal, Fachbereich für Bildungs- und Sozialwissenschaften, Study Report, `http://www.petra-buchwald.de/ExamensarbeitAmok.pdf`
12. Vossekuil, B., Fein, R., Reddy, M., Borum, R., Modzeleski, W.: The Final Report and Findings of the Safe School Initiative. U.S. Secret Service and Department of Education, Washington, DC
13. Robertz, F.J.: School Shootings. On the relevance of fantasy for teenagers that killed many (Über die Relevanz der Phantasie für die Begehung von Mehrfachtötungen durch Jugendliche). Verlag für Polizeiwissenschaft, Frankfurt am Main, Germany (2004)
14. Sanomat, H.: The trial against police officer who handled the gun license of the Kauhajoki shooter started (December 12, 2009) (in Finnish), `http://www.hs.fi/kotimaa/`
    `artikkeli/Kauhajoen+kouluampujan+aselupaa+koskevan+jutun+`
    `k%C3%A4sittely+alkoi/1135251191383`
15. Preti, A.: School Shooting as a Culturally Enforced Way of Expressing Suicidal Hostile Intentions. The Journal of the American Academy of Psychiatry and the Law 36(4), 544–550, `http://www.jaapl.org/cgi/content/abstract/36/4/544`

16. Lieberman, J.A.: School Shootings; what every parent and educator needs to know to protect our children. Kensington Publishing Corporation, NY (2008)
17. Bartol, C.R., Bartol, A.M.: Juvenile delinquency and antisocial behavior: A developmental perspective, 3rd edn. Pearson/Prentice Hall, New Jersey (2009)
18. Newman, K.: Rampage; The social roots school shootings; Why violence erupts in close-knit communities – and what can be done to stop it. Basic Books, NY (2005)
19. Welt, D.: A new turn in Ansbach, Die Wende von Ansbach (September 20, 2009),
    http://www.welt.de/die-welt/politik/article4573857/
    Die-Wende-von-Ansbach.html
20. Alueet, Y.: The trial concerning the Kauhajoki school shooting about to end tomorrow,
    http://yle.fi/alueet/teksti/pohjanmaa/2009/12/
    kauhajoen_koulusurmaoikeudenkaynti_loppusuoralla_1253891.html
21. MnoGoSearch, http://www.mnogosearch.org
22. AspSeek, http://www.aspseek.org
23. Donderler, M.E., Saykol, E., Arslan, U., Ulusoy, O., Gudukbay, U.: BilVideo: Design and Implementation of a Video Database Management System. Multimedia Tools and Applications 27(1), 79–104 (2005)
24. Maglogiannis, I., Vouyioukas, D., Aggelopoulos, C.: Face detection and recognition of natural human emotion using Markov random fields. Personal and Ubiquitous Computing 13(1), 95–101 (2009)
25. CLIPS: A Tool for Building Expert Systems,
    http://clipsrules.sourceforge.net
26. Kosch, H., Dollar, M.: Multimedia Database Systems: Where Are We Now?,
    http://www.itec.uni-klu.ac.at/~harald/MMDBoverview.pdf
27. Li, X., Yan, J., Fan, W., Liu, N., Yan, S., Chen, Z.: An online blog reading system by topic clustering and personalized ranking. ACM Transactions on Internet Technology (TOIT) 9(3), Article 9 (2009)
28. Dunker, P., Nowak, S., Begau, A., Lanz, C.: Content-based Mood Classification for Photos and Music: a generic multi-modal classification framework and evaluation approach. In: Proceeding of the 1st ACM international conference on Multimedia information retrieval, Vancouver, pp. 97–104. ACM, New York (2008)
29. Posner, J., Russell, J.A., Peterson, B.S.: The circumplex model of affect: an integrative approach to affective neuroscience, cognitive development, and psychopathology. Development and Psychopathology 17(3), 715–734 (2005)
30. Stamatatos, E.: A survey of modern authorship attribution methods. Journal of the American Society for Information Science and Technology 60(3), 538–556 (2009)
31. Zhao, W., Chellappa, R., Phillips, P.J., Rosenfeld, A.: Face recognition: A literature survey. ACM Computing Surveys (CSUR) 35(4), 399–458 (2003)
32. Chen, X., Zhang, C.: Interactive Mining and Semantic Retrieval of Videos. In: Proceedings of the 2007 International Workshop on Multimedia Data Mining (MDM/KDD 2007), in conjunction with the ACM SIGKDD International Conference on Knowledge Discovery & Data Mining, San Jose, CA, USA (2007)
33. Aiyuan, J., Roy, G.: A nearest neighbor approach to letter recognition. In: Proceedings of the 44th annual southeast regional conference, Melbourne, Florida, pp. 776–777 (2006)

# Infrastructure Aided Privacy Preserving-Authentication in VANETs

Brijesh Kumar Chaurasia[1], Shekhar Verma[2], and G. S. Tomar[3]

[1,2] Indian Institute of Information Technology, Allahabad, India
{bkchaurasia,sverma}@iiita.ac.in
[3] Malwa Institute of Technology and Management, Gwalior, India
gstomar@ieee.org

**Abstract.** The paper presents a privacy preserving authentication protocol for vehicles in a VANET. The authentication process involves authentication of the vehicle and the corresponding RSU by a fixed infrastructure (CTA). Every RSU has a public key infrastructure and continuously broadcasts public key. The vehicle encrypts its identity, RSU Id and timestamp using its symmetric key. The encrypted bits along with the pseudonym of vehicle and timestamp are again encrypted by the public key of RSU and send to the RSU. RSU forwards the encrypted part to the CTA. CTA sends its verification to the RSU. The verification of the vehicle is encrypted by the vehicle symmetric key and sends along with authentication of the vehicle to the RSU. The encrypted portion is forwarded to the vehicle which confirms the authentication of the RSU after decryption. The CTA also sends a temporary short certificate to the vehicle for vehicle to vehicle communication. The whole process needs only one request and reply between different entities. Simulation results indicate the time taken ($\sim 223\ ms$) for the whole process is small and constitutes only a small portion of the stay time of a vehicle within an RSU region.

**Keywords:** Mutual authentication, public-private key, VANETs, Vehicles, Road Side Units.

## 1 Introduction

VANETs is a network of vehicles are moving on the road exchanging information. The network membership is very volatile with members joining / leaving a neighborhood as they move on the road. Vehicles are equipped with an On Board Unit (OBU) that has an event data recorder (EDR), global positioning system (GPS), forward and backward radar, computing facility, and short range wireless interface [1]. A bandwidth of 75 MHz has been allocated in the 5.850-5.925 GHz band and vehicles use dedicated short range communications (DSRC) protocol for communication [2]. According to DSRC, each vehicle periodically broadcast information. DSRC classifies the five basic classes of applications; public safety application, traffic management, traveler information, freight/cargo transport, and transit. Messages class can be divided in two categories; safety and non-safety categories. The entails that (a vehicle) the source of message be authenticated

S.K. Bandyopadhyay et al. (Eds.): ISA 2010, CCIS 76, pp. 179–189, 2010.

beforehand joining the networks. Since message can cause / prevent life endangering situations, the variety of a message must be ascertained before an action is taken. In life threatening situations, the time for message authentication is almost negligible. Moreover, a malicious vehicle can broadcast with different identities. In vehicular network, DSRC [2], recommends the range of communication of vehicle is 500 meters and 1000 meters for road side infrastructure, a vehicle sends each message within 100-300 milliseconds time interval. However, if 50-200 vehicles present in the communication of road side infrastructure then network is high density network and in this case receiver vehicle will needs to verify near about 500-2000 messages per second. So main issue of authentication protocol is low communication overhead and fast verification.

At the time of authentication, identities of claimant vehicle must be hidden from a verifier vehicle and on the other hand, the authority should be able to trace the claimant vehicle or sender of a message by revealing its identity when required, such as liability investigation etc. So privacy must be preserve and privacy should be conditional.

Privacy preserving authentication can be achieved by using pseudonyms that are intimately linked to the original identity [1]. The pseudonym may be generated by the fixed infrastructure [3], [4] or by the vehicle itself [5]. They may be presorted [1] or downloaded from a trusted site periodically [6], [7]. During communication, the pseudonyms are switched periodically [8], or when required [9], in a crowd or a maximizing zone [10].For entity authentication public key infrastructure (PKI) [11], [12], [13] is deployed, where a large number of short-lived anonymous credentials is installed in the OBU. One of them is randomly selected used as the private key for digitally signing the messages. Verification is through the public key. However, detection of malicious sender is difficult. The CA has to exhaustively search a very large credential database to find the identity the compromised vehicle. Moreover, the security overhead is usually bigger than the useful message contents. Authentication can be done between two parties through exchange of certificates. This scheme [14] uses the short certificate based on temporary anonymous certified keys (TACKs) and uses group signature for tracing and revocation. A regional authority distributes certificates and certifies temporary key created by vehicles for authentication. Vehicles download CRLs certification revocation list to find for revoked entities [15]. Group based schemes [16], [17], [18], [19] provide anonymity as a receiver cannot distinguish a member from its group. Group based schemes achieve both privacy and authentication. However, group formation, maintenance, revocation need to be further studied [20]. To reduce the size of certificate revocation list and avoid the overheads of PKI, identity based with group signature scheme is proposed. The ID-based cryptosystem simplifies the certificate management process. The ID-based cryptosystem avoids certificate exchange and storage overheads of previous proposed schemes. However, their framework is limited by the strong dependence on the infrastructure for short lived pseudonym generation, which also renders the signaling overhead overwhelming. Timed efficient and Secure Vehicular Communication (TSVC) scheme [21] is also proposed for authentication. This scheme needs to perform symmetric MAC operation instead of any asymmetric operation at the verifier vehicle. Verification time is reduced but required tight time synchronization between vehicles. RAISE [22] is a RSU-aided scheme, responsible for verifying the authenticity of the messages sent from vehicles and for notifying the results back to vehicles. Where the message authentication code (MAC) can be used for inter vehicles authentication under the aid of a RSUs. The proposed scheme has less computation and communication overhead as compared to PKI-based and the group signature based schemes. However, this scheme is highly depend upon road side infrastructure, communication will be effected due network jammed because VANET is highly densely deployed and frequently disconnected network.

The rest of the paper is organized as follows. Section 2 describes the problem. In section 3, the architecture of VANETs is described. The protocol description is given in section 4. The scheme is evaluated through simulation and results are in section 5; section 6 concludes the work.

## 2   Problem Definition

A malicious vehicle can be an outsider or may be previously good vehicle. This malicious vehicle may inject false messages with different identities with dire consequences. This necessitates that messages and vehicles both are to be authenticated. Message authentication process needs to be repeated for each new message. Vehicle authentication should be done at the time of message sending to the verifier. At the time of communication, mutual authentication should be done for vehicle and RSU. This authentication must preserve the privacy of the vehicle. However, this privacy must be conditional. The true identity of a vehicle must be revealed if required by law. Finally, since the lifetime of a vehicle with an RSU is small, the authentication time should be almost negligible.

## 3   Architecture of VANETs

The architecture of a VANET is shown in Figure 1. It consists of national trusted authority $(TA)$, under this authority there are state level trusted authorities $(STA)$, city level trusted authorities $(CTA)$ are under in $STA$. In every $CTA$ there are many road side infrastructures $(RSUs)$ and there are vehicles moving on a road with an $RSU$, they lateral motion is very restricted and the motion is unidirectional except at the junctions. A vehicle moving in a particular direction can move at different speeds and also pause. Vehicles can take velocity as variable or profile based etc & these vehicles may overtake one another. Since the transmission range of any vehicle is more than the total width of the road, this lateral motion has no effect on communications and can therefore be neglected. An $OBU/RSU$ is equipped with private key / public key which will provided by it's adjacent higher authority like $TA$ distributes the keys and certificate to state level authorities. $STA$ will play the role of key distributors to $CTA$ and similarly $CTA$ distributes the key and short certificates to road side infrastructures and vehicles. Each vehicle has equipped with storage area named as Tamper Proof Devices (TPD) to store different keys and for prevention and detection of tampering. A vehicle store many pseudonyms along with public / private key and short certificate which will be received at the time of authentication by $CTA$ via the corresponding $RSU$. When vehicle will come within

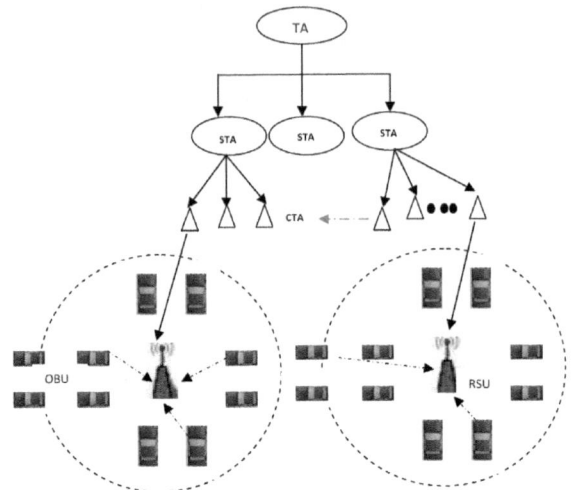

**Fig. 1.** Architecture of VANETs

**Table 1.** Notation used for this algorithm

| Notation | Description |
|---|---|
| $v_i$ | $i^{th}$ Vehicle |
| $TA$ | Trusted authority (National) |
| $STA$ | Trusted authority (State) |
| $RSU_i$ | $i^{th}$ Road Side Infrastructure / Unit |
| $CTA$ | Trusted authority (City) |
| $PK_e^+$ | The Public key of any entity in vehicular network. Entity can be a vehicles or $RSU_i$ etc. |
| $PK_{RSU_i}^+$ | The Public key of $i^{th}$ $RSU_i$ |
| $PK_v^+$ | The Private key of $i^{th}$ $v_i$ |
| $PK_{RSU_i}^-$ | The Private key of $i^{th}$ $RSU_i$ |
| $PK_v^-$ | The Private key of $i^{th}$ $v_i$ |
| $PE_{RSU_i}$ | A public-key encryption function using the $i^{th}$ $RSU_i$'s public key |
| $DE_{RSU_i}$ | A public-key decryption function using the $i^{th}$ $RSU_i$'s public key |
| $K_{CTA}$ | The securely pre-shared symmetric key with $CTA$ and vehicle |
| $ID_v$ | Unique identity of vehicle, issued by $CTA$ |
| $ID_{RSU}$ | Unique identity of $i^{th}$ road side infrastructure, issued by $CTA$ |
| $Sig_{CTA}$ | Signature of $CTA$ |

the transmission range of a *RSU* it receives its public identity. All vehicles have used pseudonyms to preserve the privacy for vehicle during the broadcast. City level trusted authority (*CTA*) plays the role as a key distributor. All vehicles register with *CTA* via any RSU or such as police station, government office, petrol pumps, and service stations etc. It is given one secret key for signing the messages, one shared secret key for communication between vehicles to city level trusted authority via *RSU*.The vehicle will receive a short certificate by *CTA* via any *RSU* during authentication process. This short certificate can be used to authenticate claimant vehicle to verifier entity of network when infrastructure is absent.

## 4  Protocol Description

The proposed authentication scheme is divided in four phases. The first three phases achieves the authentication with privacy using hashing and pseudonyms. Confidentiality is achieved by encryption of public identities and is in the fourth phase traceability and revocation is achieved by the simple cooperative scheme wherever infrastructure is absent or present. The proposed authentication scheme is as follows:

Phase I: Vehicle sends the request for association and authentication to *RSU*, Phase II: The *RSU* forwards vehicle's authentication request to *CTA*, and Phase III: *CTA* sends the authenticated short certificate to vehicle via $i^{th}$ $RSU_i$; Phase IV: Revocation.

**Phase I:**  $v \rightarrow RSU_i$
Vehicle sends the request for association and authentication to *RSU*.

*Step1.* At the time of vehicle enters in the communication range of *RSU*, it receives *RSU* $ID_{RSU}$ and $PK_{RSU_i}^+$ for sending authentication request.
*Step2:* Vehicle selects a pseudonym from its storage pool, and current time stamp $t_0$.
*Step3:* Computes a MAC value.

$$ps_0 = h(ID_v', t_0)$$

$t_0$ is the 4 byte field time stamp for freshness to prevent message by replay attack / Sybil attack.
*Step 4:*  Vehicle sends the authentication request to $i^{th}$ $RSU_i$ .

First, timestamp, vehicle identity and *RSU* identity are encrypted by the vehicle's shared key. Second, all values is again encrypted by public identity of *RSU*.

$$v_i \rightarrow RSU_i: PE_{ID_{RSU}}\{PE_{K_{CTA}}(ID_v, t_0, ID_{RSU_i}), ps_0, t_0\}$$

Encryption technique is used to provide confidentiality.

**Phase II:** *RSU* forwards vehicle's authentication request to *CTA*.
*Step 1:* $i^{th}$ $RSU_i$ decrypt received association and authentication request and store $ps_0$, for the time duration until the *CTA* does not send the response to the *RSU*.

*Step 2:* $i^{th}$ $RSU_i$ will forward the  encrypted   packet to $CTA$ .

$$RSU_i \rightarrow CTA : \{PE_{K_{CTA}}(ID_v, t_0, ID_{RSU_i})\}$$

**Phase III:** $CTA$ sends the authenticated short certificate to vehicle via $i^{th}$ $RSU_i$ .
*Step1:* $CTA$ decrypts the authentication request by its shared key and verifies the vehicle and $RSU_i$.
*Step2:* After completion of the authentication process of vehicle and $i^{th}$ $RSU_i$, $CTA$ will issue the short certificate with time to live $(t_1)$ time stamp to vehicle via $i^{th}$ $RSU_i$.

$$CTA \rightarrow RSU_i: PE_{ID_{RSU}}[PE_{K_{CTA}}(ID_{RSU}, cert[Sig_{CTA}, t_1], ID_v) \, ps_0]$$

$RSU_i$ will match the  MAC value obtained from $CTA$ from it's previously stored MAC valued if this is same then vehicle authenticates to $RSU_i$.

The certificate is valid for a time period determined by the approximate duration of stay of a typical vehicle in an $RSU$.
*Step3:* $i^{th}$ $RSU_i$ sends the authentication report to the vehicle. $RSU_i \rightarrow v$:

$$[PE_{K_{CTA}}(ID_{RSU}, cert[Sig_{CTA}, t_1], ID_v)]$$

Vehicle receives the authentication certificate and at the same time vehicle will authenticate the $RSU$.

**Phase IV:** Revocation
*Step 1:*   Vehicle found some conditions regarding $RSU$ that are such as:
(i) $RSU_i$ is malicious, (ii) $RSU_i$ is switched off, (iii) Large congestion in the network-$RSU_i$ is overloaded, hence delay occurred, and (iv) $CTA$ founds $RSU_i$ is malicious at the time of authentication process.

i. If any vehicle found the identity of  $i^{th}$ $RSU_i$ was not valid then vehicle can inform the $CTA$ connected by next $RSU_{i+1}$ or connected by next other trusted infrastructure. So that $CTA$ will verify the authenticity of that $RSU_i$. If finds $RSU_i$ is malicious then broadcast the alert messages about $RSU_i$.
ii. This condition is very rare in VANETs. If vehicle found $i^{th}$ $RSU_i$  is switched off then vehicle will report to next adjacent $RSU_{i+1}$. This will verify, if found true then broadcast the $i^{th}$ $RSU$ condition and to inform the $CTA$.
iii. In this condition vehicle will be send association & authentication request again and again and wait some more time for authentication, otherwise resend association & authentication request to the next  $RSU_{i+1}$. Vehicle will use the old certificate until didn't get new certificate.
iv. If $CTA$ founds that $RSU_i$ is malicious then it will send information to vehicle and inform the other network entities or broadcast alert messages regarding false identity of $RSU_i$  and also will take action to remove from the VANETs. $CTA$ will listed this malicious $RSU_i$ in revocation list, which stored in $CTA$. The revocation list can be seen at time to time by the connected from any type of infrastructure in VANETs such as next $RSU_{i+1}$, police station, government office , service stations and petrol pump etc. So this scheme is also able detect the false identity of network entities.

# 5   Simulation and Result Setup

## 5.1   Setup

In this section, simulation is conducted to verify the efficiency of the proposed secure protocol for inter vehicular communication applications with NCTUns [23]. For cryptographic delay we install MIRACL [24] and its library. So for these cryptographic delays we run a program that contains computational time of all standard hash function and encryption / decryption algorithms. The hardware/processor/clock of the system over which we install MIRACL is given in Figure 2.

| Intel  (R)  Core (TM)  @  Quad CPU |
| --- |
| 1.99  GB RAM |
| Q9300 @  2.50 GHz |

**Fig. 2.** CPU configuration over which we install MIRACL

We consider two types of different length of packets for authentication scheme. First when vehicle communicates to road side infrastructure then structure is as shown in figure 3a and when road side infrastructure responds to vehicle then structure is as shown in figure 3b. Lengths of packets are 108 bytes and 148 bytes respectably.

| Type ID | Message ID | Payload | Time Stamp |
| --- | --- | --- | --- |
| 2 byte | 2 byte | 100 byte | 4 byte |

**Fig. 3(a).** Packet structure from RSU to OBU

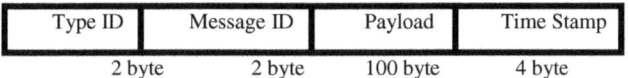

| Type ID | Message ID | Payload | Time Stamp | Signature |
| --- | --- | --- | --- | --- |
| 2 byte | 2 byte | 100 byte | 4 byte | 40 byte |

**Fig. 3(b).** Packet structure from OBU to RSU

In the simulation, speed of vehicle are $(10\text{-}30 \text{ ms}^{-1})$, while communication range of VANET is 250-300 meters. Vehicle stays within transmission range of the *RSU* for a very short duration of time (approx. 10-20 sec.). In the proposed scheme there will be two types of delays one is communication delay and another is computational delay. For communication delay we have simulated in NCTUNs because in VANET environment communication protocol 802.11(p) is used. We have simulated number of vehicles 10, 20, 40 in fixed transmission range (300 m).

## 5.2  Setup

Data packets are generated at a constant bit rate at *RSU* as well as on OBU. Figure 4a and figure 4b, shows the average and maximum delay when number of vehicles varies from 5-40. Speed of vehicles are assumed here 10- 30 ms$^{-1}$ and acceleration / deceleration = 3 ms$^{-2}$.

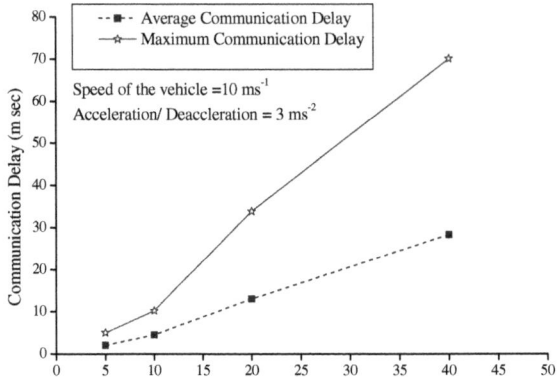

**Fig. 4(a).** Average and Maximum communication delay at speed of source vehicle 10ms$^{-1}$

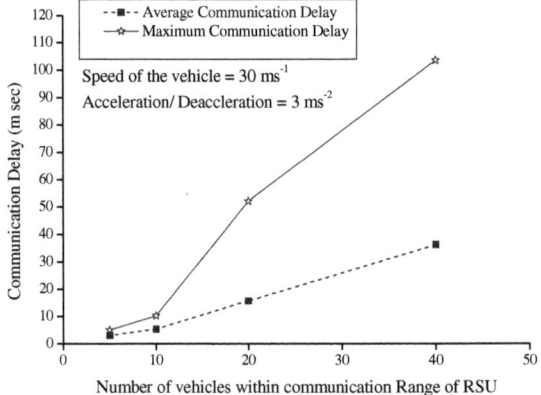

**Fig. 4(b).** Average and Maximum communication delay at speed of source vehicle 30ms$^{-1}$

## Computational delay

For calculating delay of the authentication phase we analyze each step of the phase. Here we start with first step.

i.   The delay when vehicle takes identity from *RSU*. $t_2$ is the time when vehicle send the request for authentication to *RSU* and *RSU* will send the public identity to vehicle $t_2 = t_0 + t_1$.

$t_0$ is the time when packet send by vehicle to *RSU* is 0.4081 ms.

$t_1$ is the communication delay of received packet from *RSU* when vehicles (around 40) are within the communication range of the *RSU*. Time $t_1$ is the maximum communication delay around 70ms and (~104) ms when vehicles having acceleration / deceleration of 3 ms$^{-2}$ and speed of 10 ms$^{-1}$ and 30 ms$^{-1}$ respectively.

ii.  $t_3$ is the delay when vehicle compute the hash function and encrypt the packet. Average delay of hash function (SHA-1) after multiple simulations is (~0.88) ms and similarly encryption or decryption delay $t_4$ is (~1.66) ms.

The delay of hash and encryption of the packet is $t_5 = t_3 + t_4$ .

iii. Signing delay of the *CTA* is $t_6$ = (~1.33) ms.   Verification delay $t_7$ is dependent on the computational delay of accessing the identity of claimant from its database and decryption delay $t_4$ .

Delay when *RSU* send the authentication request to *CTA* and *CTA* send the response to *RSU* along with the computational delay which is taken as 10 ms maximum.

Total time taken in authentication process is $T = t_2 + t_5 + t_7$.

Total maximum delay for authentication is $T$ shown in figure 5. In figure 5a and figure 5b shown total maximum and average delay of the authentication process when number of vehicles varies 10 to 40 and speeds of vehicle is 10 ms$^{-1}$ , and 30 ms$^{-1}$ respectively with  acceleration / deceleration taken as 3 ms$^{-2}$.

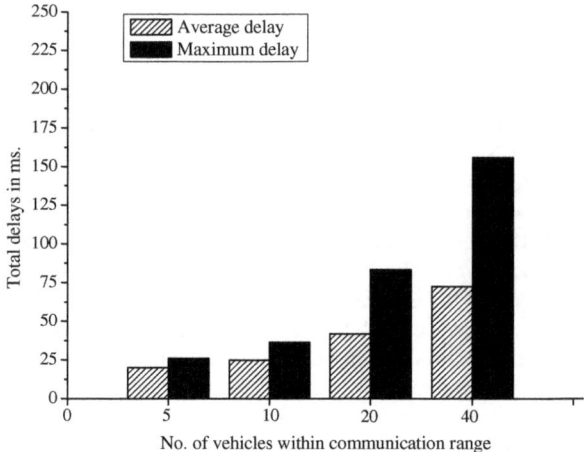

**Fig. 5(a).** Average and maximum delay at speed of source vehicle 10ms$^{-1}$

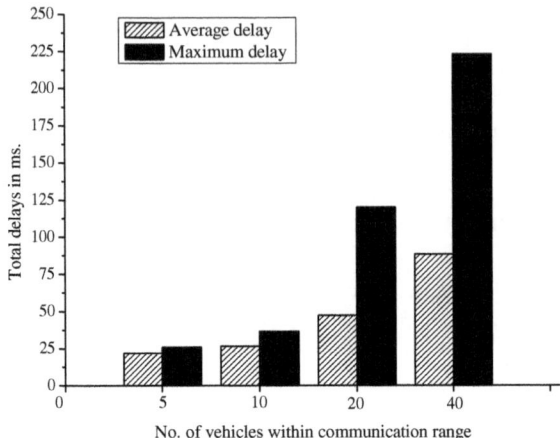

**Fig. 5(b).** Average and maximum delay at speed of source vehicle 30ms$^{-1}$

# 6 Conclusion

In this paper, we provide a solution for privacy and mutual authentication process. We use the pseudonym based scheme for privacy preservation and mutual authentication. The *RSU* was used as a mediator for authentication for both the *RSU*, itself, and requesting vehicle. Since the *CTA* is responsible for checking the credentials, the work of the *RSU* is drastically reduced. However, this requires all the *RSU* to be in continuous communication with a city level trusted authority, which may constitute a large overhead. This also solved the problem of malicious *RSU* along with the number of message exchange between different entities.

# References

1. Dotzer, F.: Privacy Issues in Vehicular Ad Hoc Networks. In: Danezis, G., Martin, D. (eds.) PET 2005. LNCS, vol. 3856, pp. 197–209. Springer, Heidelberg (2005)
2. Dedicated Short Range Communications (DSRC), http://www.leearmstrong.com/Dsrc/DSRCHomeset.htm
3. Papadimitratos, P., Buttyan, L., Hubaux, J.-P., Kargl, F., Kung, A., Raya, M.: Architecture for Secure and Private Vehicular Communications. In: International Conference on ITS Telecommunications (ITST 2007), Sophia Antipolis, France, pp. 1–6 (2007)
4. Gerlach, M., Guttler, F.: Privacy in VANETs using Changing Pseudonyms - Ideal and Real (Poster Presentation). In: Proceedings of 65th Vehicular Technology Conference VTC 2007-Spring, Dublin, Ireland, pp. 2521–2525 (2007)
5. Armknecht, F., Festag, A., Westhoff, D., Zang, K.: Cross-layer privacy enhancement and non-repudiation in vehicular communication. In: Proceedings of the 4th Workshop on Mobile Ad-Hoc Networks, WMAN 2007 (March 2007)
6. Raya, M., Hubaux, J.-P.: The Security of VANETs. In: VANET 2005, Cologne, Germany, pp. 93–94 (2005)

7. Ma, Z., Kargl, F., Weber, M.: Pseudonym-On-Demand: A New Pseudonym Refill Strategy for Vehicular Communications. In: Proc. IEEE 68th Vehicular Technology Conference, pp. 1–5 (2008)
8. Gruteser, M., Grunwald, D.: Enhancing location privacy in wireless LAN through disposable interface identifiers: a quantitative analysis. In: The Proceedings of ACM WMASH, pp. 46–55 (2003) (paper presented)
9. Chaurasia, B.-K., Verma, S., Tomar, G.-S., Abraham, A.: Optimizing Pseudonym Updation in Vehicular Ad-hoc Networks. In: Gavrilova, M.L., Tan, C.J.K., Moreno, E.D. (eds.) Transactions on Computational Science IV. LNCS, vol. 5430, pp. 136–148. Springer, Heidelberg (2009)
10. Chaurasia, B.-K., Verma, S.: Maximising Anonymity of a Vehicle. International Journal of Autonomous and Adaptive Communications Systems (IJAACS) 3(2), 198–216 (2010), Special Issue on: Security, Trust, and Privacy in DTN and Vehicular Communications
11. Raya, M., Hubaux, J.-P.: Securing Vehicular Ad Hoc Networks. Journal of Computer Security 15(1), 39–68 (2007), Special Issue on Security, Ad Hoc and Sensor Networks
12. Hubaux, J.-P., Capkun, S., Luo, J.: The security and privacy of smart vehicles. IEEE Security & Privacy magazine 2(3), 49–55 (2004)
13. Raya, M., Hubaux, J.-P.: The security of vehicular ad hoc networks. In: Proceedings of the ACM Workshop on Security of Ad Hoc and Sensor Networks (SASN), pp. 11–21 (2005)
14. Studer, A., Shi, E., Bai, F., Perrig, A.: TACKing Together Efficient Authentication, Revocation, and Privacy in VANETs. In: IEEE SECON 2009, Rom, Italy, pp. 1–9 (2009)
15. Golle, P., Greene, D., Staddon, J.: Detecting and correcting malicious data in VANETs. In: Proceedings of VANET 2004, pp. 29–37 (2004)
16. Sampigethaya, K., Li, M., Huang, L., Poovendran, R.: AMOEBA: Robust Location Privacy Scheme for VANET. IEEE JSAC 25(8), 1569–1589 (2007)
17. Guo, J., Baugh, J.-P., Wang, S.: A Group Signature Based Secure and Privacy- Preserving Vehicular Communication Framework. In: Proc. of the Mobile Networking for Vehicular Environment (MOVE) workshop in conjunction with IEEE INFOCOM, pp. 103–108 (2007)
18. Calandriello, G., Papadimitratos, P., Lioy, A., Hubaux, J.-P.: Efficient and robust pseudonymous authentication in VANET. In: Proceedings of the Workshop on Vehicular Ad Hoc Networks (2007)
19. Lu, R., Lin, X., Zhu, H., Ho, P.-H., Shen, X.: ECPP: Efficient conditional privacy preservation protocol for secure vehicular communications. In: Proceedings of the workshop INFOCOM (2008)
20. Verma, M., Huang, D.: SeGCom: Secure Group Communication in VANETs. In: 6th IEEE Consumer Communications and Networking Conference (CCNC 2009), pp. 1–5 (2009)
21. Lin, X., Sun, X., Wang, X., Zhang, C., Ho, P.-H., Shen, X.: TSVC: Timed Efficient and Secure Vehicular Communications with Privacy Preserving. IEEE Trans. on Wireless Communications 7(12), 4987–4998 (2009)
22. Zhang, C., Lin, X., Lu, R., Ho, P.-H.: RAISE: an efficient rsu-aided message authentication scheme in vehicular communication networks. In: Proc. IEEE ICC 2008, Beijing, China (2008)
23. http://nsl.csie.nctu.edu.tw/nctuns.html
24. Shamus Software Ltd. MIRACL, Multiprecision Integer and Rational Arithmetic C/C++ Library, http://indigo.ie/~mscott

# Attacks on Bluetooth Security Architecture and Its Countermeasures

Mian Muhammad Waseem Iqbal, Firdous Kausar, and Muhammad Arif Wahla

Information Security Department
College of Telecommunication Engineering (MCS),
NUST, Rawalpindi, Pakistan
waseem_iqbal@hotmail.com, {firdous.imam,arif.wahla}@gmail.com

**Abstract.** WPANs compliment the traditional IEEE 802.11 wireless networks by facilitating the clients with flexibility in network topologies, higher mobility and relaxed configuration/hardware requirements. Bluetooth, a WPAN technology, is an open standard for short-range radio frequency (RF) communication. However, it is also susceptible to typical security threats found in wireless LANs. This paper discuses some of the attack scenarios against the bluetooth network such as hostile intrusion, active Man-in-the-Middle (MITM) attack using unit key and various forms of denial of service (DoS) attacks. These threats and attacks compromise the confidentiality and availability of bluetooth data and services. This paper proposes an improved security architecture for bluetooth device which provides protection against the above mentioned attacks.

## 1   Introduction

Bluetooth an ad hoc wireless networks technology is planned to dynamically connect remote devices such as cell phones, laptops and PDAs [2]. WLANs employ permanent network infrastructure where as random network configuration is adopted in Ad hoc networks. The device communication in bluetooth technology is facilated by master-slave system connected by wireless links. The master in piconet is responsible to control both: the changes in bluetooth network topologies and the data flow among the devices having direct link to each other [1].

Bluetooth ad hoc scheme of untethered communication makes it very striking nowadays, that can outcome in increased efficiency and reduced costs. Added efficiency and cost reduction is striking for both home and business enterprise users, that is why more and more people are getting use to bluetooth technology. However bluetooth technology is subject to common attacks existing in wireless LANs. For example the hostile intrusion in piconet, MITM attack using unit key [1] is another vital attack. Similarly different kinds of denial of service attacks are also carried out.

In 2008, Suri-Rani [8] identified the vulnerability that there is no protection mechanism in piconet to detect an intruder and proposed a solution to include piconet specific information in calculating SRES, which make the attacker unable

S.K. Bandyopadhyay et al. (Eds.): ISA 2010, CCIS 76, pp. 190–197, 2010.

to guess or obtain the common secret. Jersin-Wheeler [6] identified denial-of-service attack on Bluetooth and suggested some possible fixes for this attack. In 2008, Kennedy-Hunt [7] claimed that key agreement protocol based on Diffie-Hellman key agreement can prove fatal for the countermeasure of MITM attack on bluetooth. Recently in 2009, Xin et al. [9] proposed a group key agreement scheme for bluetooth piconet, which is based on Diffie-Hellman key agreement for node authentication within piconet.

This paper proposes a security architecture which eliminates above mentioned threats and attacks. Remaining of this paper is organized as follows: Section 2 of this paper covers the existing system, link key generation and authentication procedure respectively. Section 3 highlights the existing problems in current protocol/system. Section 4 cover the solution to the identified problems and section 5 presents the security analysis of our proposed security architecture. At last section 6 ends up with conclusion.

## 2   Existing Bluetooth Security Architecture

### 2.1   Link Key Generation-Bluetooth Bonding

During intialization phase, when association or bonding between two bluetooth devices is carried out, a link key is generated. Two associated or bonded devices concurrently derive link keys during initialization phase, when identical PINs are entered into both devices by the user [1]. Figure 1 depicts the PIN entry, device association and key derivation. Unit keys are used by devices when they use the same key to connect to every device. Combination keys are used for pair wise connections and Master key is used by the piconet master to broadcast it to its slaves.

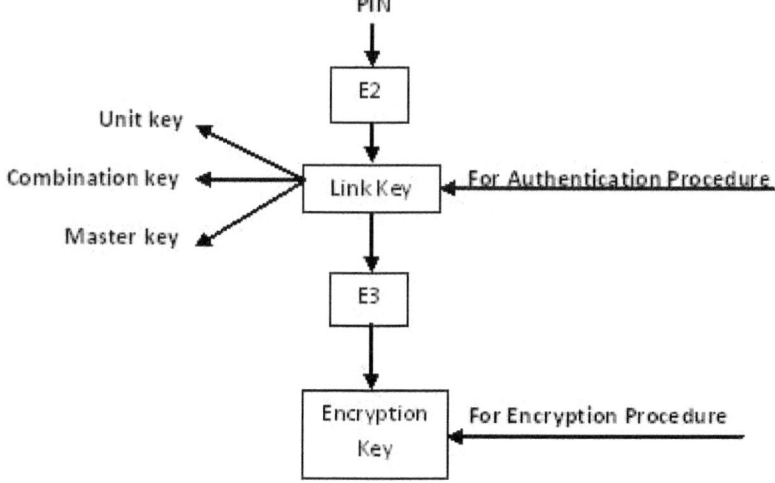

**Fig. 1.** Bluetooth link Key Generation from PIN

## 2.2   Authentication Procedure

The Bluetooth authentication process is in the form of "challenge-response" scheme. Claimant and Verifier are the two entities taking part in authentication process. Verifier validates the identity of another device whilst claimant attempts to prove its identity. The challenge-response scheme verifies devices by the acquaintance of a secret key-a bluetooth link key. Verifier decides to allow or deny the connection [5]. The challenge-response scheme is shown in the following Figure 2.

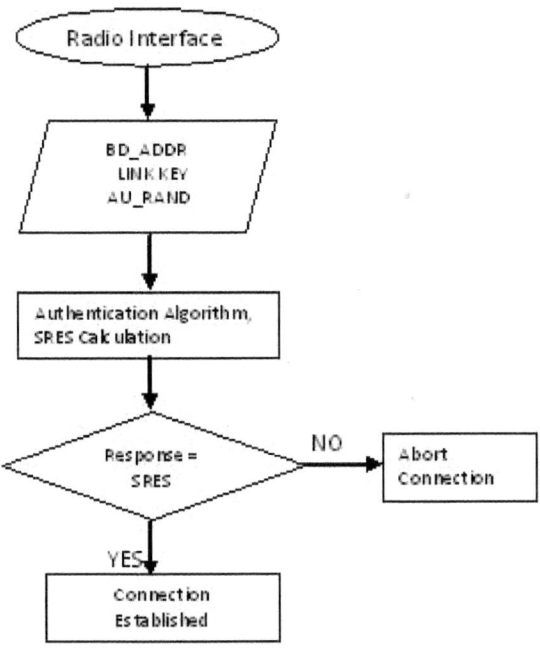

**Fig. 2.** Bluetooth Authentication

As shown, one of the Bluetooth devices (the claimant) attempts to reach and connect to the other (the verifier). The steps involved in authentication process are following:

- **Step 1.** The claimant transmits its 48-bit address (BD-ADDR) to the verifier.
- **Step 2.** The verifier transmits a 128-bit random challenge (AU-RAND) to the claimant.
- **Step 3.** The verifier uses the E1 algorithm to compute an authentication response using the address, link key and random challenge as input. The claimant performs the same operation.
- **Step 4.** The claimant returns the computed response (SRES) to the verifier.

- **Step 5.** The verifier compares the SRES from the claimant with the SRES that is computes.
- **Step 6.** If the two 32-bit SRES values are equal, the verifier will continue connection establishment.

Important to note here is that bluetooth MAC address is distinctive to each device and is a public entity. During device inquiry process it can easily be incurred. Link key is a secret entity. The pseudorandom challenge is anticipated to be different on each transaction. Pseudo-random process within the bluetooth device, derives the random number.

## 3   Weaknesses of Existing Security Architecture

Bluetooth attacks are at present more commonly associated with mobile telephony devices; however they are evenly applicable to other devices used in WPAN environment like PDAs, LAPTOPs etc. Following are the problems in the current bluetooth security architecture:

- The first problem which is found in current protocol is DoS attack as there is no check on the number of attempts of authentication request.
- The second problem is the current authentication scheme that has no protection mechanism to detect intruder in piconet. An intruder can be there as bogus device in many roles. The bogus device can be a fake slave or a fake master. It could also be an active or passive intruder [3].
- The third problem is active MITM attack using unit key. In this attack, (device C) which acts as MITM, incurs the security encryption key to monitor traffic between a network device (device A) and another network device (device B). Each device is bonded using same key, when unit key is used for association in initialization phase. When device A individually shares the unit key with two other devices, that is, device B and device C, the attacker requires such scenario to carry out this attack. For example, two devices, device A and device B are sharing some proprietary information with each other. This device B is a trusted device for device A. At the same time device A associates with another untrusted device, device C to share its personal contacts in A's PDA address book. During contact with device A, device C gets the unit key and by virtue of this unit key and a fake address, device C can scrutinize the flow of proprietary data between device A and B. This attack can be carried out by any learned malicious user who can impersonate a bluetooth address and has access to the unit key to generate the encryption key. Such attack uses prior knowledge of MAC address of the targeted Bluetooth device [1]. The biggest jeopardy in such attack is that the users of both the devices, device A and device B, never comprehend that their proprietary data is being compromised.
- The fourth problem is that there is no protection mechanism to stop a DoS attack in piconet. Once a device is authenticated, this legitimate device can carry out a DoS attack by flooding the master device with fake authentication requests.

# 4   Proposed Security Architecture

In this section, we will discuss the new link key generation and authentication scheme which will prevail over the attacks mentioned in section 4. MITM attack using link keys can be countered through the following new link key generation scheme as shown in Figure 3.

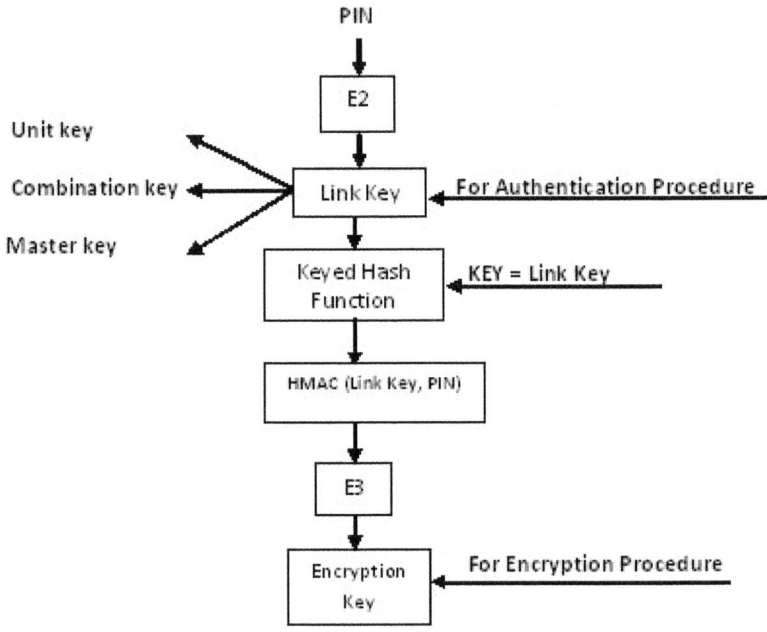

**Fig. 3.** Improved Link Key Generation

As MITM attack only requires the knowledge of unit key once the devices are associated. So in the proposed scheme every two devices which are connected through unit key will have to enter the PIN, assuming that it is securely transmitted to both the devices, into a keyed hash algorithm. The key would only be known to the specific two connecting devices which in our case is the link key. Now keyed hash of the link key and PIN would be entered in E3 algorithm to derive the encryption key. Since the PIN would only be known to the two connecting devices so the fake or untrusted devices would not be able to generate the encryption key of the other two connecting devices. In this way MITM attack can be countered.

Now to undertake DoS attack we have come up with a new authentication scheme which includes the concept of anti clogging cookies [4]. In the first message, the claimant generates and sends a Nonce-C, such that (verifier, Nounce-C) is unique with respect to claimant. Nonce's are usually generated from some local secret, some unique information about the claimant/verifier and may contain other local state information. Nounce-C = (Local Secret‖MAC-ADDRv). The verifier generates a request for confirmation i.e. (Nounce-C, Nounce-V) and sends it to the claimant. Nounce-V, which is AU_RAND = F (CAC ‖PAV ‖Nounce-C ‖ + MAC-ADDRc). Nounce-V must have the two properties:

1. The mapping from (claimant, Nonce-C) to Nounce-V is one-to-one with respect to the verifier. This implies verifier always generate same Nounce-V from same (claimant, Nounce-C).
2. Only the verifier can generate Nounce-V. This property is achieved by using some local secret in generating Nounce-V.

These properties eliminate the need for the verifier to remember Nounce-C or Nounce-V; therefore the verifier does not maintain any state information on the first and second message.

In the third message, the claimant sends (Nounce-C, Nounce-V = AU_RAND), along with BD_ADDR as the requested confirmation. The verifier computes a new Nounce-V from (claimant, Nounce-C) and checks weather the new Nounce-V matches the one in third message. If it matches then the verifier can have some absurdity that it is the supposed claimant and not an attacker, and if it does not match it simply drops the message.

Now we come to the intruder protection in piconet. We propose to use some piconet specific information in SRES calculation [8]. It could be any piconet specific information. We have proposed to generate AU_RAND as a function output. This function F is taking as parameter the concatenated value of the following: Channel Access Code (CAC), Part of MAC Address Value (PAV), Nounce-C and MAC Address of claimant. Then this value of AU_RAND is used in SRES calculation.

Now the logic behind concatenating simple AU_RAND value with CAC, PAV and Nounce-C is that in real two different devices from two different piconets will have different CAC and PAV, and if the attacker tries to gain access to the trusted piconet the messages mixes up. Improved authentication scheme is depicted in Figure 4. Original bluetooth authentication is based on challenge/response scheme with the transfer of four messages between claimant and

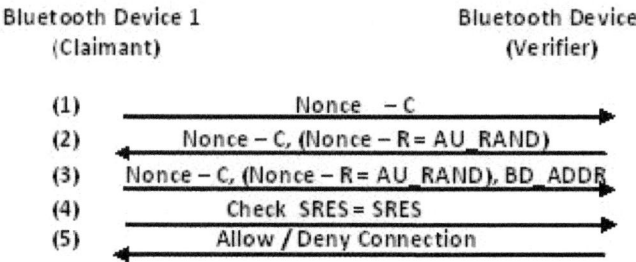

**Fig. 4.** Improved Authentication Scheme

verifier, while our proposed scheme involves five messages. With an added message our proposed scheme reduces the impact of DoS attack to much extent along with intruder detection in piconet.

Now coming to the DoS attack in piconet, once the device is authenticated, the master device should set a flag on behalf of the connected device. The master device should set the flag to "1" from "0" against the connected MAC address. Now if an authentication request from the same MAC address is received, the master device assumes the request is from an attacker and drops the connection.

In the end following points are given for the consideration of every bluetooth user as bluetooth devices are more often handled by users who are less security conscious than administrators.

1. PIN code should be long.
2. One should not use the default PINS [2].
3. Bluetooth pairing should be done in secure environment, avoiding public places [1].
4. Bluetooth application should be turned to non-discoverable mode after usage in unknown areas.
5. Agencies implementing bluetooth technology in their environment should maintain security policy regarding the use of bluetooth enabled devices and users responsibility.

## 5   Analysis

In this proposed bluetooth security architecture we have addressed MITM attack, hostile intruder detection in piconet and DoS attack in different forms on current security architecture. These threats and attacks compromise the confidentiality and availability of bluetooth data and services.

Proposed scheme overcome MITM attack efficiently as the attack requires the knowledge of unit key and a fake address, once the devices are associated. In this scheme, to get the encryption key, every two devices which are connected through unit key will have to enter the PIN, into a keyed hash algorithm. The key would only be known to the specific two connecting devices which in our case is the link key. Now keyed hash of the link key and PIN would be entered in E3 algorithm to derive the encryption key. Since the PIN would only be known to the two connecting devices so the fake or untrusted devices would not be able to generate the encryption key of the other two connecting devices.

By introducing anti clogging cookies concept in our scheme, the main objective was to minimize the impact of DoS attack. The objective of DoS attack in this case is to consume the computing resources. The goal of anti clogging cookies concept is that the verifier will not allocate much resources until the genuineness of the assumed claimant is assured.

Our proposed scheme also introduced one bit flag in the architecture for the prevention of DoS attack by the authenticated devices. The master device sets this flag to "1" after the authentication of any slave device, against its MAC address. Now if this authenticated device sends authentication request to the master device, it will drop the connection, assuming that it is an attacker device.

In the original bluetooth authentication scheme, to conduct attack on authentication method the attacker does not need to have access to the victim secrets like (PIN or current key), transfer of some messages from one victim to another without alteration carries out successful attack. Based on the deception that both victims' thinks that they are in same piconet, authentication attacks are carried out, and in reality they are in different piconets. Authentication attacks could therefore be only detected if the victim includes information about their actual piconets in SRES calculation.

# 6   Conclusion

Bluetooth devices are getting common day by day and the threats to this technology are also evolving rapidly. In this paper we highlight that current bluetooth security architecture is vulnerable to MITM attack, different forms of DoS attacks and hostile intruder detection in piconet. As a consequence, this work present a protection mechanism against these attacks. MITM can be countered to have keyed hash of the link key, that is, the unit key before generating the encryption key. DoS attack due to authentication requests can be mitigated through the concept of cookies. Hostile intruder detection can be carried out by including piconet specific information in SRES messages, which will help in detecting hostile intruder. Further DoS attack after a device is authenticated can be overcome by setting the flag "on" against the connected device MAC AD-DRESS, which will help in detecting a DoS attack from the assumed attacker. Finally we give some precautionary measures for every bluetooth user and if they follow these measures, it can prove helpful to ordinary users who do not have much knowledge about the security and threats related to bluetooth.

# References

1. Wireless network security 802.11, bluetooth and handheld devices (2002)
2. Bluetooth sig. (2006)
3. Armknecht, F.: An algebraic attack on bluetooth keystream generator (2004)
4. Cheng, P.-C., Garay, J.A., Herzberg, A., Krawczyk, H.: A security architecture for the internet protocol. IBM Syst. J. 37(1), 42–60 (1997)
5. Gehrmann, B.S., Persson, J.: Bluetooth seurity (2004)
6. John Jersin, J.W.: Security analysis of bluetooth v2.1 + edr pairing authentication protocol. CS259, Stanford University (March 2008)
7. Kennedy, T., Hunt, R.: A review of wpan security: attacks and prevention. In: Mobility 2008: Proceedings of the International Conference on Mobile Technology, Applications, and Systems, pp. 1–8. ACM, New York (2008)
8. Suri, R.S.: P.R. Bluetooth security - need to increase the efficiency in pairing, pp. 607–609 (April 2008)
9. Yu Xin, C.R., ZhaoShun, W.: Application of group key agreement based on authenticated dif?e-hellman for bluetooth piconet, vol. 2, pp. 125–128 (July 2009)

# Modified Anonymous Authentication Scheme with Enhanced Security for Wireless Communication

Muhammad Asif Khan*, Firdous Kausar, and Ashraf Masood

Information Security Department
College of Telecommunication Engineering (MCS),
NUST, Rawalpindi, Pakistan
m.aasif.khan@hotmail.com, {firdous.imam,ashrafm61}@gmail.com

**Abstract.** Authentication is the first and most important step in provision of any secure service to the users. It is used to ensure that only authentic users be able to use that secure service. Anonymous authentication is another vital aspect in wireless secure communication. Anonymous authentication is termed as authenticating the user without disclosing his/her identity. Many authentication with anonymity schemes are propose for secure communication in wireless environment. Wireless communication technology is susceptible to many common attacks. In this paper we point out security flaws in recently proposed improved anonymous authentication schemes in wireless communication, in which the inside adversary who register as a legitimate user reveals the identity of user and thus defeat the anonymity. We propose a modified anonymous authentication scheme with enhanced security, covering the security flaws identified in recent schemes.

## 1 Introduction

With the development of wireless communication technology, in recent years, the requirement of security also increased. On the air interface is used for data transmission in wireless communication instead of any conductor of wire. This communication can be of short range or long range. Short range wireless communication example is television using remote control or two mobile devices communicating using bluetooth, while for long range communication best know example is cellular telephone. For allowing people to get connected seamlessly using their mobile devices without being limited by the geographical coverage of their own home network, roaming service is deployed [1].

In roaming three parties are involved: mobile user (MU), home agent (HA) and foreign agent (FA). MU is the roaming mobile user outside from his/her home network. HA is a server located in home network, to which the MU is

---

* Please note that the LNCS Editorial assumes that all authors have used the western naming convention, with given names preceding surnames. This determines the structure of the names in the running heads and the author index.

S.K. Bandyopadhyay et al. (Eds.): ISA 2010, CCIS 76, pp. 198–208, 2010.

registered and FA is the server located at foreign network. In roaming service, when MU is out of the range of home network and want to communicate then this FA allow MU to use its services. To prevent unauthentic use of service by any illegal user, FA should first authenticate this MU to ensure that he/she is a legitimate user of home network. For this purpose FA will farward MU request to HA, to which HA will reply back to FA with legal or illegal MU.

This is wireless broadcast nature that the transmitted data by any wireless device can be intercepted by other device, kept within the range of wireless device. Due to which wireless communication is vulnerable to interception, impersonation and modification of transmitted data. The security features that should be included in wireless communication to overcome these vulnerabilities are: privacy, authentication and anonymity. A good user authentication scheme not only provide high security but also protect user privacy [2]. In wireless communication anonymity is consider as important security feature. Anonymity means to preserve the user's identity and making the identity of user securely concealed from any other entity. This makes the user untraceable by others.

We have organized the paper as follows. Section 2 outlines the related work. In Section 3, we review and analyze the security of Xinchun et al.'s and Chang et al.'s recently proposed anonymous authentication schemes. Next in Section 4, we present our modified scheme which provides enhanced security. Section 5 covers the security analysis of our proposed scheme. Finally, Section 6 concludes the paper.

## 2    Related Work

In 2004, Zhu-Ma [3] propose a new authentication scheme for wireless roaming user. This scheme claims to provide authentication with anonymity and consuming limited computing resources. In 2006, Lee et al. [4] point out many flaws in Zhu-Ma's scheme and propose his enhanced scheme. Later, Wu et al. [5] prove that the schemes proposed by Zhu-Ma and Lee et al. fails to preserve the identity of mobile user from foreign agent. In addition, Wu et al. propose an improved scheme and claim to provide anonymity. Recently in 2009, Zeng et al. [6] and Lee-Chang-Lee [7] identify weaknesses in Wu et al.'s improved scheme and show that the scheme fails to provide anonymity. Also Xinchun et al. [8] and Chang et al. [2] point out the same vulnerabilities and propose their improved version of that scheme. In this paper, we analyze the security of both recently propose Xinchun et al.'s scheme and Chang et al.'s scheme and show that they are still vulnerable to some attacks, due to which these schemes can also be defeated in provision of anonymity. Then, we propose a modified scheme that provides enhanced security without loosing the anonymity.

## 3    Improved Anonymous Authentication Schemes

In this Section, we briefly review and analyze the security of both Xinchun et al.'s Scheme [8] and Chang et al.'s Scheme [2]. The notations used in this paper are given with description in the following Table 1:

**Table 1.** The Notations used in this paper

| Notation | Description |
|---|---|
| MU | Mobile User |
| HA | Home Agent in home network |
| FA | Foreign Agent in foreign network |
| $ID_X$ | Identity of entity X |
| $PW_X$ | Password of entity X |
| $T_X$ | Timestamp generated by entity X |
| $Cert_X$ | Certificate of entity X |
| $[X]_k$ | Symmetric encryption of message X using key $k$ |
| $PU_X[M]$ | Asymmetric encryption of message M using public key of entity X |
| $PR_X\{M\}$ | Asymmetric encryption of message M using private key of entity X, that is, message M is digitally signed by entity X. |
| $DS_X$ | Variable used for digitally signed message by entity X |
| $E_X$ | Variable used for public key encryption of message by entity X |
| $A \rightarrow B : M$ | A sends a message M to B |
| $n_y$ | n obtain by mobile user Y, from his/her smart card |
| $\acute{n}_y$ | $\acute{n}$ obtain by mobile user Y, from his/her smart card |
| $x_y$ | Random value x generated by smart card of mobile user Y |
| $S_y$ | S computed by smart card of mobile user Y |
| h(.) | One-way hash function |
| ‖ | Concatenation operator |
| ⊕ | XOR operator |

### 3.1   Xinchun et al.'s Scheme

**Review:** This Scheme [8] composed of three phases: initial phase, first phase and second phase.

i. **Initial Phase**

The registration of MU to the home agent HA occurs in this phase. MU submits the identity $(ID_{MU})$ to the HA. In response HA will generate MU's password $PW_{MU} = h(N\|ID_{MU})$ and $r = h(N\|ID_{HA}) \oplus h(N\|ID_{MU}) \oplus h(ID_{HA}\|ID_{MU})$. Where $N$ is HA's sufficiently large secret random number. Then HA provides a smart card and $PW_{MU}$ to MU. This smart card contains $r$, $ID_{HA}$ and $h(.)$.

ii. **First Phase**

When MU want to communicate and access services at foreign network, then he/she has to get a temporary certificate $(TCert_{MU})$ from the foreign agent (FA). FA first authenticates the roaming MU and then issues $(TCert_{MU})$ as follows.

- **Step 1.** MU → FA: $n$, $C$, $ID_{HA}$, $T_{MU}$.
  MU computes $n = r \oplus PW_{MU} = h(N\|ID_{HA}) \oplus h(ID_{HA}\|ID_{MU})$ and $C = [h(ID_{MU})\|x_o\|x]_L$, where $L = h(T_{MU} \oplus PW_{MU})$ is a temporary key, both $x_o$ and $x$ are secret random number generated by MU. $T_{MU}$ is timestamp to prevent replay attack.

- **Step 2.** FA → HA: $b$, $n$, $C$, $T_{MU}$, $DS_{FA}$, $Cert_{FA}$, $T_{FA}$
  FA sends the message received from MU to HA with random number $b$, its Certificate $Cert_{FA}$, a timestamp $T_{FA}$ and corresponding signature $DS_{FA}$, computed as follows:
  $$DS_{FA} = PR_{FA}\{h(b, n, C, T_{MU}, Cert_{FA})\}.$$

- **Step 3.** HA → FA: $c$, $E_{HA}$, $DS_{HA}$, $Cert_{HA}$, $T_{HA}$
  HA computes $E_{HA}$ and a digital signature $DS_{HA}$ as follows:
  $E_{HA} = PU_{FA}[h(h(N\|ID_{MU}))\|x_o\|x]$
  $DS_{HA} = PR_{HA}\{h(b, c, W, Cert_{HA})\}$, where $c$ is a random number.

- **Step 4.** FA → MU: $[TCert_{MU}\|h(x\|x_o)]_k$
  FA decrypts $E_{HA}$ with its private key and verifies the signature. FA obtains $h(h(N\|ID_{MU}))$, $x_o$ and $x$. Then computes a session key $k$, between FA and MU. Session key $k$ is computed as follows:
  $k = (h(h(N\|ID_{MU}))\|x_o\|x)$

  On receiving this message from FA, MU computes the session key $k$ and obtains the temporary certificate $TCert_{MU}$.

iii. **Second Phase**

The session key is updated at every session between MU and FA. For ith session, the following message is send from MU to FA:
MU → FA: $TCert_{MU}$, $(x_i\|TCert_{MU}\|OtherInformation)_{k_i}$.

Where $k_i$ is a new session key that is derived from previous unexpired secret knowledge $x_{i-1}$ and a fixed secret knowledge $x$, as shown below:
$k_i = h(N\|IDMU\|x\|x_{i-1})$ and $i = 1, 2, , n$.

When FA receives this message from MU, FA computes the new session key $k_i$ and decrypts the message. After decryption FA gets value of $x_i$ and stores it for next session key generation.

**Security Analysis:** Here, we demonstrate the flaws in Xinchun et al.'s [8] proposed improved Scheme. One security flaw and two design flaws are point out as follows:

1. **Security flaw**

Due to this Security flaw Xinchun et al.'s Scheme fails to provide the anonymity of MU, by revealing $ID_{MU}$ to inside attacker, who has legally registered to the same HA.

Assume A is an inside attacker, who knows $ID_A$, $PW_A = h(N\|ID_A)$ and has smart card. The smart card of attacker A contains $ID_{HA}$, $h(.)$

and $r = h(N\|ID_{HA}) \oplus h(N\|ID_A) \oplus h(ID_{HA} \oplus ID_A)$. Attacker A inserts this smart card, inputs $ID_A$ and $PW_A$ to get $\acute{n} = r \oplus PW_A = h(N\|ID_{HA}) \oplus h(ID_{HA} \oplus ID_A)$. As both $ID_{HA}$ and $ID_A$ are known to attacker A, so can compute $h(ID_{HA} \oplus ID_A)$. Then from $\acute{n}$ attacker A can obtain $h(N\|ID_{HA})$ by computing:

$$h(N\|ID_{HA}) = \acute{n} \oplus h(ID_{HA} \oplus ID_A).$$

Let MU is other legal mobile user. At Step 1 of first phase, MU sends messages to FA containing $n = h(N\|ID_{HA}) \oplus h(ID_{HA} \oplus ID_{MU})$. Attacker A intercepts the value of $n$ and gets $h(ID_{HA} \oplus ID_{MU})$ by computing: $h(ID_{HA} \oplus ID_{MU}) = n \oplus h(N\|ID_{HA})$.

Generally the identity of any entity is short and has certain format. As Attacker A knows $ID_{HA}$, so can launch offline guessing attack on $h(ID_{HA} \oplus ID_{MU})$ to get real identity of MU. Thus defeat the Scheme in providing anonymity.

2. **Design Flaws**

   There are two design flaws in this Scheme. Xinchun et al. didn't consider some aspects in their scheme. We pointed out them as follows:

   (a) In Step 1, of Xinchun et al.'s Scheme MU sends message to FA, with $n = h(N\|ID_{HA}) \oplus h(ID_{HA} \oplus ID_{MU})$. Then at Step 3, HA gets this value of $n$ with other messages from FA. Now HA should obtain $ID_{MU}$ by doing computational operation on this received $n$, to authenticate MU and decrypt $C$. While HA gets $h(ID_{HA} \oplus ID_{MU})$ as:

   $$h(ID_{HA} \oplus ID_{MU}) = n \oplus h(N\|ID_{HA})$$

   It is clear that HA is unable get $ID_{MU}$ from $h(ID_{HA} \oplus ID_{MU})$ by computational operation. Without getting $ID_{MU}$, HA can't compute $PW_{MU}$ and temporaty key $L$. Hence, can't decrypt $C$ to get $x$ and $x_o$.

   (b) In Second phase, Xinchun et al. proposed that the session key will be derived as:

   $$k_i = h(N\|ID_{MU}\|x\|x_{i-1}), \text{ where } i = 1, 2, , n.$$

   In this case to compute $k_i$, both FA and MU should know the value of $N$, $ID_{MU}$, $x$ and $x_{i-1}$. However, FA doesn't know $N$ and $ID_{MU}$. Also the of $N$ is unknown to MU, because $N$ is the secret value of HA.

### 3.2   Chang et al.'s Scheme

**Review:** Chang et al.'s [2] Scheme has the same phases and steps with some procedural modification. We discuss only the modified procedures as follows:

1. In initial phase HA also stores $h(N)$ with $r$, $ID_{HA}$ and $h(.)$ into the smart card. Also in this Scheme $r = h(N\|ID_{HA}) \oplus h(N\|ID_{MU}) \oplus ID_{HA} \oplus ID_{MU}$.

2. In Step 1 of first phase, MU first computes $h(h(N)\|T_{MU})$ and then $n$ as:

$$n = r \oplus PW_{MU} \oplus h(h(N)\|T_{MU}) = h(N\|ID_{HA}) \oplus ID_{HA} \oplus ID_{MU} \oplus h(h(N)\|T_{MU}).$$

3. In Step3, HA obtains MU's identity $(ID_{MU})$ as:

$$ID_{MU} = n \oplus h(N\|ID_{HA}) \oplus ID_{HA} \oplus h(h(N)\|T_{MU}).$$

4. In Second phase, the ith session key $k$ can be generated as:

$$k_i = h(h(h(N\|ID_{MU}))\|x\|x_{i-1}), \text{ for } i = 1, 2, , n.$$

**Security Analysis:** Although, Chang et al. [2] proposed an improved version of Wu et al's [5] Scheme but still can be defeated in preserving the identity of mobile user from inside attacker.

Let us assume A is any inside attacker, who has registered to the same home agent HA. Now attacker A has $ID_A$, $PW_A = h(N\|ID_A)$ and a smart card, containing $ID_{HA}$, $h(.)$, $h(N)$ and $r = h(N\|ID_{HA}) \oplus h(N\|ID_A) \oplus ID_{HA} \oplus ID_A$. At Step 1, attacker A inserts the smart card and inputs $ID_A$ and $PW_A$. Attacker A gets $\acute{n} = r \oplus PW_A \oplus h(h(N)\|T_A) = h(N\|ID_{HA}) \oplus ID_{HA} \oplus ID_A \oplus h(h(N)\|T_A)$, where $T_A$ is timestamp generated by attacker A. Attacker A knows $ID_A$ so will compute $m = \acute{n} \oplus ID_A = h(N\|ID_{HA}) \oplus ID_{HA} \oplus h(h(N)\|T_A)$.

Let MU is other legal mobile user. At Step 1, MU sends $T_{MU}, n = h(N\|ID_{HA}) \oplus ID_{HA} \oplus ID_{MU} \oplus h(h(N)\|T_{MU})$ with $ID_{HA}$ and $C$. Attacker A intercepts this message and compare both $T_A$ and $T_{MU}$, as $T_{MU}$ is in cleartext. If he/she finds $T_A = T_{MU}$, so will easily get identity of MU $(ID_{MU})$ by computing:

$$ID_{MU} = m \oplus n = h(N\|ID_{HA}) \oplus ID_{HA} \oplus h(h(N)\|T_A) \oplus h(N\|ID_{HA}) \oplus ID_{HA} \oplus ID_{MU} \oplus h(h(N)\|T_{MU}).$$

Thus this Scheme fails to provide anonymity, when more than one mobile users generates timestamp simultaneously.

## 4   Proposed Scheme

In this Section, we propose our modified scheme which overcomes all possible vulnerabilities that were present in the previous schemes discussed. Our proposed scheme with the provision of strong user anonymity also provides security of smart card, by introducing login phase. This Scheme is divided into four phases: initial phase, login phase, first phase and second phase.

### A. Initial Phase

The MU registers to HA by providing his/her identity $(ID_{MU})$. HA generates MU's password $PW_{MU} = h(N \oplus ID_{MU}\|ID_{MU} \oplus ID_{HA})$, where $N$ is sufficiently large secret random number of HA. Then HA delivers $PW_{MU}$ and a smart card through a secure channel to MU. Smart card contains $A$, $\acute{A}$, $C$ and $h(.)$. These are secret values of smart card, that is, only be used by smart card and are not retrievable by MU. The values of $A$, $\acute{A}$ and $C$ are computed as given below:

$A = h(N\|ID_{HA}) \oplus h(N \oplus ID_{HA}) \oplus ID_{HA} \oplus ID_{MU} \oplus h(PW_{MU})$
$\acute{A} = h(N\|ID_{HA}) \oplus h(N) \oplus ID_{MU} \oplus h(PW_{MU})$
And $C = h(N \oplus ID_{HA}) \oplus h(N) \oplus ID_{HA} \oplus ID_{MU} \oplus h(PW_{MU})$.

### B. Login Phase

In this phase, the smart card authenticates MU, to ensure that the intended MU is accessing the network using this smart card. This makes unable for others to use mobile user's lost smart card. Whenever MU wants the service, he/she inserts the smart card and enters $ID_{MU}$ and $PW_{MU}$. Smart card computes $h(PW_{MU})$ and $M = A \oplus \acute{A} \oplus ID_{MU} \oplus h(PW_{MU})$. After that smart card compares $M$ and $C$, if $M = C$, allow MU to further use the smart card. Otherwise, deny the user and reject the service request. If the user is denied three times successively then smart card will be disabled.

### C. First Phase

While roaming, in order to communicate and get services, MU needs a temporary certificate $(TCert_{MU})$ from foreign agent (FA). In this phase, as shown in Figure 1 FA authenticates MU securely and issues $(TCert_{MU})$ as follows:

- **Step 1.** MU → FA: $n$, $\acute{n}$, $T_{MU}$, $[ID_{MU}\|T_{MU}]_{h(S\|H)}$, $ID_{HA}$.
  Smart card of MU takes the following steps:

  1. Generate a secret random number $x$, kept unknown to MU.
  2. Compute $S = x \oplus h(PW_{MU})$ and
     $H = \acute{A} \oplus ID_{MU} \oplus h(PW_{MU}) = h(N) \oplus h(N\|ID_{HA})$.
  3. Compute $n = A \oplus h(PW_{MU}) \oplus h(S\|H)$.
  4. Compute $\acute{n} = \acute{A} \oplus ID_{MU} \oplus x$.
  5. Encrypt $ID_{MU}$ and $T_{MU}$ using temporary key $h(S\|H)$, where $T_{MU}$ is timestamp.

  MU gets $n$, $\acute{n}$, $T_{MU}$, $ID_{HA}$ and encrypted value $[ID_{MU}\|T_{MU}]_{h(S\|H)}$ and forwards them to FA.

- **Step 2.** FA → HA: $n$, $\acute{n}$, $T_{MU}$, $T_{FA}$, $Cert_{FA}$, $[ID_{MU}\|T_{MU}]_{h(S\|H)}$, $DS_{FA}$.
  FA forwards the message received from MU to HA with its certificate $Cert_{FA}$, timestamp generated by FA $(T_{FA})$ and corresponding signature $DS_{FA}$, computed as given below:
  $DS_{FA} = PR_{FA}\{h(Cert_{FA}, T_{FA}, n, \acute{n}, T_{MU}, [ID_{MU}\|T_{MU}]_{h(S\|H)})\}$,

- **Step 3.** HA → FA: $Cert_{HA}$, $T_{HA}$, $E_{HA}$, $DS_{HA}$.
  Upon receiving message from FA, HA checks the validity of $Cert_{FA}$ and $T_{FA}$. If they are valid, HA reveals the real identity of MU from the message received as follows:

  1. HA computes $h(S\|H)$, where $H=h(N)\oplus h(N\|ID_{HA})$ and $S=\acute{n}\oplus H$.
  2. Then computes $\acute{ID}_{MU} = n\oplus h(N\|ID_{HA})\oplus h(N\oplus ID_{HA})\oplus ID_{HA}\oplus h(S\|H)$.
  3. Decrypts $[ID_{MU}\|T_{MU}]_{h(S\|H)}$ using temporary key $h(S\|H)$.

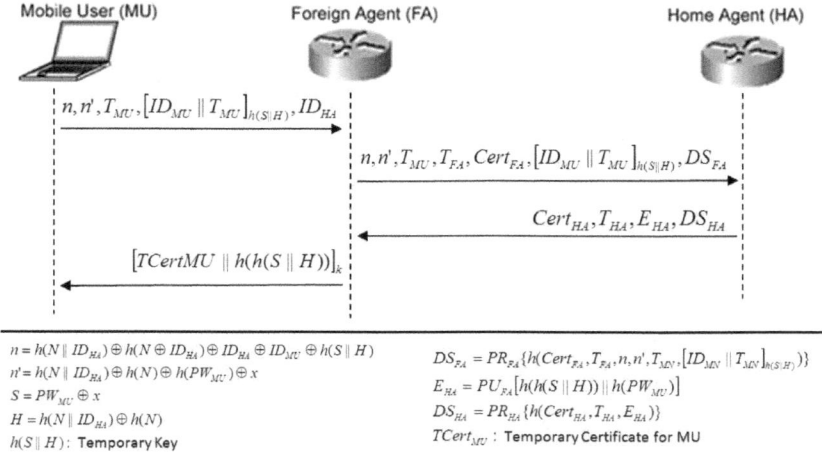

**Fig. 1.** First Phase of Proposed Scheme

HA compares the computed identity $I\acute{D}_{MU}$ and decrypted identity $ID_{MU}$. If HA gets $I\acute{D}_{MU}$ not equal to $ID_{MU}$, HA sends message "Illegal User" to FA. Otherwise HA proceeds as follows:

1. Computes $h(PW_{MU})$ and $h(h(S\|H))$.
2. Encrypts asymmetrically $h(h(S\|H))$ and $h(PW_{MU})$ using public key of FA to $E_{HA}$, computed as given below:
   $E_{HA} = PU_{FA}[h(h(S\|h))\|h(PW_{MU})]$.
3. Generates timestamp $T_{HA}$.
4. Generate digital signature $DS_{HA}$ as given below:
   $DS_{HA} = PR_{HA}\{h(Cert_{HA}, T_{HA}, E_{HA}, h(PW_{MU}))\}$.
5. Send the message to FA, which contains:
   $Cert_{HA}$, $T_{HA}$, $E_{HA}$ and $DS_{HA}$.

- **Step 4.** FA $\rightarrow$ MU: $[TCert_{MU}\|h(h(S\|H))]_k$.
  FA verifies the signature and decrypts $E_{HA}$. By decryption FA obtains $h(h(S\|H))$ and $h(PW_{MU})$ to compute session key $k$ as follows:

  $k = h(h(PW_{MU}\|h(h(S\|H))))$

  Using this session key FA encrypts temporary certificate for MU ($TCert_{MU}$) with $h(h(S\|H))$ and sends to MU. FA then stores $TCert_{MU}$, $h(PW_{MU})$ and $h(h(S\|H))$ into the database, because these values will be used in computing next session key.

- **Step 5.** On receiving the encrypted message from FA, MU also computes the session key $k = h(h(PW_{MU}\|h(h(S\|H))))$ and decrypts the message to get temporary certificate $TCert_{MU}$.

## D.  Second Phase

At every session when MU communicates with the same FA, the session key will be changed. Let MU visits FA at ith session. The session key $k_i$ will be used, derived from $h(h(S_{i-1}\|H))$ and $h(PW_{MU})$, for encrypted communication between FA and MU. As FA stored value of $h(h(S_{i-1}\|H))$ at the previous session, so both the values $h(PW_{MU})$ and $h(h(S_{i-1}\|H))$ are known to FA. MU sends message to FA as follows:

MU $\rightarrow$ FA: $TCert_{FA}, [TCert_{FA}\|h(h(S_i\|H))]k_i$

Where $k_i = h(h(PW_{MU}\|h(h(S_{i-1}\|H))))$ and $h(h(Si\|H))$ is the new value computed by MU for the derivation of session key at next session. Smart card of MU takes the following steps:

1. Generates new secret random number $x_i$.
2. Computes $S_i = x_i \oplus h(PW_{MU})$.
3. Computes $h(h(S_i\|H))$, where $H$ was computed at the time of login.

On getting the value of $h(h(S_i\|H))$ from smart card, MU encrypts this value $h(h(S_i\|H))$ with $TCert_{MU}$ using new session key $k_i = h(h(PW_{MU})\|h(h(S_{i-1}\|H)))$ and sends to FA.

When FA receives the message from MU, gets the stored values $h(PW_{MU})$ and $h(h(S_i\|H))$ from the database, using $TCert_{MU}$ as primary key of that database. FA computes new session key $k_i$ and decrypts $[TCert_{MU}\|h(h(S_i\|H))]_{k_i}$. Session key $k_i$ is computed as given below:

$k_i = h(h(PW_{MU})\|h(h(S_{i-1}\|H)))$

After decryption FA compares the two $TCert_{MU}$ to verify the integrity of message. FA then saves $h(h(S_i\|H))$ for computing session key in next session. To store $h(h(S_i\|H))$ FA updates the database by replacing $h(h(S_i\|H))$ with $h(h(S_{i-1}\|H))$.

## 5    Security Analysis

The security of the scheme is based on secure hash function and smart card. While the security between HA and FA is based on discrete logarithm problem. In this Section, we demonstrate how our scheme provides security and achieves anonymity from inside attacker. We show that no offline attacks can access any secure information. Also our scheme, by adding login phase, provides security of smart card. Thus making any other user unable to use mobile user's lost smart card. The following are some propositions regarding the proposed scheme:

- *Our scheme preserves the identity of mobile user very effectively.*

  *Proof:* Assume $MU$ and $\acute{M}U$ are two legal mobile users. After all computation of smart card at Step 1 of first phase, $MU$ gets $n_{MU}$ and $\acute{n}_{MU}$ with values as follows:

$$n_{MU} = h(N\|ID_{HA}) \oplus h(N \oplus ID_{HA}) \oplus ID_{HA} \oplus ID_{MU} \oplus h(S_{MU}\|H)$$
$$\acute{n}_{MU} = h(N\|ID_{HA}) \oplus h(N) \oplus h(PW_{MU}) \oplus x_{MU}$$

Keep in mind all the values in smart card, such as: $A$, $\acute{A}$ and $C$, including $x$ are irretrievable to MU, because of temper resistant property of smart card. MU knows $ID_{HA}$, $ID_{MU}$ and $h(PW_{MU})$, so he/she can obtain the follows:

$$K = n_{MU} \oplus ID_{HA} \oplus ID_{MU} = h(N\|ID_{HA}) \oplus h(N \oplus ID_{MU}) \oplus h(S_{MU}\|H)$$
And $L = \acute{n}_{MU} \oplus h(PW_{MU}) = h(N\|ID_{HA}) \oplus h(N) \oplus x_{MU}$.

From the value of $K$ and $L$, MU can't get the value of $h(N\|ID_{HA})\oplus h(N\oplus ID_{HA})$, $h(N\|ID_{HA}) \oplus h(N)$ and $h(S_{MU}\|H)$, only because MU is unknown to value of $x$. So without the knowledge of these values a mobile user can't get the identity of other mobile users. This shows that only by introducing a secret random number of smart card, the security of whole scheme enhanced.

- **Offline guessing/brute-force attack can't disclose any secret of mobile user.**

*Proof:* Now assume that coincidently smart card of both the mobile users $MU$ and $\acute{MU}$ selected the same random value of $x$. Then also our proposed scheme cannot be defeated in preserving the identity of any mobile user to other, because the value of $h(S_{MU}\|H)$ and $h(S_{\acute{MU}}\|H)$ are different, as $S_{MU} = x \oplus h(PW_{MU})$ and $S_{\acute{MU}} = x \oplus h(PW_{\acute{MU}})$.

While using computed value of $L$, $MU$ can compute $\acute{MU}$'s hashed password $h(PW_{\acute{MU}})$, that is, $h(PW_{\acute{MU}}) = \acute{n}_{\acute{MU}} \oplus L$. Where $\acute{n}_{\acute{MU}} = h(N\|ID_{HA}) \oplus h(N) \oplus h(PW_{\acute{MU}}) \oplus x_{\acute{MU}}$ and $L = h(N\|ID_{HA}) \oplus h(N) \oplus x_{MU}$, as in this case $x_{MU} = x_{\acute{MU}}$.

From $h(PW_{\acute{MU}})$ the value of $PW_{\acute{MU}}$ can't be derived due to one way property of hash function. Also offline guessing attack is infeasible, because $N$ is sufficiently large random secret of HA.

- **The mobile user's lost smart card is unusable by others.**

*Proof:* Assume $\acute{MU}$ has $MU$'s lost smart card. When $\acute{MU}$ inserts the smart into the device, a login interface is prompt. Now the $\acute{MU}$ has to enter the $ID_{MU}$ and $PW_{MU}$, which are the credentials of $MU$, thus only known to $MU$. If $\acute{MU}$ enters any other ID ($\acute{ID}$) and password ($\acute{PW}$), the smart card will compute $M = A \oplus \acute{A} \oplus \acute{ID} \oplus h(\acute{PW})$ and compare it with smart card's secret value C. Where the value of $A$, $\acute{A}$ and $C$ are as follows:

$$A = h(N\|ID_{HA}) \oplus h(N \oplus ID_{HA}) \oplus ID_{HA} \oplus ID_{MU} \oplus h(PW_{MU})$$
$$\acute{A} = h(N\|ID_{HA}) \oplus h(N) \oplus ID_{MU} \oplus h(PW_{MU})$$
And $C = h(N \oplus ID_{HA}) \oplus h(N) \oplus ID_{HA} \oplus ID_{MU} \oplus h(PW_{MU})$.

As it is clear that the value $M$ can't be equal to $C$, till $MU$'s correct credentials are known to $\acute{MU}$. Thus $\acute{MU}$ will be denied to use this smart card to access the wireless network. Also if the user enters wrong credentials three times successively, the smart card will be disabled.

# 6    Conclusion

In this paper, we point out security flaws in Xinchun et al.'s [8] scheme and Chang et al.'s [2] scheme. We show that both of these schemes can be defeated in providing user anonymity against inside adversary who is legal user. Our proposed scheme not only preserves the identity of user from others but also enhances the security of smart card by adding login procedure in the anonymous authentication scheme. The login procedure make unable for others to use mobile user's lost smart card, because the smart card will ask for identity of MU $(ID_{MU})$ and password of MU $(PW_{MU})$, which are unknown to any other user. The Security analysis of our proposed scheme verified that all the weaknesses and vulnerabilities present in previous schemes are effectively encountered.

# References

1. Yang, G., Huang, Q., Wong, D., Deng, X.: Universal authentication protocols for anonymous wireless communications. IEEE Transactions on Wireless Communications 9(1), 168–174 (2010)
2. Chang, C.C., Lee, C.Y., Lee, W.B.: Cryptanalysis and improvement of a secure authentication scheme with anonymity for wireless communications. In: Fifth International Conference on Intelligent Information Hiding and Multimedia Signal Processing, IIH-MSP 2009, September 2009, pp. 902–904 (2009)
3. Zhu, J., Ma, J.: A new authentication scheme with anonymity for wireless environments. IEEE Transactions on Consumer Electronics 50(1), 231–235 (2004)
4. Lee, C.C., Hwang, M.S., Liao, I.E.: Security enhancement on a new authentication scheme with anonymity for wireless environments. IEEE Transactions on Industrial Electronics 53(5), 1683–1687 (2006)
5. Wu, C.C., Lee, W.B., Tsaur, W.J.: A secure authentication scheme with anonymity for wireless communications. IEEE Communications Letters 12(10), 722–723 (2008)
6. Zeng, P., Cao, Z., Kwang Choo, K., Wang, S.: On the anonymity of some authentication schemes for wireless communications. IEEE Communications Letters 13(3), 170–171 (2009)
7. seon Lee, J., Chang, J., Lee, D.: Security aw of authentication scheme with anonymity for wireless communications. IEEE Communications Letters 13(5), 292–293 (2009)
8. Xinchun, C., Xinheng, W.: An improved user authentication scheme for wireless mesh networks. In: IEEE International Symposium on IT in Medicine and Education, ITIME 2009, August 2009, vol. 1, pp. 915–918 (2009)

# Security Risks of Cloud Computing and Its Emergence as 5th Utility Service

Mushtaq Ahmad

FCSE, GIK Institute of Engineering Sciences & Technology
Topi, NWFP, Pakistan
mushtaq@giki.edu.pk, mushtaq_ahmad@hotmail.com

**Abstract.** Cloud Computing is being projected by the major cloud services provider IT companies such as IBM, Google, Yahoo, Amazon and others as fifth utility where clients will have access for processing those applications and or software projects which need very high processing speed for compute intensive and huge data capacity for scientific, engineering research problems and also e- business and data content network applications. These services for different types of clients are provided under DASM-Direct Access Service Management based on virtualization of hardware, software and very high bandwidth Internet (Web 2.0) communication. The paper reviews these developments for Cloud Computing and Hardware/Software configuration of the cloud paradigm. The paper also examines the vital aspects of security risks projected by IT Industry experts, cloud clients. The paper also highlights the cloud provider's response to cloud security risks.

**Keywords:** Cloud, Cloud Computing, Cloud Infrastructure, DASM, 5th Utility, Cloud Security, ISP.

## 1 Introduction

The Cloud Computing concept has emerged as the off-shoot of HPC Clusters and Grid Computing paradigms. The success stories of these technologies and Internet search engines – Google, Yahoo and MSN- in the e-Science community around the globe for scientific, engineering, technical and e-business research projects and applications has resulted in attracting the attention of big IT entrepreneur companies like IBM, Google, Yahoo and Amazon towards Cloud Computing paradigm in a big way.

Simply said, Cloud Computing paradigm is Internet ("cloud") based development and use of computer technology whereby dynamically scalable and often virtualised resources are provided as a service over the Internet [1] by ISP companies. Most of the clients need not have knowledge, expertise and control over the technology infrastructure of the cloud that supports them. However, the scientific, engineering, and business research projects users must have pertinent information about hardware-software infrastructure, data servers, Internet/ISP and security risks etc. from the cloud services providers. The Cloud Computing incorporates software as a service (SaaS), Web 2.0, Web 3.0 and other recent, well-known technology trends, in which

S.K. Bandyopadhyay et al. (Eds.): ISA 2010, CCIS 76, pp. 209–219, 2010.

the common theme is reliance on the Internet for satisfying the computing needs of the clients. An often-quoted example is Google Apps [2], which provides common business applications online that are accessed from a web browser, while the software and data are stored on Google servers.

Large Hedron Collider(LHC) at CERN, Geniva, Switzerland was made operational in August, 2009 [3] for experimentation and ascertaining of reliability, safety and security. The media reported that the facility was stopped [4] on January 27, 2010 for further consultation. Some 2000 scientists, engineers in the field of High Energy Particle Physics from around 200 research institutions in Europe, North America and Asia including Pakistan will use the HDL facility. ATLAS and CMS [5] grids will provide distant access to 2000 physicists from around 200 research institutions in Europe, North America and Asia including Pakistan. These research institutions and others will have accumulated approximately100 Peta-bytes of data that must be archived, processed and analyzed by thousands of researchers at research institutions across the world. Each experiment will deploy a global data Grid and Cloud Computing services for harnessing the entire computing power and storage resources of the collaborating scientists into a single source.

These Global Grids will depend crucially on advanced networks/Internet (Web 2.0 and Web 3.0) [6] to provide throughput to allow massive datasets to be moved quickly moved between CERN and a dozen of national computing centers including those in Euro, USA, Russia, China, India and Pakistan and the facilities of the participating scientists. The ability to run thousands of simultaneous jobs on the data Grid poses the additional requirement that transfer of multi-terabyte datasets (common for many team-based research scientists/analysts) must be completed in a few minutes to maintain stability of the overall system. This will also be a great challenge for the major providers of Cloud Computing services like IBM and Google. GLORAID [7] currently provides a critical component of that vision by extending the powerful US-EU networking to Russia and regions in Asia, providing new collaborative links to high energy particle physicists of these regions.

The technological aspects can be briefly described by Cloud Computing providers' infrastructure [8], which consists of Internet-connected servers, at one site or distributed across several locations that house application packages and data. They also include virtualization, grid management, database, and other types of software. Client interfaces API i.e. communications infrastructure for connecting clients over Internet or private networks, and usage of monitoring and billing mechanism. Clients generally use browsers or dedicated software to access cloud applications, which they frequently control via APIs. The clients will have very easy access like fifth utility.

## 2 Cloud Computing Infrastructure Components

The major components of Cloud Computing infrastructure are described here to understand the implications and basic knowledge of Cloud Computing. These components play the central role in providing the services of Cloud Computing to the Clients.

## 2.1 The Grid Technology

Grid computing is an interoperable technology, enabling the integration and management of services and resources in a distributed, heterogeneous environment. Grid technology provides support for deployment of different kinds of infrastructures joining resources which belong to different administrative domains. For example EGEE [9] or TeraGrid- a large distributed cyber-infrastructure available for non-classified scientific research funded by the US National Science Foundation (NSF)- is used to federate computing resources spanning multiple sites for application execution and data processing.

## 2.2 The Virtualization in Cloud Computing

The virtualization is a very old concept of computer science. It is a broad term which means the abstraction of computer resources and has also been used by the grid computing community before arrival of Cloud Computing on the scene. The virtualization of a grid site provides several benefits, which overcome many of the technical barriers for grid adoption [10].

- Easy support for VO- Virtual Organizations- specific worker nodes
- Reduce grid cycles
- Dynamic balance of resources between VO's
- Fault tolerance of key cloud infrastructure components
- Easier deployment and testing of new middleware distributions
- Distribution of pre-configured components
- Cheaper development nodes
- Simplified training machines deployment
- Performance partitioning between local and grid services
- On-demand access to cloud providers
- The Virtualization in Cloud Computing have further characteristics of;
- Platform virtualization; which separates an operating system from the underlying platform resources
- Resource virtualization; the virtualization of specific system resources, such as storage volumes, name spaces, and network resources

Application virtualization; the hosting of individual applications on alien hardware/ software such as portable application, cross-platform virtualization, emulation or simulation Virtualization Development; the remote manipulation of a computer desktop.

The concept of Cloud Computing and how virtualization enables it, offers so many innovation opportunities that it is not surprising that there are new announcements every day. What clients [11] need to do, however, is to not take a cloud vendor's announcements at face value, but instead dig into new product offerings to understand if something is really utilizing the full potential of Virtualization and Cloud Computing.

### 2.3  Infrastructure as a Service - IaaS

Dr. Jonathan Erickson has described [12], IaaS is the ability to provide computing resources -processing power, network bandwidth, and storage - as a service. Some traditional hosting providers claim to have IaaS, but in reality what they provide is dedicated hardware to clients, put virtualization on top and call it IaaS. True IaaS offerings, however, are truly pay-as-you-go for services that can be turned on and off at any time like utility services with almost no prior notice. When a provider has the ability to serve truly transient burst requirements, then they are capable of claiming, they offer cloud-based, pay-as-you-go, IaaS.

## 3  Types of Cloud Services

There are four major types of cloud services [13] as described below:

1. **Services:** Products offer internet-based services—such as storage, middleware, collaboration, and database capabilities directly for clients.
2. **IaaS:** Infrastructure-as-a-service products deliver a full computer infrastructure via the Internet.
3. **Paas:** Platform-as-a-Service: products offer a full or partial application development environment that clients can access and utilize online, even in collaboration with others.
4. **SaaS:** Software-as-a-Service: products provide a complete, turnkey application—including complex programs such as those for ERM or enterprise-resource management via Internet.

## 4  The Cloud Computing Architecture

The Cloud Computing Architecture is essentially the Grid architecture which consists of several layers of middleware. The Fig. 1 depicts the Globus Architecture [14]

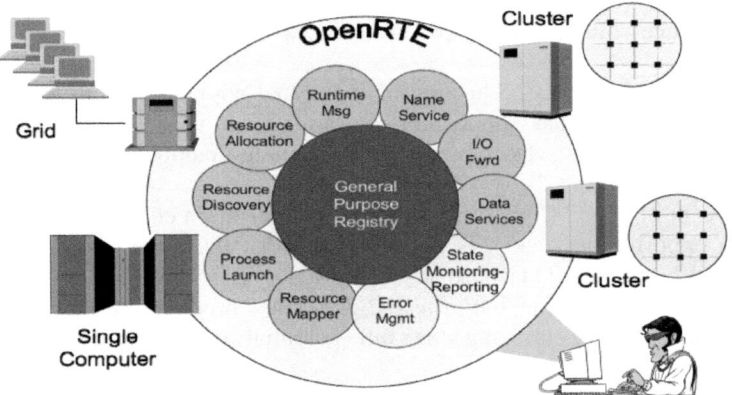

**Fig. 1.** RTE Globus Architecture

for Gird. The Cloud Computing will have additional middleware on top of it (like a Shell ) to provide the management and billing etc., for the clients. From the client's perspective, Cloud Computing is universally accessible, massively scalable with vast pools of multi-tenant on-demand resources. These resources are highly reliable, cost effective and utility priced (like electricity, gas, water and telephone). The resources have also low cost barriers to entry (for capital expenditure, professional services), but none of these attributes are absolute requirements.

## 4.1  The Worldwide Cloud

The futuristic scenario for development of worldwide cloud i.e. the cloud of clouds covering the globe has been projected in Fig. 2 by the IT experts and major could services vendor companies. However, the potential opportunities for the world wide cloud, there have been very few real world examples of applications that can take advantage of this idea.

SOASTA [15] has unveiled an ambitious plan to utilize an interconnected series of regionalized cloud providers for global load and performance testing Web applications and networks. They're calling this new service the Cloud Test Global Platform, which is commercially available today, and is said to enable companies of any size to simulate Web traffic and conditions by leveraging the elasticity and power of Cloud Computing.

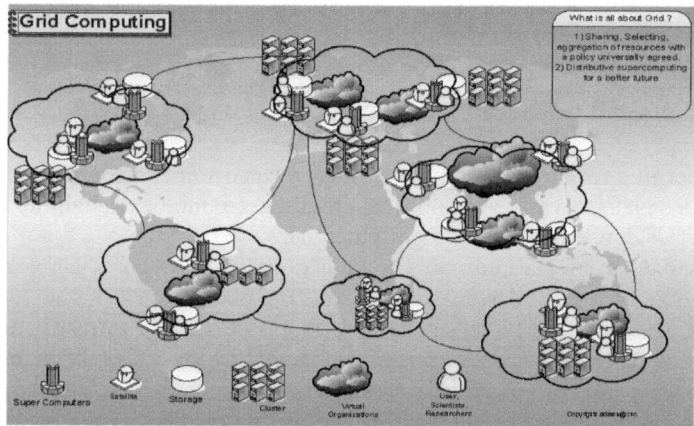

**Fig. 2.** Depicts Cloud Computing as Worldwide Cloud

## 5  Prospects of Cloud Computing

The IT experts and industry observers [16] have predicted that the Cloud Computing technology growth potential is enormous. The IT cloud services spending will grow from about $16 billion in 2008 to about $42 billion by 2012 as shown in the Fig. 3 which also depicts the breakdown of expenses into business applications, infrastructure software, application development, deployment, server and storage. They also forecast that Cloud Computing spending will account for 25 percent of annual IT expenditure growth by 2012 and nearly a third of the growth by next year.

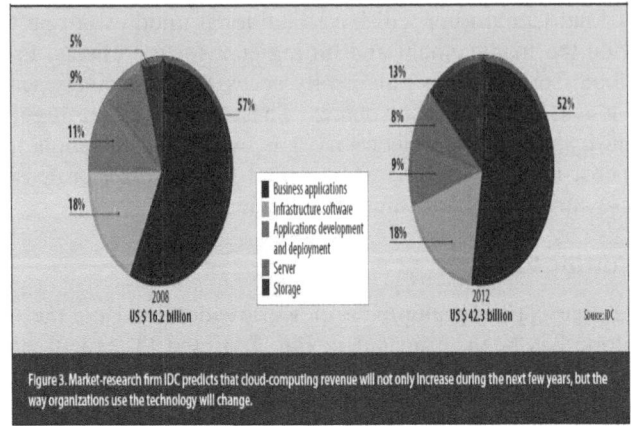

**Fig. 3.** Prospects of Cloud Computing

Working via large platforms owned by Cloud Computing providers and shared by numerous clients makes Cloud Computing less expensive. The shift to Cloud Computing will greatly reduce the cost of information technology. Cloud Computing also lowers the cost of application development and makes the process more scaleable. This technology will further encourage the global projects development teams. However, the approach is still relatively new and has not yet been widely adopted.

## 6   Challenges and Security Risks

A new emerging technology or approach has to face some challenges, apprehensions, uncertainties and security risks concerns about the technology reliability and maturity. Some of these concerns [17] are highlighted here.

IT companies are afraid of Cloud Computing because a vendor, not the organization's own staff, designs and controls the platform.

The cloud services providers generally do not design the infrastructure to support specific companies' IT business practices for applications. Clients cannot change the platform's technology to meet their requirements.

Cloud services providers can change it when and how they want it, without clients' consent. This may involve serious security risks for clients.

Performance concerns may stop some companies from using clouding computing for transaction-oriented and vital data-intensive applications such as global banking transactions among countries and stock exchange companies etc.

Some providers may run into problems of network temporarily facing short of capacity. This may happen due to either by provisioning too many virtual machines or saturating their Internet links due to high demand. This will hamper their system performance till they remedy the situation. Some clients might claim it as security risk.

The security aspect of Cloud Computing was rated as the top concern by 75 percent of IT executives and chief information officers in the recently IDC [18] conducted survey. They were worried about security, "with their businesses" information and critical IT resources outside the firewall, clients worry about their vulnerability to hacker attacks.

Data stored in the cloud might be used anywhere in the world and thus might be subject to state or national data storage laws related to privacy or record keeping.

While IT companies can save money on equipment and software with Cloud Computing. But they could face higher band-width charges from their service providers. Bandwidth costs might be low for smaller internet-based applications that are not data-intensive, but it could be very high for a company which makes a multi-terabyte database available by via Cloud Computing. The full security of very large databases might be possible by cloud service provider. In such a case it will be a very high security risk.

Currently there are no robust Cloud Computing standards for elements and processes such as APIs, the storage of sever images for disaster recovery, and data import and export. This is currently hampering adoption by limiting the portability of data and applications between systems. The portability aspect will become increasingly important as more cloud providers emerge.

Reliability is another important issue of concern for clients. Cloud Computing has not always provided reliability on the 24/7 basis. For example Salesforce.com [19] left clients without service for six hours on 12 February, 2008. Amazon's S3 (Simple Storage Service) and EC2 (Elastic Compute Cloud) services suffered a three hours outage three days later.

## 7  Risk Mitigation

Corporations or end-clients wishing to avoid losing or not being able to access their data should research Cloud Computing vendors' policies on data security before using vendor services. The software technology analyst and consulting firm,Gartner[20] has listed seven security issues in its survey report which should be discussed with a cloud-computing vendor:

1. **Privileged client access:** Sensitive data processed outside the enterprise brings with it an inherent level of risk, because outsourced services bypass the "physical, logical and personnel controls", IT shops exert over in-house programs. Get as much information as you can about the people who manage your data. Ask providers to supply specific information on the hiring and oversight of privileged administrators, and the controls over their access.
2. **Regulatory compliance:** Clients are ultimately responsible for the security and integrity of their own data, even when it is held by a service provider. Traditional service providers are subjected to external audits and security certifications. Cloud Computing providers who refuse to undergo this scrutiny are signaling that clients can only use them for the most trivial functions.
3. **Data location:** When you use the cloud, you probably won't know exactly where your data is hosted. In fact, you might not even know what country it will be stored in. Ask providers if they will commit to storing and processing data in specific jurisdictions, and whether they will make a contractual commitment to obey local privacy requirements on behalf of their clients, Gartner [20].

4. **Data segregation:** Data in the cloud is typically held in a shared environment alongside data from other clients. Encryption is effective but isn't a cure-all. "Find out what is done to segregate data at rest," (Gartner advice). The cloud provider should provide evidence that encryption schemes were designed and tested by experienced specialists. "Encryption accidents can make data totally unusable, and even normal encryption can complicate availability," a serious security risk.

5. **Recovery:** Even if you don't know where your data is, a cloud provider should tell you what will happen to your data and service in case of a disaster. Any offering that does not replicate the data and application infrastructure across multiple sites is vulnerable to a total failure. Ask your provider if it has the ability to do a complete restoration, and how long it will take.

6. **Investigative support for investigating inappropriate or illegal activity may be impossible in Cloud Computing:** Cloud services are especially difficult to investigate, because logging and data for multiple clients may be co-located and may also be spread across an ever-changing set of hosts and data centers. If you cannot get a contractual commitment to support specific forms of investigation, along with evidence that the vendor has already successfully supported such activities, then the only safe assumption is that investigation and discovery requests will be impossible.

7. **Long-term viability:** Ideally, your Cloud Computing provider will never go broke or get acquired and swallowed up by a larger company. But you must be sure that data will remain available even after such an event. Ask potential providers how you would get your data back and if it would be in a format that you could import into a replacement application. If not then it is a serious security risk.

The issue of Cloud Security and its serious repercussions have been seriously recognized by the IT Industry experts, cloud services users community and Cloud Services providers. Only seven months after their first security guide, the Cloud Security Alliance (CSA) has released a second document: The Security Guidance for Critical Areas of Focus in Cloud Computing Version 2.1. This report [21] has suggested 12 domains. Each domain provides many practical recommendations for a more secure cloud strategy. Two of these domains are highlighted as below for severity of the issue of Cloud Security.

**Domain 5: Information Lifecycle Management**

1. Make sure there is specific identification of all controls used during the data lifecycle.
2. Know where your data is.
3. Understand the compartmentalization techniques employed by a provider to isolate its customers from one another.
4. The data owner determines who should access the data, what their rights and privileges are, and under what conditions these access rights are provided.
5. Understand how encryption is managed on multi-tenant storage.
6. Perform regular backup and recovery tests to ensure that controls are effective.

**Domain 7: Traditional Security, Business Continuity, and Disaster Recovery**

1.  Understand that the centralization of data means there is a risk of insider abuse from within the cloud provider.
2.  Cloud providers should think about adopting the most stringent requirements of any customer as a security baseline.
3.  Customers should look at the cloud provider's disaster recovery and business continuity plans.
4.  Customers should identify physical interdependencies in provider infrastructure.
5.  Customers should ask for documentation of the provider's internal and external security controls, and adherence to any industry standards.

# 8  Future of Internet and Cloud Computing

In 2013, the Internet will be nearly fourtimes larger than it is today[22]. Aplications such as remote data backup, Cloud Computing, and video conferencing demand high speed access. Cloud Computing will unleash the potential of small and medium sized enterprises(SMEs) worldwide. Europe which is heavily dominated by SMEs as compared to the US, will surely benefit when companies rent, rather than buy, IT services. A recent study [23] estimated that such online business services could add 0.2 percent to the EU's annual gross domestic product growth, create a million jobs and allow hundreds and thausands of new SMEs to take off in Europe over the next five years. The Internet also offers a plateform for a new wave of smart and green growth and for tackling the challenges of an aging society. The concept and use of virtualization by cloud service providers to host virtual machines belonging to multiple customers on a shared physical infrastructure is opening up fresh data leak risks [24].

The recent news in the media about the Cyber War between USA and China  and hotline contact between President Obama and President of Peoples Republic of China and similar hackings news among other countries needs serious attention. The IT industry international experts and international regulating authorities will have to work for the evolution of robust and reliable strategy to avoid such hacking episodes in the future. The international regulation and serious imlementation by the IT international community will a have a great impact on the future security of Internet and Cloud Computing.

# 9  Conclusion

In spite of the fact that the concerns, fears, apprehensions and resevations of clients for Cloud Computing highlighted in the paper are very realistic and genuine. However, such concerns have always been there for an emerging technology and Cloud Computing is no exception to this fact. The scenario of Y2K is worth mentioning here and the outcome of it on the midnight of 31st December, 1999. It is likely that Cloud Computing is a type of deployment architecture that will be with us for a long time. Its success will depend on whether the Cloud Computing can overcome the challeges and the security concerns it currently faces.

Over the next five years, Cloud Computing services will become a solution for small and midsize companies to completely outsource their data-intensive processing projects/applications. The larger companies will have a way to get peak load capacity without building inhome larger data centers. While the corporate data-center managers are facing increasing problem with power consumption, space and IT costs. Cloud Computing will provide the means for most companies to to contain these IT costs.

Finally cloud coputing will become essential foundation for a greatly expanded IT industry by lowering the economic and technical barriers of developers to bring new offerings to market and for millions of more clients to adopt those offerings as fifth utility.

## References

1. Gruman, G.: What Cloud Computing really means. InfoWorld (April 7, 2008),
   http://www.infoworld.com/article/08/04/07/
   15FE-cloud-computing-reality_1.html (Retrieved January 13, 2009)
2. Berlind, D.: Google improves 'Apps', offers organizations clear path off Exchange, Notes, etc. to GMail. ZDNet. (June 25, 2007),
   http://blogs.zdnet.com/Berlind/?p=580
3. http://public.web.cern.ch/press/PressReleases/.../PR06.08E.html
4. LHC Computing Project, http://lhcgrid.web.cern.ch./LHCgrid
5. Buyya, R., Yeo, C.S., Venugopal, S.: Market-Oriented Cloud Computing: Vision, Hype, and Reality for Delivering IT Services as Computing Utilities, Department of Computer Science and Software Engineering, The University of Melbourne, Australia,
   http://oreilly.com/web2/archive/what-is-web-20.html
   (Retrieved July 31, 2008)
6. Running Large-Scale Apps with Massive Databases over Internet
7. http://gloriadclassroom.wordpress.com/2007/11/21/running-large-scale-apps-with-massive-databases-over-the-internet/
8. http://cloudcomputing.sys-con.com/node/579826
9. http://www.teragrid.org/eot/files/GIN-SC06-PMP.ppt
10. Leavitt, N.: Is Cloud Computing Really Ready for Prime Time, Technology News. IEEE Computer Society, Los Alamitos (January 2009)
11. Ahmad, M.: Architectural Aspects of Grid Computing and its Global prospects for e-Science community. Presented at FIT Intel., Conference, University of Terrengannu, Malaysia, January 25 (2007)
12. Erickson, J.: Cloud Computing and Virtualization (June 23, 2008)
13. Johnson, S.: Cloud Computing, Discover Cloud Computing (Web 2.0, Web Services, SaaS, PaaS, Grid, Utility, etc.)
14. http://www.globus.org/ogsa/
15. http://www.soasta.com/blog/?p=142
16. http://www.ddj.com/hpc-high-performance-computing/208800138
17. Gartner, Seven Cloud-computing Security Risks, InfoWorld,
    http://www.infoworld.com/article/08/07/02/
    Gartner_Seven_cloudcomputing_security_risks_1.html
18. http://blogs.idc.com/ie/?p=210

19. `http://www.roughtype.com/archives/2008/02/amazons_s3_util.php`
20. `http://www.gartner.com/`
    `resources/.../higher_education_qa_cloud_co_169023.pdf`
21. `http://www.cloudsecurityalliance.org/pr20091217.html`
22. Reding, V.: Commissioner for Information Society and Media. IEEE Computer Society, Los Alamitos, `http://www.computer.org/internet`
23. Etro, F.: The Economic Impact of Cloud Computing on Business Creation, Employment and Output in Europe. Rev. Business and Economics, 3 (2009)
24. Research Report,
    `http://cwflyris.computerworld.com/t/5834886/98627/233145/0/`

# Performance Evaluation of Video Streaming in Vehicular Adhoc Network

Aneel Rahim, Zeeshan Shafi Khan, and Fahad bin Muhaya

PMC, King Saud University, Kingdom of Saudi Arabia
aneelrahim@ksu.edu.sa, fmuhaya@ksu.edu.sa

**Abstract.** In Vehicular Ad-Hoc Networks (VANETs) wireless-equipped vehicles form a temporary network for sharing information among vehicles. Secure Multimedia communication enhances the safety of passenger by providing visual picture of accidents and danger situations. In this paper we will evaluate the performance of multimedia data in VANETS scenario and consider the impact of malicious node using NS-2 and Evalvid video evaluation tool.

**Keywords:** Evalvid, multimedia, malicious.

## 1 Introduction

Multimedia communication has gained the attraction of research community [1]. Multimedia Information includes the several applications like television, Chatting, gaming, internet, Video/Audio-on-Demand, video conferencing [2]. Due to rapid growth of multimedia application, Security is an important concern [3].

Authentication, Confidentiality, Integrity and non repudiation are the essential security requirement of multimedia communication in VANETs. [4] Security attacks (Denial of service, malicious node attack, Impersonation) and vulnerabilities (Forgery, violation of copywrite and privacy) exist in multimedia application due to mobility and dynamic nature of VANETs [5].

Video transmission in VANETs faces a lot of challenges due to limited bandwidth and transmission errors [6]. Security, Interference, channel fading, dynamic topology changes and infrastructure less are some other factors that degrade the performance of video streaming in VANETs [7].

We in this paper analyze the performance of multimedia traffic in VANETs with and without the interference of malicious node. We measure performance in terms of PNSR, delay, sending rate, receiving rate of vehicles.

This paper is organized as follows: In section 2, we discuss the feasibility of multimedia application in VANETs scenario and different existing frameworks for media streaming in VANETs In section 3, proposed study and results are presented using NS-2 and Evalvid. Lastly in section 4 conclusions is given.

## 2 Related Work

Moez et al. (2007) experimentally proof the feasibility of multimedia application in VANETs scenario by using IEEE 802.11[8].

S.K. Bandyopadhyay et al. (Eds.): ISA 2010, CCIS 76, pp. 220–224, 2010.
© Springer-Verlag Berlin Heidelberg 2010

Pau et al. (2008) evaluates the performance of video streaming in adhoc network [9]. He computes the quality of service by analysis different parameters like PSNR, delay and packet delivery ratio by using OLSR protocol. He demonstrates the drawbacks in the hierarchal protocols.

Stephen et al. (2008) proposed a framework for vehicular social network (VSN) called RoadSpeak [10]. The main aim of RoadSpeak is to share communication with other vehicles through voice chat.High speed of vehicles, dynamic topology and low bandwidth etc are main challenges for multimedia traffic in VANETs.

Fabio et al. (2008) presents Streaming Media Urban Grid, a distributed and dynamic multimedia solution for video streaming in VANETs scenario [11]. It depends upon inter vehicular communication for sharing multimedia data.

Paolo et al. (2008) evaluates the performance of multicast voice transmission in VANETs scenario [12]. He also presents the challenges and issues faced by multimedia traffic in adhoc network.

Junwen et al. (2008) presents priority queue algorithms to reduce the end to end delay and packet loss ratio of real time traffic in VANETs scenario [13].

# 3   Proposed Study and Results

In this study we evaluate the performance of video streaming in different VANETs scenarios. We use network simulator NS-2 [14] and EvalVid tool [15] for transmission of multimedia traffic in VANETs. We simulate the multimedia traffic in four different scenarios. First scenario in which we evaluate a performance of video scenario consider that two vehicles are moving in same direction and no malicious exist. Then we evaluate the performance in which vehicles are moving in opposite direction and they have very short interval for communication due to high speed. We also consider that no faulty node exist same like the first scenario. At the end we evaluate the both scenario i.e. same direction and opposite direction in real environment. We now consider the impact of malicious node and measure that how much it affects the performance of vehicles moving in same and opposite direction. We measure the PNSR, sending rate, receiving rate, end to end delay in ideal and real scenarios.

## 3.1   Same Direction in Ideal Scenario

In this study we have two vehicles moving at speed of 100km/hr in same direction. We also consider that no malicious node will affect the performance of network and both the vehicles are also fair nodes. Vehicles A sends video file to vehicle B at 25 frames per second and simulation runs for 100 seconds. We measure the PNSR, sending rate, receiving rate, end to end delay. Figure 1 shows the PNSR value and figure 2 shows the delay that packet faced during ideal simulation. Figure 3 and figure 4 shows the sending rate and the receiving rate that vehicles faced.

## 3.2   Opposite Direction in Ideal Scenario

In this study we have same scenario as above that two vehicles moving at speed of 100km/hr but in opposite direction and no selfish node a will affect the network.

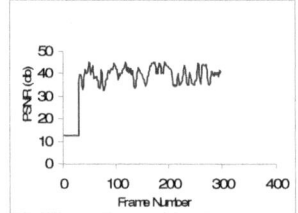
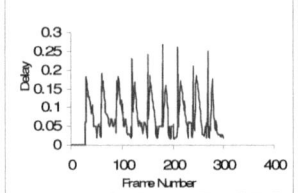
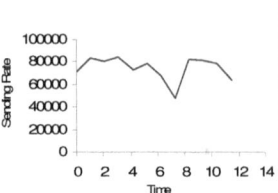

**Fig. 1.** PNSR (SD in ideal scenario)

**Fig. 2.** Delay (SD in ideal scenario)

**Fig. 3.** SR (SD in ideal scenario)

Vehicles A sends video file to vehicle B at 25 frames per second and simulation runs for 100 seconds. As the vehicles are moving at high speed and in opposite direction so that can't share all the information they have in their in buffer. We measure the PNSR, sending rate, receiving rate, end to end delay. Figure 1 shows the PNSR value and Figure 2 shows the delay. Figure 3 and Figure 4 shows the sending and receiving rate. Vehicle B can't receive all the packets because after 7 second it is no more over in range of Vehicle A.

### 3.3 Same Direction in Real Scenario

In this study we consider the impact of malicious node on the network performance. Two vehicles moving at speed of 100km/hr in same direction. Vehicles A is set to be a malicious node in network and modify it behavior and sent data to vehicle B at 15 frames per second. Figure 1 shows the PNSR value and Figure 2 shows the delay. Figure 3 and Figure 4 shows the sending and receiving rate. As Vehicles are same direction so the abnormal behavior of Vehicle A does not affect the performance of network.

### 3.4 Opposite Direction in Real Scenario

In this study we consider the impact of malicious node in opposite where vehicles are moving at high speed. Scenario is same as above Vehicle A modifies its behavior and sent 15 frames per second to vehicle B. Figure 1 shows the PNSR value and Figure 2 shows the delay. Figure 3 and Figure 4 shows the sending and receiving rate.

Due to opposite direction and malicious node, the performance of network degrades more than the opposite direction in ideal scenario.

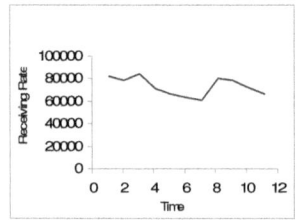
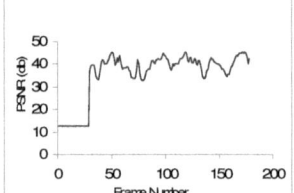
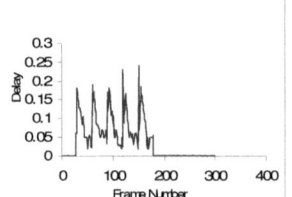

**Fig. 4.** RR (SD in ideal scenario)

**Fig. 5.** PNSR(OD in ideal scenario)

**Fig. 6.** Delay (OD in ideal scenario)

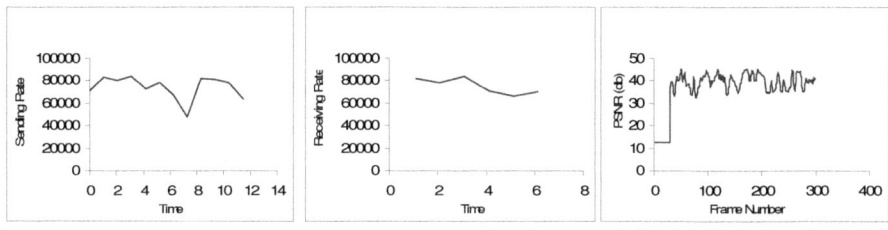

**Fig. 7.** SR (OD in ideal scenario)

**Fig. 8.** RR (OD in ideal scenario)

**Fig. 9.** PNSR (SD in real scenario)

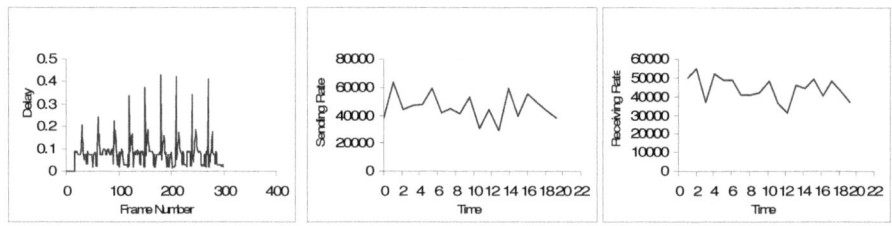

**Fig. 10.** Delay (SD in real scenario)

**Fig. 11.** SR (SD in real scenario)

**Fig. 12.** RR (SD in real scenario)

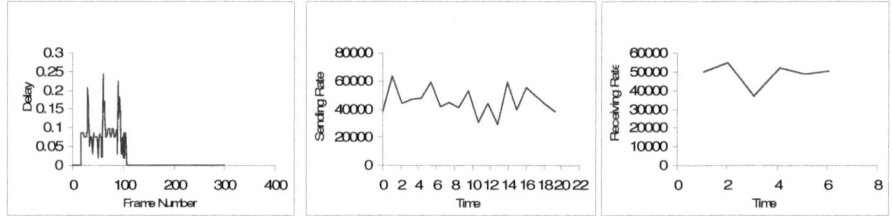

**Fig. 13.** Delay (OD in real scenario)

**Fig. 14.** SR (OD in real scenario)

**Fig. 15.** RR (OD in real scenario)

## 4   Conclusion

In this paper we evaluate the performance of multimedia data in ideal and real scenario. Simulation shows performance of multimedia traffic in VANETs scenario. We also analyze the impact of malicious vehicle on multimedia data in same and opposite direction. Results show that the Performance of network is affected by mobility, direction and malicious node.

## Acknowledgments

This research was supported by the Prince Muqrin Chair (PMC) for IT Security at King Saud University, Riyadh, Saudi Arabia.

# References

[1]  Wolf, L.C., Griwodz, C., Steinmetz, R.: Multimedia Communication. Proceedings of the IEEE 85(12) (December 1997)

[2]  Shieh, J.-R.J.: On the Security of Multimedia Video Information. IEEE, Los Alamitos (2003)

[3]  Wang, H., Hempel, M., Peng, D., Wang, W., Sharif, H., Chen, H.-H.: Index-Based Selective Audio Encryption for Wireless Multimedia Sensor Networks. IEEE Transactions On Multimedia 12(3) (April 2010)

[4]  Nahrstedt, K., Dittmnn, J., Wohlmacher, P.: Approaches to Multimedia and Security. In: IEEE International Conference on Multimedia and Expo, ICME 2000, IEEE, Los Alamitos (2000)

[5]  Raya, M., Papadimitratos, P., Hubaux, J.-P.: Securing Vehicular Communications. IEEE Wireless Communications Magazine, Special Issue on Inter-Vehicular Communications (October 2006)

[6]  Chua, Y.-C., Huang, N.-F.: Delivering of Live Video Streaming for Vehicular Communication Using Peer-to-Peer Approach. IEEE, Los Alamitos (2007)

[7]  Mao, S., Lin, S., Panwar, S.S., Wang, Y., Celebi, E.: Video Transport Over Ad Hoc Networks: Multistream Coding With Multipath Transport. IEEE Journal on Selected Areas in Communications 21(10) (December 2003)

[8]  Bonuccelli, M.A., Giunta, G., Lonetti, F., Martelli, F.: Real-time video transmission in vehicular networks. IEEE, Los Alamitos (2007)

[9]  Arce, P., Guerri, J.C., Pajares, A., Lázaro, O.: Performance Evaluation of Video Streaming Over Ad Hoc Networks Using Flat and Hierarchical Routing Protocols. Springer Mobile Netw. Appl. 13, 324–336 (2008)

[10] Smaldone, S., Han, L., Shankar, P., Iftode, L.: RoadSpeak: Enabling Voice Chat on Roadways using Vehicular Social Networks. In: SocialNets 2008, UK, April 1. ACM, New York (2008)

[11] Soldo, F., Casetti, C., Chiasserini, C.-F., Chaparro, P.: Streaming Media Distribution in VANETs. IEEE GLOBECOM 2008 (2008)

[12] Bucciol, P., Ridolfo, F., De Martin, J.C.: Multicast Voice Transmission over Vehicular Ad Hoc Networks: Issues and Challenges. In: IEEE Seventh International Conference on Networking (2008)

[13] Mi, J., Liu, F., Xu, S., Li, Q.: A Novel Queue Priority Algorithm for Real-time Message in VANETs. In: IEEE International Conference on Intelligent Computation Technology and Automation (2008)

[14] NetworkSimulator, ns2, http://www.isi.edu/nsnam/ns

[15] Ke, C.-H., Shieh, C.-K., Hwang, W.-S., Ziviani, A.: An Evaluation Framework for More Realistic Simulations of MPEG Video Transmission. Journal of Information Science and Engineering (accepted)

# Receiver Based Traffic Control Mechanism to Protect Low Capacity Network in Infrastructure Based Wireless Mesh Network

Syed Sherjeel Ahmad Gilani[1], Muhammad Zubair[2], and Zeeshan Shafi Khan[2]

[1] Foundation University, Islamabad, Pakistan
[2] Riphah International University, Islamabad, Pakistan

**Abstract.** Infrastructure-based Wireless Mesh Networks are emerging as an affordable, robust, flexible and scalable technology. With the advent of Wireless Mesh Networks (WMNs) the dream of connecting multiple technology based networks seems to come true. A fully secure WMN is still a challenge for the researchers. In infrastructure-based WMNs almost all types of existing Wireless Networks like Wi-Fi, Cellular, WiMAX, and Sensor etc can be connected through Wireless Mesh Routers (WMRs). This situation can lead to a security problem. Some nodes can be part of the network with high processing power, large memory and least energy issues while others may belong to a network having low processing power, small memory and serious energy limitations. The later type of the nodes is very much vulnerable to targeted attacks. In our research we have suggested to set some rules on the WMR to mitigate these kinds of targeted flooding attacks. The WMR will then share those set of rules with other WMRs for Effective Utilization of Resources.

**Keywords:** Mesh Networks, Targeted Attacks, Flooding Attacks.

## 1 Introduction

Wireless Mesh Network (WMN) is one of the latest technologies of wireless network. This section briefly introduces the WMNs and Infrastructure-based WMNs. WMNs are dynamic, scalable, self-organized and self-configured wireless networks with the advantages of robustness, reliability and low installation and maintenance cost.

There are so many applications of WMNs including military networks, enterprise networking [1], metropolitan area networking, broadband home networking, transportation systems, building automation, health and medical sciences, emergency response system [2], efficient support for real time applications [3], security and surveillance systems etc.

In infrastructure-based wireless mesh network (IWMN), Mesh router creates an infrastructure for clients. In this kind of network all the traffic is either forwarded to or from a gateway / mesh router. Mesh router is a device which is used by WMN to create multi-hope decentralized mesh network. WMR does not require predetermined paths as it can adjust its communication boundaries in real time. There is a gateway/bridge functionality existing in WMR, which enables it to play an important role in making IWMN.

S.K. Bandyopadhyay et al. (Eds.): ISA 2010, CCIS 76, pp. 225–232, 2010.
© Springer-Verlag Berlin Heidelberg 2010

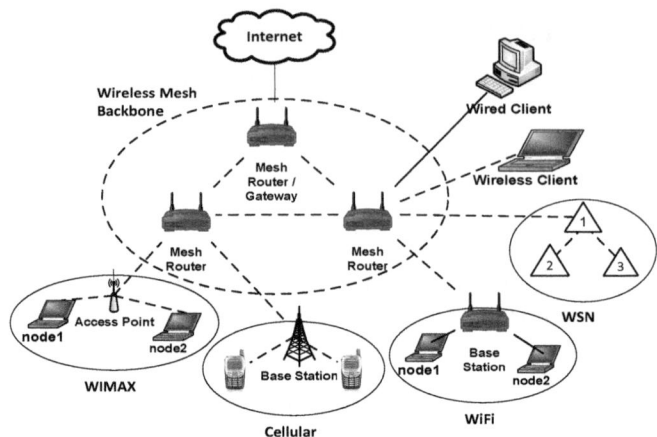

**Fig. 1.** Infrastructure based Wireless Mesh Network

WMRs form the backbone of the WMNs [4]. When a new node appears in the network, it broadcasts its address and networking capabilities. The close-by WMRs will receive the broadcast and update their list by adding the new node. When any device turns off or disappears, mesh routers will update their list accordingly. Due to this continuous adjustment, mesh routers create fault tolerant and robust networks. We can say that there is no problem of single point failure in the whole network [5].

The major drawback can be a serious security issue because of the automatic exposure of mesh routers to almost all the devices that appear in the network. In addition to this data may take longer period of time to reach its destination because of unavailability of predetermined paths.

Our research work is particularly addressing the problem of targeted flooding attacks in the IWMNs.

A Wireless Mesh Client (WMC) can be any laptop, desktop PC, palmtop, PDA, pocket PC, IP phone, RFID reader etc. In most of the cases, hardware and software for mesh clients is similar to mesh routers but gateway or bridge functions do not exist in these nodes.

## 2   Related Work

Wireless Mesh Network (WMN) is one of the most emerging and latest technologies of the present. One of the most important and current research areas is Security in WMNs. Lot of sincere and dedicated effort is required for making the WMNs more reliable and secure. WMN has many domains for research but one of the main areas of research is security. As it is relatively a new field, researchers have not worked much in this area.

Vinod et.al. in 2007 have discussed a novel end-to-end packet delay estimation mechanism with stability-aware routing policies, allowing it to more accurately follow QoS requirements while minimizing misbehavior of selfish nodes, it also guarantees QoS, to applications based on metrics of minimum bandwidth and maximum end-to-end delay, such as to support the new generation of streaming-media applications, such as voice over IP (VoIP) and video on-demand (VOD) [6]. As this approach requires proactive technique so there can be disadvantages of requiring respective amount of data for maintenance and slow reaction on restructuring and failures.

Fabian et.al. in 2009 have suggested an Open LIDS, a light weight anomaly-based intrusion detection system, simple host-based metrics to detect scanning behavior, resource consumption attacks, spam email distribution and IP address spoofing [7]. This paper explained that the devices of WMNs are typically resource constrained and their poor ability to perform intrusion detection technique. Therefore they have suggested this Open LIDS. In this Research there are some problems like this system is not as efficient for high rates of new connections and it is not possible to arbitrarily adjust time out values in this solution. Yeyan et.al. in 2009 proposed that an active cache based defense solution can detect the existence of attacking flows based on the frequency of incoming packets and eliminate the attacking flows by discarding packets by a Drop Probability (DP) [8]. In this research the solution is mainly dealing with simple client WMN but will find some difficulty to handle the Infrastructure based WMNs.

Xiawang et.al. in 2009 have proposed a cross-layer based anomaly intrusion detection system (IDS) to accommodate the integrated property of routing protocols with link information in wireless mesh networks (WMNs) [9]. According to their study, cross-layer based IDS out performs single layer based IDS: on the average it provides higher detection rate. This detection system is only suitable for local system and cannot work with distributed system. A real-time detection cannot be made with is intrusion detection system.

KuiRen in 2010 have developed PEACE, a novel Privacy-Enhanced yet Accountable security framework, tailored for WMNs. They have established an accountable security framework with a sophisticated user privacy protection model tailored for metropolitan scale WMNs. In this research some more techniques can also be used to further enhance the scheme efficiency [10].

Mehdi et.al in 2009 have discussed the drawbacks of flooding-based technique for Mobility management in Wireless Mesh Networks (WMN) and have developed a DHT-based approach, which according to them, can overcome such limitations and provide an effective solution to the mobility management problem. The solution of this research work can only handle less number of nodes so it is not efficient for larger number of nodes and for several different metrics [11].

Shafi et.al. in 2009 have introduced a three layered architecture designed for next generation technology. Authors presented a three layer architecture in which rules are configured by both sender and receiver. The main focus of the authors is on IP Multimedia Subsystem [12].

## 3   Problem Definition

As we discussed in Section 1 that IWMN connects different types of networks through Mesh Routers so it can lead towards some security issues. Nodes of different connected networks may have different capabilities like different processing speed, buffer size, battery life etc.

So a node with higher processing resources, higher buffer size and higher energy can flood a node of another network which has limited processing resources, buffer size and energy by sending too many requests [13]. (Request may be legitimate or they may be malicious).

According to our best knowledge, this area of protecting a low capacity node from a higher capacity attacker is ignored by most of the researchers.

This problem disturbs the overall structure of the WMN because wireless mesh network technology is designed to interconnect various types of networks.

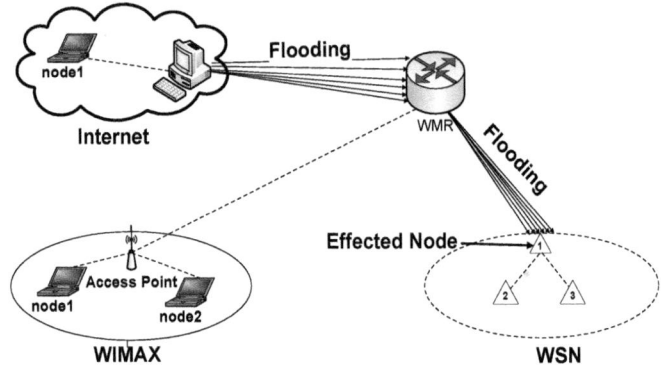

**Fig. 2.** DOS attack to a low power network client

These flooding attacks can cause the following after effects,

i)   Mesh network failure.
ii)  Converged networks success can be affected.
iii) Mesh network security can be at stake.
iv)  Discourage low capacity networks to become part of the mesh networks.

## 4   Proposed Solution and Methodology

To protect the low capacity node of a network from a high capacity attacker we introduce a Receiver Based Traffic Controlling Mechanism. In this receiver based traffic control mechanism each receiver specifies its preferences that at what time which information it wants to receive from which user. These rules are specified at the edge mesh router of that node.

Whenever edge mesh router receives a packet for any particular receiver, it matches that packet with the specified rules of that receiver. If the rules do not allow the packet to be delivered to the receiver, it is discarded by mesh router; otherwise it is forwarded to the receiver.

For instance any of the receivers belonging to a low capacity network, like a sensor network, can be saved from the targeted flooding attacks by enabling its rules on the edge mesh router, e.g. we can apply the rule to not accept any packet from any particular sender node belonging to a high speed network, like internet, between

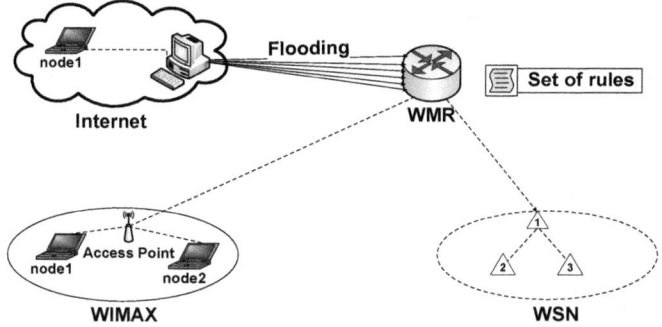

**Fig. 3.** Set of rules implemented on MR

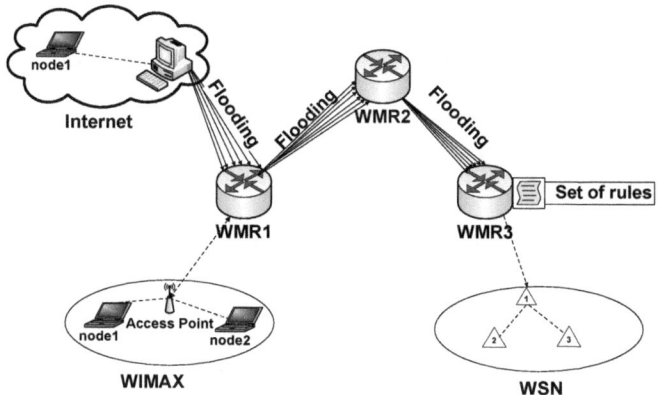

**Fig. 4.** Wastage of resources

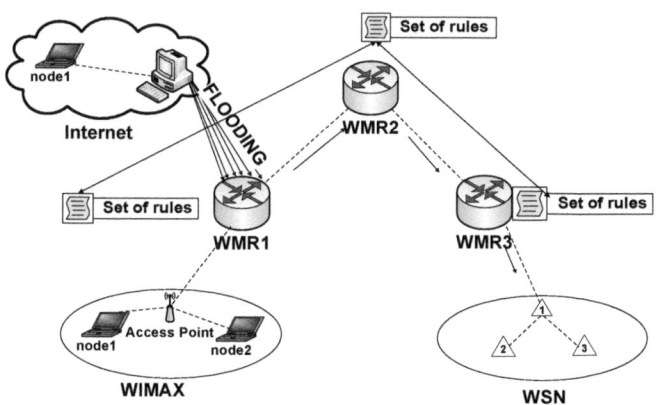

**Fig. 5.** Set of rules on MR close to sender

10 am to 10pm. Similarly a sender belonging to a high speed network can be restricted in terms of maximum number of packets it can send in particular interval of time.

Rules can be periodically updated by the receiver and in this way a node can stop some other nodes from sending too much data to it.

Configuring the rules at receiver's edge router can restrict the attacking and flooding nodes to send too many packets to the receiver but the resources consumed by the discarded request can go waste. A request that comes to the receiver's edge router may be coming by travelling 5-6 hops. So the resources consumed by that request in that case go waste.

In the second module of this work we tried therefore, to configure the receiver's rules near to the sender's end, so that a discarded request consumes very limited resources of the network.

## 5   Validation

We simulate the tests in OMNeT and writing the rules here in simple text as follows,

Receiving rules of Node '1' of WSN:

i)   Do not accept any connection / message from Node 'A' of Internet between 10 am to 10 pm.
ii)  Receive only 20 messages per hour from Node 'B' of WiMax network.
iii) Receive each and every message from Node 'C'.

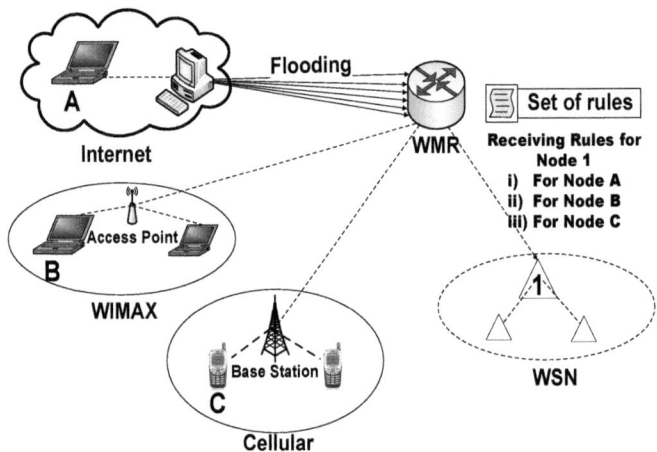

**Fig. 6.** Set of rules on MR for client 1 of WSN

**Test (1):**
**Experiment 1:**   As many as 50 connection requests were sent from Node 'A' of Internet to Node '1' of WSN between 11am to 12pm. But we observed that none of the connection request was entertained, hence validating the rule (i).

**Experiment 2:** A total of 150 more connection requests were made by Node 'A' of Internet to Node '1' of WSN within 11:30 pm and 11:50pm. This time all connection requests were entertained, validating rule (i) once again.

**Test (2):**
**Experiment 1:** Fifty connection requests were sent from Node 'B' of WiMAX to Node '1' of WSN between 9:55 pm to 10:05pm. We found that 20 requests were entertained within time range of 9:55pm to 10:00pm while additional 20 requests were entertained within the time range of 10:00pm to 10:05pm as per our defined rule, while the remaining 10 requests were discarded. Hence validating rule (ii).

**Experiment 2:** As many as 36 connection requests sent from Node 'B' of WiMAX to Node '1' of WSN within time range of 10 am to 11:15 am. We found that 20 connection requests were entertained within time range of 10 am to 11am while the remaining 16 requests were entertained within time range of 11:00 am to 11:15 am. Hence validating rule (ii).

**Test (3):**
**Experiment 1:** We sent different number of connection requests at different time frames from Node 'C' of Cellular network to Node '1' of WSN, we found that all the requests were entertained by the receiver, hence proving the validity of rule (iii).

## 6 Conclusion

WMNs are dynamic, self-organized and self-configured wireless networks with many advantages like reliability, scalability, robustness, low installation and maintenance cost. In IWMNs, mesh routers make the infrastructure-backbone and allow client nodes of different types of networks to communicate with each other. In IWMNs the client nodes belonging to low power networks are vulnerable to targeted flooding attacks. Our research proposes a Receiver Based Traffic Control Mechanism (RBTCM) which can mitigate this problem of targeted flooding attack. In the first phase of our solution, we implement the set of rules on the receiver's edge router to restrict the attacking and flooding nodes. In the second phase we try to configure the receiver's rules near the sender's end, so that the discarded request consumes very limited resources of the network.

## References

1. Akyildiz, I.F., Wang, X., Wang, W.: Wireless mesh networks: a survey Broad band and Wireless Networking, (BWN) Lab, School of Electrical and Computer Engineering, Georgia Institute of Technology, Atlanta (January 1, 2005)
2. Dilmaghani, R.B., Rao, R.R.: Hybrid Wireless Mesh Network with Application to Emergency Scenarios. Journal of Software 3(2), 52–60 (2008)
3. Yan, W., Ren, M., Zhao, T., Li, X.: A Bandwidth Management Scheme Support for Real-time Applications in Wireless Mesh Networks. In: ACM symposium on Applied computing Computer networks, Fortaleza, Ceara, Brazil, pp. 2063–2068 (2008)

4. Akyidiz, I.F., Wang, X., Wang, W.: Wireless Mesh Network: a Survey. The International Journal of Computer and Telecommunications Networking 47(4), 445–487 (2004)
5. Mynampati, V., Kandula, D., Garimilla, R., Srinivas, K.: Performance and Security of Wireless Mesh Networks, Blekinge Institute of Technology (June 2009)
6. Kone, V., Das, S., Zhao, B.Y., Zheng, H.: QUORUM: quality of service in wireless mesh networks. Mobile Networks and Applications 12(5), 358–369 (2007)
7. Hugelshofer, F., Smith, P., Hutchison, D., Race, N.J.P.: OpenLIDS: A Light weight Intrusion Detection System for Wireless Mesh Networks. In: International Conference on Mobile Computing and Networking, Beijing, China (2009)
8. YeYan, JiannongCao, ZhuLi: Stochastic Security Performance of Active Cache Based Defense against DoS Attacks in Wireless Mesh Network. In: Second International Conference on Advances in Mesh Networks, Athens/Glyfada, Greece (2009)
9. XiaWang, Wong, J.S., Stanley, F., SamikBasu: Cross-layer Based Anomaly Detection in Wireless Mesh Networks. In: Ninth Annual International Symposium on Applications and the Internet, Washington, DC, USA (2009)
10. KuiRen, ShuchengYu, WenjingLou, YanchaoZhang: PEACE: Privacy-Enhancement Yet Accountable Security Framework. IEEE transactions on parallel and distributed systems 21(2), 1045–9219 (2010)
11. Bezahaf, M., LuigiIanonne: Practical DHT-Based Location Service for Wireless Mesh Networks. In: International Conference on Emerging Networking Experiments and Technologies, Rome, Italy, pp. 47–48 (2009)
12. Khan, Z.S., Sher, M., Rashid, K., Rahim, A.: A Three-Layer Secure Architecture for IP Multimedia Subsystem-Based Instant Messaging. Information Security Journal: A Global Perspective 18(3), 139–148 (2009)

# Secure Mechanism for Handling Targeted Attacks in Infrastructure Based Wireless Mesh Networks

Rehan Shafi[2], Aneel Rahim[1,2], Fahad bin Muhaya[1],
Shehzad Ashraf[2], and Muhammad Sher[2]

[1] Prince Muqrin Chair of IT Security, King Saud University, KSA
[2] Department of Computer Science, International Islamic University, Pakistan

**Abstract.** Infrastructure based Wireless mesh networks allow heterogeneous types of networks to be connected at a time through wireless mesh routers. Since the nodes of every network have different processing power, bandwidth, amount of energy etc. so this situation can lead to targeted attacks. An Internet connected node can easily generate flood over a node of sensor network. So to handle these types of attacks we in this paper introduced a new secure authentication mechanism that works when a potential of attack is detected. Moreover we also authorized the nodes of the wireless mesh network to demand data according to their capacity by using pull data traffic control mechanism. We applied this solution first on mesh routers to discourage targeted attacks and secondly we applied the solution on an individual node that lies in between a node and mesh router.

**Keywords:** Wireless Mesh Network, Pull Data Traffic Control Mechanism, Authentication, Flooding.

## 1 Introduction

Mesh Networks, one of the latest technologies, allow different types of network technologies to be connected through wireless mesh router. On one interface of a mesh router a WiMAX based network can be attached and on the other interface sensor network can be connected. Mesh router connects different types of networks with each other. Collection of mesh routers is known as backbone. Internet may also be connected through mesh routers.

Wireless Mesh Networks (WMN) are gaining lot of reserchers as well as users' attention because of their easy deployment and many other advantages. Thers are so many applications of WMNs including military networks, enterprise networking [1], metropoliton area networking, broadband home networking, transportation systems, building automation, health and medical sciences, emergency response system [2], efficient support for real time applications [3], security and surveillance systems [4] etc.

Wireless Mesh Routers (WMR) form the backbone of the WMNs [5]. When a new node appears in the network, it broadcasts its address and networking capabilities. The close-by WMRs will receive the broadcast and update their list by adding the new node. When any device turns off or disappears, mesh routers will update their list accordingly. Due to this continuous adjustment, mesh routers create fault tolerant and

S.K. Bandyopadhyay et al. (Eds.): ISA 2010, CCIS 76, pp. 233–240, 2010.

robust networks. We can say that there is no problem of single point failure in the whole network.

A WMC can be any laptop, desktop PC, palmtop, PDA, pocket PC, IP phone, RFID reader etc. In most of the cases, hardware and software for mesh clients is similar to mesh routers but gateway or bridge functions do not exist in these nodes.

Section 2 of the paper describes the related work, section 3 highlights the problem, section 4 explains the solution in detail, and section 5 consists of conclusion and future work.

## 2   Related Work

Vinod et.al. in 2007 worked on reducing the effect of selfish nodes, [6]. Fabian et.al. in 2009 developed an intrusion detection system by focusing on anomaly based detection. [7]. The proposed solution seems to be well designed but it is not scalable in terms of number of connection. Active cache based security with drop probability is proposed by Yeyan et.al. in 2009 [8]. Xiawang et.al. in 2009 have proposed a cross-layer based anomaly intrusion detection system (IDS)[9]. First of all this solution does not work well in distributed scenario and secondly real time detection is not in the scope of this solution.

A novel Privacy-Enhanced yet Accountable security framework is proposed by KuiRen in 2010 [10]. Mehdi et.al in 2009 have discussed the drawbacks of flooding-based technique for Mobility management in Wireless Mesh Networks (WMN) and have developed a DHT-based approach, which according to them, can overcome such limitations and provide an effective solution to the mobility management problem [11].

Shafi et.al. in 2009 have introduced a three layered architecture for IP Multimedia subsystem. Sender specifies rule to avoid spoofed use and receiver specifies rules to avoid targeted attacks. Intrusion detection mechanism is deployed at core [12].

Shafi et.al. in 2010 proposed a call back authentication mechanism for web to cellular phone SMS communication. In their paper they proposed a token based authentication scheme and pull data traffic control mechanism but their solution totally focuses on GSM technology and handling of SMS flood [13].

## 3   Problem Analysis

As discussed in section 1, Infrastructure based wireless mesh network connects different types of networks with each other by using mesh routers. So on one side of a mesh router an Internet node can be connected and on the other side a sensor node may exists. So for an Internet node there is high processing speed, high bandwidth, and no battery or energy issues but for sensor node energy is a very serious issue and bandwidth is also low. Processing power of a sensor node is also very low as compared to an Internet connected high speed workstation. This situation allows the Internet connected node to launch a targeted attack on a node of sensor network.

Targeted attack can easily be launched by sending enormous number of requests to a particular receiver. For Internet connected node, generating thousands of requests per unit time is not a big issue but for a sensor node receiving and processing those requests is a big problem and it can results in expiring the battery of a sensor node. It can also cause denial of service attack on that particular sensor node.

Currently in wireless mesh networks there exists no mechanism that can handle these targeted attacks. Few intrusion detection and prevention mechanisms exist for wireless mesh networks but they mostly handle the attacks on wireless mesh routers. Handling targeted flooding attacks on a particular node is still an open issue in wireless mesh networks. Figure 1 describes the problem statement in detail.

## 4 Proposed Solution

We in this paper proposed a new solution to handle the targeted attacks in wireless mesh networks. Our solution will work in three different scenarios which are described below:

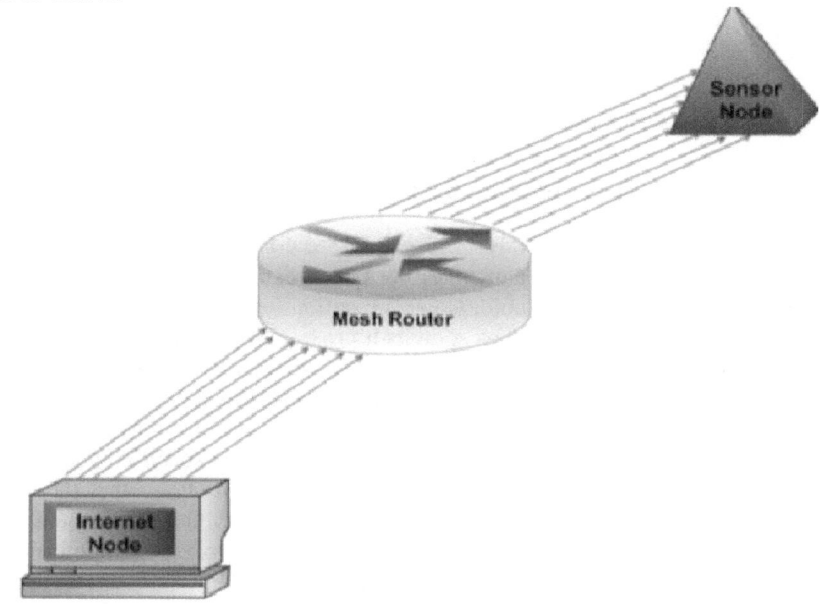

**Fig. 1 (a).** Targeted Attack Scenario

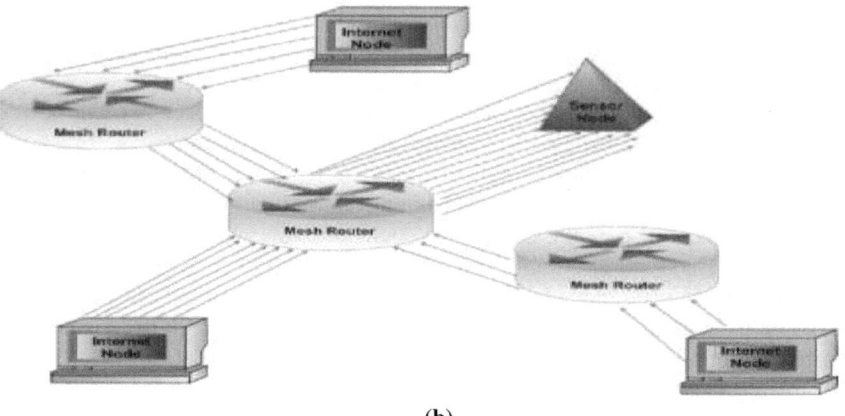

**(b)**

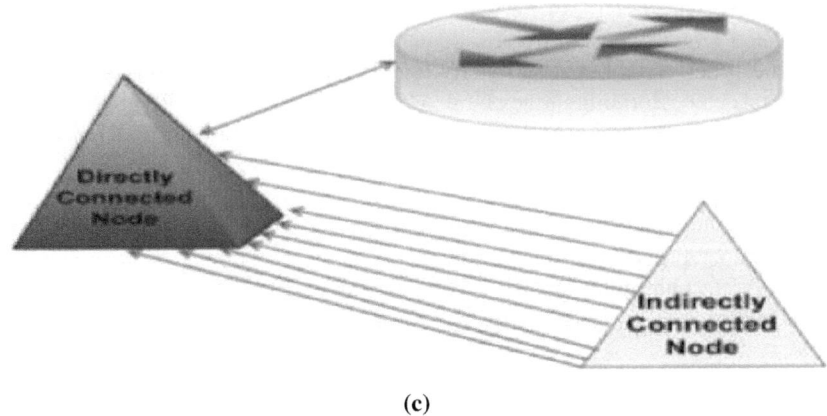

(c)

**Fig. 1 (b, c).** Distributed Targeted Attack Scenario & Flooding Attacks on Intermediate Node

### 4.1 Scenario 1: Wireless Mesh Router Detects a Targeted Attack

In this scenario first of all two threshold values are configured on the wireless mesh router. First threshold value is named as normal threshold and the second threshold value is titled as abnormal threshold. Communication between a particular sender and receiver is analyzed carefully and as soon as it crosses the normal threshold value the wireless mesh router comes into action. It verifies whether the sender is a real user or she is using a spoofed ID. For this purpose the wireless mesh router sends a simple token to the sender. Simple token is four bytes packet and the sender is required to submit the same token back to wireless mesh router within a specified period of time. If the wireless mesh router receives the same token back it shows that the sender is using real ID, she is not a spoofed user. If the received token does not match with the one issued or the wireless mesh router does not receive the token back until timeout it decides that the sender is using a spoofed ID, it blocks the communication of that particular sender for a temporary period of time and notify the node whose ID is spoofed. Receiver is also notified about this decision. If the received token is valid, communication remains in progress until the abnormal threshold arrives. As soon as sender's data touches the abnormal threshold the wireless mesh router verifies whether the sender is a legitimate user or a zombie (compromised machine) node. If it is a zombie node then it can submit the previously issued token back to wireless mesh router easily. So issuing a simple token can detect a spoofed user but can not detect the zombie machine. So when the traffic rate touches the abnormal threshold the wireless mesh router launches another mechanism to detect the zombie machine. In that mechanism wireless mesh router sends an image token (image with printed text) to the sender. Since till now there exists no such software which can read text from an image 100% correctly so a zombie machine can not return the printed image text in textual form. So if the sender is a zombie machine it can not submit the image text back and on timeout or on getting wrong image text the sender is blocked and receiver is notified. Figure 3 describes the scenario in detail.

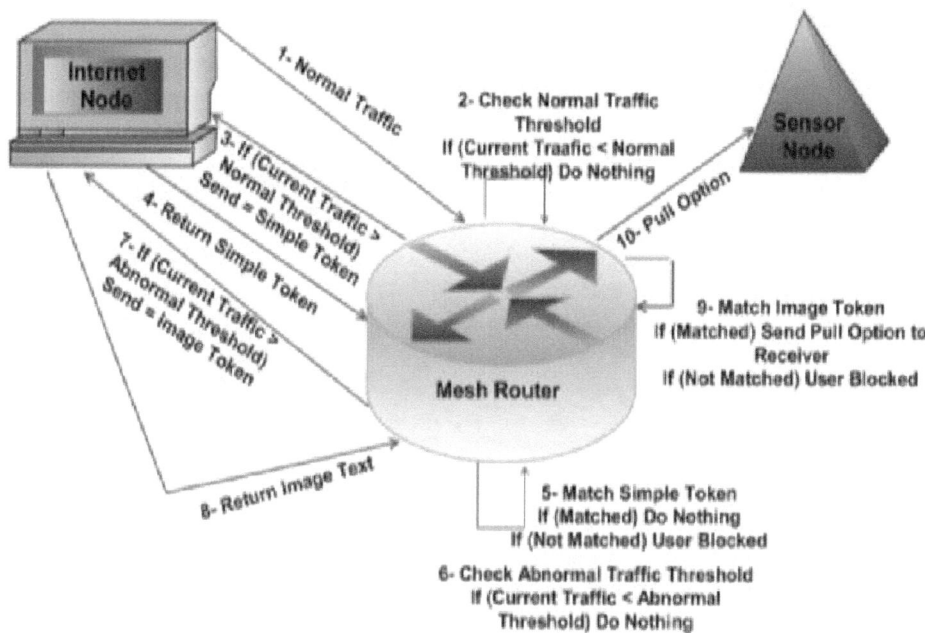

**Fig. 3.** Description of Scenario 1

## 4.2   Scenario I1: Receiver Detects a Targeted Attack

If a single sender tries to flood a particular receiver the threshold values can work to stop her. But if this attack is launched through distributed nodes then it is very hard for wireless mesh router to detect it. It may be launched by nodes those are connected with different wireless mesh routers, so in this situation it becomes more difficult to detect it. Therefore to address this situation the receiver upon him attack is launched sends a complaint to directly connected wireless mesh router. That wireless mesh router informs the other wireless mesh router that verifies the senders who are sending requests to that particular receiver. So the wireless mesh routers start token base authentication mechanism (See Scenario 1). On the same time directly connected wireless mesh router of the receiver asks the receiver whether she wants to use pull data traffic control mechanism or not. If the receiver selects the pull data traffic control mechanism the wireless mesh router stops sending data to that receiver until the receiver demands it. So in this way targeted attacks are blocked. Figure 4 describes the scenario in detail.

## 4.3   Scenario I1I: Middle Node of Multi-hop Wireless Mesh Network Detects a Targeted Attack

Wireless mesh network may also work in multi-hop mode. It is not necessary that all the nodes should directly connect to wireless mesh router, few nodes can be connected to wireless mesh router through other nodes. So if a node which is two hop away from the wireless mesh router tries to launch a targeted attack on one hop away

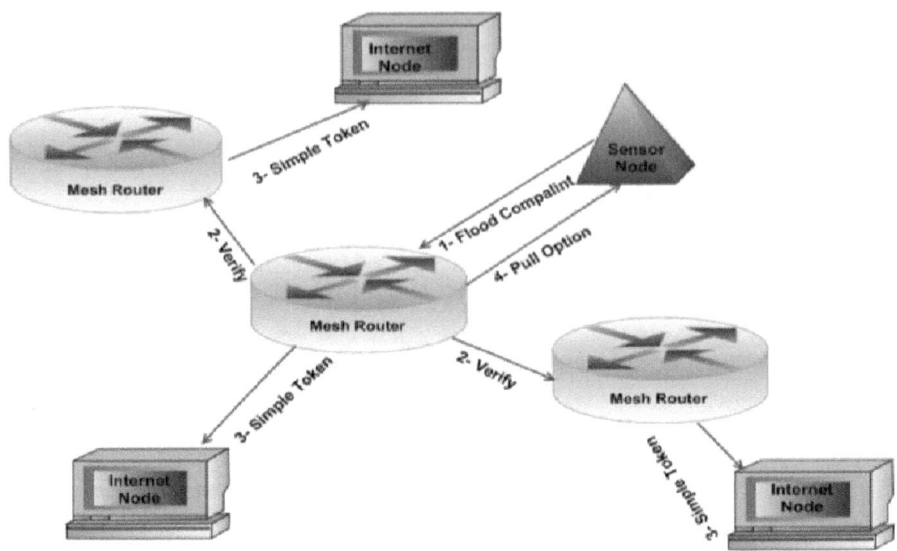

**Fig. 4.** Description of Scenario II

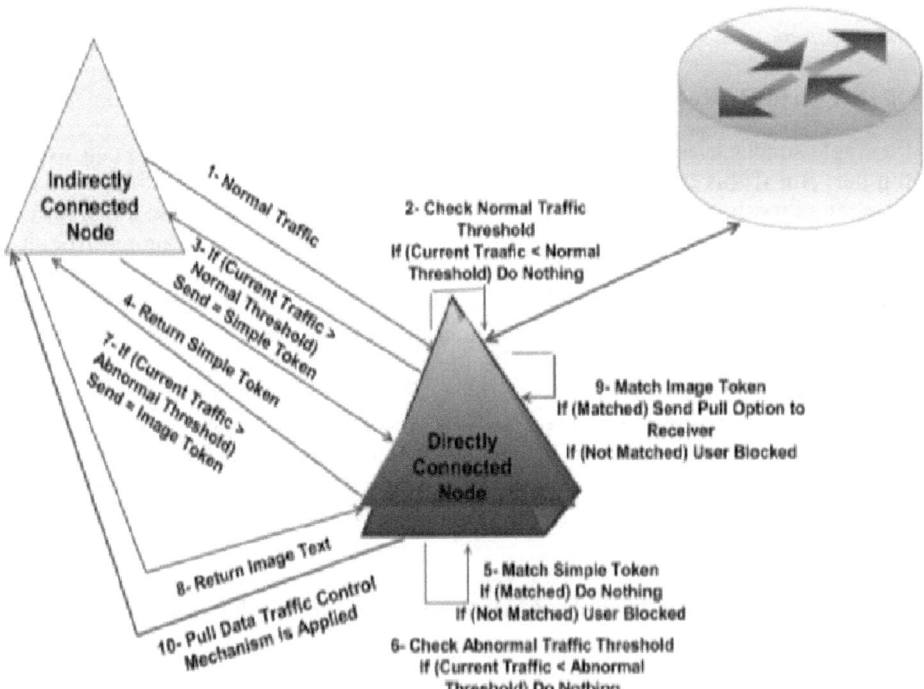

**Fig. 5.** Description of Scenario III

node (while the one hop away node is not the receiver, it is only the middle node which is connecting the sender or attacker to the wireless mesh router) then we need a mechanism to detect and prevent this attack. For this purpose when a middle node feels that the connected node is sending too many requests it first verifies the identity of the sender by issuing simple token as discussed in scenario 1. If the traffic crosses the abnormal threshold the middle node sends the image token to the connected node in order to check that the connected node is not a zombie machine. At a stage when a middle node feels that now it is not possible to accept more data from the connected node it notifies to the connected node that I am starting a pull data traffic control mechanism. After that the middle node accepts data from the connected node only when it has some resources to process it. Figure 5 describes the scenario in detail.

## 5  Conclusion and Future Work

In this paper we introduce a secure mechanism to handle the targeted attacks. We develop three scenarios in which targeted attacks can be launched and proposed solution for all the three scenarios. Simple token is used to identify the spoofed users while the image token is used to identify the zombie machine. Pull based traffic control mechanism is introduced to discourage the targeted attacks. In future we are planning to implement these solutions in some simulator to get quantitative and qualitative results of the solution. Omnet or NS-2 can be the best choices for it.

## References

1. Akyildiz, I.F., Wang, X., Wang, W.: Wireless mesh networks: a survey Broad band and Wireless Networking, (BWN) Lab. School of Electrical and Computer Engineering, Georgia Institute of Technology, Atlanta (January 1, 2005)
2. Dilmaghani, R.B., Rao, R.R.: Hybrid Wireless Mesh Network with Application to Emergency Scenarios. Journal of Software 3(2), 52–60 (2008)
3. Yan, W., Ren, M., Zhao, T., Li, X.: A Bandwidth Management Scheme Support for Real-time Applications in Wireless Mesh Networks. In: ACM symposium on Applied computing Computer networks, Fortaleza, Ceara, Brazil, pp. 2063–2068 (2008)
4. Akyidiz, I.F., Wang, X., Wang, W.: Wireless Mesh Network: a Survey. The International Journal of Computer and Telecommunications Networking 47(4), 445–487 (2004)
5. Mynampati, V., Kandula, D., Garimilla, R., Srinivas, K.: Performance and Security of Wireless Mesh Networks, Blekinge Institute of Technology (June 2009)
6. Kone, V., Das, S., Zhao, B.Y., Zheng, H.: QUORUM: quality of service in wireless mesh networks. Mobile Networks and Applications 12(5), 358–369 (2007)
7. Hugelshofer, F., Smith, P., Hutchison, D., Race, N.J.P.: OpenLIDS: A Light weight Intrusion Detection System for Wireless Mesh Networks. In: International Conference on Mobile Computing and Networking, Beijing, China (2009)
8. YeYan, JiannongCao, ZhuLi: Stochastic Security Performance of Active Cache Based Defense against DoS Attacks in Wireless Mesh Network. In: Second International Conference on Advances in Mesh Networks, Athens/Glyfada, Greece (2009)
9. XiaWang, Wong, J.S., Stanley, F., SamikBasu: Cross-layer Based Anomaly Detection in Wireless Mesh Networks. In: Ninth Annual International Symposium on Applications and the Internet, Washington, DC, USA (2009)

10. KuiRen, ShuchengYu, WenjingLou, YanchaoZhang: PEACE: Privacy-Enhancement Yet Accountable Security Framework. IEEE transactions on parallel and distributed systems 21(2), 1045–9219 (2010)
11. Bezahaf, M., Ianonne, L.: Practical DHT-Based Location Service for Wireless Mesh Networks. In: International Conference on Emerging Networking Experiments and Technologies, Rome, Italy, pp. 47–48 (2009)
12. Khan, Z.S., Sher, M., Rashid, K., Rahim, A.: A Three-Layer Secure Architecture for IP Multimedia Subsystem-Based Instant Messaging. Information Security Journal: A Global Perspective 18(3), 139–148 (2009)
13. Khan, Z.S., Rashid, K., Muhaya, F.B., Qutbuddin, Rahim, A.: Realization of call back authentication for web to cellular phone SMS communication. In: Computer and Mathematics with Application. Elsevier, Amsterdam (2009), doi:10.1016/j.camwa.2009.12.038

# MPLS Unleashed: Remedy Using IPSEC over MPLS VPN

Syed Noor-ul-Hassan Shirazi, Muhammad Asim, Muhammad Irfan, and Nassar Ikram

National University of Science and Technology, Islamabad, Pakistan
noorshirazi@gmail.com, asimonline27@hotmail.com,
{cisirfan,dr_nassar_ikram}@yahoo.com

**Abstract.** As a result of globalization, companies are striving to reach out to their customers, suppliers and partners thus extending their enterprise to provide access to critical information and offer their services upon whom their business is dependent. The bedrock of far reaching enterprise is IP network. Researchers have developed core network technology like MPLS with promising features of flexibility, scalability and security to enable enterprises to extend their businesses and transact successfully. As a result, MPLS is widely used in supporting applications like data, voice and video on the internet. It has been highly competitive from its predecessors Frame relay and ATM in terms of providing supports services. Notwithstanding its attributes, there are vulnerabilities and risks associated with MPLS. Recent papers and research reports have highlighted such issues. This paper represents a further contribution in identifying MPLS vulnerabilities and risks. In addition to discussing conventional approach of mitigating those risks, the paper also proposes IPSEC over MPLS VPN and its benefit over conventional approach.

**Keywords:** MPLS, IPSec over MPLS, MPLS Security.

## 1 Introduction

The Multi-Protocol Label Switching, commonly better known as MPLS is a technology which is transforming the networks into fast, scalable and secure global networks. This constitutes the cornerstone for delivering innovative, attractive and real time services even better than other core infrastructure technology by increasing speed and quality of services.

MPLS defines a mechanism for packet forwarding in network routers. It was originally developed to provide faster packet forwarding than traditional IP routing, although improvements in router hardware have reduced the importance of speed in packet forwarding. However, the flexibility of MPLS has led to it becoming the default way for modern networks to achieve Quality of Service (QoS), next generation VPN services, and optical signaling [1].

MPLS technology has transformed the industry and revolutionized the services that subscribers demand by reducing corporate network infrastructure costs with the elimination of private circuit and leased lines. Traditionally layer 3 routing protocols

S.K. Bandyopadhyay et al. (Eds.): ISA 2010, CCIS 76, pp. 241–248, 2010.
© Springer-Verlag Berlin Heidelberg 2010

do not have any interaction with layer 2 network characteristics, making the implementation of Quality of Service QoS and loading features difficult [2] whereas, MPLS is a layer 2.5 protocol amalgamated of layer 2 and layer 3 characteristics to improve quality of traffic engineering. MPLS draws its packet delivery speed attribute by using a label which refers to the forwarding equivalence class (FEC) for a group of data packet destined for a common destination as shown in Fig.1. Unlike traditional hop-by-hop destination routing which analyze the destination IP address contained in the network layer header for every packet at each hop.

Security and recovery times are other main advantages those are driving service providers towards MPLS based networks [3]. MPLS offers security in terms of VPN functionality by traffic separation and MPLS local protection meets the requirements of real-time applications with recovery times comparable to those of SONET rings of less than 50 ms [4, 5].

The paper is organized as follows. Section 2 compares MPLS routing with conventional routing. In Section 3 we discuss vulnerabilities and risks associated with MPLS. Section 4 briefly discusses the conventional approach to mitigate those risks. Section 5 describes proposed approach implementing IPSEC over MPLS VPN to mitigate security risks associated with MPLS and in last section conclusion has been drawn.

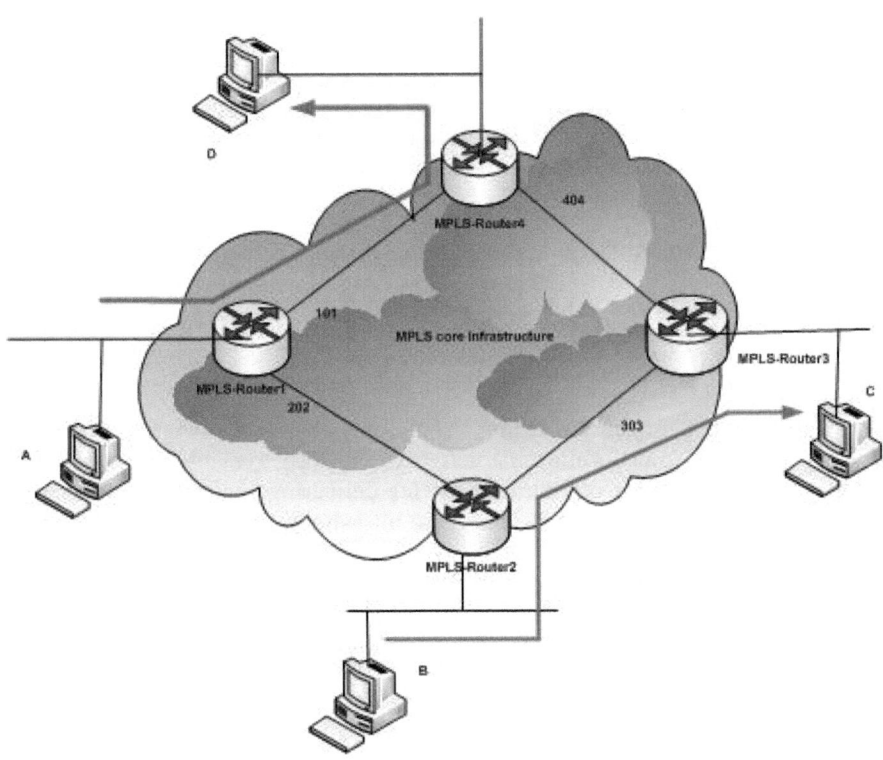

**Fig. 1.** Label Packet traversing in MPLS network

## 2  Comparison of MPLS with Conventional Routing

MPLS is more highly evolved than its predecessors frame relay (FR) and ATM. The major difference between MPLS and frame relay is that frame relay switches the frame packets based on data link connection identifiers (DLCI) and not on IP. On the contrary, in case of MPLS, the switches look at the source and destination IP of the packets to keep IP routes for building of forwarding information base (FIB).

MPLS is useful as an enabler for real-time applications because it provides asynchronous transfer mode (ATM) like capabilities with an IP network, unlike the expensive ATM links that would be required to support such applications. This service and the ability to converge real-time applications onto the data network present a tremendous opportunity to reduce operational costs and consolidate infrastructures [6].

## 3  Security Risks Associated with MPLS

There are different risks associated with MPLS which have been categorized into two types i.e., internal risks those are associated with devices inside the MPLS core and external risks those are relevant to devices outside the MPLS core.

### 3.1  External Risks

External risks are as follows:

**Scoundrel Path Switching.** An undesired path followed by a packet is known as scoundrel path. If the attacker outside the core knows the label information for such a scoundrel path and attaches those labels earlier, this will allow him to predetermine the path and to avoid the desired path of the service provider hence, disturbing the rules of segregation and traffic engineering [3].

**Scoundrel Destination Switching.** If attackers outside the core network were to know the label information for destination path, then attaching those labels earlier could allow them to encode the destination of their traffic to be of that scoundrel destination hence avoiding the traffic engineering setup of the service provider.

**Inventory of labels.** An attacker could investigate the label if MPLS device accepts labeled packet from outside the MPLS core, potentially allowing for two attacks to be realized:

i.   *expose the details of label paths*
ii.  *expose the details of targets*

In order to carry out either of the above mentioned attacks, a label brute force technique is used which increments label or label stack to a type of packet to which a reply can be expected [3]. The brute force technique attaches the labels which encode the actual label in a portion of the packet that allows it to be sealed in the related reply for TCP sequence number.TCP SYN packet or ICMP echo request are popular examples for this type of attacks.

**Detail inventory of label paths.** In order to find the complete information about the path packet takes to reach its destination when target IP is known. An attacker increments the label in anticipation of the replay from the target. The received reply then would be decoded to recover the sealed label switching path information [3].

**Deformation of Label information base.** Normally MPLS device accepts label distribution protocol (LDP) advertisement and routing information from outside because label distribution protocol is not authenticated which creates some loop hole for an attacker outside the core to poison the label information base (LIB) of one or more MPLS devices. Thus following attacks could be realized:

i. *Denial of Service- is form of attack in which the attacker redirects the traffic to a path which is not desired like the congested path. It could be done by manipulating the LIB entries in table.*

ii. *Malicious spy- the attacker can make a device part of the MPLS domain by poisoning the LIB of an MPLS domain. Taking advantage of this situation the attacker might change the LIB to forward interesting traffic to specific device where this traffic can be captured and store before forwarding it back into the MPLS domain.*

**Illicit access to the LER.** An illicit access can be gained of label edge router (LER) which could provide details of connectivity to the core infrastructure like label distribution information. Normally such attacks are due to miss configuration and improper hardening.

### 3.2 Internal Risks

By placing a device inside the core of MPLS network, the attacker might get the physical access of the core infrastructure but without the modification of the MPLS device. The above mentioned risks are also associated inside the core; in addition some of internal risks are as follows:

**Plain or unencrypted traffic.** MPLS enabled devices forward plain IP traffic which leaves a chance for an attacker to forward unlabeled IP traffic inside the core. This can be exploited by attacker inside the core to reach other core devices. Traffic engineering and other VPN capabilities which is implemented by MPLS would not protect against these sorts of attacks.

**Forwarding of traffic from the core to the outside.** If the label is known to an attacker, he can encapsulate the captured packet into UDP and spoof the source address and source port, and then configure destination IP address, port number and label to forward it through the MPLS infrastructure. Once packet is received by the listener, it strips off the UDP header and holds an exact copy of the packet captured in the core. To successfully launch an attack, label of the LSP in question should be known [7].

## 4  Conventional Approaches to Mitigation

The above mentioned risks are very critical so by using different approaches one can get rid of these vulnerabilities. Even though there is no publicly known security weakness in any MPLS implementation so far due to the fact that it differs based on implementation technique adopted by different vendors. In infrastructure like MPLS VPN, following are the conventional scenarios for IPSEC VPN as shown in Fig.2

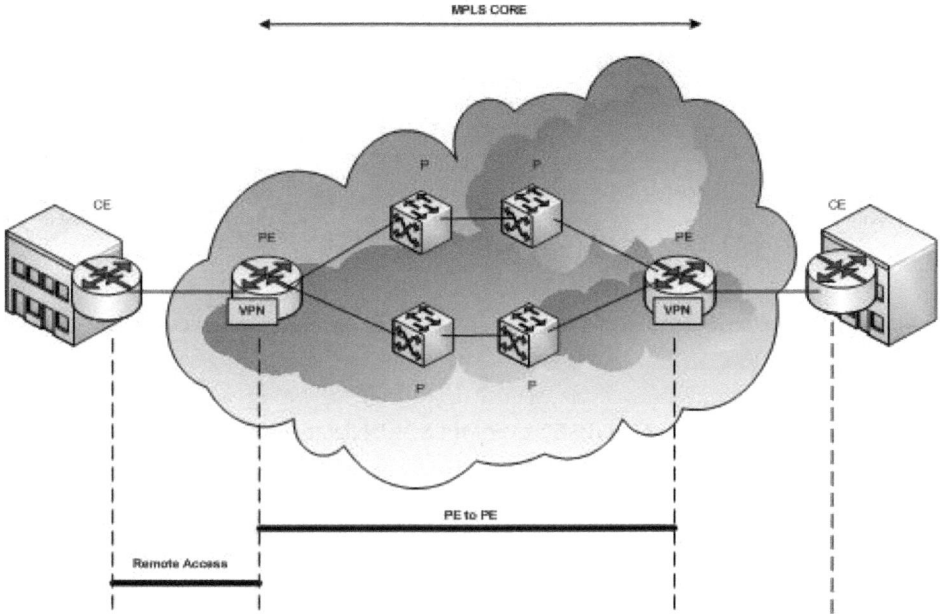

**Fig. 2.** Conventional Approach shows MPLS VPN starting and terminated location

**Scenario-I: IPSEC tunnel within VPN sites.** This approach has some limitation that security is totally independent of MPLS core infrastructure [8].

**Scenario II: Within MPLS VPN core or between provider edge router (PE).** With this approach there is a problem on customer side because it only provides security on provider's side. The customer is therefore, not aware whether the device is being secured or not. Moreover, the local loop between Customer Edge (CE) to Provider Edge (PE) is not secured in this scenario.

## 5  Proposed Approach

We propose implementation of IPSEC over MPLS VPN between CE to CE for securing an MPLS core infrastructure by addressing its different benefits compatibility and scalability issues. To implement IPSEC over MPLS between CE to CE, we first have to identify the type of target network topology. We take a generic point to point network with MPLS configured on core as shown in Fig 3.

This is the most suitable approach and more secure compared to conventional approaches discussed earlier because IPSEC gateway is placed on secure site or trusted zone. We will discuss CE-to-CE IPSEC tunnel on MPLS core infrastructure by assuming CE is on trusted site under the proper administration control and physical security of company which initiates the tunnel or VPN due to following two reasons:

MPLS CORE
CE
PE
P
P
CE
PE
VP N
VP N
P
P

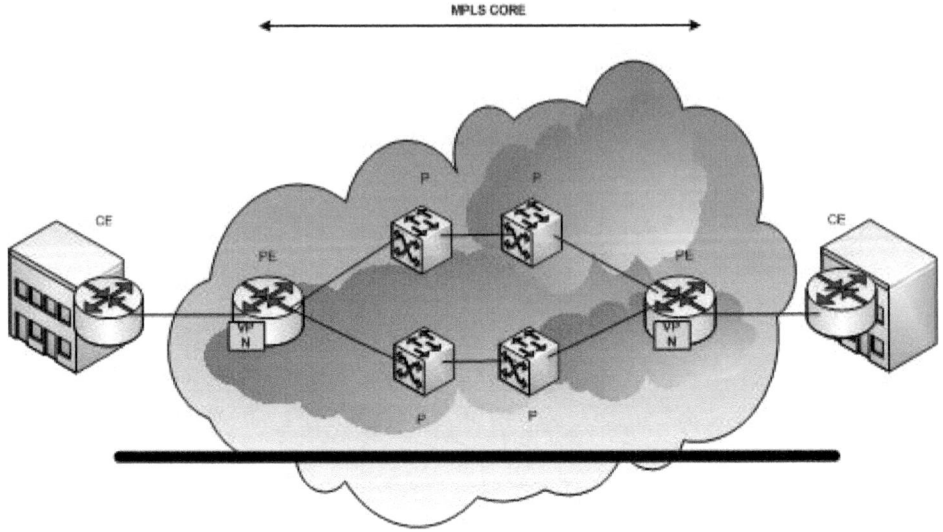

**Fig. 3.** Proposed IPSEC over MPLS VPN deployment scenario

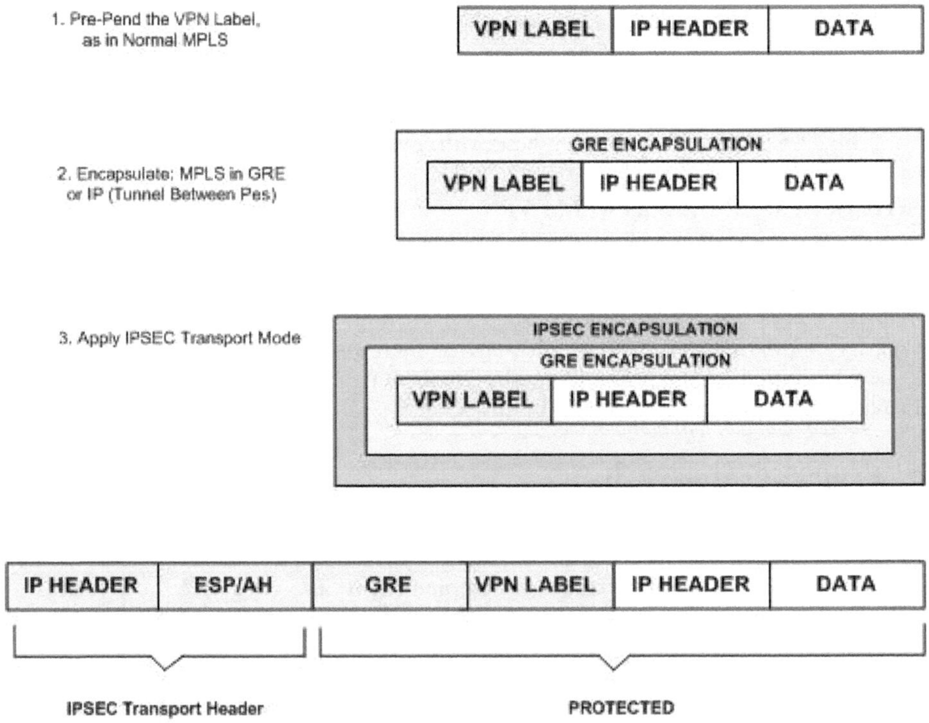

1. Pre-Pend the VPN Label, as in Normal MPLS
VPN LABEL
IP HEADER
DATA
2. Encapsulate: MPLS in GRE or IP (Tunnel Between Pes)
GRE ENCAPSULATION
VPN LABEL
IP HEADER
DATA
3. Apply IPSEC Transport Mode
IPSEC ENCAPSULATION
GRE ENCAPSULATION
VPN LABEL
IP HEADER
DATA
IP HEADER
ESP/AH
GRE
VPN LABEL
IP HEADER
DATA
IPSEC Transport Header
PROTECTED

**Fig. 4.** Proposed IPSEC encapsulation over MPLS VPN

**Reason 1.** Traffic should be secure over MPLS public infrastructure when it is outside the trusted boundaries. This includes the security of access loop, core line and inside core.

**Reason 2.** The service provided by MPLS VPN is not secured like in typical MPLS VPN networking conventional approach because customer has to trust service provider as far as device configuration and hardening is concerned.

As in usual MPLS network, VPN label is pre-pended with VPN packet but problem is that IPSEC secures the IP packet only, leaving the label packet insecure, so the proposed solution addressed this situation by encapsulating VPN label packet in GRE tunnel and runs IPSEC over GRE packet to secure the complete information traveling over MPLS core including both VPN label and VPN packet. Transport mode will be used since IPSEC and GRE have same termination points as in Fig.4.

### 5.1  Advantages of Proposed Approach

Following are the advantages of proposed approach:

**Confidentiality:** It provides defense against leakage of information in between the CE routers.

**Authenticity:** Crafted IP packet by changing port or IP cannot be inserted into the network. Hence proposed approach ensures protection against man in the middle attacks.

**Integrity:** It preserves the content of information from modification on public network keeping the originality of information.

**Anti-reply:** It provides defense against duplication of packet for legitimate attacks on customer edge router.

## 6  Conclusion

The services provided by MPLS VPN are not secured and therefore these are vulnerable to different types of internal (inside core) and external (outside core) attacks. Our proposed solution mitigates the associated risks by implementing IPSEC over MPLS VPN by encapsulating VPN label in GRE and secures it with the help of IPSEC tunnel in transport mode.

## References

1. Meta switch Network,
   http://www.metaswitch.com/MPLS/what-is-MPLS.aspx
2. Cramsession articles what you need when you need,
   http://www.cramsession.com/articles/get-article.asp?aid=329
3. Fischer, T.: MPLS security Overview. IRM PLC (December 2007)
4. Raza: Online routing of bandwidth guaranteed paths with local restoration using optimized aggregate usage information. In: IEEE-ICC (2005)

5. Li, L.: Routing bandwidth guaranteed paths with local restoration in label switched networks. IEEE journal on selected areas in communications (2006)
6. Harrell, R.: Carrier MPLS support for VOIP
7. Palmieri, F.: VPN scalability over high performance backbones evaluating MPLS VPN against traditional approaches. In: Proceeding of the Eighth IEEE international symposium on computers and communication (2003)
8. Behringer, M.H., Morrow, M.J.: How IPSEC complements MPLS. Cisco press, Networkworld (2007)

# A New Holistic Security Approach for Government Critical Systems: Flooding Prevention

Mohammed Alhabeeb, Abdullah Almuhaideb, Phu Dung Le, and Bala Srinivasan

School of Information Technology, Monash University
900 Dandenong Road, Caulfield East, Victoria 3145, Australia
maal11@student.monash.edu.au,
{Abdullah.Almuhaide,phu.dung.le}@iinfotech.monash.edu.au,
Bala.Srinivasan@iinfotech.monash.edu.au

**Abstract.** Flooding attack is a threat to services in the Internet. They can cause significant financial losses. This paper presents a new holistic security approach which prevents flooding in the government critical systems. A new corporation with local service providers has been suggested to finding the real source of the flooding attacks. In addition, a new concept of a dynamic-multi-communication-point is included to make the prevention of flooding attacks easier. Also the dynamic key encryption technique is adapted as a part of the proposed approach to enhance its functionality.

**Keywords:** Denial of Service, flooding attack, dynamic-multi-points-communication.

## 1 Introduction

Technologies in the information age offer vast opportunities for businesses to transform their services into the digital arena. For some organizations, like government departments, which have very critical systems, security is one of the important factors to provide online services. In Saudi Arabia for example, the national ID card has been changed to be a smart card as a step to offer the government services through the Internet. Information availability is one of the important security goals. It means that providing services should be uninterrupted by malicious DoS [1] [2] [3] [4]. According to Kim and Kim in [5], communication privacy is one of the importance principals for a critical system to provide online services, so a strong encryption solution must be used to attain this goal. The Internet has been designed to maximize its functionality to provide communication, and its security was not considered to be a major factor [6]. Recently, DoS attacks against highly visible Internet sites or services have become commonplace [7]. So attacks have been a danger to the Internet operations, and they have caused significant financial damages [3][8]. According to the 2009 CSI Computer Crime and Security Survey report, 29.2% of the respondents detected DoS attacks directed against them, with the respondents representing that the DoS attacks were the most costly cyber attack for them [9].

S.K. Bandyopadhyay et al. (Eds.): ISA 2010, CCIS 76, pp. 249–264, 2010.
© Springer-Verlag Berlin Heidelberg 2010

DoS attacks are committed by using victim resources to slow down or stop a key resource (CPU, bandwidth, buffer, etc) or more of these victim resources. The goal of DoS is either slowing down or stopping victim resources from providing services to the clients [6]. Flooding is one kind of DoS attacks. It occurs when an attacker sends an overpowering quantity of packets to a victim site. Some victim key resources might be crashed or delayed from responding as a result of handling this quantity of packets [6]. Encryption of communications is a significant feature that must be included in critical system security designed to achieve confidentiality [10]. However, strong encryption might lead to flooding, because the system needs more time to process an encrypted packet that might be dropped. Dropping flooding packets from their headers is the easiest solution.

DoS caused by IP packet floods is one of the major problems faced by Internet hosts. It is nearly impossible to stop packets addressed to the host. IP routers respond to dropping packets arbitrarily when an overload happens. But the question is which packet should be dropped [11]. So, flooding attacks are hard to detect [12]. It can effortlessly degrade the Quality of Service (QoS) in the network and leads to the interruption of critical infrastructure services [13]. Flooding attacks are a serious threat to the security of networks that provide public services like government portals [14]. They are more difficult to fight against if the IP has been spoofed [15]. Flooding attacks are easier to be committed when the encryption data is included in the security solutions, because an addition of overload process for communication comes from encryption and decryption of the data [5].

In this paper, a new holistic security approach, which is Holistic security Approach for Government Critical Systems (HSAGCS), is proposed. It is designed for critical systems like government portals. In these systems, higher availability of services and higher privacy of communication are important principles. The HACGSS is identified to support these systems' availability by preventing DoS attacks like flooding attacks, and to enable a suitable encryption solution. This approach divides the communications with clients into two groups: communication with non-authenticated clients and communication with authenticated clients. These two groups communicate with the system via two separate channels. This division is important to enhance the system's ability to prevent flooding attacks. In addition, this approach is designing to be integrated with local network service providers, which provide the Internet network infrastructure, in order to improve its functionality in preventing flooding. In addition, this approach chooses dynamic key encryption technique to enhance the system privacy as well as to support the approach in flooding attacks prevention. Also the HSAGCS enables a new dynamic-multi-points-communication mechanism, which makes the prevention of flooding attacks easier. In addition, this approach includes two new techniques: client's packets designing and packet stamping. These techniques are parts of the suggested solution for preventing flooding and for stopping other king of attacks like malicious packet attacks which will be discussed in future work.

In this paper we will overview the HSAGCS and its components. In addition we will illustrate how the HSAGCS prevents flooding attacks in government critical systems. The proposed approach and its components will be explained in Section 2. The last section, will discuss how this HSAGCS will prevent flooding attacks in different areas of the system and will also evaluate the HSAGCS in preventing flooding.

## 2  Holistic Security Approach for Government Critical Systems

As in the figure below (Fig. 1), our approach consists of two main components, Client Authentication (CA) and Authenticated Client Communication (ACC). Each one of these components is responsible to communicate with the client, depending on the stage in which the client communicates with the system. This division is important to identify the nature of clients' communication activities with the system, and this helps to give an appropriate powerful solution for flooding attacks in every part of the system. Client authenticity and services providence for clients will be determined in the first component. Filtering and Redirect Engine is the first element in this component. It receives clients' requests, filters them, and accepts only correct requests. In addition, it communicates with the network service providers to stop flooding from a client. The second element in the CA component is Ticket Engine. It authenticates clients and issues different categories of tickets for them. A ticket's category is determined based on the services that the client can be provided with.

Depending on the client satisfaction in the CA component, all communications for authenticated clients are moved to the ACC component. In this component, all clients' packets will be examined, and whole messages will be checked. It consists of five main elements, which are Authenticated Client Engine, Packet Manager, Stamp Engine, Determine IP Serve Engine, and Message and File Checking Engine. The first four elements work together to accept only authenticated clients' packets, to design clients' packets, and to examine received packets. The Message and File Checking Engine element checks all received clients' messages.

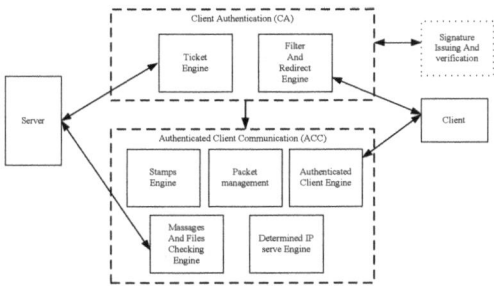

**Fig. 1.** HSAGCS Approach

### 2.1  Client Authentication (CA)

The CA component handles all unauthenticated clients' requests (Fig. 2). It filters clients' requests, authenticates clients who hold these requests, and issues tickets for each client depending on the services that each client can receive. Only correct requests are accepted to be processed in the system. The CA provides a secure channel to the client while it is authenticating the client. Each client is required to provide his/her signature to represent his/her identity. All invalid signatures are added to a list. After the client is authenticated, a ticket will be issued for the client. The type of the ticket issued depends on the type of services the client is supposed to receive, and this is decided by the server.

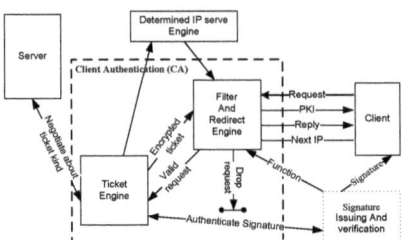

**Fig. 2.** Client Authentication (CA)

The CA contains two main parts: Filter and Redirect Engine and Ticket Engine. The Filter and Redirect Engine filters clients' requests, and the Ticket Engine will be responsible for the Clients' authentication. This Engine also communicates with Signature Issuing and Verification (SIV), a third party government organisation who is responsible for issuing signatures. In the following section, each part of this component will be explained.

**Filter and Redirect Engine:** Filter and Redirect Engine is the main window for the system to communicate with unauthenticated clients, and it provides a secure channel during their authentication stage. It has a minimum number of functions to prevent flooding (Fig. 3).

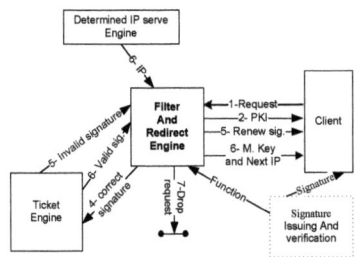

**Fig. 3.** Filter and Redirect Engine

When a client sends a packet to the system, an encrypted TAG should be attached to this packet by the network service provider (Fig. 4). The generation of this TAG is based on four elements: the ID of the network service provider which owns the first network service provider's equipment that the packet comes through, the ID of the first network equipment, client's IP address, and the time of issuing the TAG. The network service provider ID is important, because it will be essential in the case of having more than one service provider. The equipment ID is a unique ID which is identified by its network service provider.

This technique of using TAGs for packs is important to identify the source of each packet. The decision of adding these TAGs to packets can be enforced by the government, because this solution is designed for government's critical systems. For example, in Saudi Arabia, the Communications and Information Technology Commission, which is a government department, is responsible for granting licenses

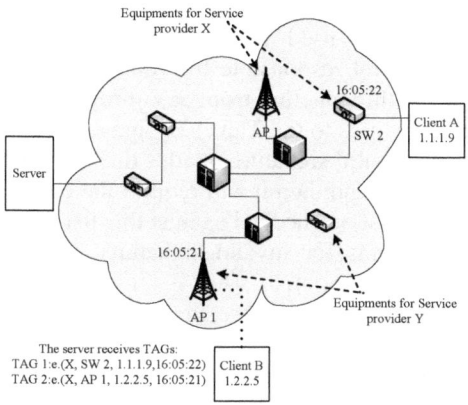

**Fig. 4.** Example for adding TAGs for clients' packets. The Client A is connected to Switch 2 which provided by the network service provider X. the Client A sends a packet to the system. So the TAG1 has been issued and attached to ClientA's packet. The ClientB, which is a wireless client, sends a packet to the system, so the Service ProviderB attaches TAG2 to this client's packet.

for building and operating public communications networks or to provide communication and information technology services. So it should have the possibility to ask current and future network services providers to offer this service of adding this TAG to each packet is sent to specific sites, like government critical systems sites. The client's privacy should not be broken, because these sites are government sites which have the right to know the clients' locations. The Filter and Redirect Engine is responsible for follows tasks:

1. It receives all unauthenticated clients' requests which have network service providers' TAGs. It processes only one request for a source in a specific time to stop flooding from the source. However this duration of time is changed dynamically, depending on the number of clients. This helps to prevent a client from engaging in the system for long time when this client's source is used in flooding attack. For example, organizations' employees which are using the Internet and the configuration of their organizations' network based on a Pool of IP addresses. In this case each packet is sent to the system will have same source, because the whole organization is connected to one source, which is the first network service provider equipment that the organization connected to. This function will be discussed later in this paper.
2. It sends its public key to the client after a correct client's request is received. This key is useful because the client's signature must be encrypted using this key when the signature is sent to the system. This will prevent sniffing and spoofing for that signature. In addition, the client will be requested to insert his/her smart card in the card reader. The client's signature, which is stored in the smart card, will be read. The client will be asked to enter his/her date of birth, and the system then will take the current time. These three data will be sent to the server after encrypted by the server's PKI.

3. Each signature is checked by a function which is provided by the SIV after it decrypted. This function is used to check the signature's form and format. However this function is not responsible for validating signatures. The Filter and Redirect Engine receives this function from SIV through a secure channel.
4. It sends new correct signatures to the Ticket Engine to authenticate them.
5. When it receives a new invalid signature, it adds this signature to a black list which contains invalid signatures, and then it will request the client to renew its signature. Any received signature must be checked against this list before it is processed. This list consists of two columns for invalid signatures and numbers of times each invalid signature has been spoofed. This list is sorted by the second column according to the frequency. Though these signatures are correct in format, they are no longer valid at the SIV. Additions of new signatures to the list take place after the signatures were rejected by the SIV. Although the checks against this list might be done partially, this still drop invalid signatures that might be used many times by attackers, and this also prevents other parts of the system from being occupied by excessive workload caused by these invalid signatures.
6. When a client is authenticated, the Filter and Redirect Engine sends the master key (encrypted by the client's PKI) to this client for dynamic key encryption. In addition, it sends this master key to the Determine IP Serve Engine to generate the keys that will be used for encryption. It also sends the next IP which this authenticated client can use to continue communication. This IP was determined by the Determine IP Serve Engine. The Filter and Redirect Engine uses the client's DOB and the time, which are attached with the signature, to authenticate the client and to generate the master key, so the mater key will be different in each time the client communicates with the system.
7. It drops any request from clients who are authenticating or have been authenticated. So it stops flooding that is caused by spoofed and reused packets of those clients. In addition, it also drops any request which is not in the specified format. Because it only accepts one request at a time from a source, it drops all following packet from that source during that time. It also drops incorrect signatures and any received signatures which exist in the black list of invalid signatures.

The Filter and Redirect Engine uses the client's IP as the source of the packet, to save time of decrypting TAGs. When the usage of the system arrives a specific percentage level (i.e. 70%), this means the system might in a flooding attack. Therefore, the system will use TAG as the source of the packet. After that, a flooding analysis system will create a table of three columns: first equipment source, IP source and number of packet received at a specific time. Then the flooding analysis system will tack a decision about sources which are trying to do a flooding attack to the system. If the flooding that comes from the first network service provider's equipment has same IP or IPs then the filter and Redirect Engine will drop any packet from these IPs for specific time, and then sends a request for their service providers to stop their packets. On the other hand if it has dynamic IPs then the filter and Redirect Engine will drop any packet from this equipment for specific time and send a request for its service providers to stop any packet comes from this equipment for a specific time.

The HSAGCS adapts the dynamic key technique to enhance our approach to stop DoS attacks and to provide a strong encryption solution. A dynamic key is a private key that is based on one time password technique. This technique will change the key for every packet. So it will be hard for the attacker to crack the keys, faster as a secret key mechanism, and non-repudiation as a public key technique [16] [17] [18] [19].

## 2.2 Authenticated Client Communication (ACC)

This is the second component of the HSAGCS (Fig. 5). It only communicates with authenticated clients via a full dynamic key encryption channel. In addition, it uses dynamic-multi-points-communication. The ACC designs clients' packets, checks received packets, and checks whole clients' messages and files before they are sent to the server. In the following the new Dynamic-Multi-points-Communication will be defined. Also each part of ACC will be explained.

### Dynamic-Multi-points-Communication technique

The dynamic-multi-points-communication technique is designed to preventing flooding for authenticated clients. This technique divides the clients' communication point into multi points. Each point has different IP. The dynamic-multi-points-communication technique seeks an appropriate communication for each client by dynamically changing between these multiple IPs. Each packet that arrives to the system must come through a specific IP. Each IP have a list of packets which should be received through this IP. Therefore, unexpected packet will be dropped. The updating of this table comes from the system. Once the system receives a correct packet, a notification will be sent to the IP, so the packet will remove from the list.

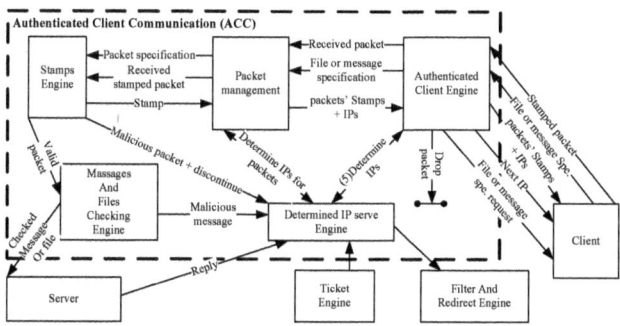

**Fig. 5.** Authenticated Client Communication (ACC)

### Authenticated Client Engine

This engine is the communication window for authenticated clients. It implements *Dynamic-multi-Points-Communication* technique. So it consists of more than one IP. Each IP handles only specific packets and requests from the specific clients. These specific packets and requests are determined by the Determine IP Serve Engine. Every unexpected packet will be dropped at this stage. After each client's communication with the system, the client should receive a next IP that can be used to continue further communication. This mechanism provides a layer of packets filtering from their headers (Fig. 6).

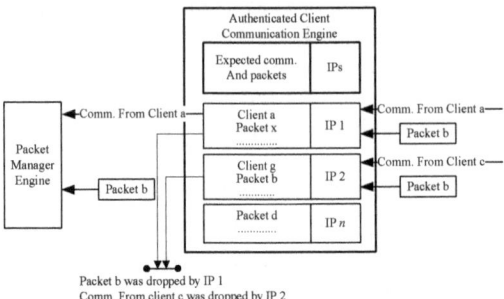

**Fig. 6.** An example of implementing the dynamic-multi-points-communication technique in the Authenticated Client Communication Engine. $IP_1$ received a communication packet from Client a and Packet b. The communication was accepted and was passed to the Packet Manager Engine, because it had been expected by $IP_1$. However the Packet b was dropped because it had not been expected in this IP. On the other hand, in $IP_2$ the communication from Client c was dropped and Packet b was accepted, because the Packet b had been expected in this IP and communication from the Client c was not.

The communication between the ACC and the client is fully encrypted by implementing dynamic key mechanism. The ACC achieve several steps in its communication with clients to prevent flooding attacks (Fig. 7). (1) When a client needs to pass a message or upload a file to the server, it is requested to give details of the message or the file, such as size, file name, etc. (2) When these details are received, they will be moved to Packet Manager. (3) The Authenticated Client Engine receives packets' stamps and their IPs from the Packet Manager, and then sends them to the clients. (4) It accepts packets only from the clients that have stamps and their details attached to the encrypted part of the packet. (5) It receives a notification from Determine IP Serve Engine about clients' requests and packet specifications that the Authenticated Client Engine should receive for each IP. (6) It sends the next IP with which the client can continue further communication. (7) It drops any packet which has not been expected by the receiver IP, so the Authenticated Client Engine drops spoofed packets after they were decrypted.

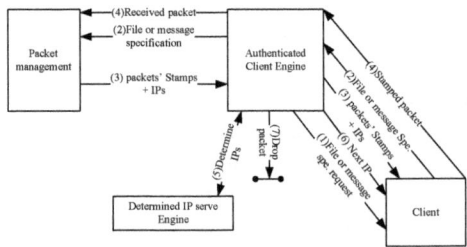

**Fig. 7.** Authenticated Client Engine

**Packet Manager Engine:** This engine is responsible for designing clients' packets templates which they can use them to pass their messages or to upload their files. In addition, the Packet Manager sends each packet header to the Determine IP Serve Engine in order to specify from which IP this packet should be received and to Stamp Engine to issue an encrypted stamp for the packet. The Packet Manager then sends all the appropriately determined packet headers, stamps and IPs through to the client.

**Stamp Engine:** This engine issues encrypted stamps for clients' packets depending on the packets' headers. In addition, it checks each received authenticated client packet's stamp. Correct packet is move to the Messages and Files Checking Engine to collect the messages and file their and check them before be moved to the server.

**Determine IP Serve Engine:** Determine IP Serve Engine determines the next IP with which the client should communicate after the client has been authenticated, and it also determines appropriate IPs for authenticated clients while communicating with the Authenticated Client Engine. In addition, it generates the dynamic key's keys. It Also determines to which IP each packet should be sent, and sends the appropriate key to the IP to be used to decrypt the packet. It also maintains load balance between these IPs.

## 3   Discussion on Security and Efficiency of the HSAGCS

This section shows how the HSAGCS helps to prevent flooding attacks in Filter and Redirect Engine and Authenticated Client Engine. Also this section discusses the benefits that the system will get of using dynamic key in term of preventing flooding. In addition, an efficiency analysis of implementing the HSAGCS will be conducted to evaluate the system in terms of flooding prevention in these two areas.

### 3.1   Security Analysis

**Filter and Redirect Engine.** This engine is designed to prevent flooding by implementing different techniques to address the following:

- This engine minimises the number of system processes for a client's request in order to process the same quantity of requests using less the existing resources. So it can handle a more number of requests at a time. This will be discussed in the Efficiency Analysis section.

- The Filter and Redirect Engine processes only one request for a source in a specific time. This decision should make the system more powerful to prevent flooding. Usually the flooding attacker repeats sending a flooding packet which is generated with its machine protocol. So the source for these packets will be the same. Then the flooding from that source will be stopped. But in the case that the flooding attacker changes the source of these packets manually or using a program, the system should be faster to drop these packets, because generating packets manually or with such programs should significantly reduce the number of packets sent to the system. However, the duration of time to stop a specific source is changed dynamically, depending on the number of clients who are served on that time. This benefits the system and the client by preventing the clients from connection in case this client IP is spoofed in the system. This will also be discussed in the Efficiency Analysis section.

- Usually flooding comes from unauthenticated clients. Once the client is authenticated, it will be moved to the Authenticated Client Engine. So more processes will then be made free to prevent flooding in this area.

- The Filter and Redirect Engine has a function which is provided from the SIV. This function can be used to know the correct formats of the signatures. This process should be simple and focus on the signatures' formats to find incorrect signatures by using less process. This should protect the system from losing time to handle incorrect signatures.

- The Filter and Redirect Engine has a black list containing invalid signatures. This list prevents the system from spending time to communicate with the SIV to verify invalid signatures. Also the sorting in this list saves time to find invalid signatures that were frequently used.

- The Filter and Redirect Engine has the flooding analysis system which use the packet's TAG to know the source of the packet. This technique stops the flooding from its first equipment that this packet comes through by the network service provider which owns this equipment. On the other hand, this decision might result in stopping other clients who are not involved in this attack (i.e. clients who are overseas and their requests comes through a local first network equipment that a flooding attack comes through). This stopping will be benefit for a lot of people who might want to connect to the system from other areas. However, a high number of packets that the system receives from same first network equipment and from different clients will never be known by the system as attack, because their TAGs should be different in the client's IP.

Using TAG mechanism for stopping flooding from a source should be more powerful than using the IP for two reasons. First of all, the attacker, who commits the flooding for the system, might use spoofed IP, so it is easy for this attacker to change his/her identity to continue flooding. Secondly, if the attacker's spoofed IP is stopped; it might result in stopping another client who is owned this spoofed IP.

These pervious techniques are incorporated together to save time for the system to find incorrect requests which the system should not spend much time to process. This saved time becomes important when more flooding attacks are received. So the availability of the system should be higher and the system should be less likely vulnerable against flooding attacks in this area of the system.

**Authenticated Client Engine.** In this Engine, the dropping of flooding is easy, because in the dynamic-multi-points-communication, the packet headers prescribe the action to be taken. Also the Authenticated Client Engine addresses the following points:

- Because each IP previously knows from which source the packet or the request should come, this engine drops any received request or packet that is not expected to be received. This saves time of processing flooding attacks, and this saved time will be helpful when more quantity of flooding occurs. This will be discussed further in the Evaluation Efficiency section for possible implementation.

- When a packet is spoofed and sent to the correct IP, this packet will be dropped after it decrypted, as the source and the destination in the encrypted part will be incorrect.

The proposed approach changes the functionality of the system so the system can serve more requests at a time within the same system resources. This happens, as shown above, by presenting a solution to drop adversary flooding attacks with less process. Therefore, more availability of the system's resources is saved in case more flooding occurs in future. Thus the HACESS improve the system availability by enhancing the capability of the same system's resources to handle more quantity of flooding.

**Using the Dynamic Key.** Both asymmetric and symmetric cryptography techniques can be used as an encryption solution for government critical systems. However, if we compare them in the key size matter, under brute-force attacks, we find that a 2304 bits asymmetric cryptography is as secure as a 128 bits symmetric cryptography [21]. Therefore, the symmetric cryptography technique is significantly faster than asymmetric cryptography technique [22]. On the other hand, asymmetric cryptography technique is more secure in term of key distribution and exchange approach [22]. However, every cryptography system can be broken in cryptoanalysis attacks by using specific computation resources for pored of time [21]. Thus, the using of re-used long term cryptographic keys is only secure for period of time. So using dynamic keys technique can minimize the key compromised risk under cryptoanalysis attacks, because different key is used to encrypt each packet and encrypting keys are different in each communication [20]. Also the dynamic key mechanism provides non-repudiation future, which is an important requirement in such government system, as the asymmetric cryptography techniques. So the dynamic key provides the fast feature as the symmetric cryptography techniques and the non-repudiation future as the asymmetric cryptography techniques. Furthermore, it is more secure than these two cryptography techniques [23].

**Efficiency Analysis.** In this section, the performance of the HSAGCS to prevent flooding will be discussed. This discussion will focus on how the HSAGCS effectively saves time while preventing flooding in Filter and Redirect Engine and Authenticated Client Engine.

**Filter and Redirect Engine.** The HSAGCS minimizes the number of processes for a request to increase the number of clients that can be served at a time. This can be verified in the following equation (1):

$$n = \frac{s}{p} , \tag{1}$$

Where $p$ is the number of processes for each single client's request, $s$ is the number of processes can system handles at a time.

As seen in (1), a smaller number of processes for each client's request would result in a large number of clients who can be served at a time $n$.

As we mentioned before, HSAGCS only accept a single request from a source at a time. The HSAGCS makes the duration of time to stop the source changing dynamically to prevent a client from communicating with the system for long time, in case this client source is used in a flooding attack. This dynamic time is determined depending on the percentage of the system's usage. It can be calculated as follows:

$$D = t \times \frac{c}{n} , \tag{2}$$

where $t$ is the fixed blocking time for a source, $c$ is the number of clients that are serving at the time, $n$ is the number of clients that the system can serve at a time.

In the (2), when the number of clients who are served at a time is small, the dynamic time for blocking multiple requests $D$ will be reduced. So when the system has an ability to receive more requests, this dynamic time is reduced to give the client a chance to reach the system.

The time $T$ is required for the systems, which prevent flooding by dropping received flooding packets from a source, to drop a flooding packet can be calculated as follows:

$$T = f + d , \tag{3}$$

where $f$ is the average time for finding a flooding packet, $d$ is the time for dropping a flooding packet.

In HSAGCS, once a source is blocked for a time, no any packet will be received for the system, because this source is stopped to send any packet of the system. So the time that HSAGCS needs to drop a flooding packet ($T'$) will be as in (4) below:

$$T' = 0 , \tag{4}$$

$$T > T'$$

From the above evaluation, HSAGCS is save time in preventing flooding in Filter and Redirect Engine.

**Authenticated Client Engine.** In the Authenticated Client Engine, the dynamic-multi-points-communication mechanism is implemented to dropping flooding packets in less time. In the (5), the number of clients that the system can serve at a time $N$ consists of all clients' requests from both clients and adversary attackers.

$$N = N_c + N_f , \tag{5}$$

where $N_c$ is the number of clients' requests which the system can serve at a time, $N_f$ is the number of adversary attackers' requests (from flooding attacks) which the system can serve at a time.

Also number of clients that can be served at a time ($N$) can be defined depending on the system processing divided by the number of processes for each request, as follows:

$$N = \frac{P}{P_{requests}} , \tag{6}$$

where $P$ is the number of processes that the system can do at a time, $P_{requests}$ is the number of processes that system does for each request.

So the number of processes P that the system can do at a time ($P$) can be defined as follows:

$$P = \left( N_c * P_{requests} \right) + \left( N_f * P_{requests} \right) \tag{7}$$

The time that the system needs to handle these processes can be defined, as in (8) below:

$$T = N_c * P_{c_{requests}} * t + N_f * P_{f_{requests}} * t \quad , \tag{8}$$

where $P_{c_{requests}}$ is the average number of processes in each client's request, $P_{f_{requests}}$ is the average number of processes in each adversary attacker's request, and $t$ is time required to handle each process.

In the HSAGCS, the communication between the client and the system is done through two system points: System and Redirect Engine and Authenticated Client Engine. In the rest of this section, we are going to investigate how the HSAGCS will respond to adversary attackers in the Authenticated Client Engine, and to analyze the time that the HSAGCS can save while preventing adversary attackers:

$$N' = N'_c + N'_f \quad , \tag{9}$$

where $N'$ is the number of clients that the system can handle at a time, $N'_c$ is the number of client's right requests which the system can handle at a time, $N'_f$ is the number of adversary attackers' requests (from flooding attacks) which the system can handle at a time.

Because is the implementation of the dynamic-multi-points-communication in this part of the system, the adversary attacker's packet might not be sent to a correct IP. A packet is sent to a correct IP when this packet's source is expected in the receiver IP. So, some of the adversary attackers' packets will be expected by the receiver IPs while the other will not. This can be calculated in the following equation:

$$N'_f = \frac{1}{I} N'_{f_{expected}} + \left(1 - \frac{1}{I}\right) N'_{f_{not\,expected}} \, , \tag{10}$$

where $I$ is the number of IPs, $N'_{f_{expected}}$ is the number of adversary attackers' packets that are expected from the receiver IPs, $N'_{f_{not\,expected}}$ is the number of adversary attackers' packets that are not expected from the receiver IPs.

The time that the system needs to handle an adversary attacker's request $T'_{f_{request}}$ can be calculated as follows using (11):

$$T'_{f_{request}} = P'_{f_{requests}} * t \quad , \tag{11}$$

where $P'_{f_{requests}}$ is the average number of processes for each adversary attacker's request.

The time of handling adversary attackers' requests $T'_{f_{requests}}$ can be calculated using (12):

$$T'_{f_{requests}} = \left( \begin{array}{c} \left(\frac{1}{I} N'_{f_{expected}} \times P'_{f_{requests}}\right) + \\ \left(\left(1 - \frac{1}{I}\right) N'_{f_{not\,expected}} \times P'_{f_{requests}}\right) \end{array} \right) * t \tag{12}$$

In the case the receiver IP is not expecting to receive the received packet, the packet will be dropped from its header, so $P_{f_{not\ expected}}$ will be equal to $0$.

$$T'_{f_{request}} = \frac{N'_{f_{expected}*t}}{I} \qquad (13)$$

So the time of processing adversary attackers' requests or packets in the HSAGCS, $T'_f$ will be smaller as a result of $T'_{f_{request}}$ is reduced by $\frac{1}{I}$, as shown in the (13) above.

$$N' > N$$

Depending on the above evaluation, the system has more saved time that comes from finding and dropping flooding attacks. So the system capability is higher to prevent more quantity of flooding attacks.

**Using dynamic key encryption.** We will compare the efficiency of using the asymmetric cryptography techniques and the dynamic key in flooding prevention. We will not include the symmetric cryptography techniques in the comparison, because they have not non-repudiation feature, which is important to be in the government critical systems.

In the following, the time that the system needs to process packets, which encrypted by using an asymmetric cryptography technique, will be shown.

$$T' = \sum_{i=1}^{n}(d'_i + t_i) \ , \qquad (14)$$

where $T'$ is the time that the system needs to process encrypted packets with asymmetric cryptography, $n$ is number of packets, $d'_i$ is the average time to decrypt the packet which is encrypted with asymmetric cryptography technique, and $t_i$ is average time to process the packet.

The time that the system needs to process packets, which encrypted by using a dynamic key technique, can be calculated as follows (15).

$$T'' = \sum_{i=1}^{n}(d''_i + t_i) \ , \qquad (15)$$

where $T''$ is the time that the system needs to process encrypted packets with dynamic key technique, $d''_i$ is the average time to decrypt the packet which is encrypted with dynamic key technique, and $t_i$ is average time to process the packet.

But dynamic key technique is significant faster than asymmetric cryptography technique [20]. So the system save $T$ time when uses the dynamic key technique as follows.

$$d''_i \ll d'_i \qquad (16)$$

$$T = T' - T'' = \sum_{i=1}^{n}(d'_i - d''_i) \qquad (17)$$

From the previous equation (17), the system save more time when uses the dynamic key techniques as an encryption solution. This time can be used to handle more additional packets which might come from flooding.

# 4 Conclusion and Future Work

Flooding is one of the DoS attacks that might cause significant losses. In this paper, we proposed a new security approach, which is the Holistic Security Approach for Government Critical Systems (HSAGCS). A new corporation with local service providers technique is suggested to stopping flooding attacks from a source. In addition, the new dynamic-multi-points-communication mechanism, the new stamp packet technique and the dynamic key encryption technique were included in the proposed solution. This comprehensive combination of these techniques makes the HSAGCS more powerful in prevent flooding attacks. This paper also discussed the advantages of the proposed approach in preventing flooding.

It is necessary to go through comprehensive surveys of each component of the HSAGCS. In addition, the HSAGCS has a great potential to be developed against malicious packet attacks. Also it is important to implement a simulation for the HSAGCS, so it can be tested practically with the flooding attacks.

**Acknowledgment.** I would like to acknowledge that the funding of this paper is supported by Prince Muqrin Chair for Information Technology Security (PMC), King Saud University, Kingdom of Saudi Arabia.

# References

1. Joshi, J., Ghafoor, A., Aref, W.G., Spafford, E.H.: Digital government security infrastructure design challenges. Computer 34, 66–72 (2001)
2. Lambrinoudakis, C., Gritzalis, S., Dridi, F., Pernul, G.: Security requirements for e-government services: a methodological approach for developing a common PKI-based security policy. Computer Communications 26, 1873–1883 (2003)
3. Alefiya, H., John, H., Christos, P.: A framework for classifying denial of service attacks. In: Proceedings of the 2003 conference on Applications, technologies, architectures, and protocols for computer communications %@ 1-58113-735-4, pp. 99–110. ACM, Karlsruhe (2003)
4. Ge, Z., Sven, E., Thomas, M., Dorgham, S.: Denial of service attack and prevention on SIP VoIP infrastructures using DNS flooding. In: Proceedings of the 1st international conference on Principles, systems and applications of IP telecommunications 978-1-60558-006-7, pp. 57–66. ACM, New York (2007)
5. Young-Soo, K., Seok-Soo, K.: Delay Model for Flooding of Service Prevention in E-Commerce System. In: Proceedings of the Future Generation Communication and Networking, vol. 1, pp. 62–67. IEEE Computer Society, Los Alamitos (2007)
6. Mirkovic, J.: D-WARD: source-end defense against distributed denial-of-service attacks, pp. 3–57 (2003) (Citeseer)
7. David, M., Colleen, S., Douglas, J.B., Geoffrey, M.V., Stefan, S.: Inferring Internet denial-of-service activity. ACM Trans. Comput. Syst. 0734-2071 24, 115–139 (2006)
8. Guangzhi, Q., Hariri, S., Yousif, M.: Multivariate statistical analysis for network attacks detection. In: Proceedings of the ACS/IEEE 2005 International Conference on Computer Systems and Applications 0-7803-8735-X, p. 9. IEEE Computer Society, Los Alamitos (2005)
9. Richardson, R.: 2009 CSI Computer Crime and Security Survey, Computer Security Institute (2009)

10. Erik, S., Carl, H., Rasika, C., Dave, B.: Modular over-the-wire configurable security for long-lived critical infrastructure monitoring systems. In: Proceedings of the Third ACM International Conference on Distributed Event-Based Systems 978-1-60558-665-6, pp. 1–9. ACM, Nashville (2009)
11. Karthik, L., Daniel, A., Adrian, P., Ion, S.: Taming IP packet flooding attacks. SIGCOMM Comput. Commun. Rev. 0146-4833 34, 45–50 (2004)
12. Josep, L.B., Nicolas, P., Javier, A., Ricard, G., Jordi, T., Manish, P.: Adaptive distributed mechanism against flooding network attacks based on machine learning. In: Proceedings of the 1st ACM Workshop on AISec %@ 978-1-60558-291-7, pp. 43–50. ACM, Alexandria (2008)
13. Salem, O., Mehaoua, A., Vaton, S., Gravey, A.: Flooding attacks detection and victim identification over high speed networks. In: Conference Flooding attacks detection and victim identification over high speed networks, pp. 1–8 (2009)
14. Jensen, M., Schwenk, J.: The Accountability Problem of Flooding Attacks in Service-Oriented Architectures. In: Conference The Accountability Problem of Flooding Attacks in Service-Oriented Architectures, pp. 25–32 (2009)
15. Wei, C., Dit-Yan, Y.: Defending Against TCP SYN Flooding Attacks Under Different Types of IP Spoofing. In: Conference Defending Against TCP SYN Flooding Attacks Under Different Types of IP Spoofing, p. 38 (2006)
16. Rubin, A.D., Wright, R.N.: Off-line generation of limited-use credit card numbers. Google Patents (2001)
17. Kungpisdan, S., Le, P.D., Srinivasan, B.: A limited-used key generation scheme for internet transactions. In: Lim, C.H., Yung, M. (eds.) WISA 2004. LNCS, vol. 3325, pp. 302–316. Springer, Heidelberg (2005)
18. Xianping, W., Phu Dung, L., Balasubramaniam, S.: Dynamic Keys Based Sensitive Information System. In: Proceedings of the 2008 The 9th International Conference for Young Computer Scientists %@ 978-0-7695-3398-8, pp. 1895–1901. IEEE Computer Society, Los Alamitos (2008)
19. Kungpisdan, S., Le, P.D., Srinivasan, B.: A secure account-based mobile payment protocol. In: IEEE Proceeding of the International Conference on Information Technology: Coding and Computing, pp. 35–39 (2004)
20. Ngo, H.H., Wu, X.P., Le, P.D., Wilson, C.: A Method for Authentication Services in Wireless Networks. In: AMCIS 2008 Proceedings, vol. 177 (2008)
21. PGP: PGP Attack FAQ: The asymmetric cipher (2005),
    http://www.iusmentis.com/technology/encryption/pgp/pgpattackfaq/asymmetric/
22. Bruce, S.: Handbook of applied cryptography. CRC, Boca Raton (1996)
23. Dandash, O., Wang, Y., Leand, P.D., Srinivasan, B.: Fraudulent Internet Banking Payments Prevention using Dynamic Key. Journal of Networks 3, 25 (2008)

# Sensor Aided Authentication

Xin Huang[1], Yang Jiang[1], Xiong Gao[2], Rong Fu[3], and Tingting Zhang[1]

[1] ITM/IKS, Mid Sweden University, 85170 Sundsvall, Sweden
[2] School of Electronics and Information Engineering, Beijing Jiaotong University, 100044 Beijing, China
[3] School of Computer Information and Technology, Beijing Jiaotong University, 100044 Beijing, China
xin.huang@miun.se, yaji0800@student.miun.se, tingting.zhang@miun.se, {xiga0900,rofu0900}@student.miun.se

**Abstract.** The sharing of sensor data globally becomes possible by the development of wireless sensor network, cloud computing, and other related technologies. These new trends can also benefit information security. In this paper, the sensor data is involved in the authentication procedure which is one main component of security systems. Sensor aided password is proposed. In addition, the architecture for sensor aided authentication corresponding to the simple authentication scenario is also designed. Sensor data aided password generation and utilization bring convenience to users without weakening the password strength.

**Keywords:** Sensor, password, authentication.

## 1 Introduction

The main issue addressed in this paper is the sensor aided authentication (SAA). The sensor data is involved in the simple authentication procedure in the SAA system. The reasons are as follows. Firstly, the developments of wireless sensor network and cloud computing technologies bring a lot of opportunities to the information system today. The authentication system is no exception. The second reason comes from the authentication system itself. Most IT systems ask users to use strong passwords which are always a torture for them. Meanwhile, biometrics based authentications are always expensive; they also require high accuracy. In addition, they are not always secure: once your biometric characteristic is captured by others, you cannot use this characteristic any more. However, the SAA is able to solve these problems. It provides an easy, cheap, and secure authentication.

The main contributions of this paper are two folds.

- Sensor aided password is proposed. The advantage is that it is much easier for the users to create and remember; meanwhile, it does not violate the strength of the authentication.

S.K. Bandyopadhyay et al. (Eds.): ISA 2010, CCIS 76, pp. 265–277, 2010.
© Springer-Verlag Berlin Heidelberg 2010

- The architecture of SAA for simple authentication is designed based on the sensor aided password which is generated by the features extracted from the sensor cloud.

Our paper is organized as follows. Section 2 discusses the related works; Section 3 describes the scenario; Section 4 talks about the sensor cloud; Section 5 includes the sensor aided authentication; Section 6 contains the result; Section 7 is the discussion; finally, some important conclusions are made in Section 8.

## 2  Related Works

### 2.1  Sensor Sharing (Internet of Things)

To understand sensor sharing of Internet of things, the Internet Fridge [1] is probably the most oft-quoted. One of the leading companies in these areas is IBM, which offers a range of RFID and sensor technology solutions [1]. Pachube [2] sets up a platform that can tag and share real time sensor data from different sources: objects, devices, buildings and environments. These sources can be physical or virtual. Neil, Raffi and Danny [3] describe the idea of Internet-0 to solve the sharing of Internet of Things; in their solution, data could be sent through a wire, clicked by a speaker, printed onto a page or engraved on a key with the same Internet-0 encoding. The context sharing architectures such as PCSM [4] and FRASCS [5] also provide solutions in order to handle the sharing of the context sensor information.

### 2.2  Authentication and Password

Nowadays, user authentication is still heavily reliant on the use of alphanumerical passwords which has been shown to have significant drawbacks [6].

Biometrics based approach can be reliable. Unfortunately, physical biometrics such as fingerprints, iris scans, and faces recognition require special hardware which could be expensive for individual to install and maintain [7]. Behavioral biometrics based on keystroke dynamics [8, 9], mouse usage patterns or signature dynamics do not require any special hardware; and it can be utilized for increasing the reliability of authentication.

Since human visual memory capabilities are far superior to the ability of remembering textual information, graphical passwords are designed and they can be divided into two main categories: Recognition based [10] method, in which users must identify images they have previously seen among new graphics, and position based [11] methods, in which user selects points of interest within a single image.

## 3  Scenario

This is a simple authentication scenario, e.g., web page, campus network and corporation network. Tom wants to authenticate himself to system. He does not like to use strong password which is hard to remember. He does not like biometric recognitions either. They are not only expensive, but also fail to recognize him sometimes. Besides, he worries about these approaches since they depend on his biometric features which are impossible to change after leakage.

Meanwhile, a lot of sensors have been deployed. They provide the hardware support for our system. And cloud computing brings possibility to use them anywhere. In SAA, Tom's password is generated based on sensor data and a short PIN code. The sensor data is selected according to his preferences. In addition, this password is easy to be updated since different sensor and feature combinations can be easily changed in his preferences.

## 4 Sensor Cloud

The sensor cloud is a hybrid cloud. The design is based on Internet of things. User can choose to store their sensor data or run applications both in privately owned infrastructures and in the public cloud space. "It offers the promise of on-demand, externally provisioned scale, but adds the complexity of determining how to distribute applications across these different environments" [12]. Sensor data is provided to the authentication services.

The architecture is shown in Fig. 1. There are five parts: sensor points, platform server, interface to user, security protection measures, and the module which is responsible to QoS.

- **Sensor points:** The sensor information is collected, stored here. They can also work as a private cloud.

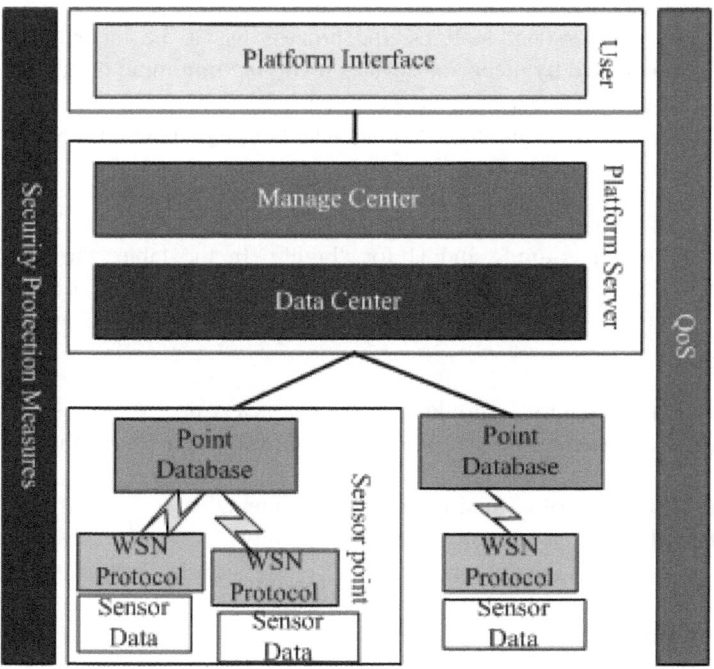

**Fig. 1.** Sensor cloud

- **Platform server:** It contains the data center and manage center. It can collect sensor information from different sensor points; and it provides information to other users.
- **Interface to user:** The user can search, view and manipulate sensor information via the interface.
- **Security protection measures and QoS module:** They provide the security related services and ensure the quality of the service, regarding the platform.

# 5 Sensor Aided Authentication (SAA)

## 5.1 Feature Sets

In order to generate password from sensor data, the fundamental procedure is the feature extraction. Since a lot of biometric technologies are already mature, the features are mainly extracted from biometric features.

### 5.1.1 Biometric Features

Biometric features have huge complexity, take face for example, from the biological point of view, everyone has different face but the distinction is confined to a really small extent; another serious disadvantage is that human face does not remain unchanged due to rich facial expressions. There are several criteria for ideal biometric features summed up from experience [13].

- Permanence and inalterability in terms of time.
- When gathering personal features, the process has to be inconspicuous; it also should be conducted by means of devices involving minimum or no contact.
- Total automation of the system should be enabled.
- The system has to be highly accurate and has high operation speed so that it enables real-time operation.

An overview of biometric features based on a survey is given in Table 1 (L stands for "low", M for "medium", and H for "high"). In the table, the rows represent several main kinds of biometric character, such as fingerprint, iris pattern, face, keystroke dynamics, signature, etc. And each column shows an attribute of each character [14]:

- **Universality:** each person should have the characteristic.
- **Permanence:** measures how well a biometric resists aging and other variance over time.
- **Collectability:** ease of acquisition for measurement.
- **Acceptability:** degree of approval of a technology.
- **Features:** richness in feature extraction
- **Durability:** invariance of biometric characters
- **Circumvention:** ease of use of a substitute.

**Table 1.** An overview of biometric features [14]

| Characteristic | Universality | Permanence | Collectability | Acceptability | Features | Durability | Circumvention |
|---|---|---|---|---|---|---|---|
| Fingerprint | M | H | M | M | H | H | M |
| DNA | H | H | L | L | H | H | L |
| Iris | H | H | M | L | H | H | L |
| Retina | H | M | L | L | H | M | L |
| Ear | M | H | M | H | M | H | M |
| Face | H | L | H | H | L | M | H |
| Thermogram | H | H | H | H | M | L | L |
| Gait | M | L | H | H | L | L | M |
| Hand Geometry | M | M | H | M | M | M | M |
| Palm-vein pattern | M | M | M | M | M | M | L |
| Keystroke dynamics | L | L | M | M | L | L | M |
| Smell | H | H | L | M | L | H | L |
| Signature | L | L | H | H | L | L | H |
| Voice | M | L | M | H | L | L | H |
| Hand Geometry | M | M | H | M | M | M | M |

### 5.1.2  Other Features
Normally, context information and object feature are also used.

- **Context information:** According to common understanding, context information is separated into four categories: location, identity, activity and time.
- **Object features:** In SAA system, users could choose any kinds of objects and features according to their preferences, for example, color, boundary, elongation, and so on.

### 5.1.3  Passive Usage of Feature
Instead of using single feature, the system today always uses multi-factor authentication. Multi-factor authentication ensures verification and validation of a user identification using multiple authentication mechanisms. It often combines two or more authentication methods for example, a three-factor authentication is based on password (what the user knows), smart cards (what the user possesses), and fingerprints (who the user is). Sometimes, these features work as the context information. For example, Tencent [15] login procedure involves the location information as one parameter. If the login IP changes, the software will ask the user re-login instead of using the pre-stored password.

## 5.2 Sensor Aided Authentication

The SAA includes two parts: sensor aided password and sensor aided authentication architecture for simple authentication.

### 5.2.1 Sensor Aided Password

Based on the multiple authentication mechanism, sensor aided password is proposed. Wireless sensor network works as feature capture devices. It is a more active way.

Take Table 1 as reference and based on an analysis of information collected by sensor cloud, we select several kinds of sensor information including both biometrics and non-biological features as a whole feature set for password generation.

- **Human face:** Every person's face is unique and face features could be changed by different expressions and poses, some common features are listed as follows. 1) Color: average RGB value of a certain area. 2) Location: coordinates of mouth corner, eyebrow, lips and nose; distance between feature points. 3) Geometrical features: squareness, elongation, invariable moment features.
- **Gesture:** Hand, as a part of body, has the same biometric features as face. Besides, hands can also convey a wealth of information by different gestures which are used as a form of non-verbal communication. From the view of image processing, we usually use two main methods: boundary extraction and skin detection.
- **Voice:** "Voice is a combination of physiological and behavioral biometrics."[14] These features can be divided into two categories, sound and speech. The sound features of the user are extracted according to the shape and size of vocal tracts, mouth, lips and so on. The synthesis of sound is exactly the combination of these appendages which are invariant for an individual. Since a person may change his speech behavior due to age, medical or emotional conditions, the speech features are more widely used. And speech recognition system is usually based on the utterance of a fixed predetermined phase.
- **Non-biological features:** object, color, shape, context information, and other features which are discussed in previous section.
- **Others:** motion, Iris pattern, hand geometry, weight, heartbeat, etc.

This system takes advantage of abundant data resources acquired by the sensor cloud and the combination of multiple authentication methods, which make the system more efficient and safer. The core idea of the system is shown in Fig.2. The characters in traditional passwords are replaced by practical features such as face, voice, fingerprint or other biometric features and some non-biological information. With these features values, the password is generated. Since there are recognition and other uncontrollable errors, the tolerance mechanisms should be applied here. These passwords are easy to be "remembered" by users and can be a pretty strong password.

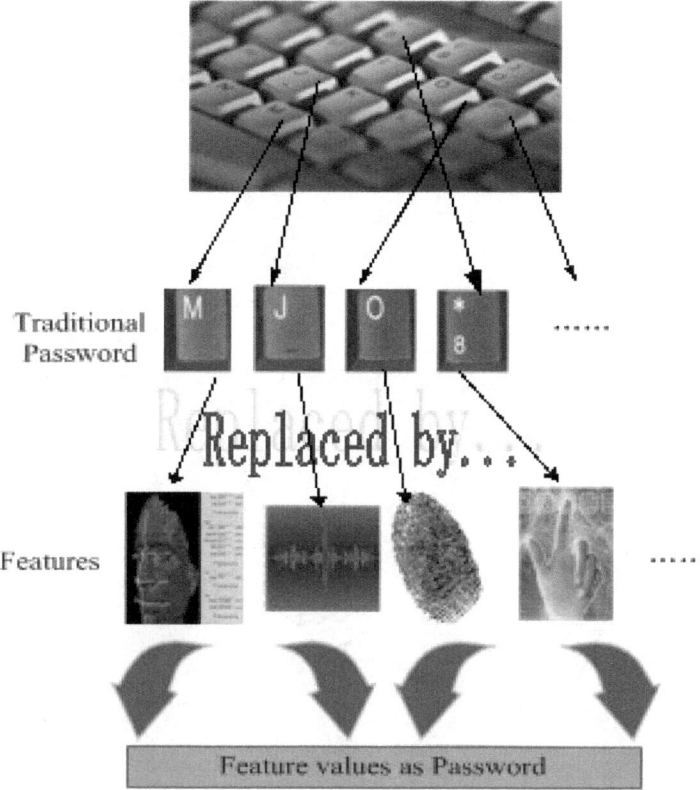

**Fig. 2.** Sensor aided password

### 5.2.2 SAA for Simple Authentication

As shown in Figure 3, the SAA process for simple authentication includes seven steps:

- When the user Tom requests access, client side PC asks for the ID, PIN code, and feature selection file (through USB stick).
- The server searches Tom's sensor selection file in its database and sends it to the cloud through a secure channel guaranteed by SSL. The sensor selection file is preconfigured by the user. And, this file can be changed by the user anytime.
- Sensors information is collected by the cloud. For instance, the camera captures image information; the microphone collects audio information, etc.
- Then the cloud returns the sensor information through the SSL channel.
- After receiving the sensor information, the server extracts the specific features according to the feature selection file provided by Tom. The Feature Selection File is private and can be changed by Tom according to his own preferences. The combination of these feature values is the password. Since there are recognition and other uncontrollable errors, the tolerance mechanisms should be applied here.

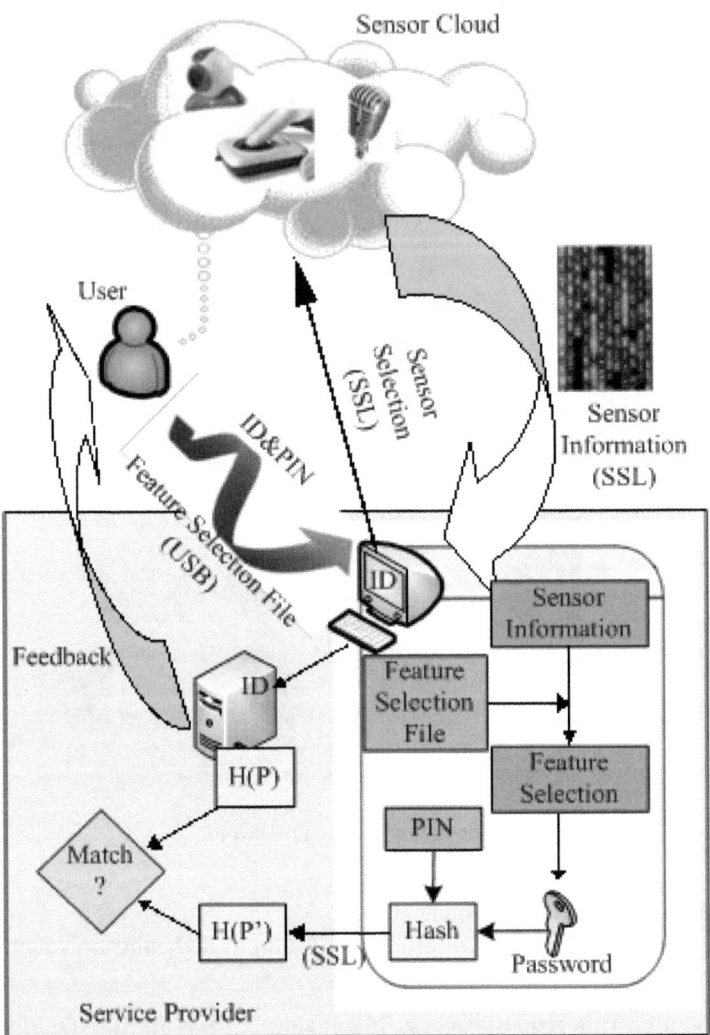

**Fig. 3.** Architecture of SAA system for simple authentication

- Then the system combines the newly generated password and PIN provided by Tom and changes them into one Hash String, then transmits it to the service provider side (SPS) through a secure channel guaranteed by SSL. The short PIN code is used to prevent the Chosen Plaintext Attack. Then the encryption module in SPS hashes the Hash String, the result is H (P'). At the same time, the server finds out the Hash form of Tom's password H (P) according to Tom's ID. So what really stored in server is H (P), not the original password (P). According to security attack analysis, if the intruder invade the system and get H (P) and use it to log in the system, then the server get H (H (P)), it does not match with H (P).

- The comparison module compares H (P') with H (P). If H (P') and H (P) match, the authentication succeeds, then the server will provide services according to Tom's access permissions. If not, he will be rejected.

## 6   Result

In this section, experiment results are shown. The related selection procedures are as follows.

Video camera is used in sensor selection procedure.

In features selection procedure, face and apartment key are selected as seeds of the features. According to Fig. 4, the left part shows that the apartment key has been recognized and surrounded by a rectangle; the right part demonstrates the face has been detected and extracted out. In the experiment, we mainly consider the BWAREA area, elongation, and invariant moment features.

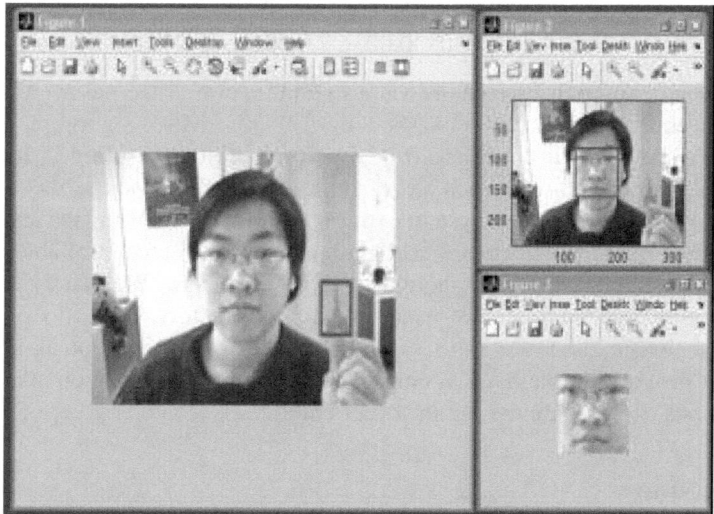

**Fig. 4.** Result

**BWAREA area:** This MATLAB function estimates "the area of the objects in binary image BW". TOTAL is a scalar and its value roughly corresponds to the total number of "on" pixels in the image [16]. Here image BW is the picture of face part or apartment key part. The combination of these two values is the first feature, which is shown as follows.

$$TOTAL = BWAREA (BW)$$

Face Feature value: 1.0e+003 * 5.3543

Apartment key Feature value: 1.0e+003 * 3.0972

**Elongation:** This feature is supposed for face feature since it is based on the biometric features that face is different in height to width ratio. Parameter H is the height of BW, W is the width of BW. This is the second feature. It is shown as follows.

$$E=\min (H, W)/\max (H, W)$$

Face Feature value: 1.0e+003*0.0013

**Invariant moment features:** Moment features can provide the properties of invariance to scale, position, and rotation [17]. Invariant moment is one of the principal approaches used in image processing to describe the texture of a region. A set of seven invariant moments can be extracted from the picture collected by camera. Their combination is the third feature (shown as below).

Face Feature value:  1.0e+003 *

[0.0004    0.0008    0.0040    0.0001    0.0007    0.0032    0.0066    0.0010]

Apartment key Feature value: 1.0e+003 *

[0.0007    0.0013    0.0010    0.0036    0.0019    0.0051    0.0015    0.0030]

Password verification: These feature values combination is the password. Combined with user's short pin-code, it is hashed by 128 bits MD5 algorithm. The server compares the result with the Hash form which is previously stored in the server. It turns out that they match with each other, so the authentication succeeds.

In the experiment, the SAA system extracts three features from face and apartment key, respectively. Since there are recognition and other uncontrollable errors, the SAA system's tolerance degree should be configured here. We briefly evaluate the performance of the SAA system according to two factors, the ratio of the users' successfully log-in, and the ratio of the attackers' failure to break-in. And the experiment proves that the SAA system has fantastic performance on attack defense, and unobvious decrease on the log-in success ratio.

## 7  Discussion

### 7.1  Attack Analysis

#### 7.1.1  Brute Force Attack
Brute-force involves trying all possible keys in the key space. For instance, people usually use keyboard as the input tool. There are totally 128 symbols. If a 8-digit password is inputted for your account, there are $128^8$ different passwords at most. It is really a piece of cake to violate it by brute force attack today.

In the SAA system, the key space depends on three factors: the sensor number, the feature number, PIN length. The sensor number in the cloud is very large; and the number of features that can be used is also very large. Thus, the key space is considerably large.

### 7.1.2  Chosen Plaintext Attack

Chosen Plaintext attack is an attack model for cryptanalysis which presumes that the attacker has the capability to choose some related sensor information, i.e. sensor cloud. The goal of the attack is to gain some further information which reduces the security of the encryption scheme.

In our case, the attacker can get some sensor information in advance. However, the features used to generate password are hard to guess. Thus, this system is strong to a guess attack.

## 7.2  Ease of Use

In the SAA system, user only needs to remember a short PIN. And, the security degree is still high. However, in traditional password system, it is to find a balance between security and user-friendly at the same time. People are certainly unwilling to remember long but irregular alphanumerical strings.

In the SAA system, the password can be changed when the user select different sensor, different feature, or different PIN. However, in the biometric authentication system, it is impossible to change your biometric features. It is awkward for the biometric system if you lose your biometric information.

## 7.3  System Requirement

For existing authentication case of single biometric, in order to ensure high security level, the system needs to be very accurate. Assume that the accuracy of an authentication system must reach 98%. For the system of single biometric, it requires high accuracy equipments and algorithms. But in SAA system, several kinds of biometrics are required, and the security level increases with an increased variety of features. Thus, SAA reduces the precision requirements of the equipment and algorithms.

Besides, authentication with multiple biometric characters efficiently defends eavesdropping and guesses attack.

## 7.4  Cost

This SAA system is based on the sensor cloud platform:

- It needs sensor information collection in the sensor cloud;
- It needs to compute features from the sensor information;
- And it requires Internet connections.

## 7.5  Miscellany

In this section, a simple comparison among SAA, one time pad, and challenge-response model is made.

One time pad is more secure than SAA. However, it is not scalable; users can not control the password themselves; and the password is endangered by lost.

SAA is suitable for simple-authentication login scenario. However, it can be used in challenge-response model. Response is a token generated from challenge (data block), counter and clock. The sensor and feature selection can be used to generate the data block by the features in client side. In this case, SAA is better than normal smart card or USB stick, because it also verifies that the user from "who the user is".

# 8  Conclusion

In this paper, sensor aided password is proposed. The advantage is that it is much easier for the users to create and remember; meanwhile, it does not violate the strength of the authentication. In addition, the architecture of sensor aided authentication for simple authentication is designed based on the sensor aided password.

However, there are some drawbacks.

- The tolerance degree should follow some rules. It is not deeply studied in this paper.
- The user's privacy is violated when the sensor cloud collects their biometric information.

These will be our future works.

**Acknowledgments.** We would like to thank Sensible Things That Communicate (STC) research for their funding.

# References

1. Top 5 Web Trends of 2009: Internet of Things,
   http://www.readwriteweb.com/archives/
   top_5_web_trends_of_2009_internet_of_things.php
2. Pachube, http://www.Pachube.com
3. Gershenfeld, N., Krikorian, R., Cohen, D.: The Internet of Things, pp. 76–81. Scientific American (2004)
4. Ye, J., Li, J., Zhu, Z., Gu, X., Shi, H.: PCSM: A Context Sharing Model in Peer-to-Peer Ubiquitous Computing Environment. In: 2007 International Conference on Convergence Information Technology, pp. 1868–1873. IEEE Press, New York (2007)
5. Lai, T., Li, W., Liang, H., Zhou, X.: FRASCS: A Framework Supporting Context Sharing. In: The 9th International Conference for Young Computer Scientists, ICYCS 2008, pp. 919–924. IEEE Press, New York (2008)
6. Yampolskiy, R.V.: Analyzing User Password Selection Behavior for Reduction of Password Space. In: Proceedings 2006 40th Annual IEEE International Carnahan Conferences Security Technology, pp. 109–115 (2006)
7. Yampolskiy, R.V.: Secure Network Authentication with PassText. In: 4th International Conference on Information Technology: New Generations (ITNG 2007), pp. 831–836. IEEE Press, New York (2007)
8. Monrose, F., Reiter, M.K., Wetzel, S.: Password Hardening based on Keystroke Dynamics. International Journal of Information Security 1(2), 69–83 (2001)

9. BioPassword, http://www.biopassword.com
10. Brostoff, S., Sasse, M.A.: Are Passfaces More Usable Than Passwords? A Field Trial Investigation. In: Proceedings of CHI 2000, People and Computers XIV, pp. 405–424 (2000)
11. Wiedenbeck, S., Waters, J., Birget, J.C., Brodskiy, A., Memon, N.: Authentication using graphical passwords: Basic Results. In: Proc. Human-Computer Interaction International 2005 (2005) (in press)
12. Take your business to a higher level with SUN. Get a free guide on getting started with cloud computing. Technical report, SUN microsystems (2009)
13. Jain, A., Bolle, R., Pankanti, S.: Biometrics: Personal Identification in Networked Society. Kluwer, Dordrecht (1999)
14. Jain, A.K., Ross, A., Prabhakar, S.: An introduction to biometric recognition. IEEE Transactions on Circuits and Systems for Video Technology 14(1), 4–20 (2004)
15. Tencent, http://en.wikipedia.org/wiki/Tencent_QQ
16. MATLAB function "BWAREA", http://www.mathworks.com/access/helpdesk/help/toolbox/images/bwarea.html
17. Gonzalez, R.C., Woods, R.E.: Digital Image Processing, 2nd edn. Prentice Hall, Englewood Cliffs (2002)

# Knowledge-Base Semantic Gap Analysis for the Vulnerability Detection

Raymond Wu, Keisuke Seki, Ryusuke Sakamoto, and Masayuki Hisada

Department of Research and Development, NST, Inc.
Aizuwakamatsu, Fukushima, Japan
{raymond,seki,sakamoto,hisada}@nstlab.com

**Abstract.** Web security became an alert in internet computing. To cope with ever-rising security complexity, semantic analysis is proposed to fill-in the gap that the current approaches fail to commit. Conventional methods limit their focus to the physical source codes instead of the abstraction of semantics. It bypasses new types of vulnerability and causes tremendous business loss.

For this reason, the semantic structure has been studied. Our novel approach introduces token decomposition and semantic abstraction. It aims to solve the issues by using metadata code structure to envision the semantic gap.

In consideration of the optimized control and vulnerability rate, we take SQL injection as an example to demonstrate the approach. For how the syntax abstraction be decomposed to token, and how the semantic structure is constructed by using metadata notation. As the new type of vulnerability can be precisely specified, business impact can be eliminated.

**Keywords:** vulnerability, security, validation, metadata, semantic.

## 1 Introduction

The existing approaches don't guarantee the completeness and accuracy of vulnerability detection, as their methods are still weak in the abstract layer. Rule base validation can leave the applications vulnerable if the developer has not correctly specified the filtering rules. Malicious data can stay undetected even if the filter and parser are well designed. Furthermore, keyword checking can result in a high rate of false positives, since an input field could legally contain words that match keywords. Much evidence indicates that existing validation methods are not sufficient to cope with new attacking patterns.

Our research aims to settle such issues, and take approach in syntax abstraction, token decomposition, metadata encoding and semantic validation. The approach differentiates its multi-dimensional vision from conventional processes. It encapsulates new attributes of light-weighted metadata to conduct validation against abstract layer. As the conversion between physical and abstract layer is reversible, we can fine-tune the analysis by recursive cyclic work. For this reason, our approach doesn't need to start from scratch, as the abstract layer can be added on top of heterogeneities, and

S.K. Bandyopadhyay et al. (Eds.): ISA 2010, CCIS 76, pp. 278–285, 2010.

performs unique semantic gap analysis based on existing physical layer's coverage. The attackers have learned to bypass existing policy and validation rules, and design new methods to perform illegal data manipulation.

Our investigation indicates that the weak identification, late responsiveness and lack of scoping capability are all common issues of web security. This implies the conventional methods have not built up sufficient capability in applying symbolic notation to represent the source codes. In a mixed-up program, as mediation is weak, the issue identification is limited to string validation and pattern matching method. Consequently, the scoping is weak and many vulnerability detection methods rely on database response, which is inefficient in its nature.

Our research proposes semantic validation by using the structure of concatenated metadata code. It applies abstract syntax analysis to produce node notation, and to serve as basic syntax element [1]. Node identification enables static analysis and capture run-time information. It stores the node information, and run-time path to the knowledge-based repository. The validation process deals with token decomposition. It first labels "hot spot" which is produced from identification process, and use parser analyzer to decompose the source codes into tokens. The semantic analyzer then encodes token by using a symbolic notation with capsulated run-time information. Thus the encapsulated metadata has sufficient information to align the hierarchical information and map to semantic structure. This builds up the foundation of our research which has been missing in the past.

For this reason, we conduct a literature review as followed; String validation mainly checks user input for keywords; it identifies known malicious patterns and escaping potentially troublesome characters [2]. As attackers have learned to embed sensitive characters in different ways [3], they are still harmful. A black-box test was proposed by Huang and colleagues [4] for testing SQL vulnerabilities. This technique improves penetration-testing techniques by using machine learning, but fails to apply static analysis in knowledge-based implementation [5].

Syntactical validation by using a key was first introduced by Boyd and colleagues [6]. Although effective, this technique could be circumvented if the key used for the randomization is exposed. The Java String Analysis (JSA) library, developed by Christensen and colleagues [7], performs string analysis and automata [8] [9] that can be useful; however, the technique can be bypassed by an alternative coding scheme. In recent approaches, a prepared statement was proposed by Kosuga et al. to separate the query variables from the SQL structure. It reduces the scope of risky variables, but meanwhile requires messaging responses from database to the front-end (i.e., HTTP), which can be inefficient in prediction [10].

## 2  Metadata Foundation

As indicated in Figure 1, a generic format of metadata messaging is critical in identification and message carrying. Generic format means that the nodes' symbolic notation and run-time messaging are common across industry, creating a system which is also language-independent.

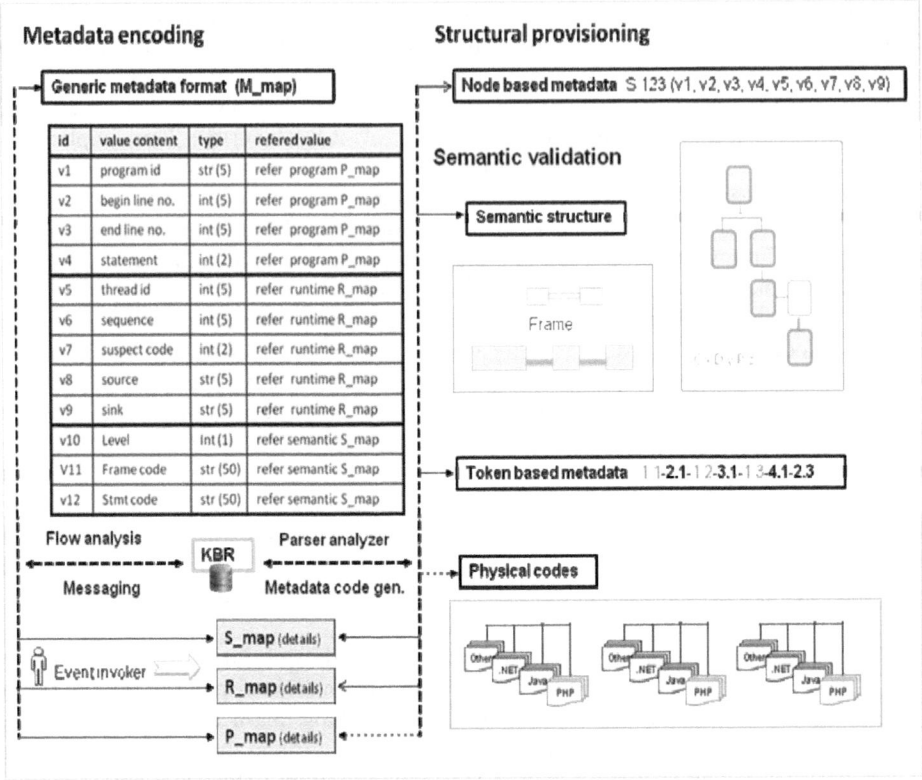

**Fig. 1.** Metadata governance and security services provisioning

In a token-based analysis, the decomposition process identifies each node and associated tokens through the parser analyzer, so the linkage between tokens and statement can be tracked at run-time. Semantic metadata serves as foundation of semantic validation. The message, embedded in the statement block as a node, captures the snapshot information when executed, so the logging messages can be generated at run-time process in HTML form, and represent the execution path. Validation process then works on the decomposition of tokens by using parser analyzer, so each token is encoded to a special code, which will then be filtered and integrated into a string code.

The formation of a string code can be representation of semantics. It differentiates its multi-dimensional approach from conventional processes by encapsulating new attributes of light-weighted metadata [11]. As the conventional methods lack token decomposition and metadata tracking capability, the validation doesn't detect truncation and replacement cases. Thus, in many instances of attack, the malicious data can still produce healthy status under the mixed-up schemes as the syntax stays steady. In order to solve this issue, metadata governance and provisioning is introduced to extend syntax validation to the semantic level.

## 3   Token-Based Semantics

Token is the atomic element from decomposition. Each token can be represented by a metadata code with exposure to the abstract metadata world with a pointer aligned to the source codes. Thus, the codes are validated at certain events under a particular format, and the integration of the metadata codes forms a semantic structure for analysis.

A token-based semantic validation has its unique characteristics in dealing with tough issues. In the first step, the token validation deals with string input and syntax check, which enables token validation at the pre-concatenation stage. In a combination case, other methods may miss the tracking or loss event for capture of the $x value, and validate directly the concatenated "C x D y P z", where the syntax matches the original while the C, x, or D violates the source code semantic but remains undetected. The first step can solve the basic issues; however it can miss the embedded non-alpha-numerical code which obfuscates the whole statement. For this reason, our second step becomes critical. From hierarchical perspectives, the original syntax structure can be represented as:   "$C_1 x_2 D_1 y_2 P_1 z_2$" as second normal form.

| Original | Switch | Shrink | Stretch | Extension |
|---|---|---|---|---|
| 1 1-2 1-2.2-3.1-3.2-4.1 | 1 1-2 1-2.2-3 2-3 1-4 1 | 1.1-2.1-2.2-3 1-3 2 | 1 1-2 1-2.2-3 1-4 1-5 1 | 1.1-2.1-2.2-3.1-3.2-4.1-4.2-4.3 |

**Fig. 2.** Digitized semantic metadata

The metadata code which represents the semantic structure is demonstrated in Figure 2. The digitized information applies graphic as its supplementary representation, so the developers and testers can visualize the semantic gap and fix the problem easily.

To take semantic analysis into use case, this paper applies a simple transaction example to demonstrate how the semantic structure is implemented [12]. The simple statement in syntactical form which follows is a daily transaction in the service industry:

"credit to: x  debit from: y  password: z"

In a symbolic notation, let  C="credit to" , D="debit from", and  P ="password"

Assume the statement is identified as a hot spot. The token-based decomposition supports tracking as each input variable (x, y, z) maintains a linkage with source code. Now we are able to present the original statement in the metadata notation such as:

"C x D y P z"

## 4   Processes for Decomposition and Validation

The graphic representation takes digitized semantic metadata into visualization. Thus the vulnerability detection and validation can be streamlined across the enterprise, to expose operational issues and reach a common practice.

In order to visualize the gap between vulnerability cases, Figure 3 demonstrates the structures of four different cases. Each token is identified by its level and token ID, that they may match the format of C x D y P z, however the gap can be easily detected for each case.

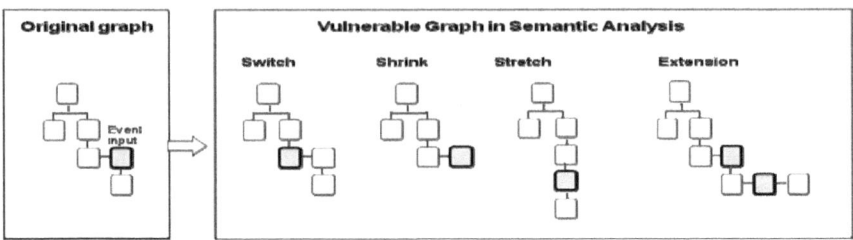

**Fig. 3.** Semantic structure and gap analysis

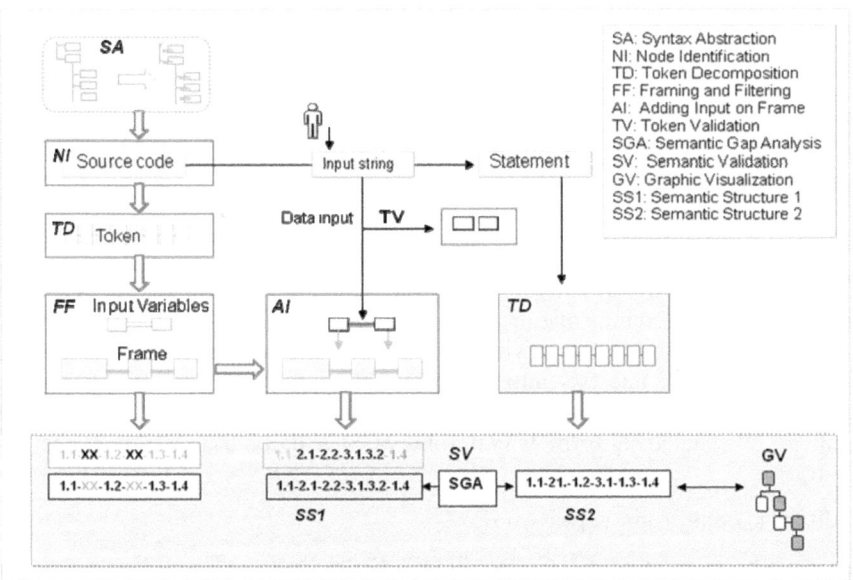

**Fig. 4.** Process for token decomposition and semantic validation

To further explain token-based semantic validation, and how the semantic structure achieves validation process, Figure 4 demonstrates the approaches. The process is supported by generic messaging format, metadata hierarchy, framing, and a tracking mechanism. In the static analysis, the process first conducts token decomposition, and applies a framing technique to derive the frame's metadata code.

At the post-entry stage, it takes the metadata code from input variables and adds them to the code of the frame, which produces SS1 (in pre-concatenation stage). It then converts the concatenated statement directly into token and metadata codes, which derive SS2. The semantic gap between SS1 and SS2 indicates whether the statement is tainted and the comparison can be automated or visualized. The semantic structure is actually a long string concatenated from individual metadata codes from the tokens (or input variables and frame). The gap analysis serves as indicator for whether the input strings are malicious, and graphic visualization provides a supplementary check of vulnerability detection [13]. The comparison is based on the semantic information captured from three different events: 1) from original source code; 2) from concatenation of frame and input variables; and 3) from the final statement. The unique contribution of our research is the addition of an intermediate stage (event 2) which contributes to the discovery of many hidden variables in vulnerability detection.

## 5  Evaluation

Currently, we may encounter certain difficulty in preparing benchmarking for the approach and other industry solutions, particularly before completing development work. However, we have tried to create scenarios which can be a reference, to evaluate the semantic validation.

In the experiments, we used Unix and Oracle servers to load a million records and consisting of organizations, employees, and attributes of employees. We identified "bugs" among the input records, such as organization impact, referential integrity, and employee's personal attributes. In 1203 events, the potential issues averaged 10 cases for each event, resulting in a total of 12,030 potential issues. As indicated by Table 1, the pattern-matching method misses most vulnerability cases and the false positive rate is high. Syntax check method capture vulnerability, however, the complexity and computing effort are high and false positives are also very high. Semantic structure achieves best results in accuracy and efficiency, as all 94 tainted cases were detected and the false positive rate was 0 in the test. The benchmarking relies on further experiments in the near future.

**Table 1.** A preliminary evaluation of Pattern matching, Syntax and Semantic validation

| Criteria vs. method | Pattern match | Syntax validation | Semantic validation |
|---|---|---|---|
| **Metadata strategy** | Non-metadata | Linear | Hierarchical |
| **Vulnerability** | 219 | 2408 | 94 |
| **Miss** | 62 | 0 | 0 |
| **Fault positives** | 90% | 99% | 0% |
| **Prediction** | negative | positive | positive |

# 6  Conclusion and Future Work

This paper aims to solve the problems such as alternative coding schemes, and semantic tautology [14]. It applies token decomposition and metadata strategy to impact semantic-layer analysis. Our review indicates that the direct comparison between original source code and run-time statement is far from sufficient to detect new types of vulnerability. Our research indicates the key issue that most of the current approaches lack a metadata strategy to perform decomposition, to take token-based identification into run-time tracking.

Our approach sheds light on metadata strategy. The validation process realizes event capture and vulnerability control. It captures the image of state at three different events. It then applies metadata to mediate physical codes, abstract syntax, and run-time conditions and takes both token and semantic analysis into validation process. Semantic analysis compares the structure from both static and dynamic analysis. Semantic gap detects the obfuscation of tautology even when the syntax remains healthy. The gap can be presented by an automation of digitized data and graphic interfaces; it can also reversely reengineer the hot spot identification by taking results from dynamic analysis back to a fine-tuning of static analysis.

To demonstrate the process for how the decomposition and validation can be implemented in the real world, this paper applies SQL injection as examples to provide the use cases and metadata codes. Since the validation process is generic in format and language-independent, there are certain points needing automation and tools in future development: 1) Syntax abstraction relies on an upward aggregation tool to construct AST. 2) Metadata should be standardized for its semantic notation such as hierarchical structure. 3) Semantic structure and notation should be standardized and generated at a suitable event, so the gap analysis can be automated for further computing and visualization. This paper coaches industry mainstream technologies such as security-as-service, service on demand, and componentization. It embraces cutting-edge technologies to streamline web security for next-generation computing.

## Acknowledgement

The present research was supported through a program for the promotion of Private-Sector Key Technology Research by the National Institute of Information and Communications Technology (NICT) of Japan, entitled "Research and development concerning the web application security with combination of static and dynamic analysis".

## References

1. Wu, R., Hisada, M., Ranaweera, R.: Static Analysis of Web Security in generic syntax format. In: The 2009 International Conference on Internet Computing, Las Vegas, USA (2009)
2. Chen, K., Wager, D.: Large-Scale Analysis of Format String Vulnerabilities in Debian Linux, UC Berkeley (2007)

3. Xu, W., Bhatkar, S., Sekar, R.: Practical Dynamic Taint Analysis for Countering Input Validation Attacks on Web Applications. Stony Brook University (2006)
4. Huang, Y., Huang, S., Lin, T., Tsai, C.: Web Application Security Assessment by Fault Injection and Behavior Monitoring. WWW 2003, 148–159 (2003)
5. Buehrer, G., Weide, B., Sivilotti, P.: Using Parse Tree Validation to Prevent SQL Injection Attacks. In: SEM (2005)
6. Boyd, S., Keromytis, A.: SQLrand: Preventing SQL injection attacks. In: Jakobsson, M., Yung, M., Zhou, J. (eds.) ACNS 2004. LNCS, vol. 3089, pp. 292–304. Springer, Heidelberg (2004)
7. Buehrer, G., Weide, B., Sivilotti, P.: Using parse tree validation to prevent SQL injection attacks. In: Software Engineering and Middleware SEM, pp. 106–113 (2005)
8. Wu, R.: Service design and automata theory. In: International Conference on Enterprise Information System and Web Technologies, EISSWT 2007 (2007)
9. Christensen, A., Møller, A., Schwartzbach, M.: Precise analysis of string expressions. In: Cousot, R. (ed.) SAS 2003. LNCS, vol. 2694, pp. 1–18. Springer, Heidelberg (2003)
10. Dysart, F., Sherriff, M.: Automated Fix Generator for SQL Injection Attacks. University of Virginia, Charlottesville (2007)
11. Pietraszek1, T., Berghe, C.: Defending against Injection Attacks through Context-Sensitive String Evaluation, IBM Zurich Research Laboratory and Katholieke Universiteit (2004)
12. Turker, K., Gertz, M.: Semantic Integrity Support in SQL-99 and Commercial Object-Relational Database Management Systems, Swiss Federal Institute of Technology, ETH (1999)
13. Pretorius, A., Wijk, J.: Bridging the Semantic Gap: Visualizing Transition Graphs with User Defined Diagrams. IEEE Computer Society, Los Alamitos (2007)
14. Halfond, W., Viegas, J., Orso, A.: A Classification of SQL-Injection Attacks and Countermeasures. In: IEEE Symposium on Secure Software Engineering, ISSSE (2006)

# TOKEN: Trustable Keystroke-Based Authentication for Web-Based Applications on Smartphones

Mohammad Nauman[1] and Tamleek Ali[2]

[1] Department of Computer Science, University of Peshawar, Pakistan
[2] Institute of Management Sciences, Peshawar, Pakistan
`recluze@gmail.com, tamleek@imsciences.edu.pk`

**Abstract.** Smartphones are increasingly being used to store personal information as well as to access sensitive data from the Internet and the cloud. Establishment of the identity of a user requesting information from smartphones is a prerequisite for secure systems in such scenarios. In the past, keystroke-based user identification has been successfully deployed on production-level mobile devices to mitigate the risks associated with naïve username/password based authentication. However, these approaches have two major limitations: they are not applicable to services where authentication occurs outside the domain of the mobile device – such as web-based services; and they often overly tax the limited computational capabilities of mobile devices. In this paper, we propose a protocol for keystroke dynamics analysis which allows web-based applications to make use of remote attestation and delegated keystroke analysis. The end result is an efficient keystroke-based user identification mechanism that strengthens traditional password protected services while mitigating the risks of user profiling by collaborating malicious web services.

**Keywords:** Remote attestation, privacy, security, keystroke-based identification.

## 1  Introduction

The increasing popularity of both smartphones and web-based applications has given rise to the deployment of non-native web-based applications targeting these mobile devices. As in any application residing in the cloud, security is an important concern for this new breed of applications and within the scope of security, user authentication is a critical factor. Traditional approaches to authentication involving 'strong passwords' have several limitations in the context of mobile phones. Miniature keyboards (and in latest devices – on-screen *touch* keyboards) tend to motivate users to choose simpler, and thus weaker, passwords. A solution to this problem, proposed and implemented on desktop computers since more than two decades back, is *keystroke-dynamics* analysis [1,2] that uses more sophisticated parameters, such as duration between each keystroke pressed, alongside password matching to strengthen authentication.

S.K. Bandyopadhyay et al. (Eds.): ISA 2010, CCIS 76, pp. 286–297, 2010.

A recent extension to this approach has been to measure keystroke dynamics [3,4] of users on *mobile platforms* alongside password-based authentication to determine their authenticity. While this approach has been shown to be highly effective [5], existing techniques fail to be applicable on web-based services. The reason that existing keystroke-dynamics analysis approaches cannot be deployed as-is for web-based services is fairly straight-forward. Keystrokes are captured on the client end, while the authentication decision needs to take place on the remote web-application server platform. There is no way for the web application to trust the measurements of keystroke dynamics taken on the client platform. Moreover, if the keystroke dynamics patterns of a user are released to any requesting web site, collaborating malicious applications may profile a user's usage pattern and lead to privacy concerns for the user. The recent hack [6] of the popular micro-blogging site Twitter, in which the hacker was able to access Twitter's confidential documents using only their compromised passwords, is evidence of the need for enabling better authenticating mechanisms for web applications.

In this work, we propose an authentication framework based on two hot security research topics – keystroke-dynamics and remote attestation – that allows the extension of the former to web-based applications using the constructs of the latter.

**Contributions:** Our contributions in this paper are the following:

1. We extend keystroke-dynamics based user authentication to web-based applications targeting mobile devices,
2. We device an infrastructure for establishing trust on keystroke patterns reported by the client platform and
3. We enable privacy protection against profiling attacks that may arise as a result of releasing keystroke patterns outside the user's device.

**Outline:** The rest of the paper is organized as follows. Section 2 provides background knowledge about both keystroke-based authentication and Trusted Computing. The problem description is detailed in Section 3 along with the challenges in solving these problems. Our proposed architecture is presented in Section 4. The paper is concluded in Section 5.

# 2    Background Work

## 2.1    Keystroke-Dynamics Analysis

The concept of keystroke-dynamics based user authentication is not a new one. Card et al [1] first proposed this method of authenticating users based on the time span between each successive keystroke. This time duration is termed as *digraph*. Further studies added more parameters to this basic metric including overlapping combinations of keys due to different time spans between key press and key release events. Rick et al. [7] reported strong empirical evidence in support of keystroke latency-based verifier for desktop systems to successfully identify impostors who had knowledge of a user's screen name and password as well as her first and last name.

These approaches were, however, limited to desktop computers and could not directly be applied to mobile devices due to the differences in keyboard types of these two types of computers. The pattern analysis techniques therefore had to be revised extensively and were studied at length in scientific literature. One of the more recent of these techniques was proposed by Clarke and Furnell [8] who used *key-hold times* and latencies on cell phones to experimentally establish the false acceptance rate of around 3%. Karatzouni and Clarke [9] however, concluded that hold-time metrics were not reliable enough at the time to be used on mobile devices. Further, each type of mobile device is equipped with a different type of keyboard and even those stochastic models that were largely successful for traditional cell phones seemed to lack in effectiveness on smartphones with QWERTY keyboards and on-screen touch pads. The most recent and most successful effort for keystroke-based user authentication on smartphones has been reported by Zahid et al. [5] in which they achieve an error rate of approximately 2% and a false negative rate of close to zero using fuzzy classifiers, Particle Swarm Optimizers [10] and Genetic Algorithms [11]. Specifically, they measure three features for their analysis:

1. *Key hold time:* The time span between the key press and key release events for one key.
2. *Digraph time:* The time between key release event of one key and key press event of another. This is further divided into four categories.
   - *Horizontal digraph ($D_h^a$):* The digraph associated with keys on a row.
   - *Vertical digraph ($D_v^a$):* The digraph associated with keys in a column.
   - *Non-adjacent horizontal digraph ($D_h^{na}$):* The digraph associated with non-neighboring keys on a row.
   - *Non-adjacent vertical digraph ($D_v^{na}$):* The digraph associated with non-neighboring keys in a column.
3. *Error rate:* Number of key press events for the backspace key.

Figure 1 shows the result in variation observed in this work between keystroke dynamics on the laptop and a smartphone. We note that this is only one facet of the problem. Not only are keystroke dynamics on smartphones significantly different from those on desktop and laptop computers, they also vary between input methods such as 'hard' and 'soft' keyboards on the smartphones themselves.

As noted earlier, all of these techniques rely on the keystroke-dynamics analysis on the mobile device itself. The problem of providing keystroke-based authentication for browser-based applications on mobile devices has received little attention. *Off-site authentication* is significantly different from *on-device analysis* because the analysis engine must reside outside the domain of control of the user/owner of the device. We argue that analyzing keystroke dynamics on the mobile device itself seriously limits the potential of this type of authentication mechanism.

Since one of the most popular uses of smartphones nowadays is to browse and use online services through the world wide web [12], there is a rather large gap

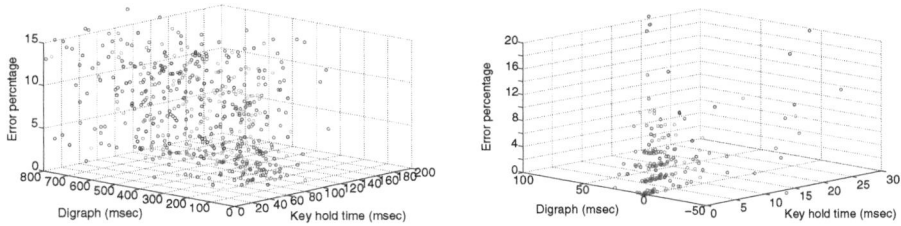

**Fig. 1.** Difference between keystroke dynamics on laptops (left) and smartphones (right) [5]

between research in this area and the requirements of today's smartphone and web application market. In the following section, we discuss the second building block of our paper, Trusted Computing, that can enable a trustable framework for extending these existing approaches for web applications.

## 2.2   Remote Attestation

In the context of social sciences, the semantics of trust and behavior are one of the more difficult concepts to define. The reasons behind this difficulty stem from the ambiguous nature of different connotations of these words in different contexts. Translating any social definition of trust to computing platforms introduces further complications. A consensus in the scientific community has not yet been reached on what 'placing trust in a computing platform' really means. The issue is further convoluted because of the different usages of the word. For example, trust is applied to concepts as further apart as SSL encryption [13], pre-established metadata corpuses [14] and secure storage through asymmetric encryption [15]. However, one of the most widely accepted definitions of trust has been proposed by the *Trusted Computing Group* (TCG) [16] who use the term to denote *"the expectation that a device will behave in a particular manner for a specific purpose"* [17]. To measure and store the behavior of a platform, the TCG has defined an open set of specifications for a *hardware root-of-trust.* This root-of-trust – termed as the Trusted Platform Module (TPM) in case of desktop systems – allows the storage of platform configurations in shielded memory locations called Platform Configuration Registers (PCRs). The TPM is a low-cost secure co-processor that is able to calculate cryptographic hashes (currently SHA-1) of executable code and configuration data and store the resulting 20-byte hashes in the PCRs. The number of PCRs is limited to a multiple of eight and are usually 24 in number. While this helps reduce hardware costs, it imposes restrictions on the number of hashes that can stored in the PCRs. To circumvent this problem, the `pcr_extend` operation is defined as an exclusive point interface for modifying the value of a PCR. This operation has the following semantics: When a new hash has to be stored in a PCR, it is concatenated with the existing value of the PCR and the SHA-1 hash over the resultant byte string is saved in the PCR. In this way, a limited number of PCRs can be used to store as many platform configurations as required [15].

Along with being able to *store* the platform configurations, the TPM also needs to be able to securely *report* them. Trust is established on the values of PCRs by having them signed with an *Attestation Identity Key (*AIK*)* that is accessible only to the TPM. The TPM never releases the private part of the AIK for use outside the TPM and a value signed by the AIK thus provides assurance that the aggregate is vouched for by a genuine hardware TPM [18].

The overall process of storage, reporting and verification of a platforms configurations for the purpose of establishing trust on a remote platform is termed as *remote attestation.* Several remote attestation techniques, achieving varying levels of success, have been proposed in the past. Integrity Measurement Architecture (IMA) [19] is one of the core techniques for establishing trust on a remote platform. It extends the concept of *chain-of-trust* (established by TCG from the BIOS to the bootloader) to within an operating system by measuring all loaded executables. The technique has been implemented on the Linux operating system to measure the boot loader, operating system kernel and all loaded executables including static and shared libraries. This approach is built around the premise that an application remains trusted as long as its binary executable remains unchanged. However, this premise has been shown to be untrue in recent findings [20,21]. Moreover, IMA also suffers from privacy issues since it forces a platform to release complete information about its configurations to a remote challenger.

To address the limitations of IMA, Property-based attestation [22] proposes the protection of a platform's privacy regarding its configuration by introducing a trusted third party in the situation. The trusted third party maps the platform's configurations to more generalized *properties* and releases this information to the remote challengers. While this solution has its benefits in terms of privacy, it still doesn't address the problem of reliance on binary code for behavior trustworthiness. Moreover, as the number of platforms and their possible configuration space increases, property-based attestation quickly becomes infeasible. One of the most novel privacy preserving solutions for measurement of a remote platform's integrity has been proposed by Lyle [23]. It uses static checkers to provide assurance of correct enforcement of a web service without releasing the measurements of the implementation of the web service. One limitation of this approach is that it is limited to the web services scenarios and cannot be implemented in general architectures. For the purposes of this paper, we use an approach we have previously developed [24] in which a small portion of the target application, called the *behavior monitor*, is established as being trusted and is then responsible for reporting the behavior of the application.

## 3    Problem Description and Challenges

The problem targeted in this contribution is that of keystroke-based authentication for web-based applications running on a mobile device. There are several facets of this problem:

1. While keystroke-based authentication on smartphones has been well-studied, all of the previous works consider native applications running on the device as the authenticating entities. In case of web applications, the native application (i.e. the browser) only acts as a conduit between the user and the web application and is not responsible for authenticating the user. The web application, on the other hand, does not have access to the user's keystroke entry pattern information.

2. The naïve approach towards the problem would be to allow the browser to release the keystroke patterns to the web service but this leads to two severe problems.

   (a) The browser operates on the user's mobile device and is outside the control of the web application. As such, it is not feasible for the web application to trust the keystroke patterns reported by the browser. For example, a malicious user may conspire with the browser application on a stolen device to present a previously stored genuine keystroke pattern to the web application.

   (b) On the flip side, it is not prudent for the user to release her keystroke patterns to different web applications operating outside her domain of control. This could lead, at the very least, to profiling attacks on the user if different web applications conspire together to find out the usage patterns of the user.

In this contribution, we propose the use of remote attestation for addressing these problems. However, this approach requires overcoming several challenges:

1. The core challenge is the lack of a hardware root-of-trust on the mobile platforms. An implementation of the proposed hardware co-processor – Mobile Trusted Module (MTM) [25] is not yet widely available. Therefore, an emulation of the hardware is required until it does.

2. Remote attestation of mobile platforms is still an open research topic. A mechanism for establishment of trust on the reporting entity is a prerequisite for trustworthiness of the reported keystroke dynamics. This requires modification to the existing remote attestation techniques to enable them to support this kind of reporting efficiently.

3. Reporting keystroke patterns to third parties will inevitably lead to privacy concerns and threats from potentially malicious third parties. A mechanism needs to be devised that can enable keystroke-based authentication while still mitigating these risks.

4. The user can use different devices and each can have different keystroke-dynamics. On modern smartphones, this problem is compounded by the presence of alternative input methods such as (multiple) on-screen and physical keyboards.

In the following section, we described how we have catered to the problems and addressed the challenges mentioned above.

## 4   Target Architecture

For addressing the issues discussed above, we propose the use of Trusted Computing constructs – specifically remote attestation for trustable reporting of keystroke dynamics to service providers (SP). Our proposed architecture is depicted in Figure 2. The protocol for our architecture is as follows. Initially, a mobile user requests a protected resource from a web-based application's SP. If the SP requires keystroke-based authentication, it responds to the user's browser requesting that a trusted token be provided to it vouching for the correctness of keystroke dynamics. The browser shows a password entry field to the user as is the usual case. However, a component of the browser known as the *keystroke monitor* records the keystroke dynamics while the user enters her password. These keystroke patterns are sent to a Trusted Third Party (TTP) which then performs attestation of the mobile device to establish trust on the reporting entity. Once trust on the keystroke monitor and thus the keystroke patterns is established, the TTP performs keystroke dynamics analysis on the patterns to establish if they match those of the user being authenticated.

After authentication, the TTP returns a token to the mobile browser that is inserted in the data posted to the SP. Finally, the SP requests the TTP for verification that the user is indeed authenticated for correct keystroke dynamics. Thus, trust on the entry pattern of the user is established without having to release any keystroke pattern to the SP.

The above description is a very brief statement of the protocol. There are several steps that need to be performed for successful deployment of this system. These are discussed below.

### 4.1   Registration with the TTP

The primary requisite for use of a TTP in our proposed architecture is registration of users' devices with the TTP. When a user wants to register her device with the TTP, it initiates a protocol that allows her to release information about the device

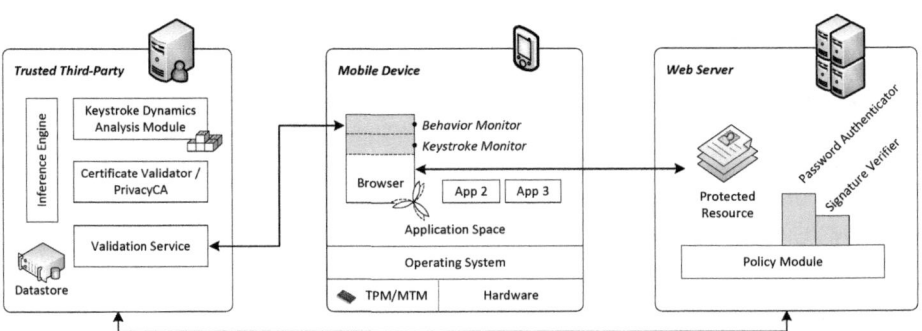

**Fig. 2.** Proposed architecture for trustable keystroke-based authentication on smartphones

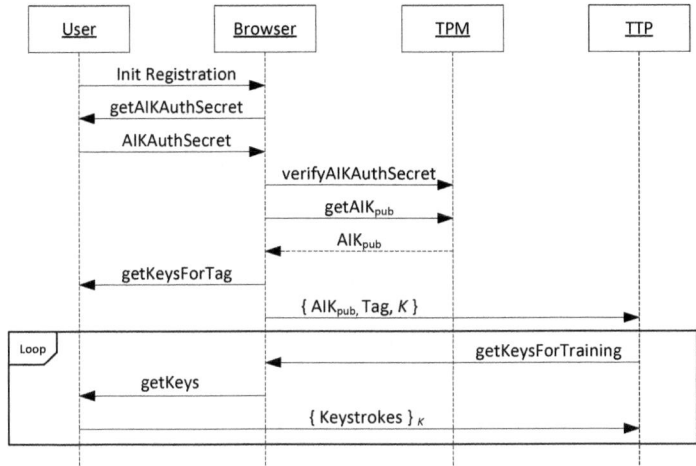

**Fig. 3.** Protocol for Device Registration with the TTP

and owner data to the TTP. Since each user may have more than one devices in her ownership, we introduce the concept of *device tags* during the registration process. The scenario for registration is shown in Figure 3. The user initiates the registration process by visiting the registration page in her mobile device's browser[1]. The browser requests the user to provide the AIK authentication secret which is then verified by issuing the `loadKey` command of the TPM. The browser then retrieves the public portion of the AIK. It also requests the user to enter a few keys using the keyboard so that a *tag* can be associated with the entry method. As mentioned earlier, modern smartphones have touch keyboards as well as hard QWERTY keyboards. Each of these will have a different tag associated with them. The user has to register each type of keyboard with the TTP that she wishes to use during keystroke-based authentication.

The public portion of the AIK, the tag and the public portion of an asymmetric key *Keystroke Signing Key (KSK)* is sent to the TTP. The private portion of the KSK will be used to sign the keystroke patterns during the authentication phase. Once the TTP retrieves these keys, it verifies that the AIK belongs to a genuine hardware TPM. This protocol is similar to the PrivacyCA protocol currently in use today. We omit the details of this verification and refer the reader to [26] for more information. After the verification is complete, the TTP requests the initiation of the training phase (cf. Section 4.3).

## 4.2 Registration with the SP

In order to be able to allow the SP to retrieve and extract meaning out of the keystroke-based authentication involving the TTP, the client first needs to

---

[1] We assume that an AIK has previously been created and that the user knows the authorization secret of the AIK.

register with the SP and convey information about the TTP to the SP. The protocol for this registration is shown in Figure 4. The client initiates the registration process by visiting the SP registration page. The SP collects all the information usually gathered from the client during the registration process and afterwards requests the client to associate a TTP with the SP from among the known TTPs. Currently, it is a limitation of our protocol that the SP must have a previously established trust relationship with the client's TTP and the two must share their metadata. This metadata includes the URLs (or service endpoints) required for communication with each other and other relevant information such as public keys etc. Once the client selects a specific TTP, the SP redirects the client to the TTP sending a *registration token*. This registration token can be used by the TTP to retrieve registration information such as the username from the SP. The TTP can then associate the username with the client on its end.

On the TTP side, the client can set fine-grained authorization credentials such as the time of the day during which the SP can be allowed to retrieve keystroke-dynamics certificates as well as selecting offline or online credential exchange. The TTP then sends a signal to the SP using the SP's metadata and the registration token in order to convey to the SP that keystroke dynamics-based authentication information about the client being registered can indeed be provided by the TTP. Once this phase is completed, the client is redirected to the SP to continue with the registration process as required by the SP.

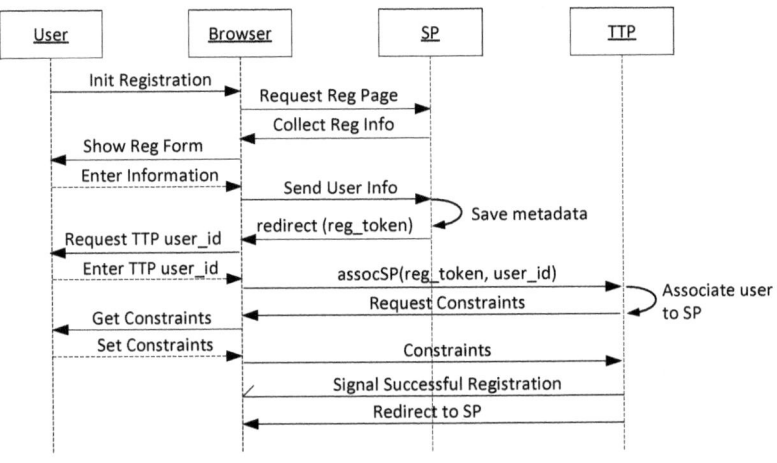

**Fig. 4.** Protocol for User Registration with the SP

## 4.3   Profile Training

In order for the TTP to make decisions about the keystroke-dynamics of a user during authentication, it needs to be able to have training data for the user for each device tag. The user may provide this training data during registration with the TTP or afterwards. However, since our protocol is not dependent on the keystroke-dynamics analysis technique being used, we omit the details of the training phase from our discussion. We refer the reader to [5] and further references of that paper for discussions regarding individual keystroke-dynamics analysis techniques.

## 5    Conclusion and Future Work

Smartphone usage is increasing at a fast pace. One of the reasons for this increased usage is the support provided by these devices to use the Internet just as with a PC. Enhanced usability of web-based applications has caused an exponential growth in the number of users browsing the web through their smartphones. On the other hand, the vulnerability of smartphones both in terms of the probability of theft and getting lost, gives rise to many security concerns. One of these is password (and identity) theft. Over the past few years, interest in alternative and supporting mechanisms to password-based authentication has been revised. Keystroke-based authentication is one such mechanism that has been successfully deployed for smartphones but only for native applications residing on the device itself. In this paper, we have proposed an architecture to enable a trustable and privacy preserving mechanism to support keystroke-based authentication on smartphones for web-based applications. This allows applications running in the cloud to take advantage of this stronger authentication metric. We have also provided details of our proposed architecture and protocols for enabling this type of authentication.

We are currently working on the implementation of our architecture on the popular Android [27] smartphone. We have successfully deployed the prerequisites of our architecture on the software stack and are currently working on the modifications required in the 'browser' project.

One of the most important future aspects of this research is to implement our proposed architecture on a real-world web-based application such as twitter[2] or facebook[3]. Detailed analysis both in terms of security and usability of our architecture will lead to new insights into this extension and provide opportunities to enhance both aspects of our architecture.

## References

1. Card, S., Moran, T., Newell, A.: Computer text-editing: An information-processing analysis of a routine cognitive skill. Morgan Kaufmann Publishers Inc., San Francisco (1987)
2. Joyce, R., Gupta, G.: Identity authentication based on keystroke latencies (1990)
3. Clarke, N., Furnell, S.: Authenticating mobile phone users using keystroke analysis. International Journal of Information Security 6(1), 1–14 (2007)

---

[2] http://www.twitter.com
[3] http://www.facebook.com

4. Karatzouni, S., Clarke, N.: Keystroke Analysis for Thumb-based Keyboards on Mobile Devices. In: International Federation for Information Processing Publications IFIP, vol. 232, p. 253 (2007)
5. Zahid, S., Shahzad, M., Khayam, S., Farooq, M.: Keystroke-based User Identification on Smart Phones. In: 12th International Symposium on Recent Advances in Intrusion Detection (RAID), Symposium on Recent Advances in Intrusion Detection, RAID (September 2009)
6. Cubrilovic, N.: The Anatomy of The Twitter Attack,
   http://www.techcrunch.com/2009/07/19/
   the-anatomy-of-the-twitter-attack/
7. Joyce, R., Gupta, G.: Identity authentication based on keystroke latencies. Commun. ACM 33(2), 168–176 (1990)
8. Clarke, N., Furnell, S.: Authenticating mobile phone users using keystroke analysis. International Journal of Information Security 6(1), 1–14 (2007)
9. Karatzouni, S., Clarke, N.: Keystroke Analysis for Thumb-based Keyboards on Mobile Devices. International Federation For Information Processing-Publications-IFIP, vol. 232, p. 253 (2007)
10. Kennedy, J., Eberhart, R.: Particle swarm optimization. In: Proceedings of IEEE International Conference on Neural Networks, vol. 4 (1995)
11. Goldberg, D.: Genetic algorithms in search, optimization and machine learning. Addison-Wesley Longman Publishing Co., Inc., Boston (1989)
12. AdMob Mobile Metrics: January 2010, Mobile Metrics Report (2010),
    http://metrics.admob.com/wp-content/uploads/2010/02/
    AdMob-Mobile-Metrics-Jan-10.pdf
13. Freier, A., Karlton, P., Kocher, P.: Secure socket layer 3.0. IETF draft (November 1996)
14. Internet2: Shibboleth: A Project of Internet2 Middleware Initiative (2010),
    http://shibboleth.internet2.edu/
15. TCG: TCG Specification Architecture Overview v1.2. Technical report, Trusted Computing Group, pp. 11–12 (April 2004)
16. TCG: Trusted Computing Group (2010),
    http://www.trustedcomputinggroup.org/
17. Pearson, S.: Trusted Computing Platforms: TCPA Technology in Context. Prentice Hall PTR, Upper Saddle River (2002)
18. Challener, D., Yoder, K., Catherman, R., Safford, D., Van Doorn, L.: A Practical Guide to Trusted Computing (2008)
19. Sailer, R., Zhang, X., Jaeger, T., van Doorn, L.: Design and Implementation of a TCG-based Integrity Measurement Architecture. In: SSYM 2004: Proceedings of the 13th conference on USENIX Security Symposium, Berkeley, CA, USA. USENIX Association (2004)
20. Shacham, H.: The Geometry of Innocent Flesh on the Bone: Return-into-libc without Function Calls (on the x86). In: Proceedings of the 14th ACM conference on Computer and Communications Security (CCS 2008), pp. 552–561. ACM, New York (2007)
21. Buchanan, E., Roemer, R., Shacham, H., Savage, S.: When Good Instructions Go Bad: Generalizing Return-oriented Programming to RISC. In: Proceedings of the 15th ACM conference on Computer and Communications Security (CCS 2008), pp. 27–38. ACM, New York (2008)

22. Sadeghi, A.R., Stüble, C.: Property-based Attestation for Computing Platforms: Caring about Properties, not Mechanisms. In: NSPW 2004: Proceedings of the 2004 Workshop on New Security Paradigms, pp. 67–77. ACM Press, New York (2004)
23. Lyle, J.: Trustable Remote Verification of Web Services. In: Chen, L., Mitchell, C.J., Martin, A. (eds.) Trust 2009. LNCS, vol. 5471, p. 153. Springer, Heidelberg (2009)
24. Nauman, M., Alam, M., Ali, T., Zhang, X.: Remote Attestation of Attribute Updates and Information Flows in a UCON System. In: Chen, L., Mitchell, C.J., Martin, A. (eds.) Trust 2009. LNCS, vol. 5471, pp. 63–80. Springer, Heidelberg (2009)
25. Mobile Phone Work Group Mobile Trusted Module Overview Document, http://www.trustedcomputinggroup.org/resources/ mobile_phone_work_group_mobile_trusted_module_overview_document
26. IAIK: About IAIK/OpenTC PrivacyCA (2010), http://trustedjava.sourceforge.net/index.php?item=pca/about
27. Google: Android – An Open Handset Alliance Project (2009), http://code.google.com/android/

# An Improved EKG-Based Key Agreement Scheme for Body Area Networks

Aftab Ali and Farrukh Aslam Khan

Department of Computer Science, FAST National University of Computer & Emerging
Sciences (NUCES), Islamabad, Pakistan
{aftab.ali,farrukh.aslam}@nu.edu.pk

**Abstract.** Body area networks (BANs) play an important role in mobile health
monitoring such as, monitoring the health of patients in a hospital or physical
status of soldiers in a battlefield. By securing the BAN, we actually secure the
lives of soldiers or patients. This work presents an electrocardiogram (EKG)
based key agreement scheme using discrete wavelet transform (DWT) for the
sake of generating a common key in a body area network. The use of EKG
brings plug-and-play capability in BANs; i.e., the sensors are just placed on the
human body and a secure communication is started among these sensors. The
process is made secure by using the iris or fingerprints to lock and then unlock
the blocks during exchange between the communicating sensors. The locking
and unlocking is done through watermarking. When a watermark is added at the
sender side, the block is locked and when it is removed at the receiver side, the
block is unlocked. By using iris or fingerprints, the security of the technique
improves and its plug-and-play capability is not affected. The analysis is done
by using real 2-lead EKG data sampled at a rate of 125 Hz taken from MIT
PhysioBank database.

**Keywords:** Body Area Network (BAN), Physiological Values (PVs),
Electrocardiogram (ECG/EKG).

## 1 Introduction

Body area network (BAN), sometimes referred as smart–clothing, is a network of
wirelessly connected sensors placed on or around the human body. This wearable sensor
network can be used for health monitoring. These sensors which are placed on the
human body measure the physiological parameters such as heartbeat, body temperature,
motion etc. The sensors collect data from the body and send it to a base station for
processing and storage, usually through a wireless multi-hop network [1]. Then the base
station sends data to the medical server via internet as shown in Figure 1. Since BANs
work on physiological values which are quite sensitive information, providing security
to the inter-sensor communication within a BAN is extremely important. BANs are used
to monitor hospital patients in an automated pervasive monitoring environment.
Ubiquitous computing and monitoring enable the doctors to predict, diagnose, and react
to situations efficiently. BANs can also play a significant role in assisted living for

S.K. Bandyopadhyay et al. (Eds.): ISA 2010, CCIS 76, pp. 298–308, 2010.
© Springer-Verlag Berlin Heidelberg 2010

elderly patients. BANs set up in the patient's home will allow earlier detection of any variation in the patient's physiological condition. BANs have the potential to develop a personalized healthcare system where only monitoring, detection and diagnosis of the patients are performed.

Since sensors are tiny devices, their battery power is an issue and the changing of batteries frequently is quite problematic. Since BAN deals with the human body and its physiological values, securing the communication among sensors is just like securing the human life. Securing the inter-sensor communication in a BAN requires the distribution of encryption/decryption keys [3], [4]. This kind of solution requires initial network setup time and also the overhead of the change if made in the BAN's topology. A mechanism for EKG-based key agreement in a BAN is provided in [8] that uses fast Fourier transform (FFT) for feature extraction. The authors use EKG signals as physiological values for generating the common keys for secure inter-sensor communication. The technique consumes a lot of power and its commitment phase is also not so secure because of the exchange of blocks in this phase.

This paper presents an improved EKG-based key agreement scheme that uses discrete wavelet transform (DWT) for feature extraction. The advantage of using DWT over FFT is that its computational cost is linear i.e. $O(n)$ whereas the computational cost of FFT is linearithmic i.e., $O(nlogn)$ [9]. The scheme has another advantage over the existing schemes; that is, it uses watermarking during the commitment phase in order to make the system more secure. The proposed scheme fulfils the requirements described in [5] for a secure system i.e., the keys should be long, random and time variant. The security is improved and its plug and play capability remains intact, i.e., the sensors are just put on the human body and they start secure communication with one another.

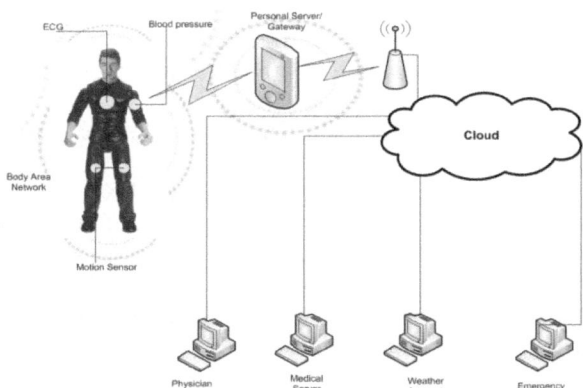

**Fig. 1.** Architecture of a typical wireless Body Area Network (BAN)

The rest of the paper is organized as follows: Section 2 presents the related work and section 3 describes the system model. Section 4 explains the key agreement scheme in detail. Section 5 discusses the security analysis. In section 6, the performance results are shown followed by section 7 which concludes the paper.

## 2  Related Work

The use of physiological values (PVs) for security purposes was introduced by Cherukuri et al. [2]. The advantage of using physiological values is their distinctiveness i.e., the PVs of a person will be unique and different from another person. Taking advantage of this property, the EKG-based key agreement scheme generates the common keys for inter-sensor communication.

In [6], the PVs are used for authentication of entities in a body area sensor network. The work provides the basic functionality of data gathering, transmitting and processing. A new functionality is provided by making use of the collected data or information for authentication or recognition of other sensors on the same individual and the communication is done over a secure channel. In [7], a wristwatch shaped wearable sensor module measures the patient's physiological data and then the data is sent to a PDA via Bluetooth technology and recognizes the patient's general context. It provides various services such as giving timely instructions on daily healthcare, displaying detailed data, and managing the data. The wearable sensor module is equipped with a character LCD and a vibrator speaker. The LCD can display simple messages and the vibrator can activate an alarm.

The authors in [8] propose an EKG-based key agreement scheme for body area networks using fast Fourier transform (FFT) for feature extraction. The authors use EKG signals as physiological values for generating the common keys for secure inter-sensor communication. The scheme also exchanges blocks during the commitment phase by simply hashing the blocks using SHA-256 hashing scheme.

## 3  System Model

A body area network is composed of sensors which have the capability of collecting PVs from a person's body. These sensors then transmit those PVs over a multi-hop body area network. Those PVs are then received by a personal server which is normally a PDA or some powerful node. This personal server has the ability to send that information to the medical server for assistance.

We assume that all the sensors can measure the EKG signal and the iris or fingerprints. The wireless medium cannot be trusted; therefore, several attacks can be launched against the BAN. The traffic can be eavesdropped, messages can be injected to the traffic, old messages can be replayed, and node identities can be spoofed. Communication from the personal server onwards uses conventional security schemes such as SSL for the secure communication. The main focus here is the inter-sensor communication in a BAN.

## 4  EKG-Based Key Agreement Scheme Using DWT

In this section, we present an EKG-based key agreement scheme using DWT for generating common encryption/decryption keys for secure inter-sensor communication. The scheme has two main steps i.e., feature generation and key agreement which are described below.

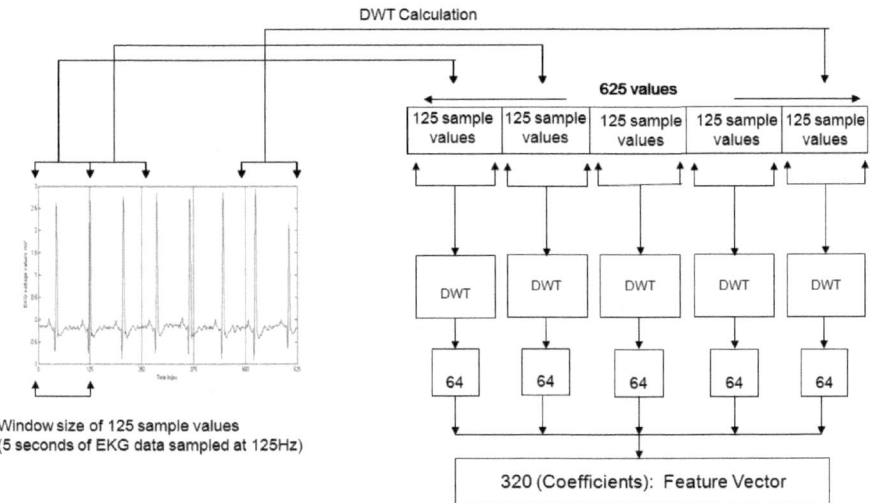

**Fig. 2.** Feature generation

## 4.1   Feature Generation

The feature generation process consists of two steps; Extraction and Quantization. For secure inter-sensor communication using EKG in BAN, the sensors first extract features from the signal. For this purpose, we use discrete wavelet transform (DWT) because DWT is localized in both frequency and time domains and is also computationally inexpensive. The process of feature generation is accomplished by the two communicating sensors. Both the sensors first sample the EKG signal at a certain sampling rate for a specific duration of time (125Hz sampling rate and 5 seconds duration). The signal is then filtered by removing the unnecessary frequency components. The five seconds sample of the EKG signal (producing 625 samples) is then divided into 5 parts of 125 samples each. After filtration, the discrete wavelet transform is applied on each part. The first 64 coefficients are selected and then horizontally concatenated to form a 320 coefficients feature vector, as shown in Figure 2.

The feature vector is then quantized into a binary stream for the sake of key generation. For this purpose, the feature vector is divided into 20 blocks and each block contains 16 coefficients and then these are quantized into a binary stream. As a result of quantization, a 4-bit binary value is produced for each coefficient, resulting in 20, 64-bit blocks at each communicating sensor.

## 4.2   Key Agreement

After the process of quantization, creation of feature vectors, and formation of blocks, we need to exchange these blocks among the communicating sensors for the sake of generating a common key. The key agreement phase itself has three steps i.e., watermarked commitment phase, processing phase, and de-commitment phase.

### 4.2.1 Watermarked Commitment Phase

Digital watermarking is the technology that embeds machine-readable information within the content of a digital media. The information is encoded through subtle changes to the signal (blocks in this case). Watermarked commitment phase is basically the step where the sensors exchange the blocks. For example, $B_{s1}= \{b^1_1, b^1_2, ..., b^1_{20}\}$ are the blocks created at sensor B. These blocks are the building blocks of the key so some security measures are required to securely exchange these blocks among the sensors. For the sake of security, the blocks are hashed using the hash function SHA-256. As the blocks exchanged are only 64 bits long, brute-forcing of these blocks is not much difficult. Therefore, after hashing the locking is performed. In locking, a watermark is added to the blocks. Locking is the process of putting the random values form the iris or fingerprint matrix into each block. The iris or fingerprint matrix is used because of its constant nature. The iris or fingerprint values for a single human will always be same and unique. So, whether these values are measured by sensor A or sensor B, the values will be the same. Taking advantage of this constant nature of these values, we first generate the indices using a random machine. The indices are generated by giving the seed to the random machine from the iris or fingerprint matrix which generate the indices and then using these indices, we put the random values from the iris or fingerprint matrix into each block. This whole process is carried out on the sender side. We call the process on the sender side the locking of the block.

For example, the random machine generates the indices like $\{4, 9, 39, 11\}$, so first the random values are picked from the iris matrix and then using the indices, these values are placed in a temporary block whose size is double the size of the original block. Here, the values will be placed on locations 4, 9, 39, and 11. After this, the original block values are put in the temporary block. On the receiver side, the block is unlocked using the same seed from the iris or fingerprint matrix. The seed specifies the location of the embedded values in the matrix, which makes it easy to recover the original matrix. The hashing is done in two steps. After these two steps, the locking (sender side) and unlocking (receiver side) is performed. This whole process is depicted in Figure 3. The following two steps explain the hashing phase:

**Step1:s1$\rightarrow$s2:<ID,N,hash($b^1_1$,N)...hash($b^1_{20}$,N),MAC(Key$_R$,ID,N,hash($b^1_1$,N)...ha sh($b^1_{20}$,N))>**

**Step2:s2$\rightarrow$s1:<ID$^-$,N$^-$,hash($b^2_1$,N$^-$)...hash($b^2_{20}$,N$^-$),MAC(Key$^-_R$,ID$^-$,N$^-$,hash($b^2_1$,N$^-$) ...hash($b^2_{20}$,N$^-$)>**

where the ID and ID$^-$ are node ids, N and N$^-$ are nonce, which are used to maintain transaction freshness and also act as salt to avoid dictionary attacks. Hash is a one-way hash function, MAC is the message authentication code, and Key$_R$ and Key$^-_R$ are random keys generated at each sensor. The presence of the MAC commits the sensors to their blocks, and is used to detect adversaries.

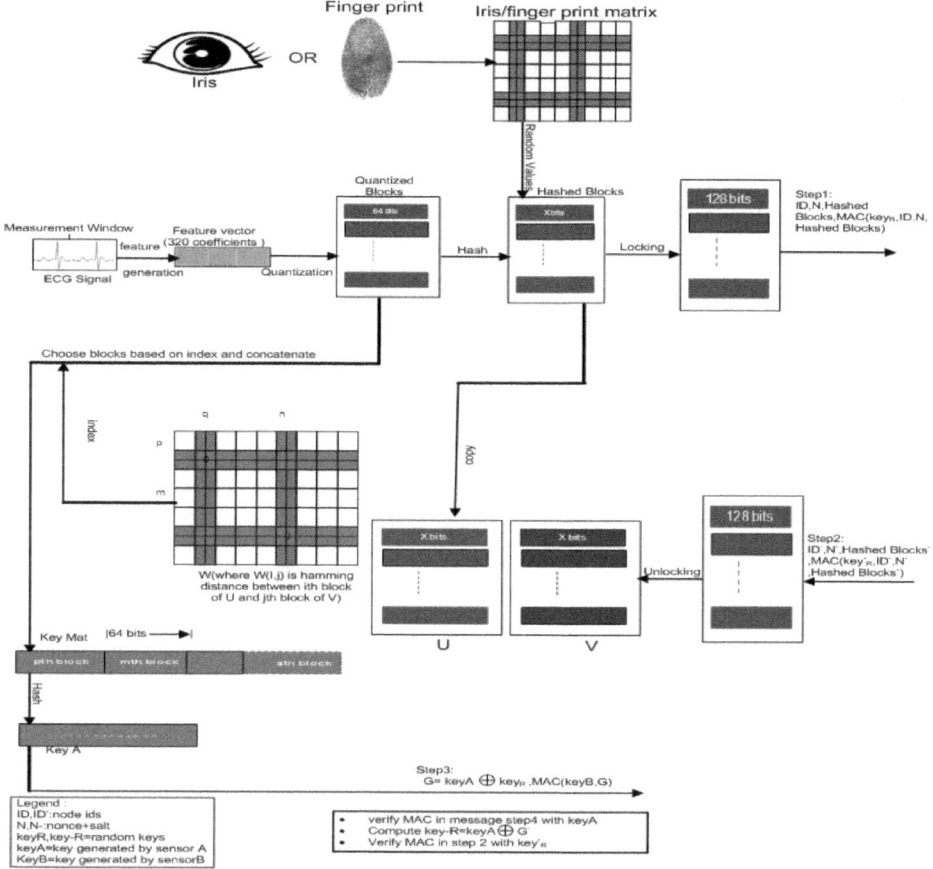

**Fig. 3.** Key agreement process at both the sensors

### 4.2.2 Processing Phase

After the successful completion of watermarked commitment phase (exchange of hashes), the received blocks (hashes) are arranged in two matrices. The hashed blocks which have been received are arranged in a matrix, say U, and the blocks of the same node (local hashed blocks) are arranged in a matrix, say V. On the basis of these matrices (U & V), the hamming distance between the $i^{th}$ row of U and the $j^{th}$ row of V is calculated in such a way that $1< i,j<20$. The matrix W is used for the identification of the blocks which are identical at both the sensors. This process is accomplished by the function KeyGen given in [8]. The blocks KeyMat are identical at both the sensors. These blocks contain the values and not their hashes. The final key (Key) is produced by hashing (SHA-256) the KeyMat [8].

### 4.2.3 De-commitment Phase

After key generation, the communicating sensors have to check their legitimacy by using MAC (message authentication code).

**Step 3:** $s1 \rightarrow s2 :< G = Key_R \oplus KeyA, MAC\ (KeyA, G)>$

**Step 4:** $s1 \rightarrow s2: <\hat{G} = \bar{Key}_R \oplus KeyB, MAC\ (KeyB, G)>$

Generated keys KeyA and KeyB during the processing phase at both the sensors s1 and s2, which are located on the same person, should be identical. The verification is performed using MAC in the messages received in de-commitment phase using their KeyA and KeyB, respectively. On the successful verification, the nodes just extract KeyR and Key¯R by XOR-ing KeyA and KeyB with G and Ĝ, respectively, which is then utilized to evaluate the MAC in the commitment phase. The keys are accepted only if the second evaluation is successful [8]. Figure 4 shows the execution of all the phases. Given the values of KeyA and KeyB, the two sensors generate temporary keys.

$Ktmp = hash\ (KeyA,\ l) = hash\ (KeyB,\ l)$

The temporary keys are generated for the sake of performing actual communication, where $l$ is a random number, which protects the key from getting compromised.

## 5 Performance Evaluation

The simulation was performed over 100 random start-times and the average hamming distance between keys was computed. The input is the EKG of 31 subjects taken from MIT PhysioBank database.

### 5.1 Security Analysis

During the locking and unlocking process, the hashed values are locked by taking advantage of the constant nature of fingerprints or iris values. We use these values as a seed to the random machine. The values produced by the random machine are the indices in the EKG blocks where we place the values from fingerprints or iris (random values). The same seed is used on the receiver side which again produces the same indices, and the values which are located at those indices are removed from the blocks. The process is simple and secure because the random machine gives different random values for every seed each time. Secondly, the random values are extracted or removed completely from the blocks without affecting the blocks. The advantages of using the hash are that the actual values are not known to the attacker who captures the packet. Modification of the blocks will make no sense because the changes will be caught when the received MAC is verified in the commitment phase. The key could not be guessed from the blocks if captured by an adversary due to the randomness of the keys (keyA & keyB). Moreover, for the rejection or protection against the replay attacks, the nonce (N) plays its role. For example, if an adversary replays a captured message and imitates itself as a legitimate node, then the nonce of the message will be identical with the previous message and hence will be rejected.

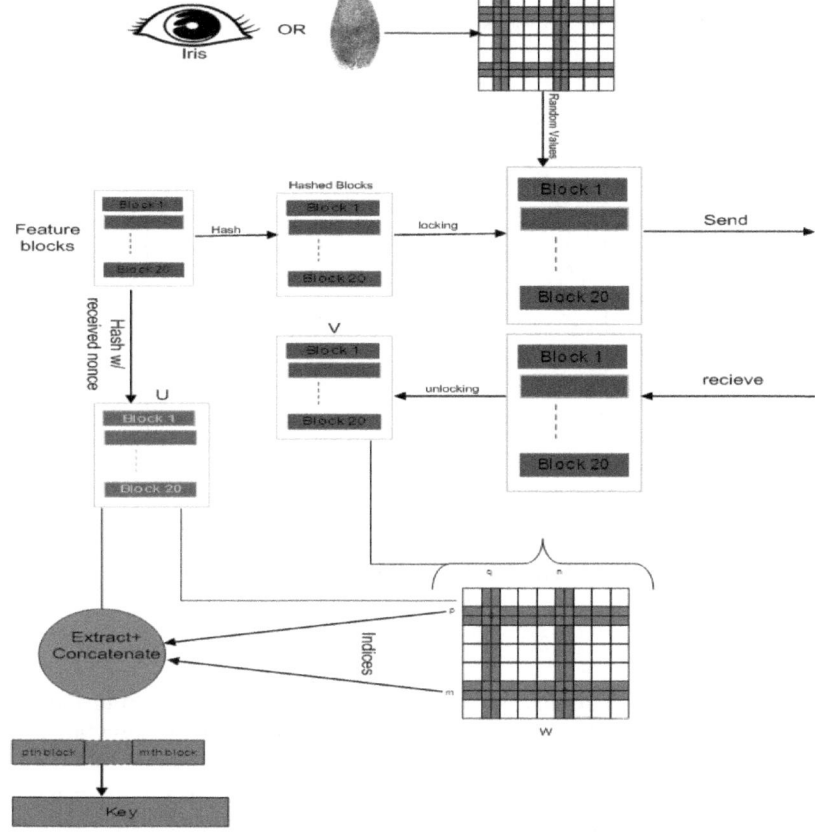

**Fig. 4.** Overall execution of all the phases

We include the watermark to increase the security in the watermark commitment phase instead of exchanging the blocks by only applying the SHA-256 algorithm. The watermarking increases the block size and makes it difficult for the adversary to brute-force it or extract the information from the contents.

## 5.2 Randomness

The keys generated are then evaluated for randomness. Randomness means that there are no patterns in the keys. This is done by calculating entropy of the keys for each subject over 100 random start-times. In our observation, the entropy value almost reaches to 1 in every case which is the confirmation that the distribution of 0's and 1's in the key are uniform, that is, there are no long strings of 1's and 0's in the key. This is shown in Figure 5. For example, if the key has a total of 16 bits then one possible combination might be that the first 8 bits are 1's and the rest of the bits are 0's. If the key is more random then it will be difficult for the adversary to guess it. There are some other patterns which could cause the guessing of the key. So, randomness removes these kinds of risks. Randomness is very important from the security point of view and the keys generated must be checked for randomness. If randomness fails then the process should be repeated for another set of EKG values which generate a random key.

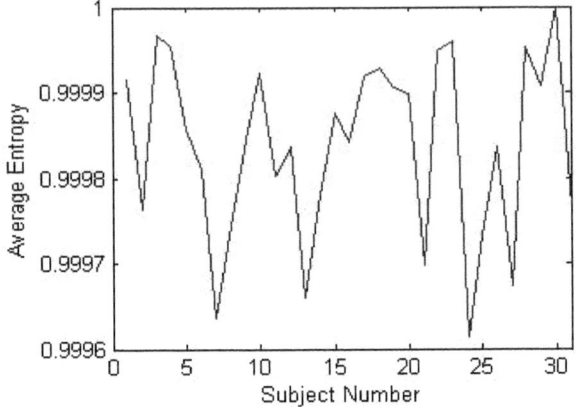

**Fig. 5.** Average Entropy of Keys for 31 subjects

### 5.3 Distinctiveness

The uniqueness or distinctiveness of the keys is verified by checking the hamming distance of the keyA and KeyB. Distinctiveness means that the keys generated are identical for the same subject and divergent for different persons. In Figure 6, the results at random start time are shown. The anti diagonal matrix indicates that the keys generated are identical for the same subject and different for the other subjects. The values at the diagonal are all zeros. This indicates that the keys generated at a particular subject are identical.

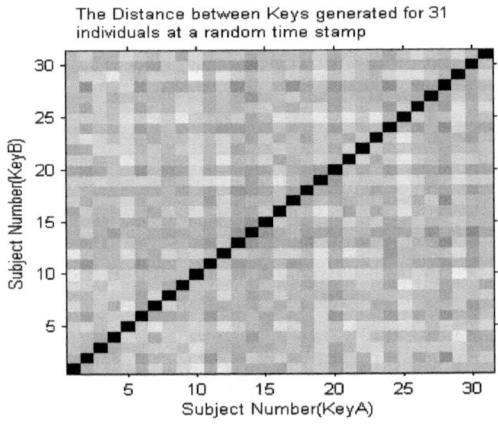

**Fig. 6.** Hamming Distance between Keys generated from Different Subjects

### 5.4 Repetition

The EKG-based keys generated are then checked for the temporal variance. We confirmed that the keys generated are different from the previous keys i.e. the EKG signal does not produce same keys for two different measurements. For this purpose, we calculate the average hamming distance between the keys which ensures that the key generated is not repeated. If the average hamming distance reaches 50% then it means that the key is not repeated, which in our case is approximately 50%.

### 5.5 Computational Cost

As the sensors are tiny devices, their battery life is not so long. We need to keep in mind this requirement of body area networks and reduce the computational cost of our solution. The FFT-based solution suggested in [8] has the time complexity of $O(nlogn)$ while that of DWT-based solution proposed in this work is $O(n)$ [9]. Hence, the wavelet-based solution is fast and robust as compared to the FFT-based solution.

## 6  Conclusion and Future Work

In this paper, we presented an electrocardiogram (EKG) based key agreement scheme for body area networks (BANs) using discrete wavelet transform (DWT) for the generation of a common key for secure inter-sensor communication. The use of physiological values brings plug and play capability and also removes the overhead of schemes like trusted server and traditional key distribution. We also have to keep in mind the computational cost since the sensors cannot afford heavy calculations due to their limited battery life. Therefore, the proposed scheme has the advantage of having linear time complexity. The process is made secure by using the iris or fingerprints to lock and then unlock the blocks during the exchange between communicating sensors. The locking and unlocking is done through watermarking. The analysis was done by using the real 2-lead EKG data sampled at a rate of 125 Hz taken from MIT PhysioBank database.

In future, we would like to improve the security scheme by using some other watermarking technique. We would also further analyze the scheme for performance as well as computational overhead. Moreover, some other physiological values that produce more efficient results are also needed to be considered.

## References

1. Venkatasubramanian, K., Deng, G., Mukherjee, T., Quintero, J., Annamalai, V., Gupta, S.K.S., Ayushman: A Wireless Sensor Network Based Health Monitoring Infrastructure and Testbed. In: Prasanna, V.K., Iyengar, S.S., Spirakis, P.G., Welsh, M. (eds.) DCOSS 2005. LNCS, vol. 3560, pp. 406–407. Springer, Heidelberg (2005)
2. Cherukuri, S., Venkatasubramanian, K., Gupta, S.K.S.: BioSec: A Biometric Based Approach for Securing Communication in Wireless Networks of Biosensors Implanted in the Human Body. In: Proc. of Wireless Security & Privacy Workshop 2003, October 2003, pp. 432–439 (2003)

3. Singel, D., Latr, B., Braem, B., Peeters, M., Soete, M.D., Cleyn, P.D., Preneel, B., Moerman, I., Blondia, C.: A secure cross-layer protocol for multi-hop wireless body area networks. In: 7th International Conf. on Ad-hoc Networks and Wireless (2008)
4. Perrig, A., Szewczyk, R., Wen, V., Culler, D., Tygar, D.: SPINS: Security Protocol for Sensor Networks. Wireless Networks 8(5), 521–534 (2002)
5. Poon, C.C.Y., Zhang, Y.-T., Bao, S.-D.: A Novel Biometrics Method To Secure Wireless Body Area Sensor Networks for Telemedicine and M-Health. IEEE Communications Magazine 44(4), 73–81 (2006)
6. Bao, S.D., Zhang, Y.T., Zhang, Y.-T.: Physiological Signal Based Entity Authentication for Body Area Sensor Networks and Mobile Healthcare Systems. In: Proc. of the IEEE 27th Conference on Engineering in Medicine and Biology, pp. 2455–2458 (2005)
7. Ouchi, K., Suzuki, T., Doi, M.: LifeMinder: A Wearable Healthcare Support System Using User's Context. In: Proc. of 22th International Conference on Distributed Computing Systems Workshops, pp. 791–792 (2002)
8. Venkatasubramanian, K., Banerjee, A., Gupta, S.K.S.: EKG-based Key Agreement in Body Sensor Networks. In: Proc. of the 2nd Workshop on Mission Critical Networks. INFOCOM Workshops, Pheonix AZ, USA (2008)
9. Wu, Y.-l., Agrawal, D., Abbadi, A.E.: A Comparison of DFT and DWT Based Similarity Search in Time-Series Databases. In: Proceedings of the 9th International Conference on Information and Knowledge Management, pp. 488–495 (2000)

# Multi-agent Reinforcement Learning Model for Effective Action Selection

Sang Jo Youk[1] and Bong Keun Lee[2]

[1] Dept of Computer Engineering, Hannam University, Korea
youksj@hannam.ac.kr
[2] Database/Bioinformatics Laboratory, Chungbuk National University, Korea
bong9065@hanmail.net

**Abstract.** Reinforcement learning is a sub area of machine learning concerned with how an agent ought to take actions in an environment so as to maximize some notion of long-term reward. In the case of multi-agent, especially, which state space and action space gets very enormous in compared to single agent, so it needs to take most effective measure available select the action strategy for effective reinforcement learning. This paper proposes a multi-agent reinforcement learning model based on fuzzy inference system in order to improve learning collect speed and select an effective action in multi-agent. This paper verifies an effective action select strategy through evaluation tests based on Robocop Keep away which is one of useful test-beds for multi-agent. Our proposed model can apply to evaluate efficiency of the various intelligent multi-agents and also can apply to strategy and tactics of robot soccer system.

## 1 Introduction

In Artificial Intelligence, the ultimate goal is to achieve an intelligent agent that is capable of performing many complex tasks with seemingly human intelligence. Intelligent agents may also learn or use knowledge to achieve their goals [1]. Typically, an acting agent has a set of feasible actions to select and many environmental variables. This paper describes reinforcement learning in robot soccer settings where multiple intelligent agents playing together as a team and act in real time. In such environments, it is significant to acquire a policy that enables intelligent agents to work cooperatively to win the game. In addition, an agent should be able to learn such a winning strategy. In a multi-agent context, the state space of each learning agent grows exponentially in terms of the number of cooperating agents present in the environment, so it is difficult to consider every option available to agents. Thus, constructing a policy must rely on human experience and knowledge that might not always be available. To address this issue, there has been research on effective action selection algorithms and agent's learning capability. This paper proposes a reinforcement learning model based on fuzzy reasoning that allows robotic soccer agents to learn an optimal policy in simulated soccer games. An assessment of the practical utility of the proposed reinforcement learning model is performed by applying the proposed model to Robocop Soccer Keep away, a well known reinforcement learning task.

S.K. Bandyopadhyay et al. (Eds.): ISA 2010, CCIS 76, pp. 309–317, 2010.

## 2  Background and Related Works

Reinforcement learning is the problem faced by an agent that learns behavior through trial-and-error interactions with an external environment [2]. Reinforcement learning relies on the association between a goal and a feedback signal, interpreted as reward or punishment. In general, the purpose of reinforcement learning system is to acquire an optimum policy that can maximize expected reward per an action. An optimum policy is represented as pairs of state and action. In reinforcement learning, the learning task is often episodic. That is, each trial involves a number of episodes such as a passage in a ball game or a maze exploration. Each episode has a feasible set of states and ends up in a certain state where further actions can be taken. Reinforcement learning allows agents to get reinforcement through rewards, and eventually to learn how to behave successfully to achieve a goal while interacting with a dynamic environment [4].

Success of agent's actions is determined via performance measures. An application area of intelligent agents varies, from a simple Chess game to mission critical space exploration. Since the appearance of the Robocop-Soccer simulator, simulated robot soccer that presents many challenges to reinforcement learning methods has been used in many research works regarding intelligent agents, such as robot movement control, vision systems, and multiple agents learning.

Minsky[10] and Sloman[11] are typical model of intelligent agent framework.

**Fig. 1.** Intelligent agent framework of Minsky

Figure 1 and Figure 2 propose the model with various function such as reflective function self-learning function reaction function, etc.

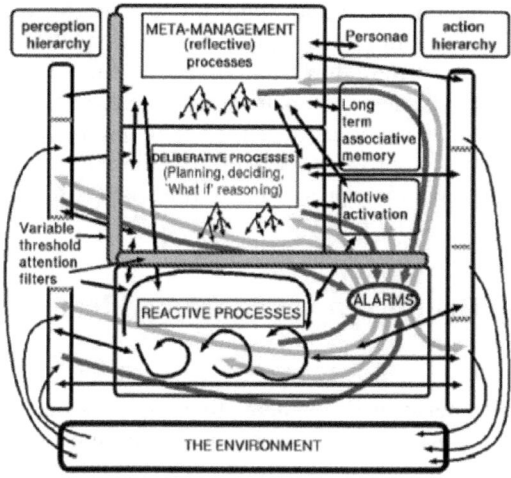

**Fig. 2.** Intelligent agent framework of Sloman

Q-Learning proposed by Watkins [5] is a most widely used reinforcement learning technique. In Q-Learning, an evaluation function over states and actions is learned. That is, Q-Learning works by learning the Q-value for a state-action pair that gives the expected utility of taking a particular action in a particular state.

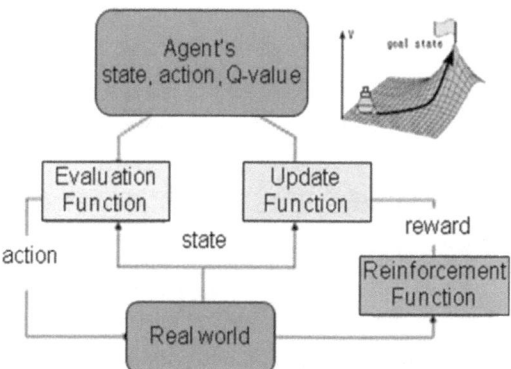

**Fig. 3.** Reinforcement Learning (Q-Learning)

The notation $Q(s, a)$ represents the Q-value of action $a$ in state $s$. In the simplest case, the Q-value for a state-action pair is the sum of all the reinforcements received, and the Q-value function is the function that maps that state-action pair to the reward value. One of the strengths of Q-Learning is that it is able to compare the expected utility of the available actions without requiring a model of the environment. If the agent learns Q-values, it can choose an optimal action even without knowing the environmental model or reward function. However, the agent initially has no idea what the Q-values of any state-action pairs are, so the Q-values are first estimated and learned through trials. The agent also needs to settle on an optimal Q-value function, the one that assigns the appropriate values for all state-action pairs. Trials of all feasible states and actions are repeated many times so as to arrive at an optimal Q-value function.

## 3   Action Select Reinforcement Learning Model Based on Fuzzy Inference

An action selection is performed by calculating the Q-values of keeper's all feasible actions in a certain state and by determining the selection ratios based on the calculated Q-values. In the action select reinforcement learning part, the efficiency of agent's learning can be enhanced by applying reinforcement learning algorithms.

Figure 4 shows that chooses its actions according to a certain action selection policy receives feedback regarding whether the chosen actions are desirable or not, and the agent learns to find optimal actions for various states in simulated soccer games based on the feedback.

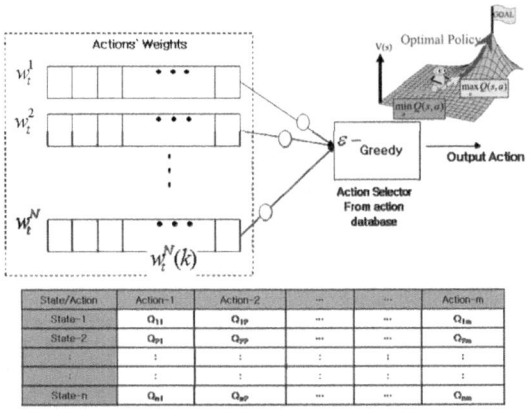

**Fig. 4.** Action Select Reinforcement Learning

In a fuzzy inference system, fuzzy rules are defined to determine actions according to state variables. The fuzzy inference system is a widely used function approximation method and thus it is suited to the representation of Q-value functions in reinforcement learning. The utilization of the fuzzy inference system in reinforcement learning brings several advantages [6].

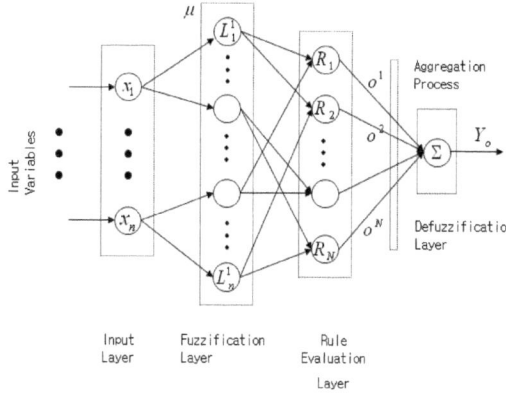

**Fig. 5.** Fuzzy Inference System's Structure

Figure 5 shows a fuzzy inference system model consisting of multiple layers. The first layer takes inputs to the system. In the second layer , the inputs are fuzzified by representing the degree of their membership in fuzzy sets. In the third layer called Rule Evaluation Layer, fuzzy inference is performed. In the Defuzzification Layer, a crisp value that best represents a fuzzy set is extracted. Finally, the fuzzy inference system outputs the extracted crisp values. When defining a fuzzy inference system, the input variables and the type and number of fuzzy sets should be determined. Besides, building the proper membership functions used in the fuzzy rules is important. The fuzzy formalism is an elegant way to pass from a continuous input variable to a discrete output variable via fuzzy membership functions. There exist several forms of membership functions. Triangle-shaped or trapezoidal membership functions are straightforward and simple to calculate, but differentiation is not possible. A Gaussian or sigmoid membership function is differentiable, but the calculation volume is relatively large.

It has the characteristics of both reinforcement learning and fuzzy inference systems, so it allows dynamic learning in an environment where precise modeling is not possible, e.g., the representation of the Q-values. In addition, fuzzy inference systems allow the integration of a priori knowledge and give the possibility to treat continuous state and action space[7].

In fuzzy inference systems, a user ought to define the input variables representing the state space of each learning module and the output variables representing the action space. If defining optimized mapping rules of the input variables to the output variables is not possible, several different output variables can be defined and then the most appropriate one is determined later through reinforcement learning. Figure 6 shows a fuzzy inference mechanism for soccer agents. It determines the membership degree based on relative distances and angles to the ball and other players, and creates fuzzy rules to determine the best action in a given state.

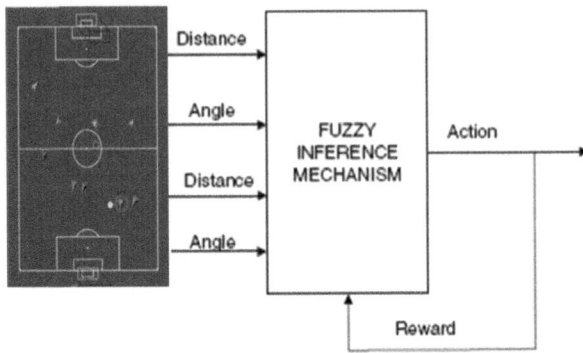

**Fig. 6.** Agent's Fuzzy Inference Mechanism

This paper proposes a learning model for agents in simulated soccer games based on fuzzy inference and reinforcement learning methods. The model aims to improve action selection and learning capability of robot soccer agents in multi-agent environments. Figure 7 shows the structure of the proposed model consisting of two parts - fuzzy inference system and reinforcement learning system. In the fuzzy inference part, agents can choose the appropriate action in each state based on fuzzy inference rules representing a priori knowledge.

In the reinforcement learning part, the efficiency of agent's learning can be enhanced by applying conventional reinforcement learning algorithms.

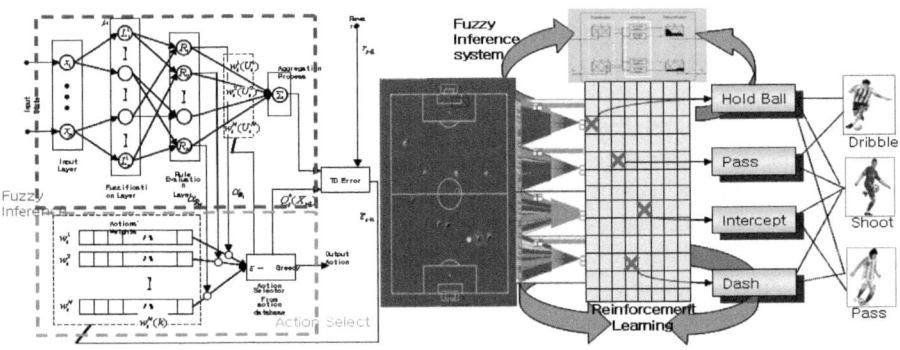

**Fig. 7.** Action Select Reinforcement Learning Model based on Fuzzy Reasoning

## 4    Experiments and Result Analysis

In order to evaluate the efficiency of the proposed fuzzy reasoning-based reinforcement learning model in selecting the best actions, experiments were performed using the

Robocop-Soccer Keep away system. Robocop-Soccer is a multi-agent domain with two opposing teams of agents trying to beat the other one in a game of simulated soccer. The Robocop-Soccer Keep away, a keep away subtask of Robocop-Soccer, is developed as a test tool for reinforcement learning, and it retrieves the information required for the keep away subtask from the Robocop-Soccer server.

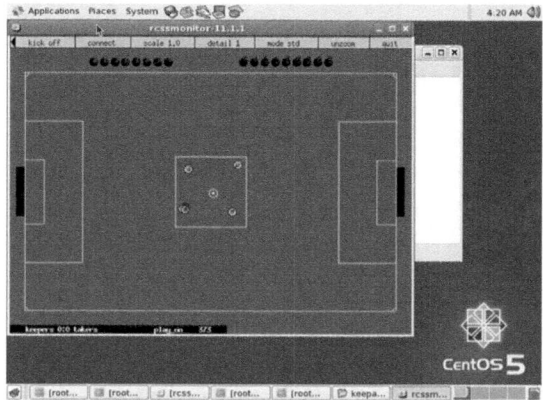

**Fig. 8.** Keep away Main Screen

In the task of keep away, one team "the keepers" tries to keep control of the ball for as long as possible while staying within a rectangular space. The other team "the takers" tries to gain possession of the ball.

Figure 8 shows three keepers and two takers. Parameters are field sizes and the number of keepers and takers. The task is episodic; takers succeed in gaining control or ball goes out of bounds are examples of episode. Each agent gets the information about the ball and the opposing agents, and performs the basic actions - kick, turn, and dash.

In the keep away experiment, each agent selects an action among the basic actions in Robocop Simulator League and five high-level macro actions. An action selection is performed by calculating the Q-values of keeper's all feasible actions in a certain state and by determining the selection ratios based on the calculated Q-values. The performance measure adopted is average episode duration.

An experiment regarding the comparison of action selection policies was carried out in terms of four different keeper's policies - Always Hold, Random, Hand-coded, and Learned (FIS). A brief description of each action policy is as follows:

- **Always Hold:** Hold Ball() is always performed.
- **Random:** Hold Ball() or Pass Ball(k) is performed randomly.
- **Hand-coded:** Hold Ball() is performed when there is no taker within 4 meters; Pass Ball(k) is performed when the keeper is located in a position where ball can be safely passed to a team-mate.
- **Learned (FIS):** The fuzzy inference mechanism presented in Figure 1 is employed. The membership degree is calculated based on distances and angles to team-mates; fuzzy rules are created and used for action selection.

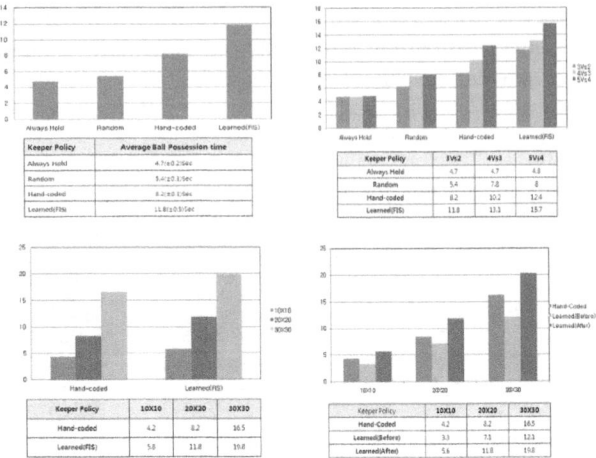

**Fig. 9.** Keeper's Average Ball Possession Time

The efficiency of each policy is measured by the average ball possession time. The experiment was repeated 10 times, and each time lasted 50 hours.

As shown in Figure 9, the average ball possession time of the learned policy through the proposed reinforcement learning model outperforms other policies. This result indicates that the efficiency of agent's action selection is enhanced when the fuzzy inference mechanism providing the exploitation of a priori knowledge is applied to reinforcement learning. As mentioned earlier, the experimented task is episodic. The suggested reinforcement learning model is effective in episodic multi-agent environments, but its effectiveness is restricted in an environment where the dynamics of the environment are unknown and cannot be obtained easily. Hence, a different learning approach is required for such an unpredictable, non-deterministic environment.

## 5  Conclusion

An agent should be able to find optimal actions with regard to its goals and the states of the environment. This paper has presented a fuzzy reasoning-based reinforcement learning model that enables robotic soccer agents to learn policies to take effective actions. An episodic reinforcement environment called Robocop Keep away has been used to evaluate the effectiveness of the proposed learning model. The conducted experiments show that keeper's chances of success are improved when the proposed learning approach is applied. The proposed learning model that combines reinforcement learning and the fuzzy inference mechanism can be used to build optimal policies for simulated soccer games as well as to evaluate the efficiency of other multi-agent action selection methods. With such information, the proposed model enables soccer agents to select the best action in each state and to acquire an optimum policy that maximizes the effectiveness of the selected actions.

For future research, going beyond deterministic episodic environments, the way to construct and learn an effective policy for the choice of action in a multi-agent environment with uncertainty and continuously evolving states, such as online game environments, will be studied.

## References

1. Taylor, M.E., Stone, P.: Representation Transfer for Reinforcement Learning. In: AAAI 2007 Fall Symposium, Arlington, Virginia (2007)
2. Yang, E., Gu.: Multi-Agent Reinforcement Learning for Multi-Robot System: A Survey, University of Essex Technical Report CSM-404 (2004)
3. Sutton, R.S., Barto, A.G.: Reinforcement Learning: An Introduction. MIT Press, Cambridge (1998)
4. Tesauro, G.: Multi Agent Learning: Mini Tutorial, IBM Watson Research Center (2000)
5. Watkins, C.J.C.H., Dayan, P.: Technical notes: Q-learning. Machine Learning 8, 279–292 (1992)
6. Fagin, R.: Combining Fuzzy Information from Multiple Systems. Computer and System Sciences 58, 83–99 (1999)
7. Jouffe, L.: Fuzzy Inference System Learning by Reinforcement Methods. IEEE Transactions on Systems, Man and Cybernetics, 338–355 (1998)
8. McAllester, D., Stone, P.: Keeping the ball from CMUnited-99. In: Stone, P., Balch, T., Kraetzschmar, G.K. (eds.) RoboCup 2000. LNCS (LNAI), vol. 2019, p. 333. Springer, Heidelberg (2001)
9. Sherstov, A.A., Stone, P.: Function Approximation via Tile Coding: Automating Parameter Choice. In: Zucker, J.-D., Saitta, L. (eds.) SARA 2005. LNCS (LNAI), vol. 3607, pp. 194–205. Springer, Heidelberg (2005)

# Author Index